Servicing
Personal Computers

To Yvonne, James and Richard

Servicing Personal Computers

Fourth edition

Michael Tooley, BA

Dean of the Faculty of Technology
Brooklands College

 NEWNES

Newnes
An imprint of Butterworth-Heinemann Ltd
Linacre House, Jordan Hill, Oxford OX2 8DP

℞ A member of the Reed Elsevier group of companies

OXFORD   LONDON   BOSTON
MUNICH   NEW DELHI   SINGAPORE   SYDNEY
TOKYO   TORONTO   WELLINGTON

First published 1985
Second edition 1988
Reprinted 1988
Revised reprint 1990
Third edition 1992
Fourth edition 1994

British Library Cataloguing in Publication Data
Tooley, Michael H.
   Servicing Personal Computers. – 4 Rev. ed
   I. Title
   621.3916

ISBN 0 7506 1757 8

Library of Congress Cataloguing in Publication Data
Tooley, Michael H.
   Servicing personal computers/Michael Tooley. – 4th ed.
   p. cm.
   Includes bibliographical references and index.
   ISBN 0 7506 1757 8
   1. Microcomputers – Maintenance and repair. I. Title.
   TK7887.T66
   621.39'16'0288–dc20   93–44369
                                              CIP

Typeset by Scribe Design, Gillingham, Kent
Printed in Great Britain by Redwood Books

Contents

Preface

In recent years the manufacture of personal computers has been a world-wide growth industry. Indeed, the expansion in the personal computer market is likely to continue for at least the foreseeable future, with personal computers becoming commonplace everyday tools to be used and enjoyed by all. Whereas it is not always possible to make clear distinctions between the lower-cost business machines and those which are intended primarily for domestic use, all of these small systems may be described as 'personal' since they are primarily intended for single-user applications.

Personal computers come with a wide variety of price tags to suit a range of budgets and applications and, despite obvious differences in the outward appearance of machines costing a little over £200 from those which cost around £2000, it is somewhat sobering to realize that, even at the extremes of the price range, one often encounters machines that use the same VLSI microprocessor.

Regrettably, there is considerable variation in both the quantity and the quality of service information provided by personal computer manufacturers. All too often technical manuals, if they can be obtained at all, are of poor quality and the service information which they contain may be extremely limited. In fairness, some manufacturers (such as Epson, IBM, and Olivetti) provide excellent service information but others are either not willing to supply any technical information or will only release such information to their own accredited service agents.

This whole sad state of affairs is often compounded by the fact that equipment regularly appears for sale well in advance of the technical manuals and service documentation. This can create serious problems since initial variants of equipment are invariably less reliable than their successors. The unfortunate user is therefore constrained to returning the equipment to the dealer who then consigns the equipment to the manufacturer. All too often this is merely the starting point in a long saga of delays and frustrations until the equipment is finally made operational.

Different problems arise when, by virtue of age, a personal computer ceases to be adequately supported by the manufacturers or by 'third party' maintenance organizations. Consider the case of an IBM PC-AT with an EGA display built in 1989. Whilst unable to support the latest Windows software such a system is perfectly adequate for most DOS applications. So, when the hard disk drive fails, why not consider upgrading the disk with a more modern and larger IDE unit?

This book sets out to describe the basic principles and practice of personal computer servicing and is intended for the enthusiast as well as the professional computer technician.

It is worth noting at the outset that this book is not merely restricted to the IBM PC and its numerous 'clones' and 'compatibles'. Rather the intention has been that of producing a handy reference manual which contains a wealth of background information that can be applied to *all* types of personal computer.

Chapter 1 begins with an introduction to microcomputers and microprocessors and continues with descriptions of typical LSI and VLSI support devices. As with other areas of electronic servicing, there is an underlying need to understand the operation and behaviour of circuitry in order to recognize and correctly diagnose faults which may arise. A large number of representative circuits and block diagrams have therefore been included so that even those with minimal experience of electronic circuitry will be able to follow the main themes contained within the later chapters.

Although Chapter 2 is entitled 'Test equipment', it covers the broader aspects of setting up a workshop as well as providing details of the equipment considered essential for effective microcomputer servicing. Advice is given on the selection of tools and test equipment and many details have been included for those about to start a small business servicing personal computers.

Chapter 3 is devoted to fault finding. It begins by discussing common faults and the level of skill required in their diagnosis. A general approach to fault finding is then introduced together with a series of diagnostic tests and flow charts which may be used to pinpoint quickly and accurately the area of a fault. The chapter concludes with a number of software diagnostic routines. While no attempt has been made to present these in their minimal or most elegant form, the majority are written in BASIC and they should provide readers with plenty of ideas for developing their own personalized software routines which can be used with a wide variety of personal computers.

Tape and disk drives are covered in Chapter 4. This chapter describes the basic principles of magnetic storage together with representative circuits. Floppy and hard disk drives are described together with common interface standards. Stock faults are discussed and suggested action is given for each symptom.

Chapter 5 deals with printer servicing. The chapter discusses the principles of the most popular types of printer; impact dot matrix and laser types. Routine maintenance procedures are described as are stock faults for both types of printer.

Personal computer displays feature in Chapter 6. This chapter describes the operation, adjustment and maintenance procedures for monochrome and colour raster scan displays. As in previous chapters, stock faults are also discussed.

The last two chapters bring together many of the principles and techniques discussed in the earlier chapters. Chapter 7 is devoted to a range of popular personal computers, each of which is based on Motorola's elegant 68000 CPU. These include machines from Commodore and Atari (the Amiga and ST range respectively), Apple's popular Macintosh series, and the somewhat lesser-known Sinclair QL.

The final chapter is devoted to servicing the immensely popular IBM PC family (and compatibles). This large chapter describes the IBM PC, PC-XT, PC-AT and PS/2 standards and provides detailed information on the hardware and software configuration of such systems as well as a wealth of practical fault-finding information.

The book concludes with a comprehensive reference section containing a great deal of information which will be required in the day-to-day servicing of personal computer equipment. The reference section includes component symbols, TTL and memory data and a comprehensive listing of IBM error codes.

Not only should this book be of value to those regularly engaged in the servicing and repair of personal computers, but it will also be useful for the enthusiast wishing to know more about the internal workings of his computer and its peripherals. For those delving into computers for the first time, a word of caution is appropriate. A good service technician takes time to develop his or her own technique of fault finding.

Finally, don't to expect too much on your first attempt - it is far better to develop experience gradually, commencing with straightforward faults before attempting to tackle more complex problems. This book will undoubtedly help you to avoid the more obvious pitfalls by providing you with a reliable and comprehensive guide at your fingertips. No book can be a complete substitute for hard-won experience and thus you should not expect to become a first-class service technician by merely reading through these pages. However, if you do put the ideas contained in this book into practice you should quickly improve both your servicing technique and your success rate.

Good luck!

M.H.T.

Conventions used in this book

In order to avoid confusion, particularly as far as the newcomer is concerned, the following conventions have been adopted throughout this book:

1. Hexadecimal quantities. Where decimal and hexadecimal numbers are used concurrently an H has been added. For example, 10 is a decimal number while 10H is a hexadecimal number (equivalent to decimal 16). (Note that some texts use $ to precede a hexadecimal quantity. Thus $FFFF is the same as FFFFH.) Where no confusion is likely to exist (e.g., where all quantities in a particular section are expressed in hexadecimal) the H suffix is omitted.

2. Block schematics and simplified circuits. Arrows have been included to indicate the direction of signal flow or data transfer. A solid arrow indicates a bus (multiple signal or data line). The following symbols have been employed:

Bi-directional bus   Uni-directional bus

Bi-directional signal line   Uni-directional signal line

Power rail (no arrow)

3. Logic signals. Logic signals and control lines are shown in block capitals and a bar is used to denote inverted signal lines. So -WE (pronounced 'not WE' or 'WE bar') is the logical complement of WE. In terms of logic levels, -WE is described as an 'active-low' signal line (a 'low' or logic 0 being required to enable the line) whereas WE is 'active-high' (requiring a 'high' or logic 1 to enable it).

4. Within the text, the words 'personal computer' should be taken to mean any micro-computer system designed for individual use, whether for business, education or pleasure. The letters 'PC', on the other hand, should be taken as referring specifically to an IBM Personal Computer System (e.g. IBM PC-XT, IBM PC-AT, etc) or a compatible microcomputer system produced by another manufacturer.

1
Microcomputer systems

In computer servicing, as with many fields of endeavour, there is a popularly held misconception that success can be guaranteed provided one has all the necessary test equipment. The skill and perception of the individual concerned is of greater importance but, to be effective, this needs to be coupled with a thorough understanding of the principles and practice of both microprocessors and microcomputer systems. This chapter aims, therefore, to provide the reader with an elementary understanding of personal computers at both a systems and a circuit level. Wherever possible, commonly used integrated circuit devices and techniques are described and representative examples of circuitry have been included where appropriate.

The basic system

The essential components of any microcomputer system are:

(a) a central processing unit (CPU), which generally takes the form of a single VLSI device, the microprocessor;
(b) a memory comprising both read/write and read only devices (RAM and ROM respectively); and
(c) interface circuits to facilitate system input and output (I/O) in conjunction with such peripheral devices as keyboards, joysticks, printers, and displays.

These components are linked together using a multiple-wire connecting system known as a 'bus'. This can be divided into three parts:

(a) an address bus, used primarily to specify memory locations;
(b) a data bus, on which data is transferred between devices; and
(c) a control bus, which provides timing and control signals throughout the system.

The basic configuration of a microcomputer system is shown in Figure 1.1. The clock generator is responsible for providing an accurate and highly stable timing signal. The clock circuitry is generally external to the microprocessor itself. A control signal of particular note is the 'interrupt'. Essentially, this is a request from an external device that requires the attention of the microprocessor. The response to an interrupt can be programmed in various ways and these will be discussed later in this chapter.

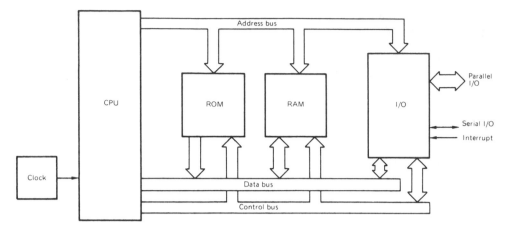

Figure 1.1   Basic internal configuration of a microcomputer

The address and data bus each consist of a number of lines depending upon the particular microprocessor employed. Most of today's microprocessors are capable of performing operations on binary numbers consisting of either 8, 16 or 32 bits. They are thus respectively known as 8-bit, 16-bit and 32-bit microprocessors.

Clearly, 32-bit microprocessors will tend to be more powerful than their 16 and 8-bit counterparts. Despite this, common application programs will run on all three types of microprocessor, the only difference being speed of operation.

In a microcomputer based on an 8-bit microprocessor, the data bus will have eight separate lines. In a 16-bit system the data bus will have 16 separate lines, and so on. The address bus used in most 8-bit systems consists of 16 lines whereas that for a 16-bit system usually has either 16, 20 or 24 lines. The address bus in a 32-bit system may comprise as many as 32 individual lines.

Signals on all lines, whether they be address, data, or control, can exist in one of two states: logic 0 (or 'low') and logic 1 (or 'high'). The largest binary number that can appear on an 8-bit bus is thus 11111111 (or $2^8 - 1$) whereas that for a 16-bit bus is 1111111111111111 (or $2^{16} - 1$). Hence the maximum number of individual memory locations that can be directly addressed in a system having a 16-bit address bus is 2^{16} or 65 536.

In order to explain the detailed operation of the microcomputer system shown in Figure 1.1 we shall examine each of the system components individually. The single most important component of the system is, of course, the microprocessor itself. We shall thus start our tour of the microcomputer with this device and then continue with the other components of the system.

Microprocessors

The microprocessor naturally forms the heart of any microcomputer and, as a consequence, is crucial to the operation of the entire system. The primary function of the microprocessor is that of fetching, decoding, and executing instructions resident in memory. As such, it must be capable of transferring data from external memory into its own internal registers and vice versa. Furthermore, it must operate in a predictable manner, distinguishing, for example, between an operation contained within an instruction and any accompanying addresses of read/write memory locations. In addition, various system housekeeping tasks need to be performed. These may include the periodic refreshing of memory devices, taking appropriate action in the event of power failure to protect the system, and responding to interrupts from such external devices as keyboards, mice and joysticks.

The principal constituents of any microprocessor are:

(a) a number of registers for temporary storage of addresses and data;
(b) a device which can perform arithmetic and logic operations; and
(c) a means of controlling and timing operations within the system.

Whereas internal architecture tends to vary widely, some components remain common to most, if not all, microprocessors. We shall discuss these common components before turning to a detailed discussion of some representative devices.

Registers

The microprocessor invariably contains a number of registers. Some of these are accessible to the programmer whereas others are used entirely by the microprocessor in conjunction with its normal activities. Registers may also be classified as either 'general purpose' or 'dedicated'. in the latter case a particular function is associated with the register, such as holding the result of an operation or signalling the result of a comparison.

Registers can be thought of as a simple pigeon-hole arrangement capable of storing as many bits as there are holes available. Generally, these devices are capable of storing eight or 16 bits. Some registers are referred to as 'double length' and may be configured as either two registers each of eight bits, or one register of 16 bits.

Registers can be used as buffers for the temporary storage of data during processing. However, they must be distinguished from the general purpose read/write memory of a microcomputer system. The reason for this is that microprocessor registers are normally in constant use whenever the system is active and furthermore their capacity for data storage is strictly limited.

Buffers for data storage can also be created within read/write memory external to the microprocessor. Data can be placed in these buffers in the form of last-in first-out (LIFO) 'stacks' and first-in first-out (FIFO) 'queues'. Those readers having programming experience will doubtless be familiar with the manipulation of data using these basic techniques for data storage.

Instruction register

The process of decoding an instruction takes place very rapidly but it does require a finite time. A temporary storage device is thus generally required to retain each instruction as it is received from the data bus and while it is being decoded. The instruction register (IR) is therefore used to retain the current instruction, i.e. the one that is actually being executed.

Instruction decoder

The instruction decoder is nothing more than an arrangement of logic elements which acts upon the bits stored in the instruction register. The outputs of the decoder relate to the operations associated with the particular instruction code received. As mentioned previously, it is very important to remember that an instruction may consist of more than just the operation that is to be performed; data and/or addresses may also be present. Other registers will be required to store this information.

Program counter

Programs consist of a sequence of instructions to be executed by the microprocessor. Such a collection of instructions is stored in the system's memory, starting at a particular address location. Instructions are fetched and executed by the microprocessor in strict sequence. Often the sequence of instructions progresses through consecutive memory addresses, though this is not always the case as it is possible to jump within a program, or call a code routine resident in the operating system. Some means is therefore required for keeping track of the program and this is achieved by means of the program counter (PC) or instruction pointer (IP) that contains the address of the next instruction byte to be executed.

The content of the program counter is automatically incremented each time an instruction byte is fetched. At the initiation of a jump instruction the program counter contains the address embodied by the jump whereas, when a system call is to be made, the program counter gives the starting address of the desired subroutine. Note that in making a subroutine call the microprocessor must remember the return address in order that the calling program may be properly resumed. This is achieved by storing the program counter's contents immediately prior to the call instruction.

Accumulator

The accumulator functions as both a source and a destination register. As a source register it may be used to contain data to be used in a particular operation. As a destination register it may be used to contain the result of a particular operation. The accumulator is thus prominent in many microprocessor instructions and more reference is made to this register than to any other.

Other general purpose registers are usually provided to supplement the accumulator. Instructions are available for transferring data to/from these registers from/to the accumulator. This is an important facility which can often only be fully appreciated when one becomes conversant with assembly language programming.

Arithmetic logic unit

The arithmetic logic unit (ALU) performs arithmetic and logical operations. The ALU has two inputs as shown in the simplified microprocessor block schematic of Figure 1.2. One input is derived from the accumulator and the other from the data bus (often via a temporary register). The output of the ALU is then fed to the data bus and hence is available to the accumulator, if required.

The operations provided by the ALU usually include addition, subtraction, logical AND, logical OR and logical exclusive-OR. In 8, 16 and 32-bit microprocessors these operations are performed on 8, 16 and 32-bit binary numbers respectively. Note that, when carrying out arithmetic operations, a means of representing negative numbers is required. A system of signed binary numbers is thus often employed. This uses the most significant bit to indicate the sign (whether positive or negative) of the binary number.

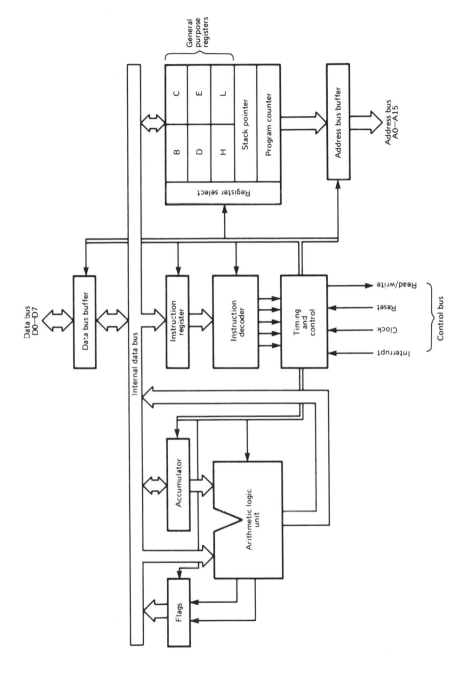

Figure 1.2 Simplified block schematic of a typical microprocessor

Status or flag register

The result of an operation taking place in the ALU is sometimes important in dictating the microprocessor's subsequent actions. A common example of this is examining two numbers to see whether they are the same or different, then branching within the program or calling a subroutine depending upon the outcome. This operation is much simplified if a 'flag' is available to indicate the result of the comparison. This flag takes the form of a single bit which can be either set (logic 1) or reset (logic 0) within a register reserved solely for indicating the current condition of the microprocessor.

Even though it is usually arranged in a group of eight or 16 bits, the status register is not a register in the conventional sense. As such it should be clearly distinguished from the other byte-orientated registers of the CPU. Flags are arranged together for convenience: the status register byte as a whole is of little relevance; what is important is the state of the individual flags.

In the foregoing example, comparison of the two numbers is carried out by means of an ALU exclusive-OR operation, then checking to see if the zero flag is set. Clearly, flags can be extremely useful and most microprocessors provide several to indicate such things as a zero result, the sign of a result, and whether a carry bit has ' :en generated.

Control and timing

The control circuitry of the microprocessor is essential in organizing the orderly flow of data to and from the microprocessor. The number and nomenclature used for control lines vary considerably from one microprocessor to another. The usual control inputs include interrupt, reset, ready (or wait) and the outputs include memory read/write.

A system clock is simply an accurate and stable high frequency oscillator which produces a logic-compatible square wave output. The clock itself is invariably crystal controlled and usually operates in the range 4 to 16 MHz although modern processors can operate with clock frequencies well in excess of 30 MHz. several megahertz. The clock frequency may be divided to produce signals having different phases, required by some processors and further divided to produce reference signals for various other support devices.

A clock cycle, known also as a clock state or 'T-state', is the fundamental timing interval of the microprocessor. A machine cycle usually comprises three to five clock states and can be thought of as the smallest indivisible unit of microprocessor activity. An instruction cycle in turn consists of one to five machine cycles and is merely the time taken to fetch and execute a complete instruction.

To put this into context it is worth considering just what sort of time interval we are actually dealing with. Consider a microprocessor with a clock at a fairly sedate 4 MHz. The fundamental clock state is 250 ns. A machine cycle will occupy from 750 ns to 1.25 µs whereas a complete instruction cycle may require some 750 ns to 6.25 µs, depending upon its complexity.

Stack pointer

Earlier we mentioned that it was necessary for the microprocessor to remember the return address whenever a call was made to a system subroutine. This is accomplished with the aid of a small area of reserved read/write memory known as a 'stack'. In the case of a call instruction, the program counter is incremented in the normal way when the call instruction is fetched and decoded. It is then placed on the stack while the subroutine is being executed and removed when it has been completed. The main program can then be resumed at the point at which it was left.

Microprocessors implement stacks in different ways. Some have in-built facilities for the storage of return addresses, but most rely on external memory. In this case an internal register must be used to point to the address of the most recent stack entry. This register is called the stack pointer (SP).

Another, most useful, facility is associated with retaining the contents of the CPU registers while a subroutine is being carried out. These can be 'pushed' onto the stack before making the call, and then 'popped' off the stack on returning.

Instruction cycle

An instruction cycle can be divided into two distinct parts: the first is devoted to the fetching of the instruction while the second is concerned with executing the desired operation. The instruction cycle is thus also commonly referred to as the 'fetch/execute' cycle. During the first part of the instruction cycle the CPU sends a memory read signal and the program counter's current contents are placed on the address bus. The next instruction word is then read from memory; the first byte is placed in the instruction register. If the instruction word consists of more than one byte, these are fetched during subsequent parts of the cycle while the program counter increments accordingly. When the instruction is complete decoding takes place and the operation specified is executed during remaining states of the instruction cycle. The instruction may require a memory read, memory write, input, output, or some internal CPU operation.

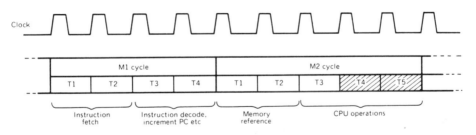

Figure 1.3   Timing diagram for the first two machine cycles of a typical instruction

The timing diagram for the first two machine cycles of a typical instruction is shown in Figure 1.3. The M1 cycle is the machine cycle in which the operation code fetch is performed. It occupies four clock states, T1 to T4. The program counter contents are placed on the address bus during T1 and T2. A memory read is performed during the T2 state and the condition of the data bus is transferred to the instruction register at the end of the T2 cycle. The latter half of the M1 cycle is used for such CPU operations as incrementing the program counter, decoding the instruction, and refreshing dynamic memory where appropriate. In the subsequent cycle, M2, an address is similarly placed on the address bus during T1 and T2 and the remaining states, T3 to T5, are used for CPU operations such as fetching an operand. Note that clock states T4 and T5 are optional and depend upon the particular instruction concerned.

Interrupts

An interrupt is a control signal that causes the processor to cease its normal operation and execute a predetermined sequence of instructions known as an 'interrupt service routine'.

With most microprocessors several different forms of interrupt are possible and it may be necessary to determine the priority of interrupts on the basis that the most important interrupt request receives the first attention of the CPU. Furthermore, it is also advantageous to provide a means whereby interrupts can be disabled under hardware or software control. In such cases the interrupts are called 'maskable', whereas, where disabling is not possible, they are referred to as 'non-maskable'. A classic example of the use of an interrupt is the reset button. This not only causes any operation in progress to cease but it also zeros the program counter and automatically disables any further interrupts.

Microprocessor families

Before we take a more detailed look at some of the most commonly used microprocessors, it is worth setting the scene by briefly describing the development of the various microprocessor families.

In 1971 Intel produced the first 4-bit microprocessor which was known as the 4004. This PMOS LSI device had a limited instruction set and required a number of other devices in order to implement a very crude microcomputer system. The first 8-bit microprocessor to become available was the Intel 8008. This was again a PMOS device with a limited instruction set. The 8008 could, however, offer an address range of 16K. At that time, this was something quite remarkable!

In 1973 the 8008 was replaced by an enhanced NMOS device, the 8080, which was immediately widely adopted by the electronics industry and which was to set the pattern for considerable future development. The 8080 offered a 64K address range and a set of 78 programming instructions. Unfortunately, the 8080 required no less than three separate supply rails and at least two further support devices to produce a fully functional CPU. To improve this situation, in 1976 Intel produced the 8085, an enhanced single supply rail version of the 8080. This device had virtually identical architecture, and was software compatible with its predecessor. It was, however, somewhat eclipsed by the arrival of the Zilog Z80.

The Motorola 6800 microprocessor was developed at about the same time as the Intel 8080 but yielded a much more compact solution, using a mere half-dozen chips in a 'minimum microcomputer system'. The 6800 achieved considerable popularity, being both easy to use and simple to understand. The 6800 yielded a particularly useful range of support devices, many of which are applicable to other 8 and 16-bit microprocessors.

The 6502 was introduced by MOS Technology as an improvement to the 6800. MOS Technology themselves were subsequently absorbed by Commodore and became part of the Commodore Semiconductor Group. Thus the 6502 was destined to become the workhorse of the Pet, Vic 20, and Commodore 64 machines. Other manufacturers who were quick to adopt the 6502 family were Apple, Atari and, in the UK, Acorn Computers. The 6502 was 'second-sourced' by Rockwell and Synertek, and both have been responsible for further development of 6502-family devices.

The natural rival to the 6502 emerged when Zilog introduced the Z80. This was a much improved version of the 8080. The Z80 was adopted by a vast number of manufacturers including Sharp, Tandy, and Sinclair. The Z80 is arguably more powerful and a good deal more complex than the 6502; it has a large instruction set comprising 158 basic programming instructions.

Whereas the 6502 has been adopted widely for use in home computers, the Z80 become the firm favourite of the 8-bit business microcomputer manufacturer. The reason for this is,

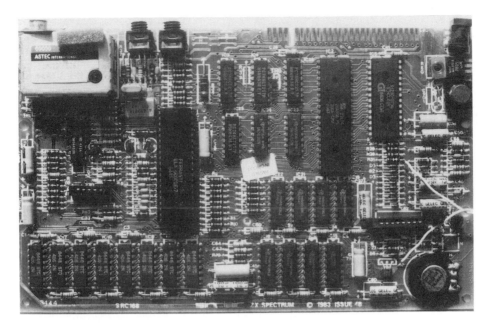

Figure 1.4   Basic home computer (48K Sinclair Spectrum)

Figure 1.5   IBM PC-XT compatible system mother board

Figure 1.6   Z80 CPU and ROM in an Amstrad Spectrum+2

at least partly, attributable to the widespread use of the 8080/Z80-based CP/M (Control Program for Microprocessors) operating system, which became, largely by default, the industry standard for 8-bit microcomputers.

The availability of a vast range of disk-based business software for use under CP/M meant that manufacturers had to provide the system in order to remain competitive in the rapidly expanding small business market. Rivals to CP/M soon appeared. Some (such as CP/M-86) were based on the original CP/M (CP/M-80) whereas others, such as PC-DOS and MS-DOS, were designed to meet the needs of the 'up-and-coming' IBM PC, PC-XT, PC-AT and compatible computers.

The first available 16-bit microprocessor was the Texas 9900. In many respects this device was ahead of its time. Unfortunately, the processor did not find immediate acceptance, even though Texas put it to use in their own TI99/4 home computer. Intel's entry to the 16-bit market was the 8086, while Zilog and Motorola quickly followed with the Z8000 and 68000 respectively. The Intel family of processors was, however, assured immediate success by virtue of its adoption by IBM for use in its PC and later the PC-XT, PC-AT and PS/2 machines. The Motorola 68000, on the other hand, was favoured by Apple, Commodore and Atari for the Macintosh, Amiga and ST microcomputers respectively.

We shall now take a closer look at several of the more popular microprocessors. Two of these devices, the Z80 and 6502, are 8-bit microprocessors and, whilst they are far from 'state of the art', they provide a useful introduction to the more powerful 16 and 32-bit microprocessors that follow. Where necessary, readers should consult the relevant manufacturer's data books and data sheets for further information. Table 1.1 provides a summary of the characteristics of the most common CPU devices.

Table 1.1 CPU data summary

Type	Originator	Address bus	Data bus	Clock freq'y (typ)	Clock phase	Supply	Pins
6502	MOS Tech.	16	8	1 MHZ	Ext, 1 phase	+5V	40
6800	Motorola	16	8	1 MHz	Ext, 2 phase	+5V	40
6809	Motorola	16	8	1 MHz	Int	+5V	40
8080	Intel	16	8	2 MHz	Ext, 2 phase	+5V, −5V, +12V	40
8085	Intel	16	8 (1)	2 MHz	Int	+5v	40
8086	Intel	20	16 (2)	5 MHz	Ext, 1 phase	+5V	40
8088	Intel	20	8 (1)	5 MHz	Ext, 1 phase	+5V	40
80186	Intel	20	16 (2)	8 MHz	Int	+5V	68
80188	Intel	20	8 (1)	8 MHz	Int	+5v	68
80286	Intel	24	16	10 MHz	Ext, 1 phase	+5V	68
80386DX	Intel	32	32	16 MHz	Ext, 1 phase	+5V	132
80386SX	Intel	32	16	16 MHz	Ext, 1 phase	+5V	132
80486	Intel	32	32	24 MHz	Ext, 1 phase	+5V	168
68000	Motorola	24	16	4 MHz	Ext, 1 phase	+5V	64
68008	Motorola	20	10	8 MHz	Ext, 1 phase	+5V	40
68010	Motorola	20	16	10 MHZ	Ext, 1 phase		
68020	Motorola	32	32	16 MHz	Ext, 1 phase	+5V	
68030	Motorola	32	32				
V20	NEC	20	8 (1)	5 MHz	Ext, 1 phase	+5V	40
V30	NEC	20	16 (2)	8 MHz	Ext, 1 phase	+5V	40
Z80	Zilog	10	8	2 MHz	Ext, 1 phase	+5V	40
Z8001	Zilog	10 (3)	16	4 MHz	Ext, 1 phase	+5V	48
Z8002	Zilog	10 (3)	10	4 MHz	Ext, 1 phase	+5V	40
9900	Texas	10	16	3 MHz	Ext, 4 phase	+5V	64

Z80 microprocessor

The Z80 CPU is an 8-bit MOS microprocessor which is packaged in a 40-pin DIL encapsulation, as shown in Figure 1.7. The functions of the principal signal lines are summarized below:

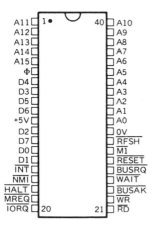

Figure 1.7   Z80 pin connections

A0–A15   16-bit tri-state address bus.

D0–D7   8-bit tri-state data bus.

M1   Output, active low. Indicates that the current machine cycle is an operation code fetch.

MREQ   Output, tri-state, active low. Indicates that the address bus holds a valid address (see also RFSH).

IORQ   Output, tri-state, active low. Indicates that the lower half of the address bus holds a valid address for an I/O operation.

RD   Output, tri-state, active low. Indicates that the CPU wants to read data from memory or from an I/O device.

WR   Output, tri-state, active low. Indicates that the CPU data bus holds valid data to be written to memory or an I/O device.

RFSH   Output, active low. Indicates that the lower seven bits of the address bus contain a refresh address for dynamic memories. A concurrent MREQ signal should then be used to signal a refresh read to all dynamic memories in the system.

HALT   Output, active low. Indicates that the CPU has executed a HALT software instruction and is awaiting either a non-maskable or maskable interrupt (with the mask enabled) before normal operation can be resumed. (Memory refresh continues in the HALT state with the CPU executing a NOP instruction.)

INT   Input, active low. An interrupt request generated by external devices will be honoured at the end of the current instruction if the internal (software controlled) interrupt enable flip-flop (IFF) is enabled and if the BUSRQ signal is not active. When the CPU accepts the interrupt an acknowledge signal is generated (IORQ) at the beginning (M1 cycle) of the next instruction.

NMI   Input, negative edge triggered. The non-maskable interrupt line has a higher priority than INT and is always recognized at the end of the current instruction independent of the state of the IFF. NMI forces the CPU to restart at location 0066H. The PC contents are automatically ·saved on the stack to facilitate an orderly return to the program.

RESET   Input, active low. Forces the PC to zero and initializes the CPU such that the IFF is reset (interrupts disabled), registers I and R are set to 00H, and interrupt mode 0 is enabled. During reset periods, the address and data buses go to a high impedance state and all output signals become inactive.

BUSRQ   Input, active low. Used by external devices as a signal to the CPU when they wish to have control of the system buses. At the end of the current machine cycle in which the signal is received the CPU will set all tri-state lines to the high impedance state.

BUSAK   Output, active low. Used by the CPU to signal to external devices that the system buses are in the high impedance state and available for their use.

Φ   Single-phase TTL clock input. Generally requires a 330 ohm pull-up resistor.

The Z80 CPU contains 18 8-bit and four 16-bit registers, jointly constituting a total of 208 bits of read/write memory accessible to the programmer. The register configuration of the Z80 CPU is shown in Figure 1.8. Note that this shows two sets of six general purpose registers

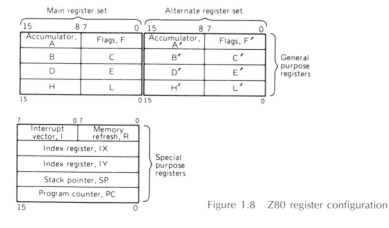

Figure 1.8   Z80 register configuration

which may be used individually as 8-bit registers or in pairs as 16-bit registers. There are also two sets of accumulator and flag registers. The functions of the registers are summarized below:

Accumulators (A, A')   Two independent 8-bit accumulator registers are provided.
Flags (F, F')   The flag registers indicate the status of the accumulator selected.
General purpose registers (BC, DE, HL, B'C', D'E', H'L')   Either of the two groups of registers can be selected using a single exchange (EXX) instruction.
Program counter (PC)   Holds the 16-bit address of the current instruction being fetched from memory.
Stack pointer (SP)   Holds the 16-bit address of the current top of the stack located in external read/write memory.
Index registers (IX, IY)   Two independent registers each capable of holding a 16-bit offset address used in the indexed addressing mode.
Interrupt vector (I)   One of the Z80 interrupt modes allows an indirect call to an address located anywhere in memory (i.e. not just zero page). The I register is used to hold the high order eight bits of this address.
Memory refresh (R)   The R register contains the output of a 7-bit refresh counter. The count is incremented after each instruction fetch. The contents of the R register are sent to the lower eight bits of the address bus during the refresh period.

The Z80 CPU contains an ALU capable of the following operations:

Addition, subtraction
Logical AND, logical OR, logical exclusive-OR
Compare
Left or right shift or rotate
Increment and decrement
Set and reset bits
Test bits

Z80 support devices

The Z80 is well supported with a family of peripheral devices suitable for a wide variety of systems applications. These devices include:

Z80CTC   Counter timer circuit having four programmable counter/timer channels.
Z80PIO   Parallel input/output arranged in two 8-bit groups.
Z80DMA   Direct memory access controller.
Z80SIO   Serial input/output controller.
Z80DART   Dual asynchronous receiver/transmitter.

The 8086 microprocessor

Intel's immensely popular 8086 processor was designed with modular internal architecture. This approach to microprocessor design allowed Intel to produce a similar microprocessor with identical internal architecture but employing an 8-bit external bus. This device, the 8088, shares the same 16-bit internal architecture as its 16-bit bus counterpart. Both devices are packaged in 40-pin DIL encapsulations, the pin connections for which are shown in Figure 1.9.

The CPU signal lines are as follows:

AD0–AD7   Multiplexed 8-bit address/data bus (8088).
AD0–AD15   Multiplexed 16-bit address/data bus (8086).
A8–A19   Address bus lines (8088).
A16–A19   Address bus lines (8086).

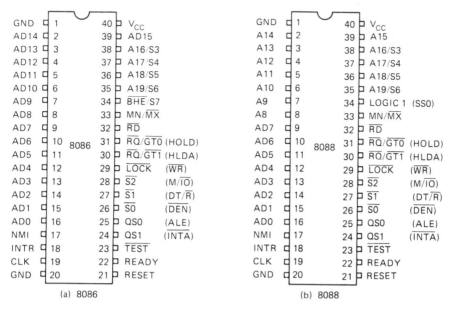

Figure 1.9   Pin connections for the 8086 and 8088 CPU

S0–S7	Status lines. S0–S2 are only available in Maximum Mode and are connected to the 8288 Bus Controller. S3–S7 all share pins with other signals.
INTR	Interrupt line. Level-triggered, active high interrupt request input.
NMI	Non-maskable interrupt. Positive edge-triggered line non-maskable interrupt input.
RESET	Active high reset input.
READY	Active high ready input.
TEST	Test. Input used to provide synchronization with external processors. When a WAIT instruction is encountered, the 8088 examines the state of the TEST line. If this line is found to be high, the processor waits in an 'idle' state until the signal goes low.
QS0,QS1	Queue status lines. Outputs from the processor which may be used to keep track of the internal instruction queue.
LOCK	Bus lock. Output from the processor which is taken low to indicate that the bus is not currently available to other potential bus masters.
RQ/GT0, RQ/GT1	Request/Grant. Used for signalling bus requests and grants placed in the CL register.
RD	Active low read line. When taken low the processor is performing a read operation.
MN/MX	Mode select line. This line is taken high or low in order to select minimum or maximum mode respectively. (Note that this line is tied low in the IBM PC and compatible equipment).
CLK	Clock input.
Vcc	Positive supply (+5 V).
GND	Ground/common 0 V.

The 8086 can be divided internally into two functional blocks comprising an Execution Unit (EU) and a Bus Interface Unit (BIU), as shown in Figure 1.10. The Execution Unit is responsible for decoding and executing instructions whilst the BIU prefetches instructions from memory and places them in an instruction queue where they await decoding and execution by the EU.

The Execution Unit comprises a general and special purpose register block, temporary registers, arithmetic logic unit (ALU), a flag (status) register, and control logic. It is important

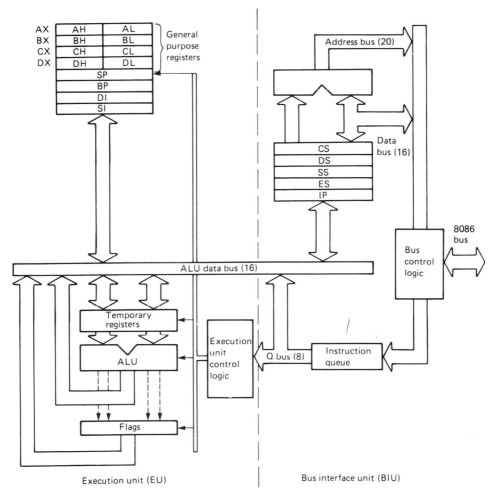

Figure 1.10   Internal architecture of the 8086

to note that the principal elements of the 8086 Execution Unit remain essentially common to each of the members of Intel's 80 × 86 microprocessor family but with additional 32-bit registers in the case of the 80386, 80486 and Pentium.

The BIU architecture varies according to the size of the external data bus. The BIU comprises four segment registers and an instruction pointer, temporary storage for instructions held in the instruction queue, and bus control logic.

The 8086 has 20 address lines and thus provides for a physical 1M byte memory address range (memory address locations 00000 to FFFFF hex.). The I/O address range is 64K bytes (I/O address locations 0000 to FFFF hex.).

The actual 20-bit physical memory address is formed by shifting the segment address four zero bits to the left (adding four least significant bits), which effectively multiplies the Segment Register contents by 16. The contents of the Instruction Pointer (IP), Stack Pointer (SP) or other 16-bit memory reference is then added to the result. This process is illustrated in Figure 1.11.

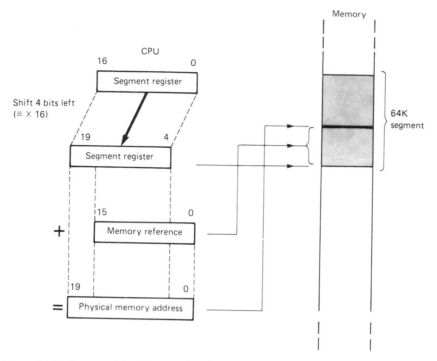

Figure 1.11   Process of forming a 20-bit physical address

As an example of the process of forming a physical address reference, Table 1.2 shows the state of the 8086 registers after the RESET signal is applied. The instruction referenced (i.e. the first instruction to be executed after the RESET signal is applied) will be found by combining the Instruction Pointer (offset address) with the Code Segment register (paragraph address). The location of the instruction referenced is FFFF0 (i.e. F0000 + FFF0). Note that the PC's ROM physically occupies addresses F0000 to FFFFF and that, following a power-on or hardware reset, execution commences from address FFFF0 with a jump to the initial program loader.

Table 1.2 Contents of the 8086 registers after a reset

Register	Contents (hex.)
Flag	0002
Instruction Pointer	FFF0
Code Segment	F000
Data Segment	0000
Extra Segment	0000
Stack Segment	0000

The 80286

Intel's 80286 CPU was first employed in the PC-AT and PS/2 Models 50 and 60. The 80286 offers a 16M byte physical addressing range but incorporates memory management

Figure 1.12   8088 CPU in an IBM PC-XT system board

capabilities that can map up to a gigabyte of virtual memory. Depending upon the application, the 80286 is up to six times faster than the standard 5 MHz 8086 while providing upward software compatibility with the 8086 and 8088 processors.

The 80286 has fifteen 16-bit registers of which fourteen are identical to those of the 8086. The additional Machine Status Word (MSW) register controls the operating mode of the processor and also records when a task switch takes place.

Table 1.3 Bit functions in the 80286 machine status word

Bit	Name	Function
0	Protected mode (PE)	Enables protected mode and can only be cleared by asserting the RESET signal.
1	Monitor processor (MP)	Allows WAIT instructions to cause a 'processor extension not present' exception (Exception 7).
2	Emulate processor (EP)	Causes a 'processor extension not present' exception (Exception 7) on ESC instructions to allow *emulation* of a processor extension.
3	Task switched (TS)	Indicates that the next instruction using a processor extension will cause Exception 7 (allowing software to test whether the current processor extension context belongs to the current task).

The bit functions within the MSW are summarized in Table 1.3. The MSW is initialized with a value of FFF0H upon reset, the remainder of the 80286 registers being initialized as shown in Table 1.2. The 80286 is packaged in a 68-pin JEDEC type-A plastic leadless chip carrier (PLCC) as shown in Figure 1.13.

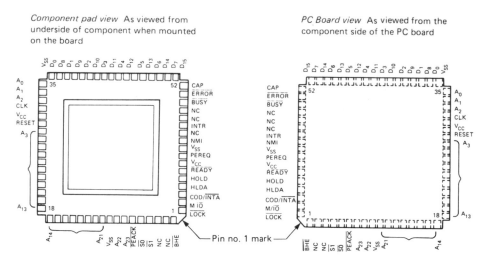

Figure 1.13   Pin connections for the 80286

The 80386

The 80386 was designed as a full 32-bit device capable of manipulating data 32 bits at a time and communicating with the outside world through a 32-bit address bus. The 80386 offers a 'virtual 8086' mode of operation in which memory can be divided into 1 Mbyte chunks with a different program allocated to each partition.

The 80386 is available in two basic versions. The 80386SX operates internally as a 32-bit device but presents itself to the outside world through only 16 data lines. This has made the CPU extremely popular for use in low-cost systems which could still boast the processing power of a '386 (despite the obvious limitation imposed by the reduced number of data lines, the 'SX version of the 80386 runs at approximately 80% of the speed of its fully fledged counterpart).

The 80386 comprises a BIU, Code Prefetch Unit, Instruction Decode Unit, EU, Segmentation Unit and Paging Unit. The Code Prefetch Unit performs the program 'looka-head' function. When the BIU is not performing bus cycles in the execution of an instruction, the Code Prefetch Unit uses the BIU to fetch sequentially the instruction stream. The prefetched instructions are stored in a 16-byte 'code queue' where they await processing by the Instruction Decode Unit.

The prefetch queue is fed to the Instruction Decode Unit which translates the instructions into microcode. These microcoded instructions are then stored in a three-deep instruction queue on a first-in first-out (FIFO) basis. This queue of instructions awaits acceptance by the Execution Unit. Immediate data and opcode offsets are also taken from the prefetch queue.

The 80486

The 80486 CPU is not merely an upgraded 80386 processor; its redesigned architecture offers significantly faster processing speeds when running at the same clock speed as its

Table 1.4 The 80x86 family

	CPU type					
	8086	8088	80186	80286	80386 (386)	80486 (486)
Supply current	340mA–360mA	340mA–360mA	3415mA–550mA	3415mA–550mA	3370mA–550mA	3750mA–900mA
Supply power (typical)	1.75W	1.75W	2.5W	2.5W	2.5W	5W
Packages	DIP	DIP	PLCC, PGA	PLCC, PGA	PGA	PGA
Pins	40	40	68	68	132	168

predecessor. Enhancements include a built-in maths coprocessor, internal cache memory and cache memory control.

The 80486 CPU uses a large number of additional signals associated with parity checking (PCHK) and cache operation (AHOLD, FLUSH, etc). The cache comprises a set of four 2K blocks (128 × 16 bytes) of high-speed internal memory. Each 16-byte line of memory has a matching 21-bit 'tag'. This tag comprises a 17-bit linear address together with four protection bits. The cache control block contains 128 sets of seven bits. Three of the bits are used to implement the 'least recently used' (LRU) system for replacement and the remaining four bits are used to indicate valid data.

8086 support devices

The 8086 family is used with the following support devices:

8087   Maths coprocessor.
8237A   Direct memory access controller.
8255   Programmable parallel interface.
8259A   Interrupt controller.
8284A   Clock generator.
8288   Bus controller.

6502 microprocessor

The 6502 is packed in a 40-pin DIL encapsulation, as shown in Figure 1.14. The functions of the principal signal lines are summarized below:

A0–A15   16-bit tri-state address bus.
D0–D7   8-bit tri-state data bus.
R/W   Controls the direction of data transfer between the CPU and support devices. Output, high to read and low to write. All transitions on this line occur during phase 1 clock pulses.
IRQ   Input, active low. Provided the interrupt status flag, I, is reset, an interrupt request signalled by this input will be honoured. The interrupt status flag may be set or reset under software control.
RDY   Input, active high. Delays execution of any cycle when held low. Used to provide a delay when data is fetched from a slow memory device.

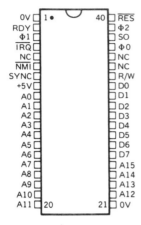

Figure 1.14   6502 pin connections

NMI   Input, negative edge triggered. The non-maskable interrupt line has a higher priority than
         IRQ. The CPU will not recognize another interrupt until this line goes high and then back
         to low. The NMI must be low for at least two clock cycles for the interrupt to be recognized,
         whereupon appropriate PC vectors are fetched.

RES   Input, active low. Initializes the CPU. When the line goes high, the CPU waits for six clock
         cycles and then fetches the PC vectors from locations FFFCH (PC low) and FFFDH (PC high).
         Execution then re-starts from this location.

SYNC   Output, active high. Indicates that the current cycles are those in which the CPU is perform-
         ing an operation code fetch.

S.O.   Input, negative edge triggered. Used to set the overflow flag, V, in conjunction with an I/O
         device.

ø0   Phase 0 clock input (see below).

ø1   Phase 1 clock output (see below).

ø2   Phase 2 clock output (see below).

The internal timing and control circuits for the 6502 require two non-overlapping square
wave clock signals, known as phase 1 and phase 2. The two signals are distinguished by
the operations that they generate. The address line changes when phase 1 is high whereas
data transfers occur when phase 2 is high. The two clock waveforms are generated by means
of an internal clock generator which itself is supplied from a single square wave input signal,

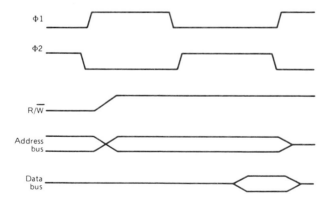

Figure 1.15   6502 read data timing diagram

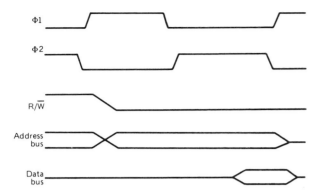

Figure 1.16   6502 write data timing diagram

phase 0. Timing diagrams for reading and writing data from memory or peripheral devices are respectively shown in Figures 1.15 and 1.16.

The register configuration of a 6502 is shown in Figure 1.17. Note that only one general purpose register (the accumulator) is available. The functions of the registers are summarized below:

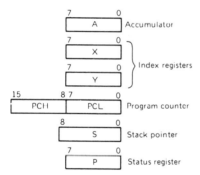

Figure 1.17   6502 register configuration

Accumulators (A)   8-bit accumulator register.
Flags (F)   Flag register that indicates the status of the CPU.
Program counter (PC)   Holds the 16-bit address of the current instruction being fetched from memory.
Stack pointer (SP)   Holds the 9-bit address of the current top of the stack located in external read/write memory. Note that the MSB (A8) is always set to 1.
Index registers (IX, IY)   Two independent registers each capable of holding an 8-bit offset address. Used in the indexed addressing mode.

6502 support devices

The 6502 is well supported with a family of peripheral devices suitable for a wide variety of systems applications. These devices include:

6520   Parallel input/output.
6522   Versatile interface adaptor (VIA) consisting of parallel input/output plus two 16-bit timers.

6532   RAM, I/O, interval timer.
6541   Keyboard/display controller.
6545   CRT controller.
6551   Asynchronous communications interface adaptor (ACIA).

68000 microprocessor

The 68000 was the first of a family of 16/32-bit microprocessors from Motorola. It contains a total of 32 registers, uses 24-bit address and 16-bit data buses respectively, and offers a massive 16 megabyte direct addressing range. The device is housed in a 64-pin DIL package, the pin connections for which are depicted in Figure 1.18. Figure 1.19 shows the principal signal lines of the 68000 grouped by their functions, which may be briefly summarized as follows:

A1–A23   23-bit tri-state address bus.
D0–D15   16-bit tri-state data bus.
AS   Output, active low. Indicates that there is a valid address on the address bus.
R/W   Output, active high. Indicates that the current data bus transfer is a memory read or write.
UDS,   Output, active low. These data strobe signals control the flow on the data bus according to
LDS   the following truth table:

UDS	LDS	R/W	Valid data bits
High	High	–	None
Low	Low	High	All
High	Low	High	0 to 7
Low	High	High	8 to 15
Low	Low	Low	All
High	Low	Low	0 to 7
Low	High	Low	8 to 15

DTACK   Input, active low. Indicates that data transfer has been completed. When the CPU recognizes DTACK during a read cycle, data is latched and the bus cycle is terminated. When DTACK is recognized during a write cycle, the bus cycle is terminated.
BR   Input, active low. This bus request input should be wire-ORed with all other devices that need to have control of the bus.
BG   Output, active low. This bus grant output indicates to potential bus users that the CPU will relinquish bus control at the end of the current bus cycle.
BGACK   Input, active low. The bus grant acknowledge input indicates that some other device has become the bus master.
IPL0,   Inputs, active low. These inputs indicate the level of interrupt priority. IPL0 is the least signif-
IPL1,   icant bit while IPL2 is the most significant bit. The three inputs allow for seven levels of
IPL2   interrupt priority. To ensure that an interrupt is recognized, it is necessary for all three inputs to remain stable until the CPU processor status lines go high to acknowledge the interrupt.
BERR   Input, active low. This input may be used to signal a bus error in the current cycle.
RESET   Input/output, active low. As an input this line may be used for system initialization. When used as an output, a reset generated by the CPU will reset all external devices connected to the reset line. In such an event the internal state of the CPU will remain unaffected. Note that a total system reset (affecting both the CPU and external devices) requires both HALT and RESET lines to be simultaneously taken low.
HALT   Input/output, active low. As an input this line causes the CPU to cease operation at the end of the current bus cycle. Thereafter, all control signals become inactive and all tri-state lines become high-impedance. The CPU may also drive the line low to indicate that the processor has ceased executing instructions.
EN   Output, active high. This signal line is provided for the control of 6800 peripheral devices. The enable signal is a free-running clock which operates regardless of the state of the CPU bus and has a period which is ten times that of the CPU clock.

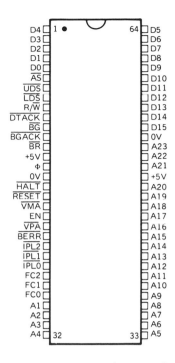

Figure 1.18   68000 pin connections

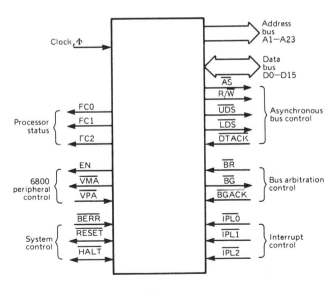

Figure 1.19   Principal signal lines of the 68000

VPA | Input, active low. Indicates a valid peripheral address for a 6800 peripheral device.

VMA   Output, active low. This signal line indicates that a valid address is on the address bus and that the CPU is synchronized to enable. The output only responds to a VPA input thus ensuring that the addressed peripheral is a member of the 6800 family.

FC0, FC1, FC2   Outputs, active high. These function code outputs indicate the state (user or supervisor, or interrupt acknowledge) and the cycle type currently being executed. information is valid whenever AS is active and conforms to the following state table:

FC2	FC1	FC0	Cycle type
Low	Low	Low	Reserved (undefined)
Low	Low	High	User data
Low	High	Low	User program
Low	High	High	Reserved (undefined)
High	Low	Low	Reserved (undefined)
High	Low	High	Supervisor data
High	High	Low	Supervisor program
High	High	High	Interrupt acknowledge

CLK   TTL compatible clock input.

The programming model of the 68000 is shown in Figure 1.20. Seventeen 32-bit registers, a 32-bit program counter and a 16-bit status register are provided. The first eight registers, D0–D7, are used as data registers for byte (8-bit), word (16-bit), and long-word (32-bit) operations. The second set of seven registers, A0–A6, and the system stack pointer may be used as software stack pointers and base address registers. In addition, the registers may be used for word and long-word operations. All of the 17 registers may be used as index registers. The status register contains the interrupt mask as well as the condition codes.

68000 support devices

Motorola supply the following support devices for 68000-based systems:

68120   Intelligent peripheral controller.
68230   Parallel interface and timer unit.
68340   Dual port RAM.
68341   Floating point mathematics ROM.
68450   Direct memory access (DMA) controller.
68451   Memory management unit.
68560   Serial DMA interface.
68454   Disk controller.

In addition, the 68000 has been designed to operate in conjunction with 6800 support devices, including:

6822   Parallel interlace adaptor (PIA).
6840   Programmable timer/counter.
6843   Disk controller.
6847   Video display controller.
6849   Dual density disk controller.
6850   Asynchronous serial I/O adaptor (ACIA).
6852   Synchronous serial I/O adaptor.
6854   Data link controller.
68488   IEEE488 bus controller.

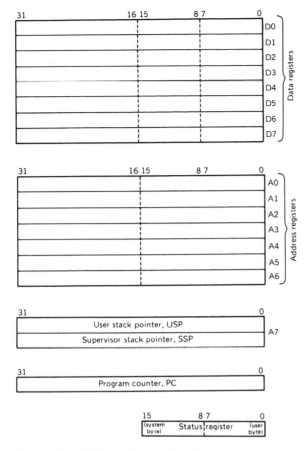

Figure 1.20   68000 register configuration

Programming

A program is essentially a sequence of instructions that tells the computer to perform a particular sequence of operations. As far as the microprocessor is concerned, each instruction comprises a unique pattern of binary digits. It should, however, be noted that the computer may also require data and/or addresses of memory locations in order to fulfil a particular function. This information must also be described to the microprocessor in the form of binary bit patterns. Clearly it is necessary for the processor to distinguish between the instruction itself and any data or memory addresses which may accompany it. Furthermore, instructions must be carried out in strict sequence. It is not possible for the microprocessor to execute more than one instruction at a time although some processors may establish an internal queue of instructions waiting for execution.

A computer program may exist in one of several forms although ultimately the only form usable by the processor is that which is presented in binary. This is unfortunate since most humans are not very adept in working in binary. The following program presented in binary for a Z80 microprocessor illustrates this point:

```
0 0 1 1 1 0 1 0
0 0 0 0 0 0 0 0
1 1 1 1 1 0 1 0
0 1 0 0 0 1 1 1
0 0 1 1 1 0 1 0
0 0 0 0 0 0 0 1
1 1 1 1 1 0 1 0
1 0 0 0 0 0 0 0
0 0 1 1 0 0 1 0
0 0 0 0 0 0 1 0
1 1 1 1 1 0 1 0
```

It is hard to tell that the program takes the contents of two memory locations, adds them together, and stores the result in a third location. Clearly a more meaningful program representation is required. An obvious improvement in making a program more understandable (at least for humans) is to write the program in a number base with which we are familiar. For this purpose, we could choose octal (base 8), decimal (base 10), or hexadecimal. The decimal equivalent of the above program code would, for example, be:

```
 58
  0
250
 71
 58
  1
250
128
 50
  2
250
```

There is clearly not much improvement, although it is somewhat easier to recognize a pattern. We would, of course, still require some means of converting the decimal version of the program into binary so that the program makes sense to the processor. A better method, and one which is much easier to convert into binary (and back again), uses hexadecimal. This is a number system having a base of 16 which uses the numerical digits 0 to 9 together with the letters A to F to represent the numbers 10 to 15.

The binary and decimal equivalent of the hexadecimal digits 0 to F are as follows:

Hex	Binary	Decimal
0	0 0 0 0	0
1	0 0 0 1	1
2	0 0 1 0	2
3	0 0 1 1	3
4	0 1 0 0	4
5	0 1 0 1	5
6	0 1 1 0	6
7	0 1 1 1	7
8	1 0 0 0	8
9	1 0 0 1	9
A	1 0 1 0	10
B	1 0 1 1	11
C	1 1 0 0	12
D	1 1 0 1	13
E	1 1 1 0	14
F	1 1 1 1	15

Larger numbers can quite easily be converted from hex to binary, and vice versa, by arranging the bits in groups of four. Note that it is good practice always to show leading zeros in a binary number. The binary equivalent of the hex number A3, for example, is found by first converting A to 1010 and then 3 to 0011. Writing this in two groups of four bits, with the most significant (A) first, gives:

```
   A          3
 ⏞          ⏞
1 0 1 0    0 0 1 1
```

Taking one further example, consider the 16-bit binary number 0010110011111. Writing this in groups of four bits (starting from the least significant bit and inserting leading zeros as appropriate) gives:

```
0 0 1 0    0 0 0 1    1 0 0 1    1 1 1 1
⏟          ⏟          ⏟          ⏟
  2          1          9          F
```

Hexadecimal-to-decimal conversion, and vice versa, is unfortunately not quite so straightforward and it is usually expedient to refer to a conversion table. The simple addition program, which we met earlier in its binary form, takes on the following appearance when written in hex:

```
3A
00
FA
47
3A
01
FA
80
32
02
FA
```

Whilst it still does not make much sense (unless the reader is familiar with Z80 machine language programming) a pattern can be easily recognized with the program written in this form. Furthermore, the conversion to and from binary is a relatively simple matter.

Instruction sets

An instruction set is simply the name given to the complete range of instructions that convey a meaning to any particular microprocessor. It should be noted that, although there are many similarities, instruction sets are unique to the particular microprocessor or microprocessor family concerned.

In most cases manufacturers have attempted to ensure that their own product range of microprocessors share a common sub-set of instructions. This permits the use of common software, simplifies development, and helps make improvements in microprocessors more acceptable to equipment designers and manufacturers. The Z80, for example, was originally designed as an enhancement of the 8080. The two processors share a common sub-set of instructions and thus a program written for the 8080 will usually run on a Z80-based system.

Complex instruction sets offer a large number of instructions. So many, in fact, that the newcomer is often bewildered by the variety of instructions that are available. It is also rather too easy to confuse the power of a microprocessor with the number of instructions contained in its instruction set; these two things are not always directly related. On the face of it, the Z80 would appear to be a very much more powerful microprocessor than the 6502. The 6502 does, however, perform some operations more quickly than its larger instruction set rival.

Instructions are presented to the microprocessor in words that occupy either 8, 16 or 32 bits depending upon the processor type. These words are sent to a register within the processor known, quite appropriately, as the Instruction Register. Instructions themselves may comprise more than one byte. The Z80, for example, has instructions that have lengths of 1, 2, 3 and 4 bytes.

Mnemonics

Most people find instructions written in hex rather difficult to remember, even though one does get to know some of the more common hex codes after working with a particular processor over a period of time. What is needed, therefore, is a simple method of remembering instructions in a form that is meaningful to the programmer. To this end, microprocessor manufacturers provide us with mnemonics for their instruction codes (but note that there is often some minor variation from one manufacturer to the next). One of the most common instructions is associated with loading a register with a particular value. The instruction code mnemonic for this operation is written 'LD' and we refer to this as an 'operation code'.

For the load instruction to be meaningful we need to tell the processor which register is to be loaded and with what. This information, which is known as an operand, must also be contained in the instruction. Thus, if we wished to load the accumulator register of a Z80 from an address in memory, FA00, we would write the instruction:

LD A,(FA00H)

This simply means 'Load the accumulator (register A) with the data stored at memory location FA00'. The 'H' simply indicates that we have specified the address in hexadecimal.

If, alternatively, we wished to load memory location FA02 with the contents of the accumulator register, we would write:

LD (FA02H),A

Each of these instructions has it own hexadecimal representation, the first being:

3A
00
FA

whilst the second is:

32
02
FA

Each of these instructions consists of three hex bytes. Notice that the operation code changes in order to distinguish whether it is the A register or a memory location that is being loaded.

Also note that the accompanying address is specified using two bytes, with the least significant byte written first.

Assembly language

A program written in instruction code mnemonics is known as an assembly language program. The process of converting the mnemonics to their hexadecimal equivalents is known as assembly. While it is possible to translate assembly language programs to hexadecimal by referring to instruction code tables (i.e. hand assembly) this is, to say the least, a somewhat tedious and repetitious task and one which is very much prone to error.

It is, in fact, a job which is ideally suited to a microprocessor. Thus we find that assemblers are available for most microcomputers, which allow us to write programs in assembly language and then have them translated into machine code by the computer itself. The assembler program translates the user's source program into an object program that can be directly executed by the microprocessor.

The simple addition program takes the following form when written in Z80 assembly language:

```
LD    A,(FA00H)
LD    B,A
LD    A,(FA01H)
ADD   A,B
LD    (FA02H),A
```

This means 'Load A with the contents of FA00, load B with the contents of A, load A with the contents of FA01, add A to B (the result stays in A), put the result in FA02'. Readers may wonder why the content of FA01 was not loaded directly into register B, rather than first placing them in A. The reason is simply that this instruction is not available in the Z80 instruction set!

High-level languages

While assembly language programming is ideal for applications where memory overhead is critical or where a great deal of input-output control is required it is, unfortunately, specific to a particular type of microprocessor and furthermore is generally more complex to write and debug. For most applications, therefore, we turn to high level languages such as BASIC or Pascal. Programs written in these languages are, with usually only minor modification, usable with a variety of microcomputers and are not specific to a particular type of microprocessor.

Programs written in high-level languages generally consist of statements that have some clearly identifiable function. Furthermore, these statements usually correspond to several machine code instructions. High-level programming is thus efficient, at least as far as the programmer is concerned!

The most common high-level language with today's microcomputers is BASIC. The letters stand for Beginners' All Purpose Symbolic Instruction Code. Most readers will be very familiar with this language. The equivalent of our simple addition program takes the form of a single statement line in a BASIC program:

```
30 S = A + B
```

Even those totally unfamiliar with BASIC will recognize such a statement and understand its function. The sum (S) is simply the result of adding the values of two variables, A and B. The number (30) simply denotes the position of the statement within the program. It is known as a line number and many versions of BASIC require such a number. The BASIC program is usually executed in strict line number sequence, but note that some versions of BASIC permit the use of multi-statement lines; i.e. it is possible to have several statements contained within a single line. An example of such a multi-statement line is:

30 S = A + B : D = A - B

This multi-statement line calculates the sum (S) and difference (D) of two numbers. The two individual statements are separated by a colon.

One important feature of a high-level language is its syntax; i.e. the accepted rules which govern the formation of statements. These have to be learnt at the outset if the user is to produce programs which are syntactically correct and acceptable to the computer. The computer uses a compiler to translate programs in high-level language into machine-code instructions. Obviously, such a compiler must be microprocessor-specific.

A complete BASIC program to input two numbers, add them together, and print their result could take the following form:

```
10      INPUT A
20      INPUT B
30      S = A + B
40      PRINT S
50      END
```

Note that there are numerous ways of achieving this result. If, for example, multi-statement lines are permissible the program could be reduced to:

10 INPUT A,B : PRINT (A + B) : END

There are, unfortunately, numerous different dialects of the BASIC language. Many are derivatives of Microsoft BASIC but others, such as Sinclair BASIC and BBC BASIC, are peculiar to particular machines. Popular versions of BASIC for the IBM PC (such as GWBASIC, Turbo BASIC and Microsoft QuickBASIC) are, however, reasonably similar and all share a common subset of BASIC commands and syntax.

Memory maps

A microprocessor having a 16-bit address bus can address any one of 65536 (2^{16}) different memory locations. This memory can be used in various ways. Some will be devoted to data and program storage, and must therefore have the capacity to be written to and read from (read/write memory), whereas some will be used for more permanent storage of the operating system which will normally only permit reading (read only memory). In addition, on many personal computers BASIC or other high-level languages are also provided. These generally also form part of the read only memory.

It is often convenient to think of the total memory space available as being divided into contiguous blocks of either 1K, 4K, or 8K. These blocks can be allocated various functions depending upon the requirements of a particular system. A simple home computer may, for example, have a total memory of 32K (note that it is not necessary to have all 64K available)

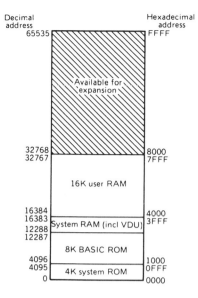

Figure 1.21   Typical memory map for a simple home computer

in which the operating system may exist in a block of 4K, a BASIC interpreter may require a block of 8K (this can be thought of as two 4K blocks end-on), and a further 4K block may contain read/write memory subdivided into 1K for a memory-mapped VDU and 3K for operating system parameters. The remaining 16K may then be devoted to read/write memory in which user programs and data are stored. Such an arrangement can most readily be illustrated by means of the memory map of Figure 1.21, which shows how the memory blocks are allocated.

In general, it is not necessary to draw memory maps to scale, nor is it necessary to show addresses in both decimal and hexadecimal formats. Fortunately, most manufacturers publish memory maps for their equipment and these can be a valuable aid to both the programmer and service technician. Simplified memory maps have been shown for six typical personal computers in Figures 1.22 to 1.27. Readers should contrast these maps and relate them to the primary function of each of the three machines. Note the differences between machines intended primarily for games/home use and those intended for more serious applications.

Random access memory

A large proportion (typically 50 per cent or more) of the total addressable memory space of a personal microcomputer is devoted to read/write memory. This area of memory is used for a variety of purposes, the most obvious of which is program and data storage. The term 'random access' simply refers to a memory device in which data may be retrieved from all locations with equal ease (i.e. access time is independent of actual memory address). This is important since our programs often involve moving sizeable blocks of data into and out of memory.

The basic element of a semiconductor random access memory is known as a 'cell'. Cells can be fabricated in one of two semiconductor technologies: MOS (metal oxide semiconductor) and bipolar. Bipolar memories are now rarely used in larger memories even though

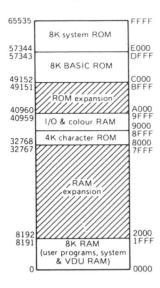

Figure 1.22   Simplified memory map for an 8K 6502-based Commodore VIC 20

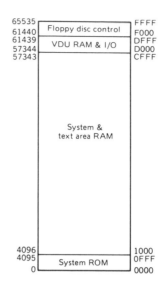

Figure 1.23   Simplified memory map for the Z80-based Sharp MZ700

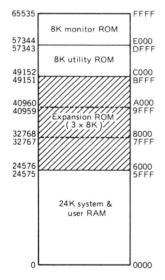

Figure 1.24   Simplified memory map for the 6301-based Epson HX20

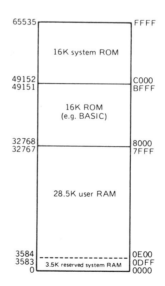

Figure 1.25   Simplified memory map for the 6502-based BBC Model B Microcomputer

they offer much faster access times. Their disadvantage is associated with power supply requirements since they need several voltage rails (both positive and negative) and use significantly more power than their MOS counterparts.

Random access memories can be further divided into static and dynamic types. The important difference between the two types is that dynamic memories require periodic

ADDRESS (hex)

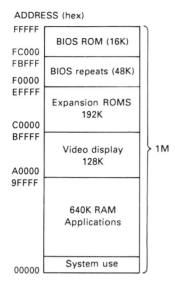

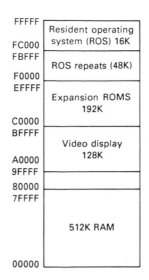

Figure 1.26   Typical memory map
for a low-cost PC compatible

Figure 1.27   Simplified memory
map for an Amstrad PPC512

refreshing if they are not to lose their contents. While, in the normal course of events, this would be carried out whenever data was read and rewritten, this technique cannot be relied upon to refresh all of the dynamic memory space and steps must be taken to ensure that all dynamic memory cells are refreshed periodically. This function has to be integrated with the normal operation of the microprocessor. Static memories do not need refreshing and can be relied upon to retain their memory until such time as new data is written or the power supply is interrupted (in which case all data is lost).

Memory cells

The circuit of a typical bipolar static memory cell is shown in Figure 1.28. The transistors form a bistable element which can be 'set' or 'reset' by means of a pulse applied to the appropriate emitter. The 'cell select' line is used to identify the particular cell concerned.

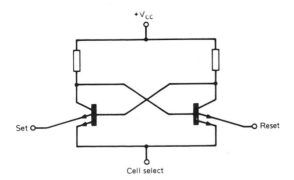

Figure 1.28   Circuit diagram of a
typical bipolar static memory cell

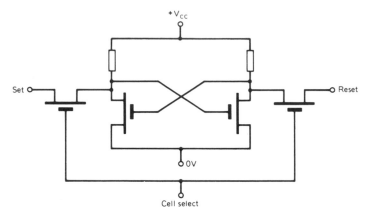

Figure 1.29   Circuit diagram of a typical MOS static memory cell

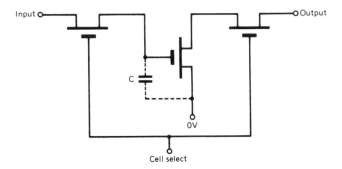

Figure 1.30   Circuit diagram of a typical MOS dynamic memory cell

This type of cell uses emitter-coupled logic (ECL) and requires both negative and positive supply rails.

The circuit of a typical MOS static memory cell is shown in Figure 1.29. This is also clearly recognizable as a bistable element. The 'cell select' line is used to gate signals into and out of the memory cell. Note that, as for the bipolar cell, the 'set' and 'reset' lines are common to a number of cells.

The circuit of a typical MOS dynamic memory cell is shown in Figure 1.30. In contrast to the previous types of cell this clearly does not use a bistable arrangement. Instead, a capacitor is used as the storage element. The capacitor is in fact the input capacitance of an MOS transistor. This is charged or discharged according to the state of the 'input', 'output' and 'cell select' lines.

RAM organization

The characteristics of a number of common random access memories are shown in Table 1.5 (a more complete table is included in the Reference section at the end of the book).

Table 1.5 RAM data summary

Type	Size (bits)	Organization	Package	Technology	Supply requirements
4116	16 384	16K words × 1 bit	16-pin DIL	D/NMOS	+5 V, –5 V and +12V (total dissipation 462 mW)
4164	65 536	64K words × 1 bit	16-pin DIL	D/CMOS	+5 V at 40 mA max.
4256	262 144	256K words × 1 bit	16-pin DIL	D/NMOS	+5 V at 78 mA max.
4416	65 536	16K words × 4 bit	18-pin DIL	D/NMOS	+5 V at 39 mA max.
5588	65 536	8K words × 8 bit	28-pin DIL	S/CMOS	+5 V at 115 mA max.
6116	16 384	2K words × 8 bit	24-pin DIL	S/CMOS	+5 V at 80 mA max.
6164	65 536	8K words × 8 bit	28-pin DIL	S/CMOS	+5 V at 80 mA max.
6264	65 536	8K words × 8 bit	28-pin DIL	S/CMOS	+5 V at 110 mA max.
43254	262 144	64K words × 4 bit	32-pin DIL	S/CMOS	+5 V at 120 mA max.
43256	262 144	32K words × 8 bit	28-pin DIL	S/CMOS	+5 V at 70 mA max.
50464	262 144	64K words × 4 bit	18-pin DIL	D/NMOS	+5 V at 83 mA max.
424256	1 048 576	256K words × 4 bit	20-pin DIL	D/NMOS	+5 V at 70 mA max.

Both static and dynamic examples of NMOS and CMOS technology have been included. Note that each of these memories is organized on a different basis. In practice this means that circuit arrangements used for read-write memories tend to be somewhat diverse! In order to illustrate this point, we shall outline the circuitry of memories based on the 4116,

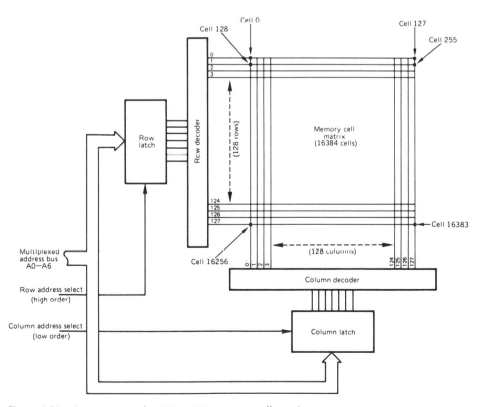

Figure 1.31   Arrangement of a 128 x 128 memory cell matrix

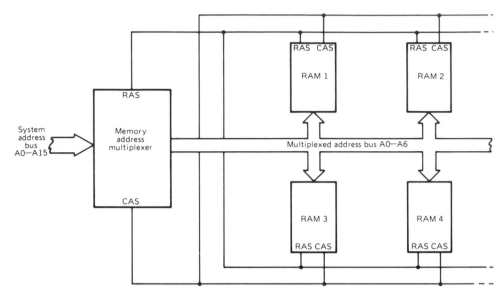

Figure 1.32   Basic arrangement for multiplexing the address bus

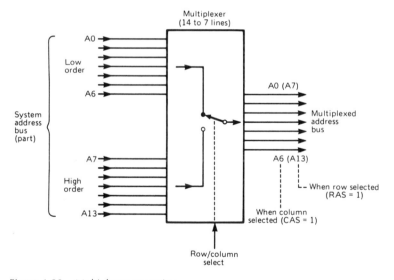

Figure 1.33   Multiplexer operation

6116, and 6264 devices. It should be a fairly simple matter for readers to extend the concepts described to any given memory arrangement.

From Table 1.5 it should readily be apparent that individual random access memories must contain some form of internal decoding in order to make each cell individually address-able. This is achieved by arranging the cells in the form of a matrix. Figure 1.31 shows one possible arrangement where 16 384 individual memory cells form a matrix consisting of 128 rows × 128 columns. Each cell within the array has a unique address and is selected by

Table 1.6 Multiplexed address decoding for a typical memory cell matrix

Order	A6	A5	A4	A3	A2	Al	A0	RAS	CAS	Row	Column	Cell No.
High	0	0	0	0	0	0	0	1	0	0	–	0
Low	0	0	0	0	0	0	0	0	1	–	0	
High	0	0	0	0	0	0	1	1	0	1	–	255
Low	1	1	1	1	1	1	1	0	1	–	127	
High	1	1	1	1	1	1	1	1	0	127	–	16383
Low	1	1	1	1	1	1	1	0	1	–	127	

placing appropriate logic signals on the row and column address lines. All that is necessary to interface the memory matrix to the system is some additional logic, but first we must consider the mechanism which allows the address bus to be connected to the memory cell.

The row and column decoders of Figure 1.31 have 128 output lines and seven input lines. Each possible combination of the seven input lines results in the selection of a unique output line. If we assume that the row decoder handles the most significant part of the address while the column decoder operates on the least significant portion, the cell at the top left-hand corner of the matrix will correspond to memory location 0 (0000H) whereas the corresponding position in the next row will be 128 (0080H). Finally, the cell at the bottom right-hand corner will be 16383 (3FFFH).

While it would be possible to have 14 separate address lines fed into the chip this is somewhat inelegant since, with the aid of some additional gating and latches, it is possible to reduce the number of address lines to seven. This is achieved by multiplexing part of the address bus and then demultiplexing it within the memory device. A typical arrangement is shown in

Figure 1.34   Upper 32K block of RAM in a Sinclair Spectrum

Figure 1.35   Lower 512K block of RAM in a Commodore Amiga A500

Figure 1.32. Separate row and column address select (RAS and CAS) control signals are required in order to enable the appropriate latches when the multiplexed address information is valid. The multiplexing arrangement for the address bus is shown in Figure 1.33. Note that, in practice, additional control signals will be required when several 16K blocks of RAM are present within the system. Such a precaution is essential in order to prevent data conflicts in which more than one memory cell (in different RAM blocks) is addressed simultaneously.

Table 1.6 shows the truth table for the address lines and decoding logic of the memory device. This table assumes that the most significant part of the address (high order) appears first and is decoded to the appropriate row while the least significant (low order) part appears second and is decoded to the appropriate column. The table shows the logic states for three address locations: 0, 255, and 16383 (0000H, 00FFH, and 3FFFH respectively).

The memory matrix described earlier is capable of storing a single bit at any of 16384 locations (16K × 1 bit). For a complete byte (eight bits) we would obviously require eight such devices. These would share the same address, RAS and CAS lines but would be responsible for different bits of the data bus. Various methods are employed for data transfer into and out of the matrix, sensing the state of either the rows or the columns of the matrix and gating with the write enable (WE) line so that data transfers only occur at the correct time. Data output is generally tristate by virtue of the shared data bus.

4116 RAM

The 4116 is a dynamic NMOS 16K word × 1 bit random access memory contained in a 16-pin DIL package. The device requires three separate supply rails; +12 V, +5 V and –5 V.

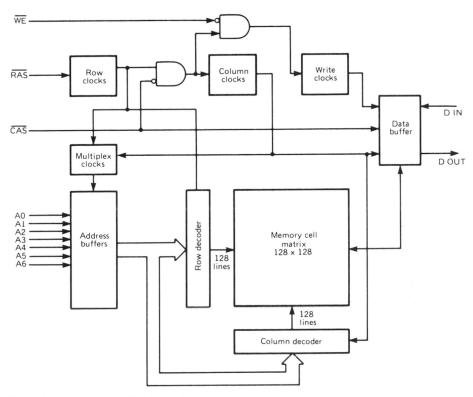

Figure 1.36   4116 simplified internal block schematic

A simplified internal block schematic of the device is shown in Figure 1.36. Note that complementary data lines are connected to opposite sides of the matrix. All input and output signals are fully TTL-compatible.

Since the device is dynamic, refresh circuitry has to be provided to compensate for the loss of charge within individual memory cells. This process must be carried out for every cell within the matrix at least once every 2 ms and is normally accomplished in the row address select (RAS) cycle. All cells can, in fact, be refreshed by scanning 128 addresses using address lines A0 to A6. Each refresh cycle then refreshes 128 cells of the selected row at a time.

The principal modes of operation are:

(a) *Memory read cycle.*   To read the contents of a particular memory cell the first part of the address is transferred to the row decoders when RAS goes low. The second part of the address is then transferred to the column decoders when CAS goes low. If the WE line is high the data output will appear for the address selected.

(b) *Memory write cycle.*   Data input is written to a particular memory cell by a similar process to that described in (a) with the WE line being taken low.

(c) *Read/modify/write cycle.*   During this cycle, first CAS and then WE are taken low so that data is read from and written to the same address within the same memory cycle.

(d) *Refresh cycle.*   CAS remains high during this cycle while RAS goes low. The address present identifies the row to be refreshed. This address is incremented on successive refresh cycles so that all rows are refreshed in 128 cycles.

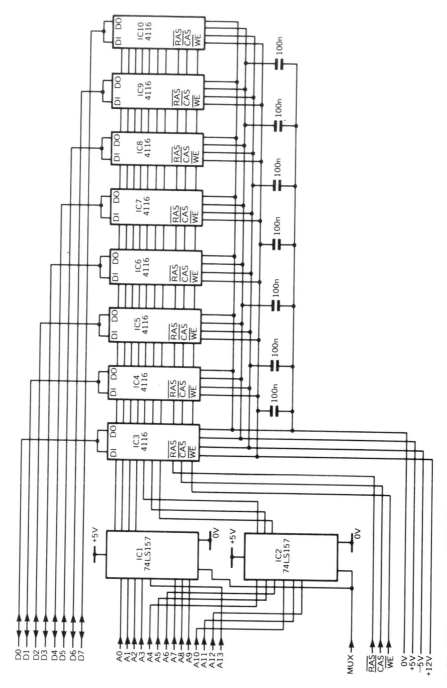

Figure 1.37   16K memory using 4116 RAM

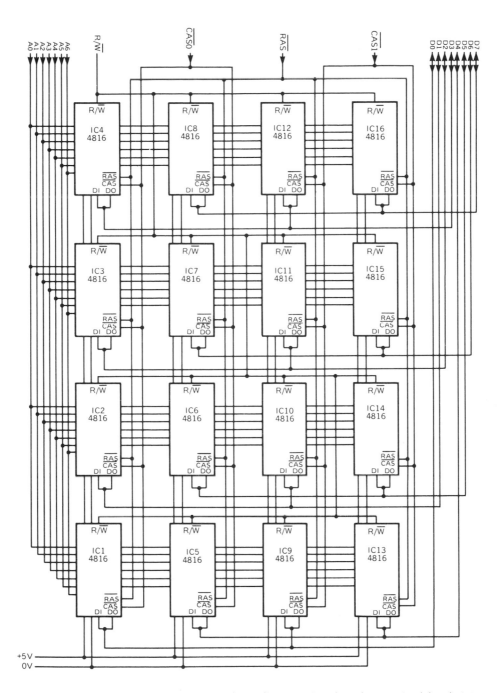

Figure 1.38   32K memory using 4816 RAM (decoupling capacitors have been omitted for clarity)

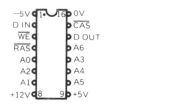

Figure 1.39   4116 pin connections]

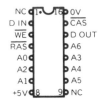

Figure 1.40   4816 pin connections

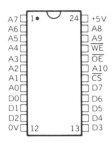

Figure 1.41   6116 pin connections

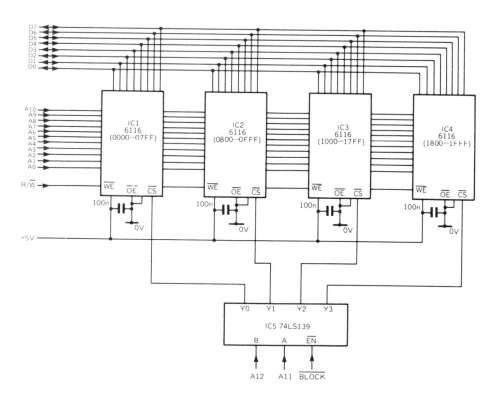

Figure 1.42   8K memory using 6116 RAM

Practical 16K and 32K memories using 4116 and 4816 RAM are shown in Figures 1.37 and 1.38 respectively. Both these memories utilize a multiplexed address bus. On the 32K memory, bank selection is accomplished by means of the column address select lines. The 4816 is very similar to the 4116 but the former device only requires a single +5 V supply rail. Pin connections for 4116 and 4816 devices are shown in Figures 1.39 and 1.40 respectively.

6116 RAM

The 6116 is a static CMOS 2048 word × 8 bit random access memory. Inputs and outputs of the 6116 are directly TTL-compatible and operation is from a single +5 V rail.

Like the 4116, the 6116 contains a 128 × 128 memory cell matrix. Address lines A1 to A7 are fed to the row decoder while A0 and A8 to A10 are fed to the column decoder, Eight data lines (input and output) are derived from the column lines, which are themselves arranged in groups of 16 (each group corresponding to one data bit).

The 6116 is contained in a 24-pin DIL package, the pin connections for which are shown in Figure 1.41. A typical 8K memory using four 6116 devices is shown in Figure 1.42. Eleven address lines (A0 to A10) are common to each 6116 whereas address lines A11 and A12 are decoded to provide chip select (CAS) signals for selection of 2K memory blocks corresponding to individual RAM chips. Data lines, D0 to D7, are common to all four memories.

6264 RAM

The 6264 is a static CMOS 8192 word × 8 bit random access memory. Only eight such devices are therefore required to provide a full 64K memory. Inputs and outputs of the 6264 are, of course, fully TTL-compatible and operation is again from a single +5V rail.

The 6264 contains a 256 × 256 matrix of memory cells. Address lines A0 to A7 are fed to the row decoder while A8 to A12 are fed to the column decoder. Like the 6116, eight data lines (input and output) are derived from the column lines. These are arranged in groups of 32 (each group corresponding to one data bit). Two chip select inputs are provided (CS2 and CS) and the truth table for the memory is shown in Table 1.7. The 6264 is contained in a 28-pin DIL package, the pin connections for which are shown in Figure 1.43.

Table 1.7 Truth table for the control inputs of a 6264 RAM

WE	CS	CS2	OE	Mode	Data line state
x	1	x	x	Not selected	High impedance
x	x	0	x	Not selected	High impedance
1	0	1	1	Output disabled	High impedance
1	0	1	0	Read	Data out
0	0	1	1	Write cycle 1	Data in
0	0	1	0	Write cycle 2	Data in

A typical 64K memory using eight 6264 devices is shown, in Figure 1.44. Thirteen address lines (A0 to A12) are common to each 6264 whereas the three most significant address lines, A13 to A15, are decoded to provide chip select (CS) signals for selection of

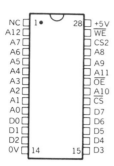

Figure 1.43   6264 pin connections

8K memory blocks corresponding to individual RAM chips. Data lines, D0 to D7, are common to all eight memory devices.

Read only memory

As its name implies, read only memory is memory which, once programmed, can only be read from and not written to. It may thus be described as 'non-volatile' since its contents are not lost when the supply is disconnected. This facility is, of course, necessary for the long-term semi-permanent storage of operating systems and high-level language interpreters. To change the operating system or language it is necessary to replace the ROM. This is a simple matter because ROMs are usually plug-in devices.

The following types are in common use:

(a) *Mask programmed ROM.* This, relatively expensive, process is suitable for high volume production (several thousand units, or more) and involves the use of a mask that programs links within the ROM chip. These links establish a permanent pattern of bits in the row/column matrix of the memory. The customer (computer manufacturer) must supply the ROM manufacturer with the programming information from which the mask is generated.

(b) *Programmable ROM (PROM).* This is a somewhat less expensive process than mask programming and is suitable for small/medium scale production. The memory cells consist of nichrome or polysilicon fuse links between rows and columns. These links can, by application of a suitable current pulse, be open-circuited or 'blown'. PROMs are ideal for prototype use and programming can be carried out by the computer manufacturer using relatively inexpensive equipment. When a PROM has been thoroughly tested, provided that volume production can be envisaged it is normal for the device to be replaced by a conventional mask programmed ROM.

(c) *Erasable programmable read-only memory (EPROM).* Unlike the two previous types of ROM, the EPROM can be re-programmed. EPROMs are manufactured with a window that allows light to fall upon the semiconductor memory cell matrix. The EPROM may be erased by exposure to a strong ultraviolet light source over a period of several minutes, or tens of minutes. Once erasure has taken place any previously applied bit pattern is completely removed, the EPROM is 'blank' and ready for programming. The programming process is carried out by the manufacturer from master software using a dedicated programming device which supplies pulses to establish the state of individual memory cells. This process usually takes several minutes (though some EPROM

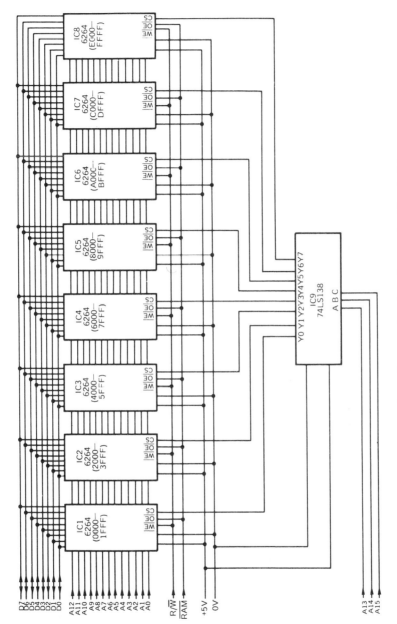

Figure 1.44 64K memory using 6264 RAM (decoupling capacitors have been omitted for clarity)

programmers can program several devices at once) and, since EPROMs tend to be relatively expensive, this process is clearly unsuitable for anything other than very small scale production. Furthermore, it should be noted that EPROMs tend to have rather different characteristics from PROMs and ROMs and thus subsequent volume production replacement may cause problems.

(d) *Electrically alterable ROM (EAROM).*   The EAROM can both be read to and written from. Unlike the random access memory (RAM) the EAROM is unsuitable for use in the read/write memory section of a computer since the writing process takes a considerable amount of time (typically a thousand times longer than the reading time). EAROMs are relatively recent and fairly expensive devices. As such, they have not found may applications in the microcomputer field. It should be noted that a reasonable compromise for semi-permanent data and program storage could take the form of low-power consumption RAM fitted with back-up batteries. In certain circumstances such a system can be relied upon to retain stored information, at relatively low cost, for a year or more. Such an arrangement is an attractive low-cost alternative to the use of EAROM devices.

ROM organization

The internal matrix structure of read only memories is somewhat similar to that employed for random access memories; i.e. individual cells within the matrix are uniquely referenced by means of row and column address lines. ROMs vary in capacity and 2K, 4K, 8K or 16K devices are commonplace. The characteristics of some common read only memories are shown in Table 1.8. To illustrate the operational characteristics of these devices we shall discuss circuitry based on 61366 ROM and 2732 EPROM devices.

Table 1.8 ROM data summary

Type	Size (bits)	Organization	Package	Technology
2716	16 384	2K words × 8 bit	24-pin DIL	uv EPROM
2732	32 768	4K words × 8 bit	24-pin DIL	uv EPROM
2764	65 536	8K words × 8 bit	28-pin DIL	uv EPROM
2816	16 384	2K words × 8 bit	24-pin DIL	EAROM
61366	65 536	8K words × 8 bit	24-pin DIL	mask ROM
613128	131 072	16K words × 8 bit	28-pin DIL	mask ROM
613256	262 144	32K words × 8 bit	28-pin DIL	mask ROM

61366 ROM

The 61366 is a mask programmed ROM containing a matrix of 64K individual memory cells arranged as 8192 words × 8 bit. The device is contained in a 24-pin DIL package, operates from a single +5 V supply, and is fully TTL-compatible. Pin connections for the ROM are shown in Figure 1.45.

The internal arrangement of the 61366 is shown in simplified form in Figure 1.46. The device has 13 address input lines, eight data output lines, and is controlled by a single output enable (OE) line. The state of this line (either OE or $\overline{OE}$ may be changed at the manufacturing stage according to the customer's requirements. It should also be noted that

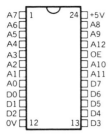

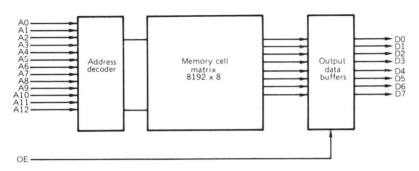

Figure 1.45   61366 pin connections

Figure 1.46   61366 simplified internal arrangement

some ROM manufacturers refer to a chip select (CS) input rather than an output enable (OE) line; in either case the function is essentially the same.

2732 EPROM

The 2732 is a UV-erasable programmable read only memory. The memory matrix contains 32K individual cells arranged as 4096 words × 8 bit. The device is fully TTL-compatible and is packaged in a 24-pin DIL encapsulation. The chip requires a +5V supply for normal read operation but an additional +25V pulse of nominally 50 ms duration is required for writing.

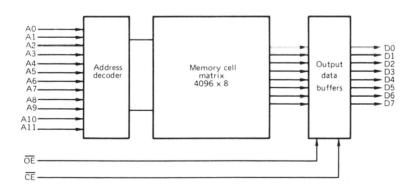

Figure 1.47   2732 simplified internal arrangement

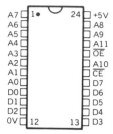

Figure 1.48   2732 pin connections

The simplified internal block schematic of the 2732 is shown in Figure 1.47. Twelve address inputs and eight data outputs are provided. The device has two control inputs, chip enable (CE) and output enable (CS). The first of these selects standby (CE high) and active (CE low) modes, whereas the second is used for requesting data output. The pin connections for the 2732 are shown in Figure 1.48.

Practical ROM arrangements

A typical arrangement of the read only memory in a 64K personal computer is shown in Figure 1.49. Three separate ROMs are provided, all three being mask programmed types.

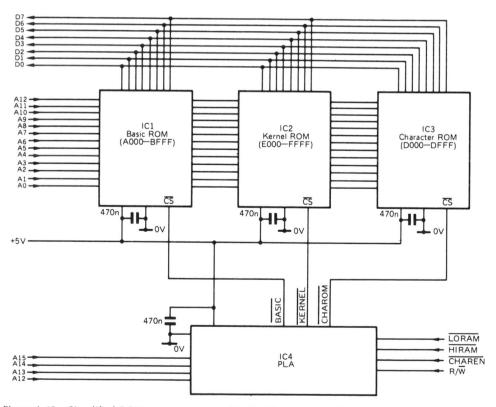

Figure 1.49   Simplified ROM arrangement used in the Commodore 64

Figure 1.50   EPROM device fitted to a PC-compatible computer (the EPROM is fitted with an adhesive label to protect the active surface of the chip from the effects of light)

IC1 contains an 8K BASIC interpreter, IC2 (8K) contains the operating system kernel, and IC3 (4K) contains the display character set. Chip select (CS) signals are derived from a programmed logic array which, in turn, derives its inputs from the four most significant address lines (A12 to A15). Note that in some machines (notably in the BBC Microcomputer) a paged ROM system is provided. Selection of ROMs is under software control and allows several ROMs to share the same memory space. This arrangement permits the extensive use of ROM-based software without necessitating the physical insertion and removal of ROM cartridges.

Parallel input and output

Most microcomputers incorporate some form of parallel input/output (PIO) facility. While an increasing number of microprocessors provide this as an in-built facility, parallel I/O invariably takes the form of one, or more, LSI devices commonly known as peripheral interface adaptors (PIA). Such devices generally provide two separate 8-bit ports in which each of the eight bit lines can be configured, under software control, as an input or output.

The interface from the PIA to the CPU usually consists of eight data lines, five address lines, and five control lines. The data lines are, of course, bidirectional whereas the address

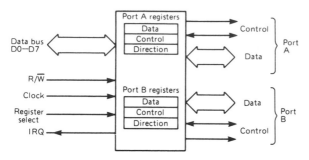

Figure 1.51   Basic arrangement of a PIA

lines are unidirectional and form a sub-set of the system address bus. The PIA thus appears as a number of specific memory addresses which may be selected by appropriate software instructions. The PIA also utilizes the CPU control bus where, for example, a R/W signal is needed in order to determine the direction of data flow from/to the PIA.

The basic arrangement of a PIA is shown in Figure 1.51. The PIA is internally divided into two independent sections, A and B. Each section is equipped with three registers, the function of which will be discussed separately. In addition, bidirectional buffers are used to interface the peripheral lines to the PIA. These buffers are generally TTL-compatible and provide a limited current drive facility, typically of the order of 1 mA or so.

Data registers

During a CPU write operation the addressed data registers are loaded with the data currently present on the system data bus. The data is then available to those lines which have been programmed as outputs. During a CPU read operation the data present on those peripheral lines programmed as inputs is transferred to the system data bus.

Control registers

The control registers allow the CPU to establish and control the operating modes of the peripheral control lines. In addition bits are reserved for use as interrupt flags and as a means of selecting either output data or data direction registers. The various bits in the control registers may be accessed many times during a program to allow the CPU to change operating and interrupt modes as required by the particular peripheral device being controlled.

Data direction registers

The data direction registers are used to determine which of the peripheral lines are configured as inputs and which are configured as outputs. Each bit position of the data registers corresponds to a particular peripheral line. A logic 1 written to the particular bit position designates the corresponding line as an output, and vice versa. Data direction and data registers often share the same address and selection between the two is made using one of the bits contained in the control register.

6522 VIA

The 6522 versatile interface adaptor (VIA) is an enhanced version of the 6520 (6820) PIA device. The 6522 differs from the 6520 in having additional internal devices: (a) two interval timers, (b) a serial-to-parallel/parallel-to-serial shift register, and (c) a means of latching input data on the peripheral ports.

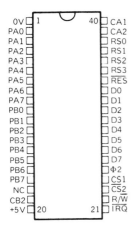

Figure 1.52   6522 pin connections

The pin connections and internal architecture of the 6522 device are respectively shown in Figures 1.52 and 1.53. The functions of the input and output signal lines may be summarized as follows:

PA0–PA7   Peripheral port A consisting of eight data lines which can be individually programmed as outputs or inputs.

CA1, CA2   Control lines for peripheral port A which can act as interrupt inputs or a handshake pair, CA1 input and CA2 output.

PB0–PB7   Peripheral port B consisting of eight data lines which can be individually programmed as outputs or inputs. These lines represent one standard TTL load in the input mode and will drive one standard TTL load in the output mode. The lines can be used to source a current of 1 mA at 1.5 V (logic 1) and can thus be used to drive a standard Darlington output stage. In addition, the polarity of the PB7 output signal can be controlled by one of the interval timers while the second timer can be used to count pulses present on the PB6 line.

CB1, CB2   Control lines for peripheral port B which can act in a similar manner to those associated with port A. These lines also represent one standard TTL load in the input mode and will drive one standard TTL load in the output mode. The lines can be used to source a current of 1 mA at 1.5 V (logic 1) and can thus be used to drive a standard Darlington output stage. In addition, the lines can act as a serial port under the control of the shift register.

R/W   The read/write line determines the direction of data transfers within the VIA. If R/W is low, data is transferred from the CPU to the VIA. If R/W is high, data is transferred from the VIA to the CPU.

IRQ   The interrupt request line goes low whenever an internal interrupt flag is set and the corresponding interrupt enable bit is a logic 1. This output may be wire-OR'ed with other equivalent signals in the system.

RS0–RS3   The four register select lines are usually connected to the system address bus in order that the CPU may select appropriate VIA registers. The 16 possible combinations are shown in the truth table below:

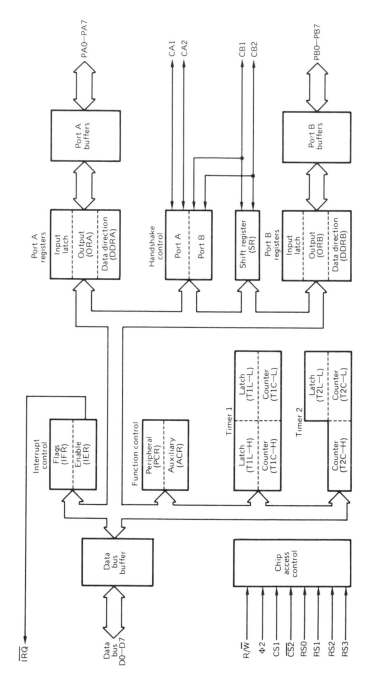

Figure 1.53 6522 internal block schematic

RS3	RS2	RS1	RS0	Register selected	Notes
0	0	0	0	ORB	
0	0	0	1	ORA	Controls handshake
0	0	1	0	DDRB	
0	0	1	1	DDRA	
0	1	0	0	T1L-L	Write latch
				T1C-L	Read counter
0	1	0	1	T1C-H	Triggers T1L-L/T1C-L transfer
0	1	1	0	T1L-L	
0	1	1	1	T1L-H	
1	0	0	0	T2L-L	Write latch
				T2C-L	Read counter
1	0	0	1	T2C	Triggers T2L-L/T2C-L transfer
1	0	1	0	SR	
1	0	1	1	ACR	
1	1	0	0	PCR	
1	1	0	1	IFR	
1	1	1	0	IER	
1	1	1	1	ORA	No effect on handshake

CS1,CS2   Chip select lines, which are normally connected to the system address bus either directly or via suitable decoding. The selected 6522 register will be accessed when CS1 is high and CS2 is low.

DB0–DB7   8-bit bi-directional system data bus. When the chip is selected (CS1 = 1, CS2 = 0) with R/W high and ø2 high, the contents of the selected register are placed on the bus. When the chip is selected with R/W low and ø2 high, the data on the bus will be transferred into the selected VIA register.

ø2   System clock phase 2. Data transfers only take place when ø2 is high. This signal also provides the timebase for the VIA timers and shift registers.

RES   Clears all internal registers (to logic 0) except for those associated with the shift register and timers. Also disables all interrupts emanating from the VIA.

Keyboards

As an example of the use of PIA devices, we shall now consider the operation of a typical keyboard decoding arrangement. On most microcomputers, the keyboard consists of a matrix of 60 or more switches, with the possible addition of further switches reserved for specific functions. The main keyboard matrix is usually arranged as eight columns and eight rows with individual switches linking rows and columns at each of the 64 locations, as shown in Figure 1.54. Various types of switch mechanism are employed, including rubber membrane and dry reed types. Early microcomputers often suffered from a problem known as 'switch bounce'. This is, to a greater or lesser extent, present with most types of switch and results from the generation of multiple pulses whenever a switch is closed or opened. Fortunately, a cure can easily be effected by introducing appropriate software delays in the keyboard processing routines.

A typical keyboard decoding arrangement is shown in simplified block schematic form in Figure 1.55. The PIA device is an 8255, which the manufacturers, Intel, refer to as a programmable peripheral interface (PPI). The 8255 provides three 8-bit I/O ports. Two of these, ports A and B, are normally configured as 8-bit ports whereas port C may be arranged as two separate 4-bit ports. The 8255 is encapsulated in the usual 40-pin DIL package, the pin connections for which are shown in Figure 1.56.

The circuit of the keyboard is shown in Figure 1.57. The key matrix is arranged in eight columns and 16 rows (not all of which are employed). Ports A and B are configured as

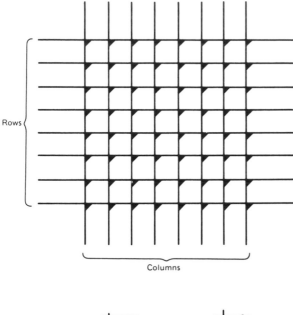

Figure 1.54   8 x 8 keyboard matrix

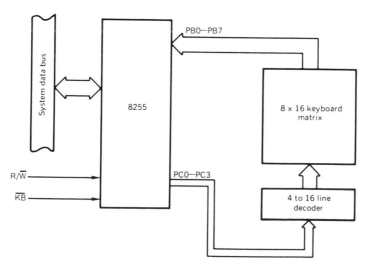

Figure 1.55   Simplified schematic of a keyboard arrangement using an 8255 PIA

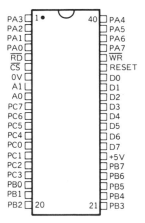

Figure 1.56   8255 pin connections

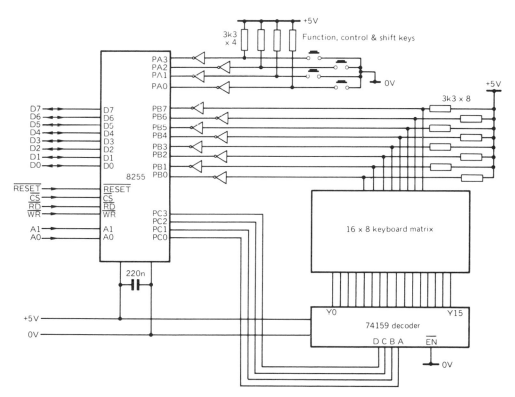

Figure 1.57   Keyboard interface using an 8255 PIA

inputs while port C is configured as an output. Note that only half of port C is utilized and that the four output lines are taken to a four-to-sixteen line decoder, IC2. This device effectively scans the keyboard rows, addressing each in turn, as the binary count on port C is cycled through its 16 states under software control. This process is repeated every 10 ms and an appropriate interrupt is generated when a key depression is detected by a return

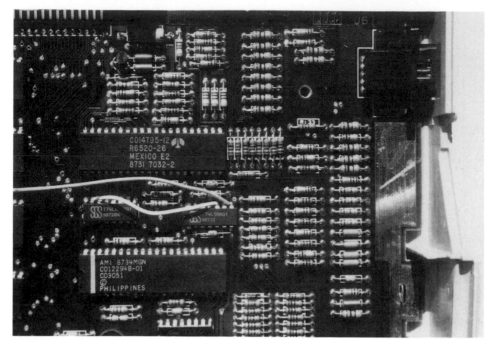

Figure 1.58   Parallel I/O devices in an Atari 65XE

signal appearing on a column line. Note that special function keys, such as 'Shift' and 'Control', do not form part of the matrix. These, higher priority, keys are treated separately as direct inputs to port A.

Serial input and output

Parallel data transfer is primarily suited to high-speed operation over relatively short distances, a typical example being the linking of a microcomputer to an adjacent dot matrix printer. There are, however, a number of applications in which parallel data transfer is inappropriate, the most common example being data communication by means of telephone lines. In such cases data must be sent serially rather than in parallel form. Parallel data from the microprocessor must therefore be reorganized into a train of bits, each following the next. An essential requirement of such an arrangement is a means of parallel-to-serial data conversion.

   This interface generally takes the form of an LSI device containing a number of registers, one of which is organized as a shift register that is loaded from the data bus with data in conventional parallel form. The data is then read out as a serial bit stream by successive shifting. The reverse process, serial-to-parallel conversion, again utilizes a shift register. In this case data is loaded in serial form, each bit shifting further into the register until it becomes full. Data is then read out from all bistables simultaneously into the parallel output lines. The basic principles of parallel-to-serial and serial-to-parallel data conversion are illustrated in Figures 1.59(a) and 1.59(b) respectively.

Figure 1.59(a)   Basic principle of a parallel-serial converter

Figure 1.59(b)   Basic principle of a serial-parallel converter

When considering serial data transmission, a distinction must be made between synchronous and asynchronous modes of transmission. The former requires a common clock signal to be present at both the transmitter and receiver. This signal is essential to both the coding and decoding processes and may be either transmitted along a separate path or regenerated from synchronizing information accompanying the data.

In the asynchronous mode of transmission individual bytes of data are sent as a series of packets. Each packet contains additional bits to assist in the decoding process. These could, for example, be present at the start and end of each byte. The rate at which data can be transmitted depends upon a number of factors not the least of which is the bandwidth of the transmission medium. The data rate, i.e. number of bits transmitted per second, is specified in 'baud'. This varies from 75 to 19200 (19.2k) baud in practical systems.

In many cases a means of detecting errors is incorporated, which relies on additional bits (not part of the data) in a parity checking system. If even parity is employed, the additional parity bit is made a 1 in order that the total number of 1s present is even. If odd parity is selected, the additional parity bit is made a 1 in order to make the total number of 1s odd. The number of data bits transmitted can vary from five to eight, with seven being the norm. The format of a typical asynchronously transmitted word consists of a start bit, seven data bits (ASCII coded), a parity bit and two stop bits, as illustrated in Figure 1.60. From this example it should be evident that the asynchronous mode of transmission uses more transmitted bits, per word, than the synchronous mode. In the foregoing example a total of 11 bits is needed to send a single ASCII character.

The binary values of 0 and 1 may be transmitted down a line as a series of alternating voltage levels. The normal convention is that the more positive level, or 'mark', corresponds to logic 1, whereas the more negative level, or 'space' is used to denote logic 0. A 'forbidden' region is assumed to exist between the two levels. This is instrumental in eliminating noise and induced pulses. It should be noted that we are not necessarily confined to standard

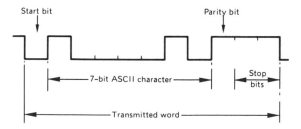

Figure 1.60   Typical format used for an asynchronously transmitted word

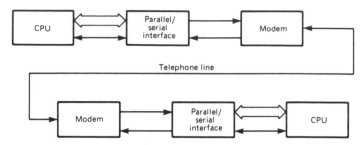

Figure 1.61   Simplified block schematic of a serial data transmission system using a telephone line

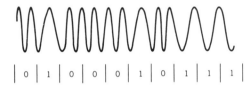

| 0 | 1 | 0 | 0 | 0 | 1 | 0 | 1 | 1 | 1 |

1650 Hz = '1', 1850 Hz = '0'

Figure 1.62   FSK transmitted waveform

TTL levels in the transmission path. The RS-232 interface standard does, in fact, employ both positive and negative voltage levels well in excess of the nominal +5 V associated with TTL systems. A further problem arises from types of transmission media in which only a.c. coupling of signals is permissible, a particular case in point being that of a telephone line.

Since it is not possible to transmit a series of voltage (or current) levels along a telephone line, some means is required for conveying the information using a signal within the audio range. This signal is frequency modulated with the binary information within a 'modem', or modulator/demodulator.

A simplified block schematic of a serial data transmission system involving a telephone line is shown in Figure 1.61. At the originating modem, the incoming train of binary information is converted to an audio signal having two frequencies, one to denote 'mark' and the other to denote 'space'. The two frequencies are chosen so as to make their discrimination relatively easy while they both remain within the passband of the telephone system. The transmitted waveform, corresponding to the previous example of asynchronous coding, is shown in Figure 1.62. A means of converting the frequency shift keyed (FSK) signal back to a train of binary data is incorporated within the receiving modem.

We shall now turn our attention to the operation of a typical LSI device designed to interface a microprocessor to a wide range of serial peripherals. This device accepts parallel data from the CPU and, depending upon its current operating status, formats, serializes and transmits the data as a serial bit stream. Serial data can also be simultaneously received, converted into parallel form and presented to the CPU.

8251 USART

The Intel 8251 is a universal synchronous/asynchronous receiver/transmitter (USART). It was designed primarily for use with Intel's 8085 microprocessor, but may also be used with a

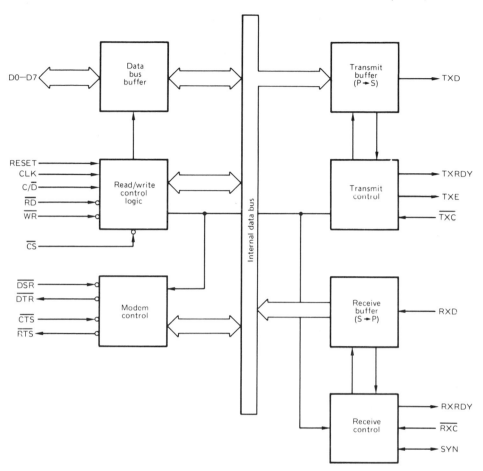

Figure 1.63   8251 internal block schematic

variety of 8-bit CPUs. The device accepts data from the CPU in parallel form and then generates a serial stream for transmission. At the same time, it can receive data in serial form and convert it to parallel data to be placed on the system data bus. The 8251 can operate in both synchronous and asynchronous modes at baud rates from d.c. to 64 kb. Various forms of error detection are incorporated.

The 8251 is shown, in simplified block schematic form, in Figure 1.63. A tristate bidirectional bus buffer is used to interface the internal data bus with the CPU data bus. Data is received or transmitted by the buffer during execution of IN or OUT (or equivalent MOV) instructions, respectively. Control words and status information are also transferred through the data bus buffer.

The transmit buffer accepts parallel data from the internal data bus and converts it to a serial bit stream adding additional bits as required by the particular mode of transmission selected. Management of the transmit buffer is assigned to the transmit controller. This device also generates external signals to indicate the status of the transmit buffer. Data is shifted out of the transmit buffer on the falling edge of the TXC signal.

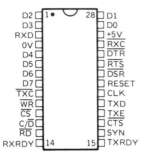

Figure 1.64   8251 pin connections

The receiver buffer accepts serial data, converts this to parallel form, checks for bits or characters that are unique to the communication mode employed, and then sends parallel data (less additional bits) to the internal data bus. Data is clocked in on the rising edge of the RXC signal. The management of the receiver buffer is assigned to the receive controller.

A useful additional feature of the 8251 is that it incorporates internal logic which can be used to control an external modem. Four control signals are involved: data set ready (DSR), data terminal ready (DTR), request to send (RTS), and clear to send (CTS).

The 8251 is housed in a 28-pin DIL package, the pin connections for which are shown in Figure 1.64. We shall now briefly discuss the function of each of the principal signal lines:

RESET   Input, active high. Used by the CPU to initiate an 'idle' mode. Once reset, the 8251 will await a new set of control words which will define its new operating mode.

CLK   Clock input, generally derived from ø2 of the system clock.

WR   Input, active low. Used by the CPU to signal the 8251 that data (or control) words are being written to it.

RD   Input, active low. Used by the CPU to signal the 8251 that data (or status) words are being read from it.

C/D   Input, used in conjunction with RD and WR inputs. A 1 on this input informs the 8251 that the word currently present on the CPU data bus is to be taken as data. A 0 on this input informs the 8251 that the word currently present on the data bus is control (or status) information.

CS   Input, active low. A 0 on this input selects the 8251. When CS is high, the internal data bus is in the high impedance (floating) state and RD and WR signals will have no effect.

DSR, DTR, The functions of these modem control signals are discussed in the section on the RS-232
RTS, CTS   interface.

TXD   Output, serial data. This line assumes the 'mark' state in the reset condition or when the transmit buffer is empty.

TXRDY   Output, active high. Used to inform the CPU that the transmitter is ready to accept a data character.

TXE   Output, active high. This output indicates that the transmitter is empty.

TXC   Input, active low. Controls the data rate of the 8251. In the synchronous mode, the baud rate is equal to the frequency of the TXC signal. In the asynchronous mode, the baud rate is a fraction of the TXC frequency. The fraction (1, 1/16, or 1/64) is determined by part of the mode instruction.

RXD   Input, serial data.

RXRDY   Output, active high. Used to inform the CPU that a character is available from the receive buffer.

RXC   Input, receiver clock. Controls the rate at which data is received. Functionally similar to the TXC signal.

SYN/BRK   Input/output, as determined by the control word. In synchronous mode this informs the CPU that a synchronizing character has been detected in the received data stream. In asynchronous mode, this pin goes high when an all-zero word of the designated length (i.e. including start, data, parity and stop bits) appears in the received data stream. This occurs whenever there is a break in the incoming serial data.

The RS-232 interface

The RS-232 interface is the most widely used method of providing serial communication between microcomputers and peripheral devices, The interface is defined by the Electronic Industries Association (EIA) standard and relates to the connection of data terminal equipment (DTE) and data communication equipment (DCE). For many purposes the DTE and DCE are the computer and peripheral respectively, although the distinction is not always clear, as for example in the case where two microcomputers are linked together via RS-232 ports. In general, the RS-232 system may be used where the DTE and DCE are physically separated by up to 20 m or so. For greater distances telephone lines are usually more appropriate.

The EIA specification permits synchronous or asynchronous communication at data rates of up to 19.2 kb. Furthermore, character length and bit codes may be varied according to the particular application. The specification allows for three distinct types of signal within the RS-232 system. These are serial data, timing signals and control signals. In addition, two separate communication channels are provided: a primary channel normally used for high speed data transfer, and a secondary channel normally employed for passing control signals.

The RS-232 system may thus be configured for a variety of operating modes including transmit only (primary channel), receive only (primary channel), half-duplex, full-duplex, and various primary and secondary channel transmit/receive combinations.

From this, it should be clear that the RS-232 is versatile and highly adaptable. Unfortunately, such flexibility does carry a penalty - the wide variation in interpretation which often results in bewildering anomalies in the physical connection and control protocol of practical RS-232 systems.

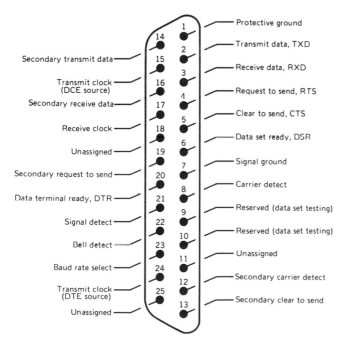

Figure 1.65   RS-232 pin connections

Figure 1.66   RS-232 ports (COM1 and COM2) in an IBM PC/XT compatible (note the line drivers and line receivers, U3 to U6)

Figure 1.67   RS-232 port on an Amiga A500

The RS-232 interface is usually distinguished by its connector; a 25-way 'D' connector. The pin arrangement for this connector is shown in Figure 1.65. Note that two lines are used for ground (signal return) and three are unassigned. In practice, few systems involving personal computers make use of the full complement of signal lines; indeed, many arrangements use only eight lines in total (including the protective ground and signal return).

The most common arrangement for a microcomputer RS-232 interface involves six signal lines and two ground connections. These use pins 1 to 7 and 20 of the D-connector and their functions, assuming that we are dealing with the computer side of the interface, are as follows:

Protective ground	Connected to the equipment frame or chassis (may be connected to an outer screening conductor).
TXD	Transmitted data. Serial output.
RXD	Received data. Serial input.
RTS	Request to send, Output. Peripheral to transmit data when an 'on' condition is present.
CTS	Clear to send. Input. When 'on' indicates that the peripheral can receive data.
DSR	Data set ready. Input. When 'on' indicates that handshaking has been completed.
Signal ground	Acts as a common signal return. Normally connected to a ground point within the RS-232 interfaces and should not be linked directly to the protective ground (even though these may both appear to be at zero potential).
DTR	Data terminal ready. Output. When 'on' indicates that the peripheral should be connected to the communication channel.

The voltage levels in an RS-232 system are markedly different from those within the computer. In the transmit and receive data paths, for example, a positive voltage of between, 3 V and 25 V is used to represent logic 0 while a negative voltage of similar magnitude is used to represent logic 1. In the control signal paths, however, conventional positive logic is employed; a high voltage in the range 3 V to 25 V indicates the active or 'on' state while a negative voltage of similar magnitude indicates the inactive or 'off' state. It should be noted that some 'quasi RS-232' systems exist in which conventional TTL logic levels are employed. Such systems are obviously not directly compatible with the original EIA system and considerable damage can be caused by inadvertent interconnection of the two.

Memory mapped input and output

Previously discussed input and output techniques have involved the use of ports through which data is transferred in response to CPU IN and OUT instructions. An alternative technique, known as memory mapped I/O, treats external devices as memory addresses. Memory mapped I/O offers both advantages and disadvantages. Chief amongst the advantages is that one is not constrained to transfer all data through the accumulator, as is the case with port I/O.

The address of a memory mapped device is usually 16 bits in length and this can be stored in an appropriate length register (e.g. AX, BX or HL). By using register addressed instructions, a memory mapped I/O transfer can be achieved with a minimum of code. Accumulator I/O, on the other hand, requires an additional 8 or 16-bit code (the port address) to distinguish individual peripheral devices. The particular device select signal is then obtained by decoding this information. To illustrate the principles of memory mapped I/O we shall discuss an alternative method of interfacing a keyboard to a CPU.

A simple 8 × 8 keyboard matrix and associated inverting buffers/drivers is shown in Figure 1.68. The keyboard rows are driven by the eight least significant address lines, A0 to A7.

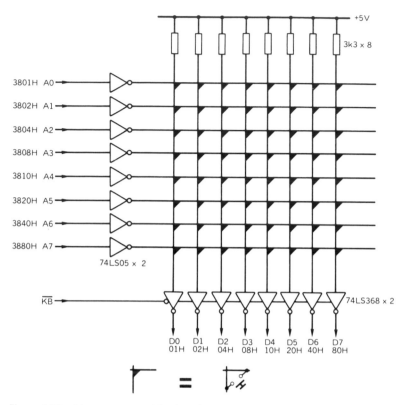

Figure 1.68   Memory mapped keyboard arrangement

The keyboard columns provide inputs to the system data bus, D0 to D7. A common enable signal is fed to the keyboard data bus buffers. This signal, KB, is derived from the address decoding logic such that the keyboard becomes enabled when the most significant address bits take the following pattern:

A15	A14	A13	A12	A11	A10	A9	A8
0	0	1	1	1	0	0	0

The remaining address bits, A0 to A7, are scanned under software control such that only one line is addressed at a time. This corresponds to the following sequence of addresses:

A7	A6	A5	A4	A3	A2	A1	A0	Hex address
0	0	0	0	0	0	0	1	3801
0	0	0	0	0	0	1	0	3802
0	0	0	0	0	1	0	0	3804
0	0	0	0	1	0	0	0	3808
0	0	0	1	0	0	0	0	3810
0	0	1	0	0	0	0	0	3820
0	1	0	0	0	0	0	0	3840
1	0	0	0	0	0	0	0	3880

When a key depression occurs, a logic 1 appears on the appropriate data bus line. This is detected by the CPU and an interrupt is generated (unless temporarily disabled under software control). The CPU then refers to a look-up table in ROM in order to determine which character has been selected. The CPU uses the eight least significant address bits together with the eight bits from the data bus to reference the look-up table.

Raster scan displays

The most common form of display used with personal computers employs raster scan techniques similar to those found in conventional television receivers. Indeed, in many cases the output of the computer is modulated onto a UHF carrier in order to be reasonably compatible with a normal received broadcast signal and thus obviating the need for a purpose-designed display. Other equipment may incorporate a CRT and associated video circuitry or may provide a video output (of nominally 1 V into 75 ohm) for connection to an external monitor. The various options may be summarized as follows:

(a) *Internal CRT display.*   Such equipment is usually intended for business applications and/or word processing. The display is generally monochrome (green or white phosphor) but some computers have colour facilities. Display resolution is invariably sufficient to cater both for high resolution graphics and 80-column text.

(b) *External monitor.*   The computer provides an output for connection to a high/medium resolution video monitor. The monitor may be monochrome (with either green or white phosphor) or R-G-B. In either case, and given suitable bandwidth, the system is generally capable of reproducing high resolution graphics and 80-column text.

(c) *TV receiver.*   The computer provides a low-level PAL-compatible modulated UHF output suitable for direct connection to the aerial input socket of a conventional monochrome (black and white) or colour receiver. Sound may also be present, modulated on the composite signal. This is the most popular display method used for low-cost home computers. Unfortunately, due to bandwidth limitations, such an arrangement is generally limited to medium resolution graphics and 40-column text. Furthermore, accurate tuning is essential and both the receiver and modulator must be drift-free.

(d) *VDU terminal.*   As an alternative to the above, some computers provide serial outputs suitable for connection to a conventional computer VDU terminal by means of an RS-232 interface. Such a terminal contains its own read/write memory (necessary for storing a full screen of information) and can generate the necessary logic control signals. A keyboard may also be provided and this may be used as an alternative to the keyboard that is integral with the computer. This arrangement is ideal for the smaller portable machines which only have small liquid crystal displays. The system is generally only monochrome (either green or white phosphor) but is capable of medium/high resolution.

(e) *A combination of methods (a) to (d).*   Many personal computers provide for several alternative display methods. In particular, methods (b) and (c) are often simultaneously available. The user may thus initially use a broadcast television receiver and later up-grade to a purpose-built monitor.

We shall now continue with a brief description of the method of picture generation and the characteristics of the video signal itself. A detailed discussion of raster scan techniques is, however, beyond the scope of this book and readers needing further information are recommended to consult more specific texts.

The standards for computer raster scan displays are invariably based upon the standards used for broadcast television in the country concerned. In the UK, therefore, the display normally uses 625 lines, has an aspect ratio (picture width:height) of 4:3, and a field frequency of 50 Hz. The scanned display, or raster, can be thought of as comprising an array of rectangular cells arranged in rows and columns. Cells themselves consist of a matrix of dots, each of which may be either dark or bright. A typical form of matrix has dots grouped in eight rows and eight columns. Hence there are 256 points within a cell and these can be individually addressed using eight bytes (one for each column within the matrix). For text and block graphics representations we can economize on memory overhead by using a single byte to represent a particular cell pattern of bright and dark points. This byte acts as a pointer to the full set of eight bytes stored in character ROM that define the complete cell pattern.

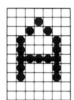

Figure 1.69   Display cell pattern for character 'A'

The cell pattern itself may constitute a particular character or graphics symbol, as shown in Figure 1.69. The number of such characters and symbols tends to vary from system to system. Personal computers typically offer 100 or more individual characters (including upper and lower case letters, numbers, punctuation and graphic symbols). The characters defined in ROM are referenced by 8-bit values placed into screen memory (an area of RAM reserved for the display). The video processing circuitry then produces the correct waveform from the character data stored in ROM.

The number of cells available over the display area tends to vary. Some smaller home computers provide screens of as few as 22 × 23 cells, others cater for as many as 80 × 32 cells. Note that the amount of screen memory provided must increase as the number of cells (and consequently the display resolution) increases. A typical 40 × 24 or 64 × 16 display requires about 1K of screen memory. By contrast, an 80 × 32 character display requires 2.5K of memory. In addition, extra memory must be provided for colour information, where appropriate.

Various techniques are used for high-resolution graphics rather than text/graphics block displays and it is dangerous to generalize about the techniques involved. Popular methods involve bit-mapping the entire screen such that individual pixels may be addressed.

Colour displays require both luminance (brightness) and chrominance (colour information). Coding schemes are used to minimize the memory overhead and there is often some limitation on the total number of colours which can be present at the same time. Red, green and blue outputs (plus composite synchronization) are generated separately for colour monitors. These outputs may be summed to produce a monochrome video output. Alternatively the R-G-B outputs may be encoded (using an encoder i.c. such as the National Semiconductor LM1889) and then used to modulate a UHF signal. A complete multi-purpose colour encoder is shown in block schematic form in Figure 1.70.

The following information must be recovered from a composite monochrome video signal:

(a) vertical synchronizing pulses to control the field scan generation;
(b) horizontal synchronizing pulses to control the line scan generation; and

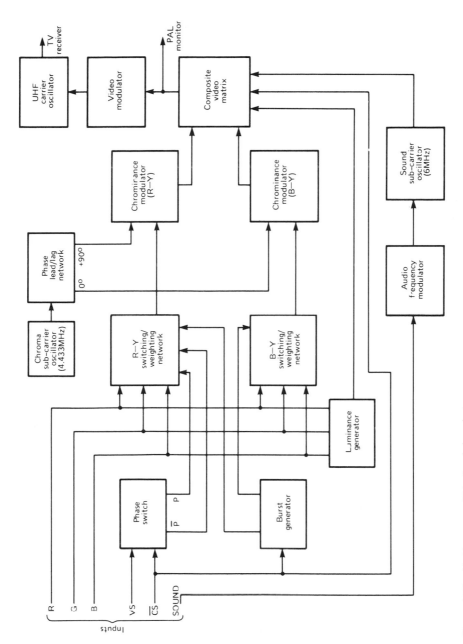

Figure 1.70 Multi-purpose PAL signal decoder

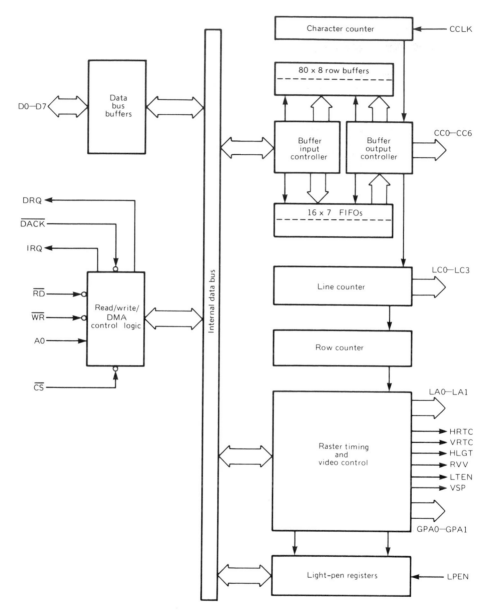

Figure 1.71   8275 internal block schematic

(c) brightness information, which is used to modulate the electron beam generated within the cathode ray tube.

The normal amplitude required of a signal for connection to a standard video monitor is 1 V into 75 ohm. Some monitors will, however, accept separate video and synchronizing signals at TTL level. Such an arrangement obviously simplifies the video signal generating

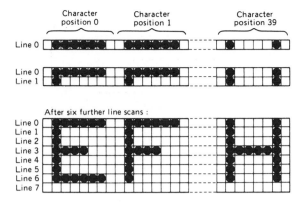

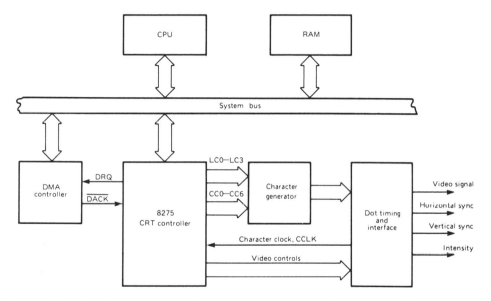

Figure 1.72   Process of building successive lines of a display

Figure 1.73   Simplified arrangement of a raster scan display controller using an 8275

circuitry. In a composite system, the synchronizing pulses may be separated quite easily from the brightness information and then applied to the field and line oscillators of the television receiver or monitor.

The problem of video signal generation is greatly simplified by the use of VLSI controllers such as the National Semiconductor 8350, Motorola 6845 and Intel 8275 (whose block schematic is shown in Figure 1.71). Such devices are responsible for management of the video processing within the microcomputer and include such functions as periodic refreshing of the display, providing various programmable screen and character formats, and generating synchronizing and blanking signals. Characters to be displayed are usually retrieved from memory and displayed on a row-by-row basis. Direct memory access (DMA) techniques are used to permit fast data transfer without requiring the attention of the CPU.

Figure 1.74   Video interface and connector on an Amiga A500

Figure 1.75   Video interface buffer on an Amstrad PPC512

Internal registers are provided to buffer several lines of the display during scanning. The process of building up lines of the display is illustrated in Figure 1.72. Note that although this example shows a row of 40 8 × 8 characters, both the number of characters per row and the composition of the cell matrices can be altered by means of appropriate software. The simplified block diagram of a raster scan display controller using an 8275 is shown in Figure 1.73.

Small computer systems interface (SCSI)

In recent years, personal computers have become increasingly more powerful and as a result have required a means of communicating with high-speed peripheral devices, such as hard disk and tape drives. The Small Computer Systems Interface (SCSI) which has its roots in the minicomputers of a decade ago, provides a means of transferring large volumes of data between devices connected in a 'local bus' configuration. The SCSI bus supports a total of eight devices (including the host computer). Communication is allowed between two devices at any one time. Each device present must have its own unique SCSI ID (usually selected by means of PCB links or DIP switch settings). The ID is established by placing a single data bit (driven low) on to the bus according to Table 1.9.

Table 1.9 SCSI ID

Data bit	SCSI ID
DB(0)	0
DB(1)	1
DB(2)	2
DB(3)	3
DB(4)	4
DB(5)	5
DB(6)	6
DB(7)	7

When two devices communicate on the SCSI bus, the unit originating the operation is designated as the 'initiator'. The unit performing the operation, on the other hand, is known as the 'target'. Any desired combination of initiators and targets may be present in a SCSI bus system (provided, of course, that the total number of devices present does not exceed eight). Data transfers on the SCSI bus are asynchronous and follow a defined protocol in which signals are exchanged on the Request (REQ) and Acknowledge (ACK) handshake lines. The SCSI interface employs a total of nine control signals and nine data signals (including an optional parity bit).

SCSI signals and bus phases

The SCSI signals and bus phases are shown in Table 1.10.

Table 1.10 SCSI signals and bus phases

Signal	Abbreviation	Function
Busy	BSY	Asserted to indicate that the bus is in use (these lines are OR-tied).
Select	SEL	Asserted by an initiator when selecting a target or by a target to reselect an initiator.
Control/data	C/D	Driven by a target to indicate whether control information or data is present on the bus.
Input/output	I/O	Driven by a target to determine the direction of data flow on the data bus. The direction is quoted relative to the initiator. True (low) indicates input to the initiator.
Message	MSG	Driven by the target during the message phase.
Request	REQ	Driven by the target to indicate a request for a data transfer handshake sequence.
Acknowledge	ACK	Driven by an initiator to acknowledge a data transfer sequence.
Attention	ATN	Driven by an initiator to indicate the attention condition.
Reset	RST	An OR-tied signal which indicates a reset condition.

Table 1.11 indicates the source of each SCSI signal during each of the eight bus phases.

Table 1.11 Sources of SCSI signals during different bus phases

Bus phase	BSY	SEL	Signal C/D, I/O	ACK/ATN	DB(7-0,P)
Bus free	None	None	None	None	None
Arbitration	All	Winner	None	None	ID
Select	Both	Init.	None	Init.	Init.
Reselect	Both	Target	Target	Init.	Target
Command	Target	None	Target	Init.	Init.
Data-in	Target	None	Target	Init.	Target
Data-out	Target	None	Target	Init.	Init.
Status	Target	None	Target	Init.	Target
Message-in	Target	None	Target	Init.	Target
Message-out	Target	None	Target	Init.	Init.

Notes:
All	the signal must be driven by all actively participating devices
Both	the signal is driven by the initiator and/or target as specified in the arbitration and selection phases
Init.	driven only by the active initiator
None	this signal must not be driven by any device (the bias circuitry within the bus terminator will ensure that the signal is pulled into the false state)
ID	SCSI ID (a unique data bit) must be placed on the bus by a device that is arbitrating

The truth table of Table 1.12 applies to the data, command, and message phases.

Signal levels and bus termination

SCSI signals are either true (low) or false (high). A bus terminator ensures that each signal line assumes the false state by pulling the line high when it is not driven into the low (asserted) state.

Each signal driven on to the bus by a device should conform to the following electrical specification:

Table 1.12 SCSI data, command and message phases

Phase		Signal		Direction of transfer
	MSG	C/D	I/O	
Data-out	1	1	1	Initiator to target
Data-in	1	1	0	Target to initiator
Command	1	0	1	Initiator to target
	1	0	0	Target to initiator
Message-out	0	0	1	Initiator to target
Message-in	0	0	0	Target to initiator

Voltage (asserted state) = 0.0 V min. and 0.4 V max.
(released state) = 2.5 V min. and 5.25 V max.

Signals received by a device from the bus, on the other hand, should conform to the following electrical specification:

Voltage (true state) = 0.0 V min. and 0.8 V max.
(false state) = 2.0 V min. and 5.25 V max.

Table 1.13 SCSI pin connections

Signal	Pin No.
DB(0)	2
DB(1)	4
DB(2)	6
DB(3)	8
DB(4)	10
DB(5)	12
DB(6)	14
DB(7)	16
DB(P)	18
GND	20
GND	22
GND	24
Terminator power	26
GND	28
GND	30
ATN	32
GND	34
BSY	36
ACK	38
RST	40
MSG	42
SEL	44
CD	46
SEQ	48
I/O	50

Note: 1. All odd numbered pins, with the exception of pin-25, are connected to ground (GND). Pin-25 is not connected.
2. Pin-1 is marked by a triangle indentation on the 50-way connector.

It should be noted that, in order to provide the maximum possible data transfer rate on the bus without risk of signal corruption due to reflections resulting from an impedance mismatch, a bus terminator must be installed on the last (furthermost) device connected to the bus. Furthermore, the physical length of the bus cable should not exceed 6 metres (approx. 20 feet) and its characteristic impedance should be 100 ohms ±10%.

SCSI connector

The SCSI interface uses a 50-way connector arranged in two rows, each of 25 ways. Typical part numbers for the female cable-mounting connector with integral strain relief are AMP 1-499506-2 and DuPont 66900-350. The connector pin assignment is shown in Table 1.13.

Other bus systems

Proprietary bus systems are employed within a number of other computers (such as the IBM PC and compatibles). Such bus systems provide a flexible system expansion by means of adaptor cards. Bus systems also tend to vary in complexity according to the capability of the processor. Details of the popular ISA, EISA and MCA bus systems are included in Chapter 7.

2
Test equipment

A well-equipped workshop is a sound investment for those who intend to service personal computers on a regular basis. The facilities offered, and in particular the type and range of test gear that must be provided, will depend not only upon the type of work to be undertaken but also on the available budget. It is, in fact, quite possible to set up a modest test facility with only a minimal outlay and it is not essential to start out with brand-new laboratory-standard equipment. Second-hand test gear is plentiful and all that is required, at least initially, are a few items of basic test gear. These can be added to as, and when, funds become available. Alternatively, several equipment hire organizations exist and major items of test equipment, such as logic analysers, can be rented at moderate cost as and when required. However, one should not forget that besides the major items of test equipment there is also a requirement for small items, not the least of which is a comprehensive set of small tools.

Consideration must also be given to the work area itself and a separate workshop well away from the normal hub of domestic or business activity is highly desirable. One should be able to keep equipment safely in a partially dismantled state well away from curious fingers! In this chapter we shall start by considering the requirements of the work area itself and then continue to examine the most useful items of test equipment it should contain.

Setting up a workshop

Location

Unfortunately one seldom enjoys the luxury of being able to choose the exact location of a workshop. Usually the site and available space are dictated by circumstances beyond one's direct control. For most of us, therefore, the purpose-built workshop must remain something of an ideal. This should not, however, deter the reader from making the best of what is actually available. To consider the essentials first: the workshop must be warm, dry and secure. Adequate lighting and ventilation must be provided, as should sufficient space for the installation of a suitably large workbench and for the storage of equipment and components.

The workshop should be physically separate from the normal domestic or business environment. This helps to avoid repeated interruption or distraction. It should not, however, be so far away as to be inaccessible. In connection with retail premises a workshop is often located in either an adjoining room or at first-floor level.

It is important to remember at the outset that you will spend a considerable proportion of your time in the workshop, so careful consideration should be given to its layout, decor and facilities. In practice this is, unfortunately, rarely the case and all too often the planning of a workshop is somewhat haphazard and is rarely accorded the high priority it deserves!

The workbench

The workbench itself should provide a continuous flat working surface with an area of at least 1.5 square metres (15 square feet approximately). The bench should be constructed from a substantial piece of timber or chipboard and must be adequately supported. The bench should be capable of supporting a surface load of at least 60 kg (150 lb). The optimum height for the work surface is a matter of personal preference but is usually between 70 and 78 cm (28 and 31 in) though a slightly higher level may be preferred if stools are to be used.

A common fault of workbenches is lack of depth. Large items of test equipment can require a depth of several feet (60 to 80 cm) and there is nothing worse than building a workbench only to find that the test gear does not fit on it! Furthermore, a large proportion of the work area (say 70 per cent or more) should be kept free and many of the smaller items of test gear should be consigned to a smaller 'equipment shelf' located above the main workbench. This shelf can also support items of peripheral equipment such as monitors and printers.

Another important requirement is that all items of test equipment likely to be in regular use should be within easy reach. Where necessary, each should be connected to the mains supply ready for immediate use when called upon. It should also not be necessary to get up from a central sitting position in order to retrieve commonly used items such as multi-meters, probes, etc.

The bench top should be covered with a hard-wearing and heat resistant surface. Several forms of decorative laminate are available from DIY outlets which are ideal for this purpose. If you wish to make scratches less noticeable choose a patterned rather than a plain finish. Also note that although components and other small items will stand out against a lighter colour, the penalty is that surface dirt and marks will be more obvious. Bench mats are another essential item. These will protect both equipment and workbench and can offer at least temporary resistance to the ravages of a hot soldering iron.

Where space is plentiful consideration should be given to the provision of an area where 'heavy' work can be carried out. This area can be fitted with a bench vice and the inclusion of a separate 'soldering station' is recommended. This would comprise a range of soldering irons, appropriate power units where necessary, and ancillary items such as desoldering pumps. This arrangement helps minimize the risk of damage to equipment and test gear which, unfortunately, can all too easily be caused by having several hot soldering irons on the test bench. In all cases, soldering irons should be fitted with stands and rigid discipline should be exercised in their use.

Finally, an anti-static mat can be useful in avoiding occasional static problems. Such a mat should be manufacturered from bulk conductive material (e.g. carbon-loaded neoprene rubber) rather than just a surface coating and it should be connected to earth at the metal trunking used for mains distribution.

Storage

Often the last but by no means the least important item to be considered when setting up a workshop is the provision of storage space. This must take a variety of forms and should not merely be restricted to test equipment and 'work in progress'. In a business environment as many as ten or more personal computers may be present in the workshop at any one time. These may be in various stages of repair and some will be awaiting spare parts from manufacturers or importers. For these items a storage rack is essential. This may easily be assembled from commercially available shelving and should consist of one or more bays of six to eight shelves. The shelving should have adequate depth; 30 cm (12 in) should be considered a minimum.

Components and spare parts should be stored in one or more multiple drawer units. These can be purchased as complete units housed in an exterior steel frame or can be assembled from modular interlocking drawers, which are usually provided with internal dividers and slots to accommodate labels. An alternative though somewhat more bulky storage system involves the use of polypropylene bins, which may either be stacked or mounted directly on a metal panel. While these are ideal for larger components they are generally unsuitable for smaller components such as resistors, capacitors and integrated circuits. Readers may wish to consider a mixture of both storage systems, which is the arrangement preferred by the author.

A separate area should be reserved for housing paperwork, books and manuals. The best method of accommodating general paperwork, such as handbooks, service manuals and service records, is in one or more standard filing cabinets. Although such units are relatively large, a two-drawer unit may be placed neatly beneath a work surface. Two such filing cabinets, placed at either end of a flat bench top, can provide a very effective work surface. This simple method of constructing a workbench is one which demands an absolute minimum of carpentry skill! Four-drawer filing cabinets are too tall to provide support for work surfaces and should thus be left 'free-standing' in a less used corner of the workshop. Note that a completely filled four-drawer filing cabinet can be extremely heavy and it is wise to consider the consequent floor loading in its vicinity.

The workshop should also be fitted with a conventional open bookshelf. This will unfortunately have to cope with a variety of book sizes and due allowance should be made during its construction. Accommodation should be provided for at least 20 books and, where a filing cabinet is not available, a similar number of service manuals. Don't forget that each item of test equipment should have its own service manual and operating handbook and these should also be carefully retained in the workshop filing cabinet or bookshelf.

Test leads and tools should ideally not be stored in drawers even though this appears to be the most commonly used method of storing them. Tools should be readily accessible and visible from the work position and the best method for storing them is with the aid of a tool board. This is a plane chipboard or plywood panel, securely fastened to the wall of the workshop. A total area of about 0.5 square metre (between 4 and 6 square feet approximately) will satisfy most requirements. Tools are then laid out upon this surface and retained by means of spring clips. If desired, the profile of each tool may be outlined on the board. This will not only help identify the correct position of each item on the board but will also alert the service technician to the fact that something is not in its proper place!

When stored in a drawer, test leads seem to develop an instant affinity for one another! The result is a tangled mass of assorted cables and wires which often takes considerable time to sort out. Again, an open storage method is much preferred. This may take the form of a ready-made test lead rack. One such proprietary system comprises a metal rail which accommodates a number of moulded hooks. Each hook then retains one test lead or cable. A less expensive alternative is the use of a board, or short length of timber, on to which is secured a number of cup-hooks. Each cup-hook supports an individual test lead or cable and it is a good ideal to label each hook so that leads can be returned to their proper places. The user soon gets to know the whereabouts of a particular item and it can thus be located quickly.

Lighting

Good lighting can make a very positive contribution to workshop safety and efficiency. Poor lighting, on the other hand, can cause eye-strain, which in turn can lead to discomfort and fatigue. There is nothing worse than a gloomy workshop in which the only light source shines directly into one's eyes! Care should be taken to ensure that as well as an adequate level of general illumination a local light source is provided for close work.

Undoubtedly the most efficient method of illuminating a large work area is with the aid of one or more fluorescent strip lights. A single 6 ft (1.8 metre approximately) fitting will provide adequate illumination over an area of around 11 square metres (120 square feet). While a diffused light source is extremely good for general illumination, shadows may still be prevalent in the work area, particularly if one sits or stands between the central light source and the workbench. In any event, a higher degree of illumination is desirable in the vicinity of the work area and this can best be provided by an 'Anglepoise' or similar counter-balanced desk lamp. These lamps can be swivelled, rotated, and extended into almost any position and must be considered essential if fine inspection work is to be carried out.

For very close work, the use of a bench magnifier is highly recommended. Such an item consists of a sizeable dual convex glass lens supported by an adjustable stand. The magnification produced is usually of the order of two or so, and some units also incorporate a light source of either the filament or fluorescent variety.

Fluorescent light fittings should be ceiling mounted in as central a position as possible. The fitting should be aligned so that its major axis is parallel to the main workbench. 'Anglepoise' or similar desk lamps may be mounted on wall brackets, bench clamps or can be fitted with heavy table bases.

Security

The value of items in any computer workshop is likely to be considerable. Furthermore, being easily sold on the second-hand market, such equipment is attractive to the would-be thief. It is, therefore, particularly important to consider the security of a workshop particularly if it is situated in an isolated position.

The first step in any security appraisal is to consider how an intruder could gain entry. Doors should be fitted with BS approved locks. The doors themselves should be substantial and strong hinges should be used. There is, after all, little point in fitting secure locks to a door if its hinges can be easily broken! Windows should similarly be fitted with adequate locks. These must be easy to operate and push-button types are to be preferred. A general point worth noting is that where locks are difficult to operate in business premises, staff tend to be less conscientious in their use. Windows themselves should not be easy to break. If the workshop is located on a ground floor it may be desirable to fit a security grille to each window. This consists of a substantial metal mesh which makes entry via a window extremely difficult.

A variety of electronic security devices can also be fitted. These not only provide a means of alerting those nearby but can also act as a deterrent to the more casual thief. In any event it is wise to seek expert advice from the Crime Prevention Officer at your local Divisional Police Station. He will be only too pleased to offer assistance and the best time to consult him is at the planning stage.

Finally, it is a good idea to keep a record of serial numbers, together with invoices, receipts, and a brief description of each major item of equipment. The serial numbers of equipment being serviced should, of course, already appear on your service dockets. This information will not only be useful in the event of a break-in but it may also be essential when making an insurance claim. Copies of such information should be lodged in a secure place away from the workshop.

Safety

A section on 'Setting up a workshop' would not be complete without some mention of the Health and Safety at Work Act. This important document sets legal standards for safety in the workplace that must be observed by employers and employees alike. Safe working methods and practices are essential at all times and all workshop users should remain alert to particular hazards that may be present.

The following paragraphs summarize the main points that should be observed. Those setting up a workshop for the first time should seek the advice of a qualified Industrial Safety Officer regarding specific interpretation of the Health and Safety at Work Act.

Special care must always be exercised with all mains operated equipment since the 240 V mains supply can be lethal. Mains operated equipment should always be switched off and disconnected from the supply before dismantling and while removing or replacing components. There should be absolutely no exceptions to this rule!

A single mains isolating switch should be fitted which can be used to interrupt the supply to all outlets simultaneously. The lighting circuit should, of course, be separate. The mains isolating switch should be fitted in a prominent position and an earth leakage circuit breaker (ELCB) should preferably also be incorporated. Mains plugs should always be correctly fitted since incorrect wiring may cause the external metal cases of equipment to become 'live'. This is a potential cause of severe electric shock. In the UK, wiring to mains plugs should follow the accepted colour code: brown = live; blue = neutral; green/yellow = earth.

A portable appliance tester (PAT) should be regularly used to check all items of mains operated equipment in the workshop. Such testers can now be obtained from a number of suppliers and they are quick and easy to operate. It is also worth getting into the habit of checking equipment with a PAT when carrying out routine maintenance.

Mains cables with integral moulded IEC connectors should be used whenever possible. Screw connections on mains plugs should be carefully tightened and no loose strands of wire should be evident. Correctly rated fuses should be fitted; for test gear and most mains operated equipment a 3 A fuse will normally be required. Where fitted, cable retaining clamps should be tightened so that the outer insulating covering of the cable is securely held. Mains leads and plugs should be regularly inspected; damaged leads or plugs should be replaced and not repaired using insulating tape!

Basic considerations of fire safety in the workshop involve:

(a) the provision of a means of escape in the event of fire;
(b) a means of safeguarding such an exit so that it never becomes blocked;
(c) an adequate range of fire fighting equipment; and
(d) an effective means of alerting others by the provision of an appropriate alarm signal.

Only dry powder, carbon dioxide (CO_2) or halon (BCF) fire extinguishers should be used for the control of electrical fires. 'Domestic' type fire extinguishers are generally inadequate for use in larger workshops. A fire blanket is, however, a useful item and can be effective in the event of clothing catching fire. Water must never be used as a means of extinguishing a workshop fire.

It should be remembered that the products of combustion of most plastics materials are toxic and the fumes generated by fires in an electrical workshop can be extremely dangerous. Inexpensive smoke detectors are readily available and one or more should be fitted. To be effective such devices should have an alarm signal that is audible throughout the premises and care should be taken to site them in the best positions, e.g. in a hallway or at the top of a stairway. The detector should incorporate a test facility to indicate that it is operational and should also provide warning of low battery condition.

A particular hazard present in all electronic workshops is the soldering iron and, while such a device can be a good friend, it can also be a deadly enemy. Soldering irons should be inspected regularly both for satisfactory earth continuity and for leakage from the element to earth. Low voltage soldering irons are, from safety considerations alone, much to be preferred. The connecting cable from the iron to the power supply (or mains) should preferably be heat resistant. Soldering irons should be mounted in heat-proof bench stands and these should be strategically positioned on the workbench.

A telephone should be available in the immediate vicinity of the workshop and a list of emergency numbers should be kept in a prominent place beside it. As well as the usual emergency services, the list should include the nearest hospital with an accident unit, the nearest eye hospital, and local doctors.

A first-aid kit should be available in the workshop and it should contain materials for the treatment of minor cuts and burns. In a workshop where several people are employed, at least one person should receive some form of recognized first-aid training.

Tools

Good quality tools can be expected to last a lifetime provided that they are properly used and cared for. It is therefore wise to purchase the best quality that you can afford. There is little sense in buying inferior items that will need replacing every few years. Many of the basic tools required will already be available and it should not therefore be necessary to spend a lot on new items.

As a guide, 'minimum' and 'extended' lists of tools are given. The 'minimum' list represents the minimum complement of tools necessary for even the most basic service work. The 'extended' list includes items that will undoubtedly not be used in everyday service work. There will still, however, be occasions when they may be invaluable.

Minimum list of tools
1 small pair of side cutters
1 small pair of snipe-nose (half-round) pliers
1 pair combination pliers and cutters
1 small flat-blade screwdriver
1 large flat-blade screwdriver
1 small cross-point screwdriver
1 large cross-point screwdriver
Set of trimming tools
Set of hexagon keys
1 general-purpose soldering iron (25 to 30 W)
1 miniature soldering iron (15 to 18 W)
1 desoldering tool

Extended list of tools
As 'minimum' list plus the following additional items:

1 small pair flat-nose pliers
1 pair of wire strippers
1 medium mains tester screwdriver
Set of jeweller's screwdrivers
Set of small files
1 hand drill
Set of twist drill bits
1 p.c.b. drill
Set of p.c.b. twist drill bits
1 junior hacksaw
1 small G-clamp vice
1 trimming knife
1 pair of tweezers
1 bench magnifying glass
1 combination wire-wrapping/unwrapping tool
Set of open ended metric spanners (M2.5 to M6)
1 portable soldering iron (12 V or rechargeable type)
1 temperature controlled soldering iron (40 to 50 W)

Choosing test gear

Not only will the range of test equipment available in the workshop dictate the type and complexity of service work undertaken but it will also determine the ease with which it can be done. A good service technician gets to know his test gear extremely well. He soon knows which instrument to use for a particular application, which he can rely on and which he should treat with caution. Choosing the right instrument for the job can be all-important and there are a number of pitfalls to be avoided. Familiarity is the key to getting the best from your test gear and, at least in the initial stages, it is wise to learn how to use one instrument at a time.

As in the previous section, 'minimum' and 'extended' lists have been prepared. The 'minimum' list includes those items which, in the author's experience, are most regularly used in the servicing of personal computers and peripheral equipment. It is not absolutely essential to have all of these items available in order to tackle basic repairs and a good deal of elementary fault finding can be carried out using nothing more than a logic probe and a good quality multi range meter. What is of fundamental importance is the interpretation that is put into the readings obtained. This skill can really only be satisfactorily acquired in the time-honoured fashion, as a direct result of many hours of experience!

Items on the 'minimum' list became essential if all of the faults likely to be encountered are to be adequately dealt with. This should not, however, deter the enthusiast from making a start. Test equipment can be acquired over a period of time, starting of course with a good multi-range meter and a logic probe. Additional items, including those on the 'extended' list, can be added when time and money permit. It is best not to be in too much of a hurry to extend the range of facilities available. Readers will soon get to know which instruments they derive most benefit from and this will help point the way to future purchases.

We shall now briefly consider each of the basic items of test equipment in turn and, whereas the majority of these items have been selected from the 'minimum' test equipment list, certain items from the 'extended' list have been included with which readers may be unfamiliar. Where appropriate, desirable performance specifications will be given and typical measurement applications discussed. Full operating principles have not been included as these are beyond the scope of this book. Where further information is required, readers are advised to consult an appropriate text on test equipment design and operation.

Minimum list of test equipment
Multi-range meter (good quality analogue or digital type)
Oscilloscope (preferably dual beam 30 MHz type)
Logic probe
Logic pulser
Test prods
Selection of IC test clips
Selection of leads and connectors

Extended list of test equipment
Current tracing probe
Logic comparator
Logic monitor
Digital frequency meter
Oscilloscope with digital storage facility
Break-out box (RS-232)
Logic analyser/signature analyser (as appropriate)
Regulated variable d.c. power supply
Specialist test ROMs and adaptors (as appropriate–see Chapter 3)

The multi-range meter

The multi-range meter is undoubtedly the most often used instrument in any service shop. As many as eight or nine measuring functions may be provided with a maximum of six or eight ranges on each. Besides the normal voltage, current and resistance functions, some meters also include facilities for checking transistors and measuring capacitance. Multimeters, which may be either analogue or digital, normally operate from internal batteries and thus are usually independent of the mains supply. This leads to a high degree of portability, which can be all-important when measurements are to be made away from the workshop.

Analogue instruments employ conventional moving coil meters and the display takes the form of a pointer moving across a calibrated scale. This arrangement is not so convenient to use as that provided by digital instruments. It does, however, offer some advantages, not the least of which is that it is very difficult to make adjustments using a digital readout to monitor varying circuit conditions, and in this application the analogue meter is therefore superior. Its scale can be easily interpreted; a movement in one direction represents an increase and in the other a decrease. The principal disadvantage of many analogue meters is the rather cramped and sometimes confusing scale calibration. To determine the exact reading requires first an estimation of the pointer's position and then the application of some mental arithmetic based on the range switch setting.

Digital meters, on the other hand, are usually extremely easy to read and have displays that are clear, unambiguous, and capable of providing a very high resolution. It is thus possible to distinguish readings that are very close. This is just not possible with an analogue instrument. The seven-segment readout used in digital multimeters employs either a liquid crystal (LCD) or light-emitting diode (LED) display. The former type requires very little electrical power and thus is to be preferred on the grounds of low battery consumption. LCD displays are, however, somewhat difficult to read under certain light conditions and, furthermore, the display response can be rather slow. LED displays, on the other hand, can be extremely bright but unfortunately consume considerable power. A mains power unit should therefore be used, if at all possible, with a unit that has an LED readout.

Figure 2.1 A multi-range meter offering a sensitivity of 100 kohm/V (courtesy Eagle International)

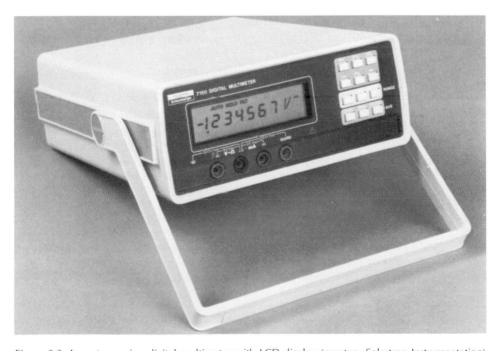

Figure 2.2 An auto-ranging digital multimeter with LCD display (courtesy Solartron Instrumentation)

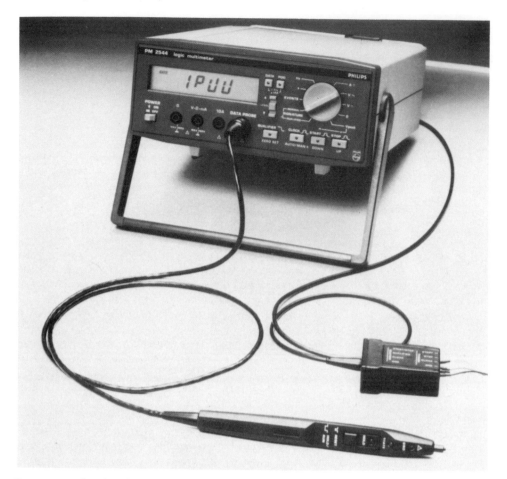

Figure 2.3 A digital multimeter designed specifically for work on digital logic circuits (courtesy Philips)

Another very significant difference between analogue and digital instruments is the input resistance that they present to the circuit under investigation when taking voltage measurements. The resistance of a reasonable quality non-electronic analogue instrument can be as low as 50 kohm on the 2.5 V range. With a digital instrument the input resistance is typically 10 Mohm on the 2 V range. The digital instrument is thus to be preferred when accurate readings are to be taken. While this may be of little concern when checking voltages of supply rails and in TTL circuits generally, it does become extremely important when measurements are to be made on high impedance circuits.

The following example, illustrated in Figure 2.4, compares readings of the open circuit input voltage of a TTL gate using representative analogue and digital multimeters. The example clearly shows the effects of loading and resolution provided by the two instruments. The digital multimeter was a 3 1/2-digit type used on the 2 V range. The input impedance, constant on all ranges, was 10 Mohm whereas, by contrast, the 20 kohm/V analogue multimeter (also used on the 2 V range) exhibited an input resistance of only 40 kohm.

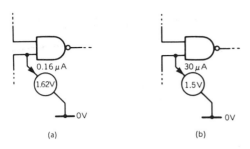

(a)   (b)

Figure 2.4 Effect of voltmeter internal resistance: (a) digital multimeter (10 Mohm internal resistance); (b) analogue multimeter (40 kohm input resistance)

Meter type	Input resistance	Reading produced	Current taken
Digital	10 Mohm	1.622 V	0.16 μ
Analogue	50 kohm	1.5 V	30 μA

It should be noted, however, that even though these results show a significant difference in voltage, the action of making the voltage measurement was not instrumental in producing a change in the logic level. Therefore, provided the user is aware of its limitations, the analogue multimeter may still be used with a reasonable degree of confidence.

Due to their different operational characteristics it is often desirable to have both analogue and digital multi-range instruments available. Where a choice has to be made between the two, the author recommends that a good quality analogue instrument should be purchased first. Although this may appear to be the less attractive of the two instruments, it does offer a number of advantages particularly where adjustments have to be made on circuits in which analogue voltages and currents are present. A high degree of accuracy and resolution is not always essential and problems of voltmeter loading can, to a large extent, be avoided.

In either case, readers should select an instrument with as many functions as possible. However, do not be too anxious if the instrument does not possess a 'dB' or 'capacitance' measuring range as these are, in normal usage, of little importance. The functions that must be considered essential are 'd.c. voltage', 'd.c. current', 'a.c. voltage', and 'resistance'. An 'a.c. current' range is also highly desirable, though not essential.

Accuracy should be better than 2 per cent on the d.c. ranges and 5 per cent on a.c. Note, however, that the accuracy of a digital instrument is not only specified in terms of the full-scale value but a further error in counting the last (least significant) digit must also be taken into account. It is also important that a digital meter should provide a clear and unambiguous over-range indication, and a battery condition indication is also highly desirable.

Voltage ranges should extend from, say, 2 V to 1 kV full-scale and the current ranges from 50 μA to 10 A full-scale. The resistance scale, which incidentally is non-linear in an analogue instrument, should extend from 10 ohms, or less, to at least 100 kohm.

When selecting an analogue instrument take a careful look at the meter scale. This should not be cramped and should be sufficiently large to be read at a distance. An anti-parallax mirror scale can undoubtedly help improve the accuracy of readings obtained although this is by no means an essential feature. Check that the range switching is logical and can easily be accomplished with one hand. Avoid instruments with a multiplicity of input sockets. They can be confusing and repeated swapping of leads from socket to socket can be frustrating, to say the least.

The meter should sit comfortably on the workbench. A tilt-up handle can improve readability but care must be exercised when using analogue meters in anything other than the horizontal plane since a small zero offset error may occur. A matching hard carrying case should be used to protect analogue instruments whenever they are carried around and ideally the case should incorporate a small compartment for test leads and prods.

It is also wise to check that meters incorporate some form of protection. This is particularly the case with analogue instruments, which can have expensive moving coil movements. While these movements are usually able to withstand overloads of several hundred per cent they are very susceptible to damage and an effective repair may not be an economic proposition. A simple form of protection is with the aid of a pair of anti-parallel diodes wired directly across the meter movement, as shown in Figure 2.5. In normal operation the diodes are non-conducting and no current flows through them. Under an inadvertent overload condition the diodes conduct when the voltage developed across the movement exceeds several hundred millivolts and, hopefully, most of the current is bypassed. More expensive instruments incorporate more sophisticated forms of protection. These include the use of sensitive fuses and mechanical cut-outs. Digital instruments generally include fuses in order to protect the shunt resistors on the a.c. and d.c. current ranges.

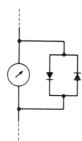

Figure 2.5 A simple method of protecting a meter movement using a pair of anti-parallel connected diodes

Low-cost digital multimeters have been made possible by the advent of mass-produced LSI devices and liquid crystal displays. A three-digit display is the norm, consisting of three full digits which can display 0 to 9 and a fourth (most significant) digit which can only display 1. Thus, the maximum display indication, ignoring the range switching and decimal point, is 1999; anything greater over-ranges the display. Nearly all digital meters contain automatic zero and polarity indicating facilities and some also have auto-ranging. This feature, which is usually only found in the more sophisticated instruments, automatically changes the range setting so that maximum resolution is obtained without over-ranging. There is thus no need for manual operation of the range switch once the indicating mode has been selected. This is an extremely useful facility since it frees the user from the need to make repeated adjustments to the range switch while measurements are being made.

For portable applications an LCD instrument is, by virtue of its small size, low weight, and minimal power consumption, much to be preferred. Most LCD meters will provide around 200 hours of continuous operation from one set of batteries but a comparable LED instrument may only operate for some 20 to 30 hours. As with analogue multimeters, it is wise to select an instrument that has a clear display and sensible range switching. Many digital multimeters use a multiplicity of push buttons and this can be particularly confusing when a combination of several push-buttons have to be used to select a particular range. In general, the author's preference is for instruments that employ a conventional rotary switch, augmented if necessary by one or two push-buttons or slide switches.

Oscilloscope

An oscilloscope is an extremely comprehensive and versatile item of test equipment that can be used in a variety of measuring and troubleshooting applications when it can be advantageous to display time-related waveforms of signals present within a microcomputer system. However, since such an item represents a considerable capital investment, it is important that full benefit is derived from it.

The oscilloscope display is provided by a cathode ray tube (CRT) which has a typical screen area of 80 mm × 100 mm. The CRT is fitted with a graticule, which may be either integral with the tube face or a separate translucent sheet. The graticule is usually ruled with a 1 cm grid to which further lines may be added to mark the major axes on the central viewing area. Accurate voltage and time measurements may be made with reference to the graticule, applying a scale factor taken from the appropriate range switch. A word of caution is appropriate at this stage: before taking meaningful measurements from the CRT screen it is absolutely essential to ensure that the front panel controls are set to the calibrate (CAL) position. Readings will almost certainly be inaccurate if this is not the case! The use of the graticule is illustrated by the following example.

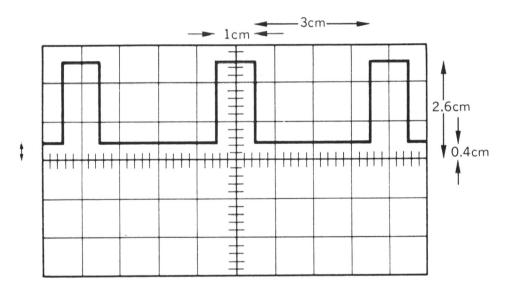

Figure 2.6 Using the oscilloscope graticule

An oscilloscope screen is depicted in Figure 2.6. This diagram is reproduced actual size and the fine graticule markings are shown every 2 mm along the central vertical and horizontal axes. The oscilloscope is operated with all relevant controls in the 'CAL' position. The timebase (horizontal deflection) is switched to the 1 ms/cm range and vertical attenuator (vertical deflection) is switched to the 1 V/cm range. The vertical input selector is initially set to the 'gnd' position (this disconnects the signal and short-circuits the oscilloscope input to earth) and the vertical position is adjusted so that the trace is exactly aligned with the horizontal axis. The input selector is then placed in the 'd.c.' position and the resulting waveform display is shown. This consists of a pulse of minimum voltage 0.4 V and maximum voltage 2.6 V. The pulse is repetitive and is 'high' for 1 ms and 'low' for 3 ms.

The time for one complete pulse cycle is thus 4 ms and hence its pulse repetition frequency is 250 Hz. Its mark-to-space ratio (ratio of 'high' to 'low' time) is 1 : 3 and its duty cycle (ratio of 'high' to 'high' plus 'low' time) is 0.25 or 25 per cent.

Having already mentioned some of the more common oscilloscope controls, we shall now continue by briefly examining the function of each of them in turn. It is worth mentioning that there is a considerable variation both in the function of the controls provided and in the terminology used by oscilloscope manufacturers. The list that follows, therefore, is necessarily general and contains details that may not be applicable in all cases. Figure 2.7 shows a typical front panel layout.

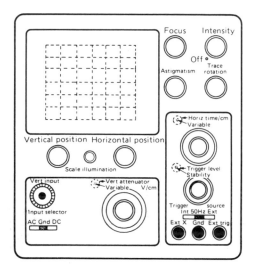

Figure 2.7 Typical front panel layout of a general purpose oscilloscope

Cathode ray tube display

Focus	Provides a correctly focused display on the CRT screen.
Intensity	Adjusts the brightness of the display.
Astigmatism	Provides a uniformly defined display over the entire screen area and in both planes. The control is normally used in conjunction with the 'focus' and 'intensity' controls.
Trace rotation	Permits accurate alignment of the display with respect to the graticule.
Scale illumination	Controls the brightness of the graticule lines.

Horizontal deflection system

Timebase (time/cm)	Adjusts the timebase range and sets the horizontal time scale. Usually this control takes the form of a multi-position rotary switch and an additional continuously variable control is often provided. The 'CAL' position is usually at one or other extreme setting of this control.
Stability	Adjusts the timebase so that a stable displayed waveform is obtained.
Trigger level	Selects the particular level on the triggering signal at which the timebase sweep commences.
Trigger slope	This usually takes the form of a switch that determines whether triggering occurs on the positive or negative-going edge of the triggering signal.
Trigger source	This switch allows selection of one of several waveforms for use as the timebase trigger. The options usually include an internal signal derived from the vertical amplifier, a 50 Hz signal derived from the supply mains, and a signal which may be applied to an 'external trigger input'.
Horizontal position	Positions the display along the horizontal axis of the CRT.

Vertical deflection system

Vertical attenuator (V/cm)
Adjusts the magnitude of the signal displayed and sets the vertical voltage scale. This control is invariably a multi-position rotary switch; however an additional 'gain' control is sometimes also provided. Often this control is concentric with the main control and the 'CAL' position is usually at one or other extreme setting of the control.

Vertical position
Positions the display along the vertical axis of the CRT.

Input selector (a.c.–gnd–d.c.)
Normally an oscilloscope employs d.c. coupling throughout the vertical amplifier, hence a shift along the vertical axis will occur whenever a direct voltage is present at the input. When investigating waveforms in a circuit one often encounters a.c. signals superimposed on d.c. levels; the latter may be easily removed by inserting a capacitor in series with the signal. With the input selector in the 'a.c.' position, a capacitor is inserted in the input lead, whereas in the 'd.c.' position the capacitor is shorted. If 'gnd' is selected, the vertical input is taken to common (0 V) and the oscilloscope input is left floating. This last facility is useful in allowing the accurate adjustment of the 'vertical position' control. The input selector may then be switched to 'd.c.' and the magnitude of any d.c. level at the input may be easily measured by examining the shift along the vertical axis.

Chopped-alternate
This control, which is only used in double-beam oscilloscopes, provides selection of the beam-splitting mode. In the 'chopped' position, the trace displays a small portion of one vertical channel waveform followed by an equally small portion of the other. The traces are, in effect, sampled at a relatively fast rate, the result being two apparently continuous displays. In the 'alternate' position, a complete horizontal sweep is devoted to each channel alternately.

A reliable trigger circuit is absolutely essential and a 'delayed trigger' facility will also be found extremely useful. This enables a predetermined time interval to elapse after the arrival

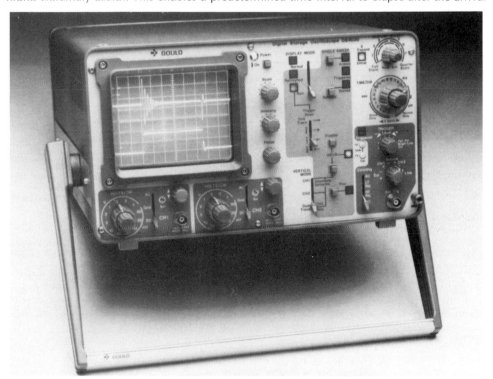

Figure 2.8 Dual trace digital storage oscilloscope (courtesy Gould Electronics)

Figure 2.9 Combined oscilloscope and logic analyser (courtesy Philips)

of the trigger signal and before the timebase sweep commences. Pulse waveforms in micro-computers are often non-repetitive and thus an oscilloscope that has a display storage facility is much to be preferred. While such instruments are unfortunately considerably more expensive, several manufacturers have introduced 'low-cost' digital storage 'scopes into their product ranges.

For servicing personal computer equipment it is essential to have an oscilloscope with a vertical bandwidth of at least 30 MHz. The timebase ranges should similarly extend to at least 0.1 μs/cm, or less. Ideally the oscilloscope should have a dual trace capability although this is not absolutely essential. A vertical amplifier sensitivity of 10 mV/cm is quite adequate and an input impedance of 1 Mohm shunted by about 30 pF is the norm.

Oscilloscope probes

A requirement of the oscilloscope is that it should faithfully reproduce pulses of fast duration and should not significantly load, and thereby affect, the circuit to which it is connected. Unfortunately, the input capacitance of the oscilloscope (i.e. that quoted by the manufacturer at the Y-input connector) appears in parallel with the capacitance of the coaxial input cable. This capacitance is usually in the region of I50 pF or so, and hence the total capacitance loading the circuit will often be in the region of 200 pF or so. While such a capacitance is almost negligible at low frequencies, it represents a reactance of only some 800 ohms at 1 MHz and may thus cause severe problems where high frequency, or fast rise-time, pulse trains are concerned.

Fortunately, this problem can be easily resolved with the aid of an oscilloscope probe. The most common type of probe provides a ten-times attenuation and is usually marked '×10'. The effect of such a probe is to raise the input resistance by a factor of 10 and reduce the input capacitance by a similar amount. A typical oscilloscope probe offers an input resistance of 10 Mohm and a capacitance of 16 pF.

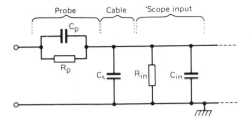

Figure 2.10 Equivalent circuit of an oscilloscope input incorporating a '×10' probe

The equivalent circuit of an oscilloscope Y-amplifier and its associated input probe is shown in Figure 2.10. In order to facilitate connection of the probe to various components, a range of probe tips should be provided.

Logic probes

Surprisingly, the most useful item of digital test gear in the author's workshop is also the least expensive. It is, as you may have guessed, nothing more than a simple logic probe. Such instruments can be a valuable aid in trouble-shooting even the most complex digital equipment. Furthermore, logic probes can offer speeds that are only equalled by the very fastest of oscilloscopes and logic analysers.

In essence, logic probes consist of a small hand-held case to which a probe is fitted. The supply to the probe is connected via a short length of cable terminated in a pair of crocodile clips. These may be attached to the positive supply and 0 V rails at suitably accessible points on the circuit under investigation. Most probes will accept supplies in the range 4.75 V to 18 V and are usually protected against inadvertent polarity reversal. Some manufacturers provide interchangeable probe tips, which can be an asset when the probe is to be attached to a variety of components.

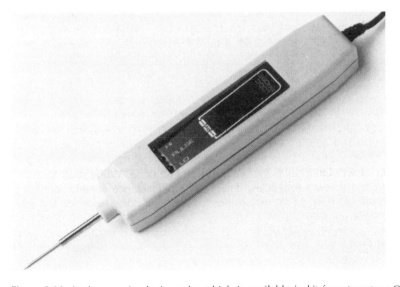

Figure 2.11 An inexpensive logic probe which is available in kit form (courtesy Global Specialities)

As with other items of test equipment, there is some variation in the facilities offered by logic probes but invariably three LEDs are provided to indicate the logical state of the probe tip, which may be either 'HIGH' (logic 1), 'LOW' (logic 0), or 'PULSE' (alternating between the two states). The relative brightness of the 'HIGH' and 'LOW' indicators gives an approximate indication of the duty cycle of the pulse train. The indications provided by a typical low-cost logic probe are shown in Table 2.1.

Table 2.1 Indications produced by a typical low-cost logic probe

LED indicator			State	Waveform
Low	Pulse	High		
OFF	OFF	ON	Steady logic 1	
ON	OFF	OFF	Steady logic 0	
OFF	OFF	OFF	Open circuit or undefined level	
OFF	BLINK	OFF	Pulse train of near 50% duty cycle at >1 MHz	
ON	BLINK	ON	Pulse train of near 50% duty cycle at <1 MHz	
OFF	BLINK	ON	Pulse train of high mark:space ratio	
ON	BLINK	OFF	Pulse train of low mark:space ratio	

More sophisticated logic probes provide pulse-stretching facilities so that pulses of very short duration can be recognized. Other types incorporate a 'memory' mode that can catch a narrow pulse and display it continuously until the mode is cancelled or the probe is disconnected from its supply. Note that when using such a probe it is usually necessary to ensure that the probe tip is connected to the circuit at the point under investigation before switching to the memory mode. If this precaution is not observed, the action of connecting the floating probe tip is likely to produce an erroneous trigger pulse.

Logic probes are usually available in two varieties or, alternatively, may be switched into one of two modes; either TTL or CMOS. In the TTL mode 'HIGH' and 'LOW' signal levels are defined as greater than 2.25 V and less than 0.8 V respectively, whereas in the CMOS mode these levels are represented by 70 per cent and 30 per cent of the probe supply voltage. While it is possible to use a high input impedance TTL logic probe for fault tracing in CMOS circuits, the use of a CMOS probe in TTL circuits is not generally to be recommended.

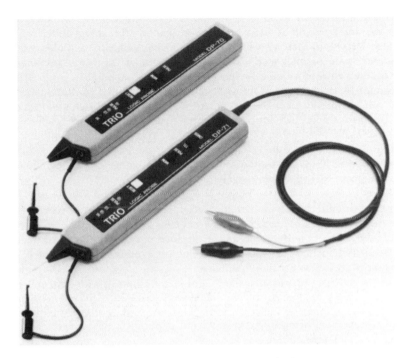

Figure 2.12 Logic probes incorporating pulse memory facilities (courtesy Trio-Kenwood Corporation)

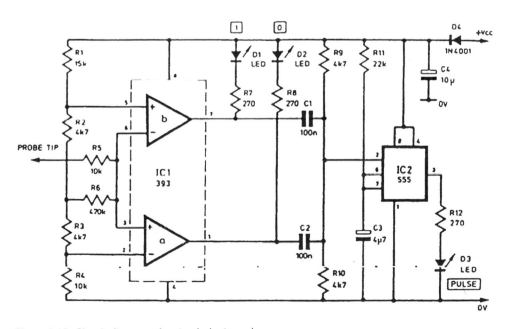

Figure 2.13 Circuit diagram of a simple logic probe

The complete circuit of a simple multi-purpose (CMOS and TTL) logic probe is shown in Figure 2.13. The probe has an input resistance of approximately 400 kohm and it will operate at frequencies of up to 10 MHz and detect pulses having widths of as little as 50 ns. The probe uses two low-cost integrated circuits and makes an ideal constructional project for those with little or no previous experience.

IC1, a dual comparator, is used to detect the voltage level at the probe tip by comparing it with reference voltages produced in the potential divider R1 to R4. When connected to a normal +5 V TTL supply, the voltage appearing at the junction of R1 and R2 is approximately 2.5 V, while that at the junction of R3 and R4 is 1.2 V. In the absence of any input (i.e. when the probe tip is left 'floating'), the voltage appearing at the inverting input of IC1b and the non-inverting input of IC1a will be the same as that appearing at the junction of R2 and R3 (i.e. approximately half the supply voltage).

The inputs of IC1 are arranged so that the output of IC1a (pin 1) will go low whenever a logic 0 appears at the probe tip whilst the output of IC1b (pin 7) will go low whenever a logic 1 appears at the probe tip. In either case, the respective LED (D2 or D1) becomes illuminated to indicate the state of the probe tip. In the absence of either a logic 0 or logic 1 input (i.e. an indeterminate, open circuit, or tri-state condition) both of the outputs of IC1 will go high and neither of the LEDs will be illuminated.

IC2 is a 555 timer operating in monostable mode and it is used to provide the necessary pulse stretching facilities. The monostable timing period is initiated by means of a negative-going (falling) edge formed by either C1 or C2 in conjunction with R9 or R10, respectively. This falling edge will occur whenever one of the outputs of IC1 goes low.

The monostable timing period (and time for which D3 will remain illuminated) is governed by the timing components, R11 and C3. The logic probe supply is decoupled by means of C4 while D4 is included in order to protect the probe from inadvertent reversal of the supply.

The logic probe can be assembled using a small piece of matrix board comprising 9 strips of 37 holes and then mounted in a proprietary probe case (available from several of the major electronic component suppliers). Construction is not critical but care should be taken to ensure that links and track breaks are correctly placed and that no dry joints or solder splashes are present.

Logic pulsers

Like logic probes, pulsers are also hand-held test instruments that derive their power supply from the circuit under investigation. A narrow pulse of short duration is generated whenever a push-putton is pressed. Alternatively, a continuous train of pulses is generated if the button is held down. When the button is released, the probe assumes a high impedance state. The output of the probe can typically source or sink currents of up to several hundred milliamps (equivalent to 50, or more, conventional TTL loads). The pulse width is made fairly narrow, being typically 1 µs and 10 µs in the TTL and CMOS modes respectively.

The primary function of the logic pulser is to achieve a momentary change of state at a node in a circuit. More sophisticated pulsers use comparator techniques to sense the state of the node before applying a pulse of the correct opposite polarity. If the test point is high the pulse goes low, and vice versa. After the pulse has been emitted another comparison is made and, if a change of node state has occurred, the next pulse generated will be of opposite polarity. This useful facility permits continuous triggering of the circuit under investigation regardless of its actual logic state.

When using a logic pulser it should be remembered that, since an appreciable current may be sourced or sunk by the device, the return current flowing in the supply common lead will also be considerable. Thus, to prevent erroneous triggering, it is essential to derive the pulser's supply from a low impedance point on the supply rails and not merely clip the leads to the nearest available integrated circuit. While this latter technique may prove satisfactory for use with logic probes, it is definitely not recommended where logic pulsers are concerned. A suitable connecting point is directly across the terminals of an electrolytic supply decoupling capacitor of 100 μF minimum.

The following examples illustrate the combined use of the logic probe and logic pulser:

1. It is necessary to check a two-input NAND gate without removing the IC from the circuit. A logic 1 is present at one input and a logic 0 at the other. The logic probe is connected to the output of the gate, as shown in Figure 2.14(a), and indicates a 'HIGH' (logic 1) state which is, of course, commensurate with the truth table for the gate (see the Reference Section at the end of the book). In order to verify that the gate is operational, the pulser is introduced to the low input (B) and a positive pulse applied. This pulse will produce a momentary logic 1 at the B input which, in turn, should cause a change of state (logic 0) at the output before reverting to logic 1. The presence of this output pulse can be detected by using the pulse stretching or 'memory' facility of the logic probe as shown in Figure 2.14(b).

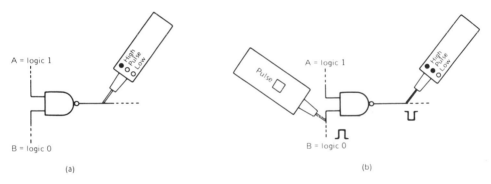

Figure 2.14 Checking a two-input NAND gate using a logic probe and logic pulser

2. It is necessary to check the operation of a J-K bistable in a circuit in which the clock pulse is absent. The logic probe can first be used to check that the Q and $\overline{Q}$ outputs are complementary, as shown in Figures 2.15(a) and 2.15(b). The pulser is then connected to the clock input and a single pulse generated, as shown in Figure 2.15(c). The logic probe is then used to verify that a change of state has occurred in the Q and $\overline{Q}$ outputs, as shown in Figures 2.15(d) and 2.15(e). Finally, the trigger button is held down to generate a continuous train of pulses to clock the bistable. The output states are checked again, as shown in Figure 2.15(f) and 2.15(g).

Another useful application for the logic pulser is to replace a single-phase clock. This allows single-stepping of the CPU, during which a logic probe can be used to display logic states at relevant points (e.g. R/W line). This subject is dealt with in further detail in Chapter 3.

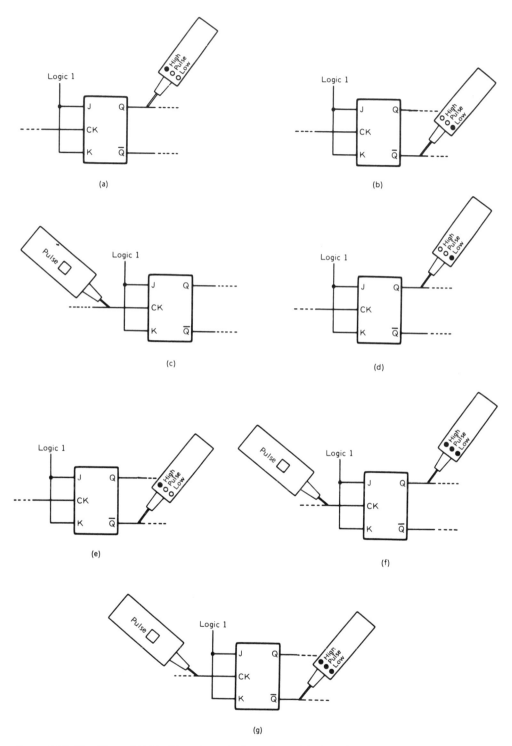

Figure 2.15 Checking a J-K bistable using a logic probe and logic pulser

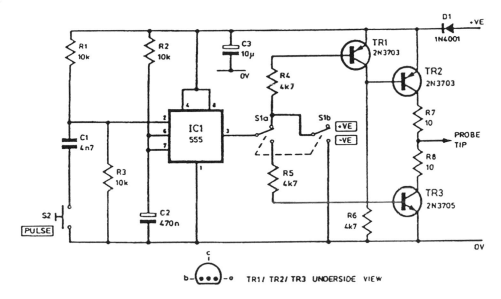

Figure 2.16 Circuit diagram of a simple logic pulser

The complete circuit of a simple logic pulser is shown in Figure 2.16. This circuit produces a switched positive- or negative-going output pulse of 5.2 ms duration with a peak current capability of about 200 mA (short-circuit output). The quiescent resistance at the probe tip is greater than 200 kohm.

IC1, a 555 timer, is connected as a monostable pulse generator. The output of IC1 (at pin 3) goes high for a period determined by the time constant R2 ×C2, whenever the pulse button S2 is depressed. With the values specified, the pulse duration is approximately 5 ms.

The polarity of the output pulse is switched by means of S1. TR1 acts as an inverter whilst TR2 and TR3 operate as saturated switches (providing positive and negative output drive respectively). The output current is limited by R7 and R8. With the component values shown, and assuming a standard +5 V supply, the peak current sourced or sunk into a short circuit will be limited to a few hundred milliamps.

When no output pulse is being produced, TR1 conducts but both TR2 and TR3 are in a non-conducting (switched off) state. The output at the probe tip thus floats in a high-impedance state. In common with the logic probe circuit described earlier, a diode (D1) is incorporated to provide protection against inadvertent reversal of the supply leads. Construction follows the same lines as those previously described for the logic probe.

IC test clips

The clearance between the pins of a conventional dual-in-line integrated circuit is of the order of 1.3 mm or less. In view of this, the use of conventional test prods is likely to be a hazardous process since there is a considerable risk of inadvertent short circuits when making a connection to a device. Spring-loaded dual-in-line test clips facilitate the attachment of a variety of test instruments using conventional hook-type test prods. Test clips come in a variety of sizes and it is wise to have several available including 16-pin, 28-pin and 40-pin types.

Logic monitors

Various forms of logic state monitor are available, ranging from simple clip-on indicators to sophisticated multi-channel bench instruments. In all cases, however, LEDs are used to display the logical state of each of the pins of the IC under investigation. It is then possible to monitor, simultaneously, the logical state of all of the inputs and outputs of a digital IC.

Simple logic monitors generally contain 16 LEDs and can be used in conjunction with 8-pin, 14-pin and 16-pin devices. These are invariably circuit powered, automatically deriving their supplies from the highest and lowest voltages appearing at the 16 points of connection. Since only one LED is available for each pin, a single logic threshold is recognized. This is usually the same as that for a logic probe 'HIGH' (i.e. greater than 2.25 V or 70 per cent of the supply voltage for TTL and CMOS monitors respectively). Pulse trains appear as LEDs with less than full intensity, the relative brightness giving an approximate indication of the duty cycle. More complex logic monitors may provide remote display facilities, a choice of logic thresholds (appropriate to either TTL or CMOS), and up to 40 display channels.

Current tracers

When fault tracing it is sometimes advantageous to be able to measure the current at strategic points in a circuit. Such a measurement may become necessary when, for example, we are concerned with the supply current drawn by an IC. Where devices are mounted in sockets, conventional multi-range meters may be used. The procedure involves first removing the IC from its socket, bending the relevant pin through 90 degrees, then re-inserting the IC and connecting the milliammeter between the bent-out pin and the appropriate point in the circuit. This method is, of course, inappropriate when an IC is soldered into the PCB. There is, however, no need to cut the PCB tracks if a current tracer is available. Such an instrument can measure, to a reasonable approximation, the current flowing in standard size PCB tracks without the need to break the circuit.

Two forms of current tracer are available; one operates by sensing the magnetic field in the vicinity of the track and the other measures the voltage drop across a short length of track. For accurate measurements, the PCB is assumed to be standard 35 μm (306 g/m²) track and calibration is usually supplied for 1 mm or 2 mm width track. Current tracers will typically respond to currents of 10 mA or less, and it is thus possible to check the operating current of a single TTL gate with a reasonable degree of accuracy. More sophisticated current tracers of the magnetic sensing variety may be used to 'follow' the path of direct current in the PCB. Such devices can thus be extremely useful in detecting such PCB faults as dry joints, hair-line cracks, solder splashes, shorted tracks, and open-circuit plated through holes.

Logic comparators

It is often necessary to determine whether or not a logic gate is functioning correctly and, while a simple method of checking an IC using a logic probe has already been described, this may not cover every case and a more rigorous substitution test may be preferred. Such a test would verify all of the gates contained within a single IC at the same time without the need to transfer a logic probe from pin to pin.

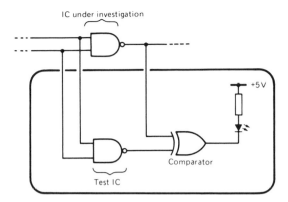

Figure 2.17 Principle of the logic comparator

Substitution testing is a relatively easy matter when devices are mounted in sockets but it may not even be considered when a device has to be desoldered (particularly when a double-sided PCB is involved). We have therefore to leave the IC in circuit. However, since we have immediate access to all of its pins, it is possible to duplicate its operation externally, using a known good device, and then compare the results obtained. A device that performs this function is a logic comparator and such an instrument can permit rapid in-circuit dynamic testing of a wide variety of logic devices.

The principle of the logic comparator is illustrated in Figure 2.17. The output of the gate on test is compared with that derived from a reference gate using an exclusive-OR gate, the output of which goes low (illuminating the LED) whenever its two inputs are similar (i.e. both logic 0 or both logic 1). If the outputs of the test and reference gates are different, as would be the case if the test gate were faulty, the exclusive-OR output goes high and the LED is extinguished.

The logic comparator is connected to the suspect device by means of an IC test clip and multi-way ribbon cable. To be useful, the logic comparator must be accompanied by a wide range of known reference devices. So if you are lucky enough to own such an instrument it is worth building up a reasonable stock of logic gates, over and above those one would normally keep in stock for replacement purposes.

Logic analysers

For most of us, a logic analyser represents the ultimate microprocessor test instrument offering extensive hardware and software debugging facilities. Whereas such instruments have, in the past, been somewhat restricted to use in general microprocessor system development, prices have fallen so that they are now readily available in most development laboratories and may thus also be considered a useful investment for those concerned with trouble-shooting specialized or prototype microcomputers.

The cost and performance of logic analysers tend to vary so much it is hard to generalize about the facilities offered. There is, however, some common ground which distinguishes such instruments from other items of digital test gear and we shall thus confine our discussion to this, leaving the finer points and detailed specifications to be gleaned from the manufacturers' own publications.

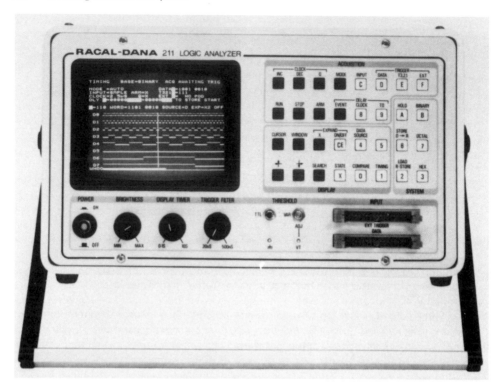

Figure 2.18 A portable 20 MHz 8-channel logic analyser (courtesy Racal-Dana)

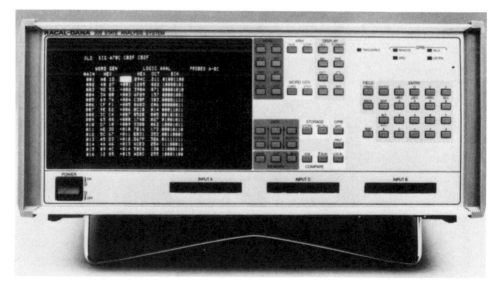

Figure 2.19 A sophisticated 48-channel logic analyser incorporating 12 kbytes of non-volatile memory (courtesy Racal-Dana)

Logic analysers, unlike other items of test equipment previously described, are so complex that they must themselves be microprocessor-based. They are thus capable of processing and displaying the logical state of a large number of channels (usually eight or 16) simultaneously on either a time-related or state-related basis. In addition, such processor and system-specific activities as disassembly and signature analysis may be provided.

Since a typical CPU is capable of executing a million or more instructions every second, a meaningful real-time display of this rapidly changing data is just not possible. A requirement of the logic analyser is that it must be able to capture a very small proportion of this data throughput so that it can be displayed and examined at leisure. In addition, a useful facility is that of being able to compare the actual data obtained with a set of reference data obtained previously.

Most of the incoming data may be irrelevant to the actual fault that we are dealing with. We may, for example, be only concerned with half a dozen bytes of erroneous data among several million. An important requirement, therefore, is to be able to capture the data both immediately before and after a particular point in the software execution. It is thus essential to have a reliable means of triggering the analyser whenever the suspect data appears. This normally involves a comparison of the incoming data with a word pre-set by the user. When a match occurs, a trigger qualifier circuit initiates a pulse that 'freezes' the acquisition memory in its current state. The memory may then be examined in one of several ways, as described later.

An alternative method of triggering the logic analyser involves deriving a pulse directly from one of the input lines; a typical example is the display of a section of memory immediately before and after the occurrence of an interrupt.

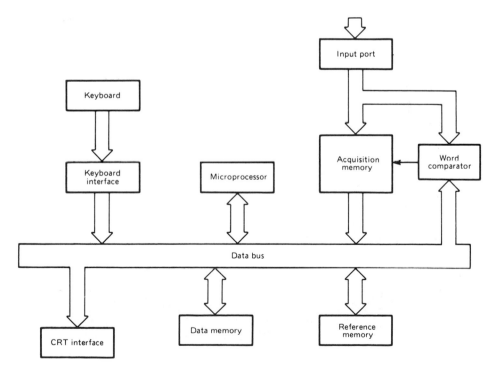

Figure 2.20 Simplified block diagram of a logic analyser

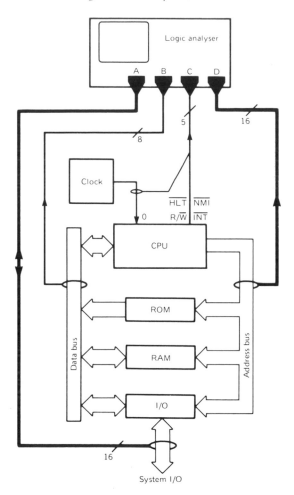

Figure 2.21 Connection of a logic analyser to a microcomputer

The simplified block diagram of a logic analyser is shown in Figure 2.20 and its typical connection to a microcomputer is illustrated in Figure 2.21. In the remaining paragraphs we shall discuss the two principal modes of logic analyser operation - time domain and state domain displays - and the signature analysis facility.

A typical logic analyser operating in the time domain mode can simultaneously display 256 data words on the screen of a CRT. The display takes the form of a timing diagram in which an individual line is devoted to each data bit, as shown in Figure 2.22. In addition, expansion facilities are often provided so that a display 'window'can be selected for more critical examination. The window is usually positioned on the display using a keyboard-controlled cursor.

Time displays permit asynchronous operation and this is important in the diagnosis of such hardware-related faults as propagation delays, race conditions, and glitches. Such faults would not be immediately apparent using the alternative state domain display mode.

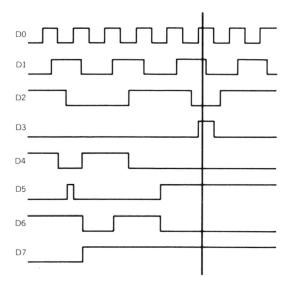

Figure 2.22 Typical time domain display (the cursor is positioned over a data byte having a value of 10101011)

In appearance, the time domain CRT display is somewhat similar to that which can be obtained using an oscilloscope. There are, however, several important differences, which may be summarized as follows:

1.   Logic analysers are capable of displaying eight or more channels, whereas oscilloscopes can normally only display two, or four at most.
2.   Logic analysers are digital instruments in which the display can only exist in one of two states. Since we are not usually concerned with actual voltage levels, the analogue display capabilities of an oscilloscope are largely redundant.
3.   The triggering facilities provided by oscilloscopes make them unsuited to the capture of specific small blocks of data when very large amounts of data are being continuously supplied at very fast rates.

At least one major manufacturer is attempting to bridge the gap between the logic analyser and the oscilloscope by combining the essential facilities of the two instruments in one package. This combined instrument operates as both a logic analyser and an oscilloscope, effectively sharing a common CRT display and permitting real-time as well as stored displays.

State domain displays are principally used as a means of investigating the software operation of a system. Unlike time domain displays, operation is synchronous with the system clock and data present at each clock transition is captured and displayed in either binary, hex, octal, or ASCII format. State domain analysis is a powerful tool in software debugging and is invariably required at the system development stage. A typical state domain display is shown in Figure 2.23.

Signature analysis is a facility that allows the compression of large amounts of data to form a characteristic 'signature' for the equipment concerned. Whenever there is a deviation in the data sequence, this signature changes and so a particular fault can be quickly recognized. The process involves cyclic redundancy code (CRC) techniques and a database of predefined signatures and stimuli.

```
TRIGGER EVENT * F01A   7E
TRACE                  FXXX   XX
SEARCH   WORD ** FXXX   XX   0001 0X11
===========================================================
                 HHHH   HH   BBBB BBBB

         495     F017   01   0000 0011

         496     F018   26   0001 0111

         497     F019   03   0000 0011

         498     F01A   FF   1111 1111

         499     F01D   FF   1111 1111

         500 *   F01A   7E   0111 1111

         501     F01B   F2   1111 0011

         502     F01C   80   1000 0011

         503     F280   86   1000 0111

         504 **  F281   20   0001 0011

         505     F282   C6   1010 0111
===========================================================
   SELECT CODE :-   0 = LINE,   1 = PAGE,   2 = WORD,   3 = TRIG
```

Figure 2.23 State domain display (showing five bytes before and after the trigger word)

Figure 2.24 A comprehensive and highly versatile field logic tester which combines signature and trace analysis with the functions of a conventional digital multimeter and logic probe (courtesy Solartron Instruments)

Data communications test equipment

A number of specialized test instruments and accessories are required for testing asynchronous serial data communications systems. The following items are available from a number of manufacturers and suppliers:

Patch boxes

These low-cost devices facilitate the cross connection of RS-232 (or equivalent) signal lines. The equipment is usually fitted with two D-type connectors (or ribbon cables fitted with a plug and socket) and all lines are brought out to a patching area into which links may be plugged. In use, these devices are connected in series with the RS-232 serial data path and various patching combinations are tested until a functional interface is established. If desired, a dedicated cable may then be manufactured in order to replace the patch box.

Gender changers

Gender changers normally comprise an extended RS-232 connector which has a male connector at one end and a female connector at the other. Gender changers permit mixing of male and female connector types (note that the convention is male at the DTE and female at the DCE).

Null modems

Like gender changers, these devices are connected in series with an RS-232 serial data path. Their function is simply that of changing the signal lines so that a DTE is effectively configured as a DCE. Null modems can easily be set up using a patch box or manufactured in the form of a dedicated null-modem cable.

Line monitors

Line monitors display the logical state (in terms of MARK or SPACE) present on the most commonly used data and handshaking signal lines. Light emitting diodes (LED) provide the user with a rapid indication of which signals are present and active within the system.

Breakout boxes

Breakout boxes provide access to the signal lines and invariably combine the features of patch boxes and line monitors. In addition, switches or jumpers are usually provided for linking lines on either side of the box. Connection is almost invariably via two 25-way ribbon cables terminated with connectors.

Interface testers

Interface testers are somewhat more complex than simple breakout boxes and generally incorporate facilities for forcing lines into MARK or SPACE states, detecting glitches, measuring baud rates, and also displaying the format of data words. Such instruments are, not surprisingly, rather expensive but could be invaluable for anyone who is regularly carrying out fault finding on asynchronous serial equipment.

3
Fault diagnosis

In the two previous chapters we have considered the operating principles of personal computers and the test equipment available for diagnosing faults that may arise within them. In this chapter we shall continue by describing some typical fault diagnosis procedures which bring together many of the principles and techniques previously introduced.

Unfortunately, personal computers are, by their very nature, somewhat diverse and hence the procedures described must be rather more general than specific. Readers should, however, be able to apply these techniques to those items of equipment with which they are currently dealing - the equipment may differ but the procedure remains essentially the same.

The overall aim of this chapter is to improve the reader's effectiveness at dealing with faults but, before describing methods employed in fault diagnosis, it is well worth attempting to identify the particular skills required of the service technician.

Skills

The precise skills required for fault finding are hard to define - they are easily acquired by some while others find the lessons difficult to learn. Fault finding is a logical pursuit but there is still plenty of room for flair and imagination. Fortunately, those who have already acquired such skills in another area of electronics, such as radio and TV, will quickly adapt to servicing microcomputers. The skills are essentially the same but the techniques are different.

The popular definition of skill is 'knowledge combined with dexterity'. Put like that, it neatly encapsulates the work of the service technician. Three levels of skill can be defined as appropriate to the general field of microcomputer servicing. These relate to broad areas of work between which there is no distinct boundary. Indeed, the correct diagnosis of many faults may involve skills drawn from more than one area.

The most 'basic' level skill involves simple processes of observation and deduction, and is limited to routine measurement, substitution and replacement techniques. This level of skill can be easily acquired in a very short time with a minimum of training. Next, and somewhat more demanding, the 'intermediate' skill level involves an elementary understanding of the behaviour of digital circuitry in general and microprocessors in particular. The technician must be able to relate events and make inferences based upon his measurements and observations. Such a skill level can be acquired by practical experience augmented, preferably, by a formal course of instruction leading to NVQ level 3, a BTEC National Certificate (or Diploma), or a City and Guilds Part Two Certificate.

Table 3.1 Typical faults and level of skill required in their diagnosis

Skill level	Fault
Basic	Fuse blown
	Defective connector
	Incorrectly configured card or board
	Failed hard disk drive
	Faulty printer cable
Intermediate	Intermittent connector
	Power supply fault
	Faulty capacitor or resistor
	Defective transistor
	Defective IC
	Failed CPU
	Defective memory device (ROM or RAM)
	Supply-borne noise spike
	Stuck line (high, low, or floating)
	Interrupt request conflict
Advanced	Intermittent VLSI device
	Timing error
	Temperature induced fault
	Race condition
	Glitch
	Bus conflict
	Incorrectly configured software driver

The 'advanced' skill level demands a thorough understanding of the principles and practice of microprocessors and microcomputers. It is demanding in terms of both powers of deduction and analytical ability. In some cases it may involve the development of testing methods that are specific to particular types of equipment and fault and which thus may not have been previously documented. Such a level of skill is usually only achieved as the result of considerable practical experience coupled with technical education to a standard of at least NVQ level 4, a BTEC Higher National qualification, or a City and Guilds Part 3 Certificate in a relevant subject (e.g. Microprocessor Computer Systems).

Typical faults relevant to the three skill areas previously defined are shown in Table 3.1. It should be noted at the outset that considerable damage can sometimes result from the use of inappropriate fault location and repair techniques. The relatively inexperienced reader should, therefore, only attempt to diagnose and repair faults with which he feels thoroughly competent to deal. For the newcomer, at least, this means restricting one's work to the 'basic' skill area as typified by the faults listed in Table 3.1. Expert advice or assistance should be sought before attempting faults in the 'intermediate' or 'advanced' areas. This cautionary note will, it is hoped, not deter the enthusiast from progressing from the more straightforward faults to those which are more demanding, as both confidence and experience are developed.

Fault finding technique

Contrary to popular belief, the majority of faults in microcomputer equipment are relatively trivial and require little skill to locate and repair. There are, however, some occasions when faults may be so complex that they will prove to be demanding of even the most experienced technician. There is, therefore, an underlying need to develop a systematic approach to fault diagnosis that will cope with the everyday, as well as the more obscure, fault.

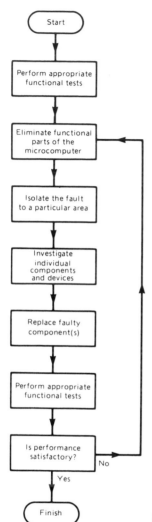

Figure 3.1 Flow chart to illustrate the basic principles of fault finding

Systematic fault finding is usually carried out in seven stages, as shown in Figure 3.I. The first stage consists of a number of functional tests to ascertain which of the equipment's functions are impaired. These allow us to eliminate those parts of the microcomputer that are working normally and which therefore do not merit our immediate attention.

The next step involves isolating the fault to a particular area of the non-functioning part of the equipment. This may involve voltage measurements, logic level checks, or substitution methods as appropriate. Once the particular area has been identified, an investigation of individual components can be carried out. In-circuit voltage, current, and resistance measurements may then be made in order to determine the precise nature of the fault. Component removal should normally be left to the last possible moment and it should not be necessary to remove a number of components before arriving at the faulty one.

Once removed from the circuit, the suspect component can be checked using resistance measurements or an appropriate component tester. Having confirmed that the component

Date	Equipment	Serial Number	Symptom	Fault	Action
26/05/93	Amiga A500+	1444566	Fails to load Workbench from system disk.	Faulty system disk.	System disk replaced.
26/05/93	Atari 520ST	A400360	Intermittent system lock up.	Faulty contact on 'Glue' VLSI socket.	Remove and re-seat 'Glue' VLSI chip.
27/05/93	Atari 1040STFM	A400205	Disk drive noisy. Displays TOS error message when program icons are double clicked.	Drive faulty.	Drive replaced.
28/05/93	Amiga A500i	1718980	TV screen displays computer video but with TV sound.	Faulty SCART connector.	Connections resoldered inside SCART connector.
31/05/93	Sinclair Spectrum Plus	A01/051064	Fails to display copyright message. Flashing squares on screen.	Faulty RAM chip.	Defective RAM chip replaced.
31/05/93	IBM PC-XT	272000391	Fails to complete boot sequence. Displays error code and then runs BASIC.	Faulty hard drive connector.	Checked supply to hard drive. Removed and cleaned PCB edge connectors.
31/05/93	DSC Turbo (AT-compatible)	D390021	Drive B not responding. Displays DOS error message.	Read/write heads damaged.	Drive replaced.
02/06/93	Olivetti M-24	3160366	Faulty keyboard (some keys missing).	Keyboard contacts dirty.	Keytops removed and PCB contacts cleaned.
03/06/93	Atari 1040STFM	A400205	Faulty keyboard (some key rows missing).	Faulty keyboard membrane.	Keyboard membrane replaced.
03/06/93	Toshiba T1200XE	05132040E	System crashes after indeterminate period.	RAM expansion card not seating correctly.	Card contacts cleaned and re-seated.
04/06/93	Amstrad PPC512	X79001219	Vertical lines on display.	Display damaged.	LCD display replaced.
05/06/93	Amstrad PC1512	00184091	Intermittent boot from floppy drive. GEM error message when loading programs.	Drive heads dirty.	Heads cleaned.
05/06/93	386SX PC (unknown)	no serial	System locks up after booting.	Virus infection.	Booted from clean system floppy and ran virus scan program.

Figure 3.2 Typical entries in a fault logbook

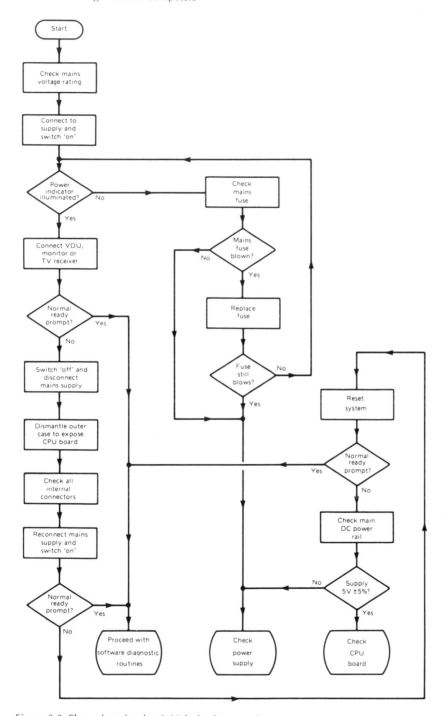

Figure 3.3 Flow chart for the 'initial check' procedure

really is defective, it may be replaced by another of the same type and then functional tests carried out to ascertain whether or not the fault has been cleared. In some cases, however, the fault may recur and it will then be necessary to examine the cause of failure. This may lie elsewhere in the circuit since some faults give rise to a 'knock-on' effect where one component failure leads to another.

Wherever possible during the fault finding process, reference should be made to the manufacturer's service manual for the microcomputer concerned. Owner's operating manuals supplied with the equipment rarely contain sufficient technical information, and very few include a circuit diagram. If a full service manual for the equipment is unobtainable, as may be the case where manufacturers go out of business or are reluctant to divulge such information, reference can often be made to service data for a similar device.

Where the reader is engaged in the regular servicing of a particular type of computer, it is recommended that a log be kept to provide a permanent record of all work carried out. While this may appear to be something of a chore, it can be extremely valuable at a later date by avoiding repetition and pointing the way to 'stock' faults that occur regularly in most types of equipment. A typical format for such a document is shown in Figure 3.2.

Initial check procedure

Assuming that one has no previous knowledge of the fault symptom, a few initial checks are required before making detailed functional tests on the equipment. These initial checks merely establish whether or not power is arriving at the equipment and whether the system reset switching is functional. The procedure, summarized in the flow chart of Figure 3.3, is as follows:

1.   Ensure that the equipment is switched off, and before connecting to a suitable mains supply outlet check that the correct mains supply has been selected. Few microcomputers include a fully tapped mains input transformer and operation is usually specified for a range of input voltages from, say, 220 V to 240 V. In such cases, compensation for changes in the mains supply voltage is achieved by means of the internal low voltage regulator. Note that a 110 V mains option is sometimes provided and, if this operating voltage is selected and the equipment is subsequently connected to a 240 V mains supply, extensive damage is likely to occur. Furthermore, in such cases the protection offered by the mains input fuse cannot be relied upon to operate quickly enough to avoid over-voltage in the power supply rails.

2.   Having ensured that the mains input voltage is correct, connect the supply and switch on the equipment. Nearly all microcomputers, other than the most basic, provide some form of power indication. Often this is a single red LED located in the front panel of the equipment. Check that this is illuminated and, if it is not, check both the 'in-line' fuse fitted to the equipment and, if necessary, the fuse fitted in the mains plug. If the equipment does not have a power indicator it will, of course, be necessary to connect a monitor or television receiver to the appropriate output connector and use this to determine the functional state of the equipment.

      If the 'in-line' fuse has blown, replace it by a fuse of the correct rating (do not up-rate it!). If the replacement fuse blows, check the mains input circuitry and d.c. supply rails for short-circuits. Where possible, disconnect the power supply module from the rest of the circuitry and check it in isolation. If the unit then operates correctly, the fault can safely be assumed to be associated with one of the other boards.

      In order to reduce equipment weight and size, some manufacturers have removed the mains transformer from the equipment and encapsulated it within the mains input

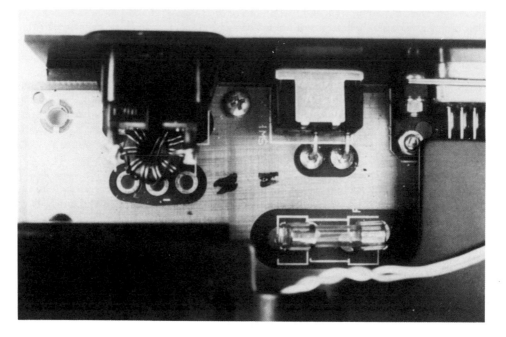

Figure 3.4 Typical fuse and input filter arrangement in a low-cost home computer

supply lead. The equipment is thus supplied from a low a.c. voltage (often this is in the region 9 V to 12 V). In such cases it is a relatively simple matter to check first the a.c. voltage supplied to the equipment before going further.

3. Assuming that there is evidence that the supply voltage is reaching the equipment, we can now refer to the display produced on the VDU, monitor, or television receiver connected to the equipment. Most equipment will provide the user with an initial prompt on 'power-up'. If no such prompt appears, the system reset button should be operated. Some of the lower cost computers do not incorporate such a facility and, in order to reset the equipment, it is necessary temporarily to disconnect it from the mains and then reconnect it. An alternative method of resetting the equipment involves directly operating on the internal microprocessor reset line. But to do this it will be necessary to remove the outer case of the equipment.

4. Before attempting to dismantle the equipment from its case, it is essential to switch off and temporarily disconnect the mains supply. The procedure for removing the case and exposing the PCB tends to vary from one manufacturer to another. In some cases, as few as two or four screws need to be removed. In others there may be 12 or more. Care must be taken to select the correct screws since not all may be involved with retaining the case. Some may, for example, be used for supporting the PCB or retaining the mains transformer. In any case, it is important to retain carefully all of the screws removed, noting where screws of differing length or thread have been used so that they may be later returned to their correct location. For this purpose, the author recommends the use of a water-based (non-permanent) felt-tip pen or Chinagraph pencil to mark the holes on the base of the enclosure.

5. We will now assume that access has been gained to the main CPU board such that measurements can be made. At this stage it is probably worthwhile checking the

Figure 3.5 Fuse sub-panel in the Amstrad PPC512

Figure 3.6 Internal keyboard connector in the BBC Microcomputer

Figure 3.7 Battery and speaker connector in the Amstrad PPC512

Figure 3.8 Various board connectors in the Amstrad PPC512

Figure 3.9 Internally fitted switched-mode power supply sub-chassis in the Atari 1040 STFM

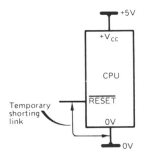

Figure 3.10 Method of resetting a system when no reset button is provided

inter-PCB connectors within the equipment. These can take various forms, from simple PCB edge connectors to more elaborate multi-pole indirect types. Unfortunately, connectors are a regular cause of problems and, before going any further, it is worth giving each connector a gentle push home with a slight sideways motion, which may help to reduce the contact resistance.

The mains supply should now be re-connected and the equipment switched on. The display on the VDU, monitor, or television receiver should then be checked again for the appearance of the initial user prompt. If no such prompt appears, or if the screen is filled with garbage, a further attempt should be made to reset the system. If no system reset button is available a typical method of resetting the system using the microprocessor's reset line is shown in Figure 3.10.

Table 3.2 Supply pin connections for a selection of CPUs

CPU	Pin numbers		Supply voltage	Other supplies
	+ve supply	common 0 V		
6502	8	1	+5 V	None
6800	8	1,21	+5 V	None
6809	7	1	+5 V	None
8080	20	2	+5 V	−5 V pin 11
				+12 V pin 28
8085	40	20	+5 V	None
8086	40	1,20	+5 V	None
8088	40	1,20	+5 V	None
9900	2	26,40	+5 V	−5 V pin 1
				+12 V pin 27
68000	14	53	+5 V	None
80188	9,43	60	+5 V	None
80186	9,43	60	+5 V	None
80286	62	60	+5 V	None
80386DX	A1,A5,A7	A2,A6,A9	+5 V	None
80386SX	48	49,50	+5 V	None
80486DX	B7,B9,B11	A7,A9,A11	+5 V	None
Z80	11	29	+5 V	None
Z8001	11	36	+5 V	None
Z8002	10	31	+5 V	None

If there is still no change to the display, it will be necessary to check the main internal d.c. power rail. This invariably provides a +5 V supply to the CPU and associated circuitry (ROM, RAM etc). The voltmeter may be connected to an existing test point, the terminals of one of the larger supply decoupling capacitors, or to the supply pins of the CPU itself. Note that at this stage we have not excluded the possibility that a fault may lie in the video processing circuitry; the CPU may, in fact, by operating correctly even though there is no confirmation that a system reset is occurring!

To assist readers, Table 3.2 shows some typical CPU supply pin connections. In all cases, voltages should be within 5 per cent of those stated. Where this is not the case, it will be necessary to carry out a detailed examination of the power supply unit. We should now have excluded the mains supply input, the d.c. power supply, and the internal connectors from our investigation and, depending upon the outcome of the initial checks and the resulting display on the VDU, there are three remaining options, as was shown in the flowchart of Figure 3.3. We shall now examine each of these options in turn, starting with the most severe, which is associated with a catastrophic failure within the CPU board.

Testing the CPU board

We shall assume that the CPU board contains these principal items: (a) the CPU itself; (b) system ROM and RAM; (c) I/O devices; and (d) video processing. If the last item is relegated to a separate board, it is well worth checking this first since a failure in this area will almost certainly inhibit the normal video display while the remainder of the system may be operating quite normally.

Visual and thermal inspection

Having established that a fault exists in the CPU board, our first task is to carry out a detailed examination of the board for any obvious signs of component or device failure. It is all too easy to overlook the obvious and before delving into the realms of voltage and logic level tracing it is well worth spending a few minutes taking a close look at the circuitry.

Inspection should take two forms: an initial 'cold' check with the supply disconnected, and a second 'hot' check with the supply connected and the equipment switched on. The cold check allows us to examine closely all of the components and devices for signs of mechanical defect or discoloration, the usual causes of which are respectively mechanical shock and over-dissipation.

The hot check allows us to examine the state of the components when power is applied and, in particular, lets us make some estimate of the consequent temperature rise. Signs of overheating should quickly become obvious. Integrated circuits, and in particular ROM or RAM chips which are noticeably hotter than other similar devices, are immediately suspect. However, this does not always mean that they have failed, since a failure in one component or device may produce consequent over-dissipation in other devices.

A classic example is associated with the failure of a three-terminal series regulator. When such a device becomes short circuit, all devices operated from the particular supply rail will be liable to over-dissipation. Hopefully, such an obvious failure as this will have been diagnosed previously as part of the 'initial check' procedure.

When a device has been recognized as suspect it should be removed from the PCB after first switching off and disconnecting from the supply. Tests may then be carried out 'out-of-circuit' or, alternatively, a known good device may be substituted. This process is, of course, greatly simplified where integrated circuits are fitted in sockets.

Where this is not the case the offending device has to be removed from the PCB by desoldering. This is a relatively simple task where the PCB is of the single-sided variety. If, on the other hand, it is double-sided the job is somewhat more complex. In some cases it may even be expedient to cut the IC away from its pins and then desolder each in turn. In this case it will, of course, not be possible to salvage the device should it later prove to be operating correctly!

When refitting the device, the author recommends the use of a low-profile DIL socket. This will greatly assist with the removal and replacement of the device in the event of its subsequent failure. In any event, the cost of an additional socket is usually negligible compared with the time and inconvenience associated with desoldering the IC from the board.

Depending upon whether an internal fault is present, replacing a device that is overheating may or may not effect an immediate cure. If the replacement device behaves in the same manner as its predecessor it will be necessary to look elsewhere for the cause, but we now have an additional symptom to aid with pin-pointing the real fault. A more detailed examination of the associated components should then be carried out. These components and devices will usually be reasonably adjacent to the IC that is overheating, but note that there are exceptions to this general rule.

Where, on the other hand, an internal failure has been confirmed, it is important to carry out the visual diagnostic routines. This allows the system some time in which to fail again. If failure does subsequently occur, it will be necessary to look for the cause of failure; we can no longer assume that it was just a random event!

The flow chart of Figure 3.11 illustrates the typical chain of events in the visual and thermal inspection of the CPU board. Again, there are three options depending upon the outcome of our investigation. We shall continue with the most severe of these, which demands more rigorous testing of the CPU and its immediate support devices.

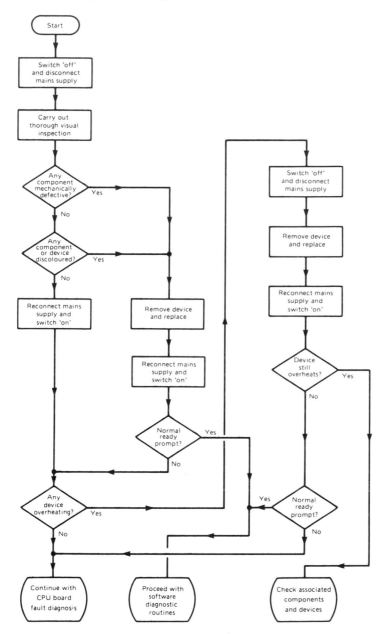

Figure 3.11 Flow chart for the CPU board inspection

Testing the system clock

Having carried out some of the more obvious tests and measurements, we now find ourselves in an area of the microcomputer in which some resort to more sophisticated items

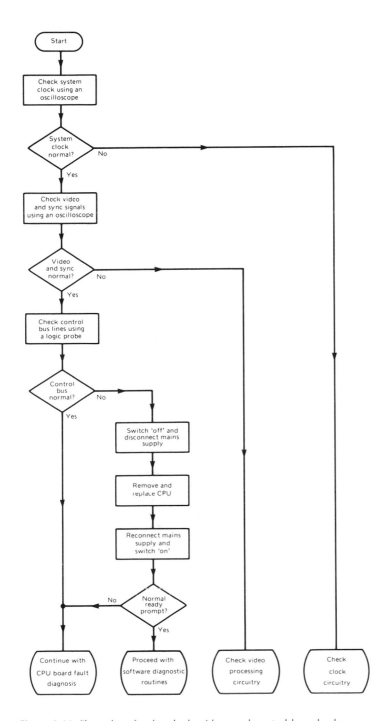

Figure 3.12 Flow chart for the clock, video, and control bus checks

Table 3.3 Typical clock frequencies and clock input pins for some common CPUs

CPU	Clock input pin number (see note 1)	Typical clock frequency (MHz)
6502	37	2
6800	3 and 37	1
6809	38 and 39 (see note 2)	4
8080	22 and 15	2
8086	19	5
8088	19	5
80186	58 and 59 (see note 2)	10
80188	58 and 59 (see note 2)	10
80286	31	12
80386DX	F12	25
80386SX	15	25
80486DX	C3	33
9900	8, 9, 28, and 29	3
68000	15	8
Z80	6	6
Z8001	35	4
Z8002	30	4

Notes: 1. Where more than one pin is shown the clock is a multi-phase type.
2. Internal 'on-chip' clock oscillator.

of test equipment is essential. The measurements that follow are outlined in the flow chart of Figure 3.12 and require the aid of the items mentioned in the 'minimum' list of test equipment quoted in Chapter 2.

The first and perhaps easiest test to perform is concerned with verifying that the system clock is operating correctly. This requires the use of an oscilloscope to observe the waveform at the clock input of the CPU. To assist readers, Table 3.3 lists some popular CPUs together with their respective clock input pin numbers and typical clock frequencies.

The clock waveform should appear reasonably square and of TTL-compatible amplitude. If the clock waveform is noticeably distorted, of insufficient amplitude, incorrect frequency, or missing altogether, this will almost certainly point to a defect in the system clock. Typical clock circuits are shown in Figures 3.13 and 3.14. The IC devices should be checked with the logic probe and pulser using the techniques described in Chapter 2.

For no immediately apparent reason, quartz crystals sometimes fail due to lack of 'activity'. In such cases, a replacement crystal should be fitted. One should, of course, exercise reasonable care when removing and resoldering these devices as they are easily damaged by excessive heat.

Testing the video processing circuits

The next measurement involves checking the video and sync signals at the output of the video processing circuitry. Unfortunately, there is wide variation in the circuitry used to generate video signals and it is very difficult to generalize about the techniques, and hence the measurements, that should be employed.

Where a computer generates a composite video signal (i.e., video plus sync) this may be available either as an output for the connection of an external monitor, or for modulation of a UHF carrier for use with a conventional TV receiver. In either case it is relatively easy

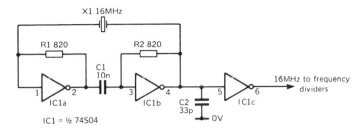

Figure 3.13 Typical clock oscillator circuit (1)

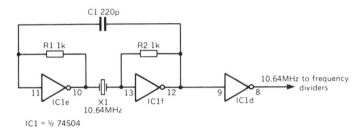

Figure 3.14 Typical clock oscillator circuit (2)

Figure 3.15 Typical system clock and associated components

Figure 3.16 Clock circuitry in an Atari 65XE

Figure 3.17 Amstrad PPC512 clock circuitry

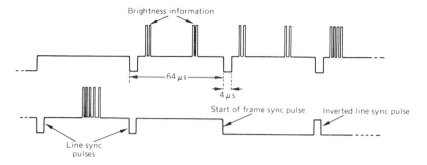

Figure 3.18 Typical video waveforms showing lines from various points on the display

to locate a suitable test point (in the first case we can simply connect the oscilloscope to the composite video output socket whilst in the latter case we simply attach the test probe to the composite video input of the modulator).

A typical signal waveform at this point is shown in Figure 3.18. Note that in the event of a failure in the CPU the positive-going brightness information may be missing and only the negative-going synchronizing information may be present.

Other displays make use of separate video and sync signals and, furthermore, the video signals may be either digital or analogue R-G-B (red-green-blue). In such cases, signals on each line can be checked independently at the video output connector using a conventional oscilloscope.

If the video waveform is completely absent, of abnormally low amplitude, or lacking in either sync or brightness information, it will of course be a matter of checking the video processing circuitry, starting with the output stage and working back through the video/sync combining stage towards the sync processing and video generating circuitry. Note that several manufacturers use custom video interface chips to take care of the majority of these functions. Such devices are invariably socketed and thus a substitute device can readily be fitted.

Testing the CPU

Assuming that one is reasonably satisfied that the video processing is normal and that some evidence of sync information is found, it is now worth checking the system control bus using a logic probe and pulser. The obvious point at which to check the state of the control bus is at the CPU itself. An IC test clip should be fitted to this device and each of the control lines should be examined in turn using the logic probe. The logical state of each line should be noted.

Unfortunately, there is some variation in the function and nomenclature used for the individual CPU control lines. It is, however, relatively easy to recognize lines that are 'stuck', or are permanently 'floating', using nothing more than a logic probe and pulser. If possible, the effect of a system reset and an interrupt request should be observed, noting the response of each of the control lines.

If the CPU is diagnosed as suspect it should, of course, be substituted by a known good device. Fortunately, this is a relatively easy process since the CPU is invariably fitted in a socket. The results of the substitution will confirm whether or not the device has failed.

If the CPU is found to be normal we must then turn our attention to the immediate support devices (ROM, RAM, I/O chips and bus buffers) which are connected to the CPU via the system bus lines. An internal failure in any of these devices may cause a fault condition to appear on the appropriate bus line and thus the first step will involve an examination of the state of the address and data bus lines as they appear to the CPU.

Testing the system bus

It is possible to carry out continuity checks on each individual bus line in turn but this can be a somewhat lengthy and tedious process when a bus fault is present. Fortunately, assuming that a fully functional CPU is available, it is possible to carry out such tests in a fraction of the time with the aid of the CPU itself.

The basis of these measurements is a device called an 'NOP exerciser'. This simple tool can be quickly constructed from low-cost readily available materials and can prove invaluable. In emergency, such a device can even be constructed using nothing more than a low-profile DIL socket and a few short wire links.

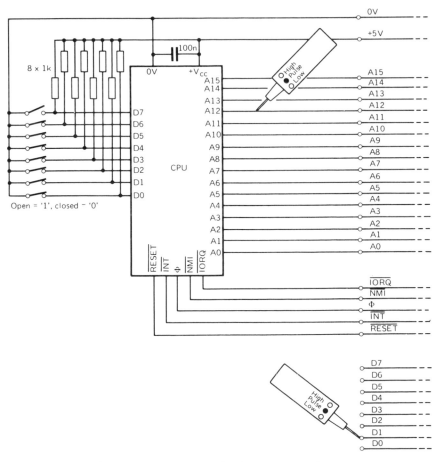

Figure 3.19 Using the NOP exerciser to check address and data lines

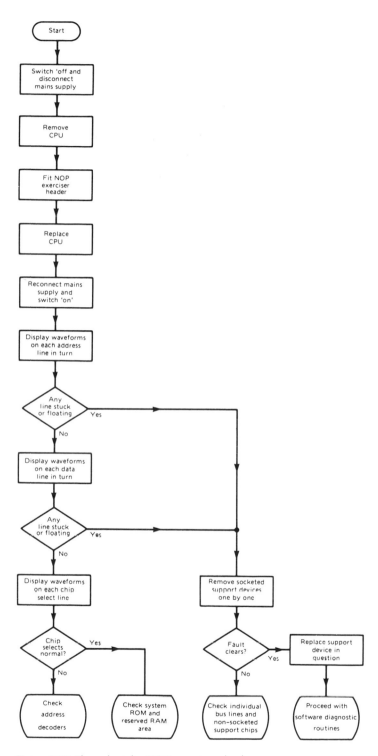

Figure 3.20 Flow chart for NOP exerciser checks

The NOP exerciser consists quite simply of a modified header that links all pins of the CPU, with the exception of the data lines, to its original socket. The data lines are connected to a row of DIP switches or, alternatively, are simply 'hard-wired' to produce an NOP instruction, as shown in Figure 3.19. Most instruction sets include this particular single-byte instruction, which simply does nothing except increment the program counter (PC).

Table 3.4 Data bus pin numbers and NOP bit patterns for some popular eight-bit CPUs

CPU	Pin numbers								NOP bit pattern							
	D7	D6	D5	D4	D3	D2	D1	D0	D7	D6	D5	D4	D3	D2	D1	D0
6502	26	27	28	29	30	31	32	33	1	1	1	0	1	0	1	0
6800	26	27	28	29	30	31	32	33	0	0	0	0	0	0	0	1
8080	6	5	4	3	7	8	9	10	0	0	0	0	0	0	0	0
8086	9	10	11	12	13	14	15	16	1	0	0	1	0	0	0	0
8088	9	10	11	12	13	14	15	16	1	0	0	1	0	0	0	0
Z80	13	10	9	7	8	12	15	14	0	0	0	0	0	0	0	0

Various other single-byte instructions could also be used, provided no data transfer is involved. Examples of these include the Z80 CCF, CPL and DAA instructions. The NOP is, however, preferred and is reasonably universal. Assembly language programmers will of course be familiar with this instruction as the means by which breakpoints are inserted in programs when testing and debugging. A flow chart for NOP exerciser checks is shown in Figure 3.20.

To assist readers, Table 3.4 shows the NOP instruction data bit patterns for some common 8-bit CPUs. A logic 0 is obtained by switching (or wiring) the relevant data line to common 0 V, whereas a logic 1 is generated by switching (or wiring) the relevant data

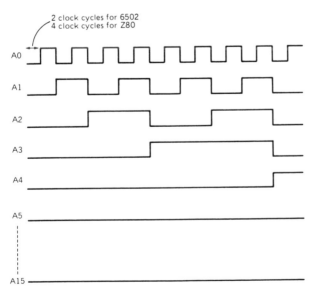

Figure 3.21 Address line waveforms obtained with the NOP exerciser

line to +5 V via a 1 kohm resistor. Due to variations in pin connections and NOP bit patterns it may be necessary to have several NOP exercisers available depending upon the types of CPU predominantly encountered.

The result of a forced NOP instruction is that the CPU successively increments the program counter and thus increments through its entire address range. Hence a binary count sequence is performed with the waveform on each address line appearing as a square wave. The frequency of the square wave on address line 0 (A0) will be twice that appearing on address line 1 (A1) and so on, as depicted in Figure 3.21. This can be a most useful test since the repetitive waveforms generated on each address line are ideal for display on a conventional oscilloscope. It is simply a matter of connecting the oscilloscope probe to each address line in turn, checking that a square wave of the appropriate frequency or period is present.

Figure 3.22 Use of an IC test clip and probes to obtain waveforms for display using an oscilloscope

If necessary the period of each signal can be checked by reference to the period of the system clock, the number of the particular address line in question, and the number of clock cycles required for the execution of the NOP (or equivalent) instruction. As an example of this, the 6502 NOP instruction requires two clock cycles for its execution and hence, for a 6502 running at 1 MHz, the frequency and period of the NOP exerciser address line square waves will be as shown in Table 3.5.

As a further example, consider an IBM PC-XT. This machine uses an 8088 CPU running at 4.7 MHz. The frequency of each of its address bus lines is shown in Table 3.6.

Although the address bus waveforms shown in Figure 3.21 are relevant to the majority of straightforward CPUs, there are some notable differences when the CPU in question incorporates facilities for refreshing dynamic memories or where a shared address/data bus

Table 3.5 Address line square wave frequencies for an NOP exerciser fitted to a 6502 CPU with a 1 MHz clock

Address line	Frequency
A0	500 kHz
A1	250 kHz
A2	125 kHz
A3	62.5 kHz
A4	31.25 kHz
A5	15.625 kHz
A6	7.8125 kHz
A7	3.9062 kHz
A8	1.9531 kHz
A9	976.56 Hz
A10	488.28 Hz
A11	244.14 Hz
A12	122.07 Hz
A13	61.03 Hz
A14	30.51 Hz
A15	15.25 Hz

Table 3.6 Address line square wave frequencies for an NOP exerciser fitted to an 8088 CPU with a 4.7 MHz clock

Address line	Frequency
AD0	
AD1	
AD2	*Note*: multiplexed address/data
AD3	lines hard-wired for NOP code,
AD4	please see Table 3.4
AD5	
AD6	
AD7	
A8	2.33 kHz
A9	1.165 kHz
A10	582.6 Hz
A11	291.3 Hz
A12	145.6 Hz
A13	72.8 Hz
A14	36.4 Hz
A15	18.2 Hz

is employed. In the Z80, for example, an NOP instruction requires four clock cycles for its execution. The instruction fetch is performed during the first two clock cycles while a memory refresh is performed using the last two clock cycles, as shown in Figure 3.23. During the refresh period, the lower seven bits (A0 to A6) of the address bus contain a refresh address while the upper nine bits (A7 to A15) are all returned to logic 0. The refresh process thus only affects the waveforms that appear on address lines A7 to A15, as depicted in Figure 3.24.

If the address lines are completely inactive, this points either to a defective CPU or to the complete failure of a bus buffer. In the latter case, a simple comparative test of the input

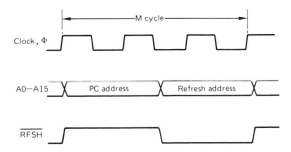

Figure 3.23 Relationship between clock, address bus, and refresh signals in a Z80 CPU

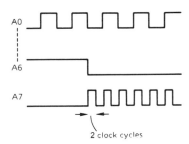

Figure 3.24 Effect of memory refresh on the address lines of a Z80 CPU

and output lines of the buffer should provide confirmation of failure. If the CPU is suspected, a substitution test should be made; although, if readers have been following the flow chart of Figure 3.20, this test should have already been carried out!

If one (or more) of the address lines appear to be stuck at either logic 1 or logic 0, this usually indicates failure in one of the support chips, each of which may now be removed in turn until the fault clears. The last device removed must be then treated as suspect. The suggested sequence for removing devices is: system ROM; BASIC (or alternative interpreter) ROM; disk controller ROM; I/O devices; and RAM. Note that these last devices may be soldered into the PCB and, if this is the case, it may be better to start with the logic gates that provide memory decoding and multiplexing (where applicable).

In any event, it is well worth consulting the circuit diagram of the equipment in order to eliminate those devices that are not operated from the particular address line in question. Some knowledge of the memory decoding is therefore invaluable at this stage.

Having checked the address lines, the oscilloscope probe should be transferred to the chip select (CS) lines of each support chip. This will confirm that the memory decoding is correct and that devices are being selected when required. The waveforms at these points will also be repetitive though not necessarily of unity mark-to-space ratio.

It is, of course, a relatively simple matter to determine the shape of the particular chip select waveform by reference to the memory decoding. A simple home computer with 16K ROM (0000H to 3FFFH in four 4K × 8-bit chips) and 48K RAM (4000H to FFFFH in three 16K × 8-bit blocks) would have the chip select waveforms shown in Figure 3.25 when the NOP exerciser is connected.

If desired, and particularly when an oscilloscope is not available, it is possible to run the CPU at low speed (or even single-step some CPUs) using nothing more than a logic pulser.

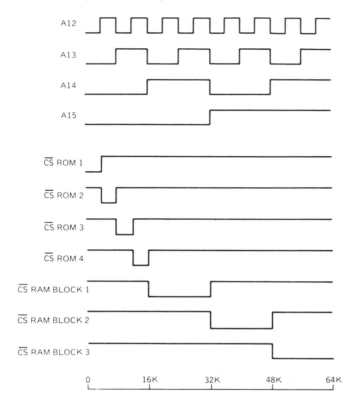

Figure 3.25 Chip select waveforms in a typical system (see text)

A similar technique can be employed for checking the data lines and for verifying that the contents of the ROM and RAM are present on the the CPU bus when the appropriate chip select signals are generated. The logic probe is simply transferred to each of the data bus lines in turn (not to the CPU pins as these will still be wired for the NOP instruction) and the state of the bus is examined as the NOP exerciser advances the address count. Blocks of data in either ROM or RAM should be seen to be present; if a particular bus line

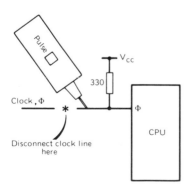

Figure 3.26 Using a logic pulser to clock a CPU (the 330 ohm resistor is essential since most pulsers have tri-state outputs in the inactive state)

shows no variation it should be further investigated, checking CPU bus and expansion connectors, removing ROM, RAM and I/O devices until the fault clears.

Using the system monitor or debugger

Although monitors and debuggers are often thought of as being solely a means of debugging machine language programs, they are in fact capable of carrying out a variety of other tasks and can be equally useful to the programmer and hardware specialist. A monitor/debugger can thus be considered to be a set of basic software 'tools' which allow the user both to probe and manipulate a system using simple commands entered from the keyboard. It is worth noting at the outset that the benefit derived from these tools will depend not only upon the level of sophistication of the particular monitor/debugger concerned but also upon the expertise of the user.

```
Copyright <c> 1983 by Hubert S. Howe, Jr.
Command?HE
DA   Display ASCII      RD   Return to DOS     IB   Initialize Block
DH   Display HEX        RB   Return to Basic   IR   Initialize RS232
DI   Disassemble        LC   Load Cassette     TM   Terminal
DX   Decimal to HEX     WC   Write Cassette    TB   Transmit Block
XD   HEX to Decimal     IS   Input Sectors     RM   Receive in Memory
MB   Move Block         OS   Output Sectors    DR   Display Registers
VB   Verify Block       RF   Read Data File    SR   Set Registers
RP   Relocate Program   WF   Write Data File   SB   Set Breakpoint
UP   Unload Program     LP   Load Program      EX   Execute Location
FB   Find Byte          WP   Write Program     SS   Single Step
FW   Find Word          KF   Kill File         SC   Single Step-Call
FS   Find String        EM   Edit Memory       HE   Help!
JP   Jump               TY   Type to Memory
Command?_
```

Figure 3.27 Commands available in a basic system monitor

Monitors and debuggers vary greatly in their complexity with, perhaps, a minimum capability of displaying and editing the contents of memory. More sophisticated monitors may incorporate extensive debugging facilities (they would then be referred to as 'debuggers'). Figure 3.27, for example, shows the complete list of commands available in a monitor program designed for use on a simple Z80-based system. While many of these routines are of limited use to the service technician, the following routines are of particular interest:

1. those which display the contents of blocks of memory in either hex or ASCII format;
2. those which display the contents of the CPU registers;
3. those which allow setting of the CPU registers;
4. those which will initialize blocks of memory;
5. those which will move, compare, or verify blocks of memory;
6. those which will transfer data between memory and I/O devices.

Fortunately, monitors will usually contain most if not all of these facilities. Hence, provided the CPU, support devices, system RAM and VDU are operating normally, the system monitor can be invoked and used as a diagnostic aid. (Figure 3.28 shows a screen dump of a memory block obtained using a simple hex monitor.)

```
5400>DF DA 85 53 1B 2A A4 40 01 2C 01 09 EB DF DA 85
5410>53 11 CE FF 22 B1 40 19 22 A0 40 CD 4D 1B 21 00
5420>52 CD A7 28 2A A9 53 2B D7 FE 0D CA 19 1A E5 7E
5430>FE 20 38 03 23 18 F8 36 00 CD 8B 03 CD AC 41 CD
5440>F9 20 21 FF FF 22 A2 40 E1 2B C3 81 1A 4F FE 40
5450>D2 4A 1E 13 1A 1B FE 20 20 7D 1A CB AF 06 31 FE
5460>4E 28 05 04 FE 58 20 6F D5 C5 CD 9B 54 C1 E1 11
5470>18 43 06 00 ED B0 3E 0D 12 21 19 43 11 80 44 C3
5480>33 44 4C 42 41 53 49 43 2F 4F 56 43 61 6E 27 74
5490>20 6C 6F 61 64 20 4F 56 33 0D 00 78 21 82 54 11
54A0>80 44 01 09 00 ED B0 12 13 AF 12 C9 3A 0E 43 3D
54B0>CA 00 4E 06 33 E5 CD 9B 54 11 80 44 21 0F 43 CB
54C0>D6 CD 30 44 E3 C8 F6 C0 CD 09 44 21 BB 54 CD A7
54D0>28 01 18 1A C3 AE 19 EB 11 18 43 06 00 ED B0 3E
54E0>0D 12 CD 50 47 21 98 F0 39 ED 5B FD 40 AF ED 52
```

Figure 3.28 Typical screen dump of a memory block, obtained with a simple hex monitor

Routines (1) and (4), for example, may be employed to check blocks of system RAM; the chosen memory block is first initialized to FFH (setting all bits on) and then displayed and examined. Subsequently, the entire block can then be set to 00H and again displayed and examined. It is thus possible simultaneously to verify blocks of memory (up to the permitted screen capacity) merely by inspecting the hex pattern displayed. A 16K RAM can typically be checked using this method in just two or three minutes. Figure 3.29 shows a typical hex screen dump of a memory block in which errors are present and Figure 3.30 shows the output obtained with a monitor providing both hex and ASCII displays.

Alternatively, if a verify memory facility is available as in (5), the entire memory can first be initialized and then verified in blocks of a suitable size. The appearance of an error message will then indicate a suspect memory device.

Routines (2) and (3) are useful for checking intermittent faults that may affect the operation of the CPU. Figure 3.31 shows the state of the CPU registers upon first entering the monitor. However, it should be noted that the monitor maintains a pseudo-register set and it is the content of these that is actually being displayed on the VDU. One further point should be made: if the CPU or system ROM itself is suspected, the results of tests made using the system monitor should be treated with some caution. Finally, readers should note that use of the MS-DOS debugger is described in detail in Chapter 7.

```
D000>FF FF FF FF FF FF FF FF FF FF FF FF FF FF FF FF
D010>FF FF FF FF FF FF FF FF FF FF FF FF FF FF FF FF
D020>FF FF FF FF FF FF FF FF FF FF FF FF FF FF FF FF
D030>FF FF FF FF FF FF FF FF FF FF FF FF FF FF FF FF
D040>FF FF FF FF FF FF FF FF FF FF FF FF FF FF FF FF
D050>FF FF FF FF FF FF FF FF FF FF FF FF FF FF FF FF
D060>FF FF FF FF FF FF FF FF FF FF FF FF FF FF FF FF
D070>FF FF FF FF FF FF FF FF FF FF FF FF FF FF FF FF
D080>FF FF FF FF FF FF FF FF FB FF FF FF FF FF FF FF
D090>FF FF FF FF FF FF FF FF FF FF FF FF FF FF FF FF
D0A0>FF FF FF FF FF FF FF FF FF FF FF FF FF FF FF FF
D0B0>FF FF FF FF FF FF FF FF FF FF FF FF FF FF FF FF
D0C0>FF FF FF FF FF FF FF FF FF FF FF FF FF FF FF EF
D0D0>FF FF FF FF FF FF FF FF FF FF FF FF FF FF FF FF
D0E0>FF FF FF FF FF FF FF FF FE FF FF FF FF FF FF FF
```

Figure 3.29 Screen dump of a memory block in which three errors are present (the block was first initialized to FFH)

```
5400   DFDA 8553 1B2A A440 012C 0109 EBDF DA85   _Z.S.*$@.,..k_Z.
5410   5311 CEFF 22B1 4019 22A0 40CD 4D1B 2100   S.N"1@." @MM.!.
5420   52CD A728 2AA9 532B D7FE 0DCA 191A E57E   RM'(*)S+W~.J..e~
5430   FE20 3803 2318 F836 00CD 8B03 CDAC 41CD   ~ 8.£.x6.M..M,AM
5440   F920 21FF FF22 A240 E12B C381 1A4F FE40   y !""@a+C..O~@
5450   D24A 1E13 1A1B FE20 207D 1ACB AF06 31FE   RJ....~ }.K/.1~
5460   4E28 0504 FE58 206F D5C5 CD9B 54C1 E111   N(..~X oUEM.TAa.
5470   1843 0600 EDB0 3E0D 1221 1943 1180 44C3   .C..mO>..!.C..DC
5480   3344 4C42 4153 4943 2F4F 5643 616E 2774   3DLBASIC/OVCan't
5490   206C 6F61 6420 4F56 330D 0078 2182 5411   load OV3..x!.T.
54A0   8044 0109 00ED B012 13AF 12C9 3A0E 433D   .D...mO../.I:.C=
54B0   CA00 4E06 33E5 CD9B 5411 8044 210F 43CB   J.N.3eM.T..D!.CK
54C0   D6CD 3044 E3C8 F6C0 CD09 4421 8B54 CDA7   VMODcHv@M.D!.TM'
54D0   2801 181A C3AE 19EB 1118 4306 00ED B03E   (...C..k..C..mO>
54E0   0D12 CD50 4721 98F0 39ED 5BFD 40AF ED52   ..MPG!.p9m[}@/mR
54F0   DA7A 1921 2D40 1103 5401 0600 EDB0 2109   Zz.!-@..T...mO!.
5500   440E 04ED B02A FD40 1100 AE19 2261 55E5   D..mO*}@....."aUe
5510   1100 F219 2299 55D1 2A49 4022 9E55 2100   ..r,".UQ*I@".U!.
```

Figure 3.30 Screen dump of the same block of memory as shown in Figure 3.28. obtained with a monitor which provides a display in both hex and ASCII

```
AF = 0000    BC = 0000    DE = 0000    HL = 0000    C  Z  P  S  N  H

AF'= 0000    BC'= 0000    DE'= 0000    HL'= 0000    0  0  0  0  0  0

IX = 0000    IY = 0000    SP = 0000    PC = 0000    (SP)= AFF3

0000   F3                 DI                        ;s
```

Figure 3.31 State of the CPU registers when first entering the monitor (the content of the program counter is F3H, which is the Z80 DI instruction)

Software diagnostic routines

An inherent advantage of microprocessor-based equipment is that self-diagnostic routines can be performed. While it is not of course possible to perform such operations on a system in which there has been a catastrophic failure of the power supply, CPU, immediate support devices, or system RAM, software diagnostic routines can be invaluable. This is particularly true in the case of intermittent faults where the equipment can be left continuously executing a routine until the fault appears.

Some diagnostic routines may be contained within the operating system of the computer but they are usually limited to the detection of specific faults in areas of the system that are prone to failure. A memory diagnostic is perhaps the best example of this. Such routines require only a few bytes of machine code within the system ROM and may be executed whenever the system is booted.

Regrettably, comprehensive diagnostic software is not generally available and only a few software companies have shown an interest in supplying programs of this type. Of the few diagnostic programs that are available, nearly all are 'menu driven' and provide the user with the choice of carrying out detailed tests on particular areas of the system. In addition, a facility may be included that permits the continuous testing of all or part of the system, thus freeing the technician from the need to run the program repeatedly in the hope that an intermittent fault may subsequently develop. A screen dump of the main menu of a

```
            System Diagnostic
Copyright <c> 1983 by Howe Software
            Version 3.0

    Select device to be tested:

        <1> ROM
        <2> RAM
        <3> Video Display
        <4> Keyboard
        <5> Line Printer
        <6> Cassette Recorder
        <7> Disk Drives
        <8> RS-232-C Interface
        <9> Return to master menu

            Your choice?
```

Figure 3.32 Screen dump of the main menu of a simple system diagnostic program

simple system diagnostic program is shown in Figure 3.32. Chapter 7 includes examples of the use of Microsoft's System Diagnostic program (MSD) which is currently supplied as part of Microsoft Windows for the IBM PC and compatibles.

Test ROMs, disks and diagnostic adaptors

Many manufacturers use test ROMs or specialized diagnostic adaptor cards in the production test process. These devices are sometimes also made available to accredited service agents and they can be invaluable when a system refuses to boot in the normal way. Test ROMs must usually be fitted in place of existing system ROMs or in expansion ROM sockets. Diagnostic adaptor cards, on the other hand, interface directly with existing expansion sockets (in some cases existing expansion cards may have to be removed in order to accommodate them).

Other manufacturers (e.g. IBM) have provided disk-based diagnostic software which can be used by 'end-users' to identify major system components that may require service. These disks are simply inserted in the floppy drive and the system is booted in the normal way. The user then follows a predefined sequence of tests, observing and noting the results of each together with any diagnostic error messages that may be displayed.

Diagnostic routines in BASIC

Where a system monitor/debugger is unavailable or if, as sometimes happens, a monitor does exist but the technician is either unaware or unfamiliar with its operation, it is possible to carry out a number of diagnostic routines using the system's own BASIC interpreter. Programs may be loaded from either disk or tape, or entered directly from the keyboard.

Diagnostic routines are greatly enhanced where the BASIC interpreter provides direct access to user-specified memory addresses. The PEEK and POKE commands found in the majority of BASICs allow just such a facility. If, for example, the operating system maintains a particular byte in reserved system memory as part of a device control block (DCB) it is possible, from BASIC, to investigate the contents of this block by simply PEEKing at the appropriate addresses.

Alternatively, it is possible to select, or de-select, a particular device or driver routine by simply POKEing appropriate data into the DCB. One does, of course, need to know the relevant DCB addresses and have some idea of the function of each individual byte! This technique is very powerful since it is the means by which logical devices (such as the keyboard, VDU, printer, etc.) may be interchanged, permitting for example the routeing of the keyboard output directly to the printer.

As an example, consider a DCB which is resident in reserved system memory from 4025H (16421 decimal) to 402CH (16428 decimal). A BASIC program to display the contents (in decimal) of this DCB is shown in Listing 3.1. The corresponding screen dump obtained from this program is depicted in Figure 3.33.

If it is required to alter the contents of the DCB, the BASIC program of Listing 3.2 may be employed. The two programs may, of course, be incorporated as subroutines within a larger program designed specifically for manipulating the DCBs.

```
100 REM ** DISPLAY CONTENTS OF DCB **
110 CLS
120 N=0
130 PRINT "BYTE NO.","ADDRESS","CONTENTS"
140 FOR X=16421 TO 16428
150 PRINT N,X,PEEK(X)
160 N=N+1
170 NEXT X
180 END
```

Listing 3.1 BASIC program to display (in decimal) the contents of a device control block

BYTE NO.	ADDRESS	CONTENTS
0	16421	6
1	16422	141
2	16423	5
3	16424	66
4	16425	35
5	16426	0
6	16427	80
7	16428	82
READY		
>_		

Figure 3.33 Typical screen display obtained from the program of Listing 3.1

```
200 REM ** MODIFY CONTENTS OF DCB **
210 CLS
220 INPUT "WHICH BYTE NO. IS TO BE CHANGED";N
230 INPUT "NEW CONTENTS OF THIS BYTE       ";Z
240 X=16421+N
250 POKE(X),Z
260 PRINT "DONE - DO YOU WISH TO CHANGE ANOTHER BYTE <Y/N> ?"
270 R$=INKEY$
280 IF R$="Y" GOTO 210
290 IF R$="N" CLS: END
300 GOTO 270
```

Listing 3.2 BASIC program to modify the contents of a device control block (input in decimal)

A more sophisticated and much enhanced program for examining the contents of memory locations is shown in Listing 3.3. This program will accept an input address in either hex or decimal and will then display the address (in both hex and decimal) together with its contents in hex, decimal and binary. This program employs user-defined functions in the hex-to-decimal and decimal-to-hex conversion routines which are, unfortunately, available in some versions of BASIC. Typical screen dumps obtained from this program are shown in Figure 3.34.

BASIC is, unfortunately, extremely slow in a number of applications and, furthermore, minor variations in the language prevent routines and programs being truly portable. Machine language is therefore much to be preferred on the grounds of both portability (for

```
100 REM **************************************************
110 REM **                                              **
120 REM **   PEEK MEMORY / DECIMAL, HEX AND BINARY       **
130 REM **                                              **
140 REM **************************************************
150 CLEAR 200
160 U$=STRING$(63,CHR$(140))
170 REM
180 REM ** DECIMAL TO HEX **
190 REM
200 DEFFNH1$(A1%)=MID$("0123456789ABCDEF",INT(A1%/16)+1,1)+MID$("0123456789ABCDE
F",A1%-INT(A1%/16)*16+1,1)
210 DEFFNH2$(A1%)=FNH1$(ASC(MID$(MKI$(A1%),2)))+FNH1$(ASC(MKI$(A1%)))
220 REM .
230 REM ** HEX TO DECIMAL **
240 REM
250 DEFFND3'(A$)=INSTR("123456789ABCDEF",MID$(A$,1,1))*4096+INSTR("123456789ABCD
EF",MID$(A$,2,1))*256+INSTR("123456789ABCDEF",MID$(A$,3,1))*16+INSTR("123456789A
BCDEF",MID$(A$,4,1))
260 REM
270 REM ** DISPLAY MENU **
280 REM
290 CLS
300 PRINT TAB(18) "PEEK MEMORY IN DECIMAL OR HEX"
310 PRINT TAB(18) "HEX OR DECIMAL INPUT <H/D> ?"
320 R$=INKEY$
330 IF R$="H" GOTO 500
340 IF R$="D" GOTO 370
350 GOTO 320
360 REM
370 REM ** MAIN PROGRAM / DECIMAL INPUT **
380 REM
390 PRINT: INPUT "MEMORY LOCATION IN DECIMAL";A!
400 IF A!<0 OR A!>65535 GOTO 390
410 IF A!>32767 THEN A%=A!-65536 ELSE A%=A!
420 GOSUB 640
430 H$=FNH2$(A%): CD%=PEEK(A%): CH$=FNH2$(PEEK(A%))
440 GOSUB 710
450 PRINT A! TAB(10) H$ TAB(30) CD% TAB(40) CH$ TAB(46) CB$
460 PRINT U$
470 GOTO 770
480 GOTO 370
490 REM
500 REM ** MAIN PROGRAM / HEX INPUT **
510 REM
520 PRINT: INPUT "MEMORY LOCATION IN HEX";A$
530 IF LEN(A$)<>4 GOTO 520
540 A!=FND3!(A$)
550 IF A!>32767 THEN A%=A!-65536 ELSE A%=A!
560 CD%=PEEK(A%): CH$=FNH2$(PEEK(A%))
570 GOSUB 710
580 GOSUB 640
590 PRINT A! TAB(10) A$ TAB(30) CD% TAB(40) CH$ TAB(46) CB$
600 PRINT U$
610 GOTO 770
620 GOTO 500
```

```
630 REM
640 REM ** TABLE HEADINGS **
650 REM
660 PRINT: PRINT TAB(4) "LOCATION" TAB(42)"CONTENTS"
670 PRINT U$
680 PRINT TAB(2) "DEC" TAB(10) "HEX" TAB(31) "DEC" TAB(40) "HEX" TAB(53) "BIN"
690 RETURN
700 REM
710 REM ** DECIMAL TO BINARY CONVERSION **
720 REM
730 CB$="": N=CD%
740 CB$=STR$(N-(INT(N/2)*2))+CB$: N=INT(N/2): IF N<>0 THEN GOTO 740
750 RETURN
760 REM
770 REM ** END OF PROGRAM **
780 REM
790 PRINT "<Q> = END THE PROGRAM, <A> = RUN AGAIN, <R> = RESTART"
800 C$=INKEY$: IF C$="Q" GOTO 850
810 IF C$="A" AND R$="H" GOTO 500
820 IF C$="A" AND R$="D" GOTO 370
830 IF C$="R" GOTO 270
840 GOTO 800
850 CLS: END
```

Listing 3.3 Sophisticated BASIC program for displaying the contents of a byte of memory in hex, decimal, and binary

```
                    PEEK MEMORY IN DECIMAL OR HEX
                    HEX OR DECIMAL INPUT <H/D> ?

MEMORY LOCATION IN HEX? 3000

        LOCATION                              CONTENTS
   .............................................................
     DEC       HEX                 DEC       HEX           BIN
    12288     3000                 205       00CD   1 1 0 0 1 1 0 1
   .............................................................
   <Q> = END THE PROGRAM, <A> = RUN AGAIN, <R> = RESTART

                    PEEK MEMORY IN DECIMAL OR HEX
                    HEX OR DECIMAL INPUT <H/D> ?

MEMORY LOCATION IN DECIMAL? 12288

        LOCATION                              CONTENTS
   .............................................................
     DEC       HEX                 DEC       HEX           BIN
    12288     3000                 205       00CD   1 1 0 0 1 1 0 1
   .............................................................
   <Q> = END THE PROGRAM, <A> = RUN AGAIN, <R> = RESTART
```

Figure 3.34 Typical screen dumps obtained from the program of Listing 3.3

a given processor) and speed. Those familiar with assembly language programming will know that it is possible to incorporate a machine language module within a BASIC program. This compromise approach simplifies the process of writing and entering the program (particularly if an assembler is not available) yet allows the speed and flexibility of machine language in areas of the program which are time-critical.

An example of embedding a machine language routine within a BASIC program is shown in Listing 3.4. This program uses an array into which the machine code is loaded from a DATA statement. The machine code uses the versatile Z80 LDIR instruction, which permits a block transfer of memory. In this particular case, 512 bytes of memory, starting at an address specified by the user, are transferred into the last 512 bytes of screen memory. This results in the lower half of the screen being filled with ASCII and graphics characters which represent the contents of the memory block in question. Typical screen dumps generated by this program are shown in Figure 3.35.

```
100 REM ***********************************
110 REM **                              **
120 REM **  M E M O R Y   D I S P L A Y  **
130 REM **                              **
140 REM ***********************************
150 REM
160 DEFINT A-Z : J=0 : A$=""
170 REM
180 REM ** LOAD Z80 MACHINE CODE INTO ARRAY **
190 REM
200 DATA 8448,0,4352,15872,256,512,-20243,201
210 DIM US(8): FOR X=0 TO 7: READ US(X): NEXT
220 REM
230 REM ** TITLE AND MAIN PROGRAM **
240 REM
250 CLS: PRINT "******* MEMORY DISPLAY *******"
260 PRINT@64,"START ADDRESS   (DEC)    ";: INPUT S!
270 IF S!<0 OR S!>65535 GOTO 260
280 IF S!>32767 THEN US(1)=S!-65536 ELSE US(1)=S!
290 PRINT@128,"NUMBER OF BYTES DISPLAYED =512"
300 DEFUSR=VARPTR(US(0)): J=USR(0)
310 PRINT@256,"HIT ANY KEY FOR NEXT 512 BYTES"
320 K$=INKEY$
330 IF K$="" GOTO 320
340 IF S!<0 THEN B!=(65536+S!) ELSE B!=S!
350 S!=US(1): S!=S!+512: IF S!>32767 THEN US(1)=S!-65536 ELSE US(1)=S!
360 PRINT@384,"START ADDRESS OF BLOCK =";(B!+512)
370 GOTO 300
```

Listing 3.4 Example of embedding a machine code module within a BASIC program which displays (in ASCII) the contents of a block of memory

It is thus possible to examine rapidly the entire memory of the system (ROM and RAM) and to check for such obvious errors as missing or non-functional blocks. Furthermore, the position and appearance of programs and data loaded into memory can also be checked. This can be important where one suspects that a memory conflict (where wanted data or programs are inadvertently overwritten by injudicious choice of starting addresses) may exist.

The diagnostic routines discussed so far have been somewhat limited in that they have only been capable of displaying the contents of memory, leaving the user to decide whether or not the data displayed is valid. Diagnostic routines should, ideally, be capable of examining blocks of memory and generating an appropriate message whenever a fault is suspected. These routines consequently place less reliance on the ability of the user to distinguish between what is normal and what must be considered to be of doubtful integrity. We shall now discuss routines of this type.

ROM diagnostic routines

System and interpreter ROMs can easily be checked for errors using a simple checksum of the contents of the particular ROM concerned. It is of course, necessary to know what the

```
****** MEMORY DISPLAY ******
START ADDRESS   (DEC)    ? 12288
NUMBER OF BYTES DISPLAYED =512

HIT ANY KEY FOR NEXT 512 BYTES

START ADDRESS OF BLOCK = 16384

..\..c..\..%..K..D.XEE..M.∂KI6xC.=∂DOF.EB8∂PR>..>....D∂∂∂∂∂∂A∂Q∂
g5_∂T\B;.....:E:E:E:E:E:E)FrE!OC.. U.^(KA.A!'D~.w.y....CC!∂?" ∂!
.∂o!.∂gx..G>∂.C.∂.M......∂∂∂∂∂∂O∂Q.,A1m∂CSZ∂∂∂∂∂B∂...∂FOAAKs∂∂∂∂∂
.................FOA].o.∂∂.∂.p∂.....oO...rA∂S∂∂∂.o.C∂∂.p.p.p.
nBBBBBBBBBBBBBBBBBBBBBBBBBBBBB∂∂∂∂∂∂∂∂∂6.∂∂∂∂∂∂∂∂∂∂ 16384∂O∂∂∂∂∂∂∂∂
...................[..U..[..V..[.._./`.4`.u[.x[.{[..W..X.Xa..^.
.`..`..^.C]..\.J^..b.aY.V_.U_..X.i^..[..X..V.?^.3Z.U^.X[.%[..^.o
X.b7.p7..\.\W.?Γ.1Γ.∂Γ.vX..Y..Γ..X..R...........   ..........

****** MEMORY DISPLAY ******
START ADDRESS   (DEC)    ? 12288
NUMBER OF BYTES DISPLAYED =512

HIT ANY KEY FOR NEXT 512 BYTES

START ADDRESS OF BLOCK = 16896

∂∂∂∂∂∂∂∂∂∂∂∂∂∂∂∂∂∂∂∂∂∂∂∂∂∂∂∂∂∂∂∂∂∂∂∂∂∂∂∂∂∂∂∂∂∂∂∂∂∂∂∂∂∂∂∂∂∂∂∂∂∂∂∂∂
PBtk∂MEMDISP BAS.B.BD∂J∂........PBt.∂RAM    BAS.B.BB∂L∂........
PB!.∂DISDCB  BAS.B.BA∂Y∂........PBL.∂RAMTP  OBJ.B.BB∂\∂........
PBtS∂IOTEST  BAS.B.BI∂"A........PA4J∂PRTOP  BAS.B.BC∂D∂........
.∂∂.∂∂R.AB.d.H.∂vH∂∂∂..DLBASICMA,P)M               .∂∂∂B∂∂.
9∂F∂F∂]!................G_.qCOD._7{..RE7.[~£.(.XD~£.O.J..nC.+D..
D.~E.(Awy. .FE....D.}D>..∂∂∂∂∂∂∂∂∂∂∂∂∂∂∂∂∂∂∂.{.:∂8∂g:B.CxC.E!∂
H∂∂∂∂∂JLHU∂∂∂∂S IH]∂∂∂∂S O∂∂∂∂∂∂∂∂∂∂∂∂∂∂∂∂∂∂∂∂∂∂∂∂∂∂∂∂∂∂∂∂∂∂∂∂∂
```

Figure 3.35 Typical screen dumps obtained from the program of Listing 3.4

```
** WARNING - ROM CHECKSUM ERROR **

    ROM1   Checksum = A28E   O.K.
    ROM2   Checksum = BFE4   O.K.
    ROM3   Checksum = 84A0   O.K.
    ROM4   Checksum = 3E3E   UNKNOWN
```

Figure 3.36 Typical ROM diagnostic message

checksum should be and, furthermore, readers should be aware that these have been known to change with different variants of particular computers! A simple ROM diagnostic error message is shown in Figure 3.36.

RAM diagnostic routines

A full RAM test usually involves writing, and subsequently reading, every possible byte value (from 0 to 255) to every possible memory address. After each byte is read it is checked with the value which was previously written and an error message is generated when a discrepancy is detected. The BASIC program of Listing 3.5 is an example of such a routine.

```
100 REM ** RAM TEST ROUTINE 1 **
110 CLS
120 INPUT "START ADDRESS ";B
130 INPUT "END ADDRESS    ";E
140 FOR A=B TO E
150 PRINT@512,"ADDRESS "A
160 IF A>32767 THEN A=A-65536
170 FOR X=0 TO 255
180 PRINT@576,"DATA     "X
190 POKE A,X
200 R=PEEK(A)
210 IF R<>X GOTO 270
220 NEXT X
230 IF A<0 THEN  A=65536+A
240 NEXT A
250 GOTO 100
260 END
270 REM ** RAM ERROR MESSAGE **
280 CLS
290 IF A<0 THEN A=65536+A
300 PRINT "ERROR IN MEMORY LOCATION "A
310 PRINT "DATA STORED              "R
320 PRINT@512,"PRESS ANY KEY TO CONTINUE"
330 INPUT Z
340 GOTO 240
```

Listing 3.5 BASIC program for the complete testing of a block of memory

This process may unfortunately take a considerable time when the memory block concerned is of any appreciable size. An alternative, yet perfectly adequate method, is that of simply setting all of the bits stored at a particular address to 0 and then to 1, checking at each stage that the correct change has occurred, as shown in Listing 3.6.

```
100 REM ** RAM TEST ROUTINE 2 **
110 CLS
120 INPUT "START ADDRESS ";B
130 INPUT "END ADDRESS    ";E
140 FOR A=B TO E
150 PRINT@512,"ADDRESS "A
160 IF A>32767 THEN A=A-65536
170 POKE A,0
180 R=PEEK(A)
190 IF R>0 GOTO 270
200 POKE A,255
210 R=PEEK(A)
220 IF R<255 GOTO 270
230 IF A<0 THEN A=65536+A
240 NEXT A
250 GOTO 100
260 END
270 REM ** RAM ERROR MESSAGE **
280 CLS
290 IF A<0 THEN A=65536+A
300 PRINT "ERROR IN MEMORY LOCATION "A
310 PRINT "DATA STORED              "R
320 PRINT@512,"PRESS ANY KEY TO CONTINUE"
330 INPUT Z
340 GOTO 240
```

Listing 3.6 An improved version of Listing 3.5

Routines of this type, although very much faster than the complete RAM diagnostic described earlier, are still too slow when written in BASIC. Furthermore, both methods destroy the previous contents of the memory and, although this may be of little consequence for the greater proportion of the memory, severe problems arise when the memory diagnostic destroys the contents of reserved areas of memory or when the diagnostic routine attempts to verify the area of RAM in which the program itself is resident!

Clearly, some form of non-destructive test is much to be preferred. All that is needed is a routine that will read the existing byte stored, perform the core of the diagnostic routine, and finally rewrite the original byte before moving on to the next byte. A routine of this type, written in Z80 assembly language, is shown in Listing 3.7. This program is fully relocatable

```
                  00100 ;    **************************************
                  00110 ;    **                                  **
                  00120 ;    **            R A M C H E C K        **
                  00130 ;    **                                  **
                  00140 ;    **************************************
                  00150 ;
                  00160 ;         VERSION 2.1          01/02/84
                  00170 ;
                  00180 ;    PROGRAM VERIFIES A 4K BLOCK OF MEMORY
                  00190 ;    AND RETURNS AN ERROR MESSAGE IF THE
                  00200 ;    BLOCK IS NOT FUNCTIONAL
                  00210 ;
                  00220 ;    @ = SYSTEM CALLABLE ROUTINE
                  00230 ;    $ = POINTER TO STORAGE LOCATION;
                  00240 ;
                  00250 ;    Z80 CODE
                  00260 ;
5200              00270           ORG       5200H       ; MAY BE RELOCATED
5200 ED7B4940     00280           LD        SP,(HIGH$)       ; TO AVOID RESERVED MEMORY
000A              00290 LF        EQU       0AH         ; LINE FEED CHARACTER
000D              00300 CR        EQU       0DH         ; RETURN CHARACTER
0033              00310 @VDCHAR   EQU       33H         ; OUTPUT TO DISPLAY
0049              00320 @KBCHAR   EQU       49H         ; ACCEPT KEYBOARD INPUT
01C9              00330 @VDCLS    EQU       01C9H       ; CLEAR DISPLAY
402D              00340 @DOS      EQU       402DH       ; START OF DOS
4049              00350 HIGH$     EQU       4049H       ; HIGH MEMORY POINTER
4467              00360 @VDLINE   EQU       4467H       ; OUTPUT STRING TO DISPLAY
                  00370 ;
                  00380 ;    ****   TITLE AND INPUT ROUTINE   ****
                  00390 ;
5204 CDC901       00400 TITLE     CALL      @VDCLS
5207 21D552       00410           LD        HL,MESS1
520A CD6744       00420           CALL      @VDLINE
520D 21F552       00430           LD        HL,MESS2
5210 CD6744       00440           CALL      @VDLINE
5213 211553       00450 INPUT     LD        HL,MESS3
5216 CDBF52       00460           CALL      VIDOUT
5219 B7           00470           OR        A
521A F5           00480           PUSH      AF
521B CD3752       00490           CALL      GNYB
521E 67           00500           LD        H,A
521F 3006         00510           JR        NC,GLBYT
5221 F1           00520           POP       AF
5222 7C           00530           LD        A,H
5223 37           00540           SCF
5224 C36252       00550           JP        MAIN
5227 CD3752       00560 GLBYT     CALL      GNYB
522A 6F           00570           LD        L,A
522B 3006         00580           JR        NC,REST2
522D F1           00590           POP       AF
522E 7D           00600           LD        A,L
522F 37           00610           SCF
5230 C36252       00620           JP        MAIN
5233 F1           00630 REST2     POP       AF
5234 C36252       00640           JP        MAIN
5237 CD4952       00650 GNYB      CALL      HEXIN
523A D8           00660           RET       C
```

```
523B  C5          00670          PUSH    BC
523C  07          00680          RLCA
523D  07          00690          RLCA
523E  07          00700          RLCA
523F  07          00710          RLCA
5240  47          00720          LD      B,A
5241  CD4952      00730          CALL    HEXIN
5244  3801        00740          JR      C,REST1
5246  80          00750          ADD     A,B
5247  C1          00760  REST1   POP     BC
5248  C9          00770          RET
5249  CD4900      00780  HEXIN   CALL    ƏKBCHAR
524C  CD3300      00790          CALL    ƏVDCHAR
524F  FE30        00800          CP      '0'
5251  D8          00810          RET     C
5252  FE3A        00820          CP      '9'+1
5254  3809        00830          JR      C,CONV
5256  FE41        00840          CP      'A'
5258  D8          00850          RET     C
5259  FE47        00860          CP      'F'+1
525B  3F          00870          CCF
525C  D8          00880          RET     C
525D  D607        00890          SUB     7
525F  D630        00900  CONV    SUB     30H
5261  C9          00910          RET
                  00920  ;
                  00930  ; ****   MAIN LOOP   ****
                  00940  ;
5262  110010      00950  MAIN    LD      DE,4096 ; SIZE OF BLOCK TO BE VERIFIED
5265  AF          00960          XOR     A       ; TO CLEAR ERROR FLAG
5266  7E          00970  LOOP    LD      A,(HL)  ; GET BYTE
5267  2F          00980          CPL             ; COMPLEMENT IT
5268  77          00990          LD      (HL),A  ; RETURN IT
5269  BE          01000          CP      (HL)    ; DID IT GO ?
526A  2022        01010          JR      NZ,ERROR ; IF NOT, JUMP
526C  2F          01020          CPL             ; ORIGINAL BYTE
526D  77          01030          LD      (HL),A  ; REPLACE IT
526E  23          01040          INC     HL      ; NEXT ADDRESS
526F  1B          01050          DEC     DE      ; COUNT DOWN
5270  7A          01060          LD      A,D     ; EXAMINE COUNT
5271  B3          01070          OR      E       ; FINISHED ?
5272  20F2        01080          JR      NZ,LOOP ; IF NOT, DO AGAIN
                  01090  ;
                  01100  ; ****   PRINT OUT RESULTS   ****
                  01110  ;
5274  213C53      01120  NOERR   LD      HL,MESS4
5277  CD6744      01130          CALL    ƏVDLINE
527A  215D53      01140  REPEAT  LD      HL,MESS5
527D  CD6744      01150          CALL    ƏVDLINE
5280  CD4900      01160  EXIT    CALL    ƏKBCHAR
5283  FE4E        01170          CP      'N'
5285  CA2D40      01180          JP      Z,ƏDOS
5288  FE59        01190          CP      'Y'
528A  2887        01200          JR      Z,INPUT
528C  18F2        01210          JR      EXIT
528E  E5          01220  ERROR   PUSH    HL
528F  217B53      01230          LD      HL,MESS6
5292  CD6744      01240          CALL    ƏVDLINE
5295  E1          01250          POP     HL
5296  F5          01260          PUSH    AF
5297  7C          01270          LD      A,H
5298  CDA352      01280          CALL    PBYT
529B  7D          01290          LD      A,L
529C  CDA352      01300          CALL    PBYT
529F  F1          01310          POP     AF
52A0  CD7A52      01320          CALL    REPEAT
52A3  F5          01330  PBYT    PUSH    AF
52A4  0F          01340          RRCA
52A5  0F          01350          RRCA
52A6  0F          01360          RRCA
52A7  0F          01370          RRCA
52A8  CDAC52      01380          CALL    PHEX
52AB  F1          01390          POP     AF
52AC  F5          01400  PHEX    PUSH    AF
```

```
52AD  E6OF        01410              AND      OFH
52AF  FEOA        01420              CP       OAH
52B1  3802        01430              JR       C,CVERT
52B3  C607        01440              ADD      A,7
52B5  C630        01450  CVERT       ADD      A,30H
52B7  CDCB52      01460              CALL     OUTPUT
52BA  F1          01470              POP      AF
52BB  C9          01480              RET
52BC  CD7A52      01490              CALL     REPEAT
52BF  7E          01500  VIDOUT      LD       A,(HL)
52CO  23          01510              INC      HL
52C1  B7          01520              OR       A
52C2  C8          01530              RET      Z
52C3  CDCB52      01540              CALL     OUTPUT
52C6  FEOD        01550              CP       CR
52C8  20F5        01560              JR       NZ,VIDOUT
52CA  C9          01570              RET
52CB  D5          01580  OUTPUT      PUSH     DE
52CC  FDE5        01590              PUSH     IY
52CE  CD3300      01600              CALL     @VDCHAR
52D1  FDE1        01610              POP      IY
52D3  D1          01620              POP      DE
52D4  C9          01630              RET
                  01640  ;
                  01650  ; ****   MESSAGES   ****
                  01660  ;
52D5  52          01670  MESS1       DEFM     'RAMCHECK VERSION 2.1 - 01/02/84',CR
      41 4D 43 48 45 43 4B 20
      56 45 52 53 49 4F 4E 20
      32 2E 31 20 2D 20 30 31
      2F 30 32 2F 38 34 OD
52F5  2D          01680  MESS2       DEFM     '--------------------------------',CR
      2D 2D 2D 2D 2D 2D 2D 2D
      2D 2D 2D 2D 2D 2D 2D 2D
      2D 2D 2D 2D 2D 2D 2D 2D
      2D 2D 2D 2D 2D 2D OD
5315  OA          01690  MESS3       DEFM     LF,'Input start address of block in hex: ',C
R
      49 6E 70 75 74 20 73 74
      61 72 74 20 61 64 64 72
      65 73 73 20 6F 66 20 62
      6C 6F 63 6B 20 69 6E 20
      68 65 78 3A 20 OD
533C  OA          01700  MESS4       DEFM     LF,'No error detected in this block',CR
      4E 6F 20 65 72 72 6F 72
      20 64 65 74 65 63 74 65
      64 20 69 6E 20 74 68 69
      73 20 62 6C 6F 63 6B OD
535D  OA          01710  MESS5       DEFM     LF,'Try another 4k block (Y/N) ?',CR
      54 72 79 20 61 6E 6F 74
      68 65 72 20 34 6B 20 62
      6C 6F 63 6B 20 28 59 2F
      4E 29 20 3F OD
537B  OA          01720  MESS6       DEFM     LF,'Error detected at memory address: ',CR
      45 72 72 6F 72 20 64 65
      74 65 63 74 65 64 20 61
      74 20 6D 65 6D 6F 72 79
      20 61 64 64 72 65 73 73
      3A 20 OD
0000              01730              END
```

```
@DOS        402D  @KBCHAR     0049  @VDCHAR     0033
@VDCLS      01C9  @VDLINE     4467  CONV        525F
CR          000D  CVERT       52B5  ERROR       528E
EXIT        5280  GLBYT       5227  GNYB        5237
HEXIN       5249  HIGH$       4049  INPUT       5213
LF          000A  LOOP        5266  MAIN        5262
MESS1       52D5  MESS2       52F5  MESS3       5315
MESS4       533C  MESS5       535D  MESS6       537B
NOERR       5274  OUTPUT      52CB  PBYT        52A3
PHEX        52AC  REPEAT      527A  REST1       5247
REST2       5233  TITLE       5204  VIDOUT      52BF
```

Listing 3.7 Z80 assembly language program for testing RAM

and is capable of testing the entire memory with the exception of the area of RAM into which the program is loaded. The program verifies a 4K block of RAM virtually instantaneously. The core of the program (i.e. that which actually operates on the RAM) has been 'commented' in order to explain its action. A typical screen dump obtained from this program is shown in Figure 3.37.

```
RAMCHECK VERSION 2.1 - 01/02/84
---------------------------------

Input start address of block in hex:
8000
No error detected in this block


Try another 4k block (Y/N) ?


Input start address of block in hex:
FE00
Error detected at memory address:
0000
Try another 4k block (Y/N) ?
```

Figure 3.37 Typical screen dumps obtained from Listing 3.7

More sophisticated RAM diagnostics may also incorporate some form of 'glitch' test in which a checksum of the contents of a block of RAM is taken before and after various peripheral devices are switched on and off. If any difference is detected between the two checksums the contents of RAM have been corrupted. Some provision may also be incorporated for running such a routine continuously, thus allowing the user to test for the effects of externally generated electrical noise and stray fields.

I/O diagnostic routines

A BASIC program for testing I/O ports is shown in Listing 3.8. This program uses the INP and OUT commands available in some versions of BASIC. The user is given the choice of outputting data to a selected port in either decimal or binary format. Alternatively, input data from a selected port may be displayed in both decimal and binary. This routine can be useful in checking the status of devices connected to I/O ports, and particularly for testing such devices as RS-232 interfaces and printers. A typical screen dump obtained from this program is shown in Figure 3.38.

A typical Z80 assembly language program that can be used for checking the character generator ROM, display memory, and VDU interface is shown in Listing 3.9. This program displays each character in turn using the entire screen area. A delay loop is used to slow the program so that the user can inspect the display produced. Any missing or incorrect characters will easily be identified, together with screen memory errors.

Diagnostic routines designed specifically for checking disk and cassette drives, printers and displays are described separately in Chapters 4 to 6.

```
100 REM *********************************
110 REM **                            **
120 REM **  I / O    P O R T   T E S T  **
130 REM **                            **
140 REM *********************************
150 REM
160 REM ** DISPLAY MENU **
170 REM
180 CLS: PRINT TAB(18) "I/O PORT TEST ROUTINE"
190 PRINT TAB(18) "----------------------"
200 PRINT: PRINT TAB(28),"MENU"
210 PRINT TAB(18) "<1>  OUTPUT TEST - DECIMAL VALUE"
220 PRINT TAB(18) "<2>  OUTPUT TEST - BINARY PATTERN"
230 PRINT TAB(18) "<3>  INPUT   TEST"
240 PRINT TAB(18) "<4>  EXIT PROGRAM"
250 PRINT: PRINT TAB(18) "ENTER YOUR CHOICE...."
260 C$=INKEY$
270 IF C$="" GOTO 260
280 IF ASC(C$)<48 OR ASC(C$)>52 THEN 250
290 C=ASC(C$)-48
300 ON C GOTO 320, 480, 710, 890
310 REM
320 REM ** OUTPUT TEST - DECIMAL VALUE **
330 REM
340 CLS: PRINT"OUTPUT TEST - DECIMAL VALUE"
350 PRINT"---------------------------"
360 PRINT: INPUT "SELECT PORT NUMBER  <1 TO 255>"; PN%
370 IF PN%<0 OR PN%>255 THEN 360
380 INPUT "SELECT OUTPUT DATA   <1 TO 255>"; D%
390 IF D%<0 OR D%>255 THEN 380
400 OUT PN%, D%
410 PRINT "DONE: PRESS <A> TO RUN AGAIN <M> TO RETURN TO MENU"
420 K$=INKEY$
430 IF K$="" GOTO 420
440 IF K$="M" GOTO 170
450 IF K$="A" GOTO 320
460 GOTO 420
470 REM
480 REM ** OUTPUT TEST - BINARY PATTERN **
490 REM
500 CLS: PRINT "OUTPUT TEST - BINARY PATTERN"
510 PRINT "----------------------------"
520 PRINT: INPUT "SELECT PORT NUMBER  <1 TO 255>"; PN%
530 INPUT "BINARY PATTERN  <MSB FIRST>   "; B$
540 IF LEN(B$)<>8 GOTO 530
550 IF LEFT$(B$,1)="1" THEN V=128
560 IF MID$(B$,2,1)="1" THEN V=V+64
570 IF MID$(B$,3,1)="1" THEN V=V+32
580 IF MID$(B$,4,1)="1" THEN V=V+16
590 IF MID$(B$,5,1)="1" THEN V=V+8
600 IF MID$(B$,6,1)="1" THEN V=V+4
610 IF MID$(B$,7,1)="1" THEN V=V+2
620 IF RIGHT$(B$,1)="1" THEN V=V+1
630 OUT PN%, V
640 PRINT "DONE: PRESS <A> TO RUN AGAIN <M> TO RETURN TO MENU"
650 K$=INKEY$
660 IF K$="" GOTO 650
670 IF K$="M" GOTO 170
680 IF K$="A" GOTO 480
690 GOTO 650
```

```
700 REM
710 REM ** INPUT TEST **
720 REM
730 CLS: PRINT "INPUT  TEST"
740 PRINT "------------"
750 PRINT: INPUT "SELECT INPUT PORT NUMBER  <1 TO 255>"; PN%
760 IF PN%<0 OR PN%>255 THEN 750
770 D=INP(PN%)
780 N=D: A$=""
790 A$=STR$(N-(INT(N/2)*2))+A$: N=INT(N/2):IF N=0 THEN 800 ELSE 790
800 PRINT "DECIMAL VALUE  "; D
810 PRINT "BINARY  VALUE  "; A$
820 PRINT "PRESS <A> TO RUN AGAIN <M> TO RETURN TO MENU"
830 K$=INKEY$
840 IF K$="" GOTO 830
850 IF K$="M" GOTO 170
860 IF K$="A" GOTO 710
870 GOTO 830
880 REM
890 REM ** EXIT PROGRAM **
900 REM
910 CLS: END
```

Listing 3.8 BASIC program for testing I/O ports

```
I/O PORT TEST ROUTINE
---------------------


              MENU
<1>  OUTPUT TEST - DECIMAL VALUE
<2>  OUTPUT TEST - BINARY PATTERN
<3>  INPUT  TEST
<4>  EXIT PROGRAM

ENTER YOUR CHOICE....


OUTPUT TEST - DECIMAL VALUE
---------------------------

SELECT PORT NUMBER  <1 TO 255>? 255
SELECT OUTPUT DATA  <1 TO 255>? 127
DONE: PRESS <A> TO RUN AGAIN <M> TO RETURN TO MENU


OUTPUT TEST - BINARY PATTERN
----------------------------

SELECT PORT NUMBER  <1 TO 255>? 255
BINARY PATTERN  <MSB FIRST>  ? 01111111
DONE: PRESS <A> TO RUN AGAIN <M> TO RETURN TO MENU


INPUT  TEST
-----------

SELECT INPUT PORT NUMBER  <1 TO 255>? 255
DECIMAL VALUE   127
BINARY  VALUE   1 1 1 1 1 1 1
PRESS <A> TO RUN AGAIN .<M> TO RETURN TO MENU
```

Figure 3.38 Typical screen dump obtained from Listing 3.8

```
              00100 ;  ****************************************
              00110 ;  **                                    **
              00120 ;  **        V D U   C H E C K           **
              00130 ;  **                                    **
              00140 ;  ****************************************
              00150 ;
              00160 ;         VERSION 1.1        05/02/84
              00170 ;
              00180 ;  PROGRAM DISPLAYS FULL CHARACTER
              00190 ;  AND GRAPHIC SET ON THE VDU SCREEN
              00210 ;
              00220 ;    @ = SYSTEM CALLABLE ROUTINE
              00230 ;    $ = POINTER TO STORAGE LOCATION
              00240 ;
              00250 ;    Z80 CODE
              00260 ;
5200          00270        ORG     5200H    ; MAY BE RELOCATED
3C00          00280 $VIDMEM EQU    3C00H    ; START OF SCREEN MEMORY
402D          00290 @DOS   EQU     402DH    ; START OF DOS
5200 169F     00300        LD      D,9FH    ; SIZE OF CHARACTER SET
5202 1E21     00310        LD      E,21H    ; FIRST CHARACTER
5204 21003C   00320 MAIN   LD      HL,$VIDMEM      ; POINT TO START
5207 010004   00330        LD      BC,400H  ; 1K SCREEN LOCATIONS
520A 73       00340 LOOP1  LD      (HL),E   ; WRITE TO FIRST SCREEN LOCATION
520B 23       00350        INC     HL       ; NEXT LOCATION
520C 0B       00360        DEC     BC       ; COUNT DOWN
520D 78       00370        LD      A,B
520E B1       00380        OR      C
520F 20F9     00390        JR      NZ,LOOP1         ; ALL DONE ?
5211 1C       00400        INC     E        ; NEXT CHARACTER
5212 21FFFF   00410        LD      HL,OFFFFH        ; INITIALISE DELAY LOOP
5215 2B       00420 LOOP2  DEC     HL       ; COUNT DOWN
5216 7C       00430        LD      A,H
5217 B5       00440        OR      L
5218 20FB     00450        JR      NZ,LOOP2         ; ALL DONE ?
521A 15       00455        DEC     D
521B 20E7     00460        JR      NZ,MAIN  ; GO FOR THE NEXT CHARACTER
521D C32D40   00465        JP      @DOS     ; BACK TO DOS
0000          00470        END
```

Listing 3.9 Z80 assembly language program for checking the character generator ROM and display memory

Fault finding on an RS-232 interface

Fault finding on an RS-232 interface usually involves the following basic steps:

1. Ascertain which device is the DTE and which is the DCE. This can usually be accomplished simply by looking at the connectors (DTE equipment is normally fitted with a male connector whilst DCE equipment is invariably fitted with a female connector). Where both devices are configured as DTE (as is often the case) a patch box or null modem should be inserted for correct operation.

2. Check that the correct cable has been used. Note that RS-232C cables are provided in a variety of forms; 4-way (for 'dumb' terminals), 9-way (for normal asynchronous data communications), 15-way (for synchronous communications), and 25-way (for 'universal' applications). If in doubt, use a full 25-way cable.

3. Check that the same data word format and baud rate has been selected at each end of the serial link.

4. Activate the link and investigate the logical state of the data (TXD and RXD) and handshaking (RTS, CTS, etc.) signal lines using a line monitor, breakout box, or interface tester. Lines may be looped back to test each end of the link.

5.   If in any doubt, refer to the equipment manufacturer's data in order to ascertain whether any special connections are required and to ensure that the interfaces are truly compatible. Note that some manufacturers have implemented quasi-RS-232 interfaces which make use of TTL signals. These are not electrically compatible with the normal RS-232 system.
6.   The communications software should be initially configured for the least complex protocol (e.g. basic ASCII character transfer without handshaking). When a successful link has been established, more complex protocols may be attempted.

Listing 3.10 shows a simple GWBASIC program which can be used to test an asynchronous RS-232 link in full-duplex mode between two PCs (or PC compatibles). Similar programs can be used in other environments or between two quite different machines. The two computers should be linked using a null-modem cable and then loaded and run on both computers.

The program can be easily modified to test the COM2 asynchronous port (rather than COM1) by changing the OPEN statement in line 150. This line may also be modified in order to test the link at different baud rates (other than 300 baud) and with different data formats. The OPEN command has the following syntax when used with a communications device:

OPEN 'COMN: [speed], [parity], [data], [stop]' AS #filenum

where: n   refers to the asynchronous port number (1, 2, 3 etc.)
       speed   is the baud rate (150, 300, 600, etc.)
       parity is the parity selected (N = none, E = even, and 0 = odd)
       data   refers to the number of data bits (5, 6, 7 or 8)
       stop   refers to the number of stop bits (1, 1.5 or, 2)

Readers are advised to consult the appropriate Microsoft GWBASIC or QuickBASIC manuals for further information.

```
100 REM Simple full duplex communications
105 REM test routine using PC COM1 serial port.
110 REM Data format; 300 baud, even parity,
115 REM seven data bits, one stop bit
120 KEY OFF
130 CLS
140 PRINT "GWBASIC full duplex communications"
150 OPEN "COM1:300,E,7,1" AS #1
160 K$=INKEY$
170 IF K$="" THEN GOTO 210
180 IF K$=CHR$(3) OR K$=CHR$(27) THEN GOTO 250
190 PRINT #1,K$;
200 PRINT K$;
210 IF EOF(1) THEN GOTO 160
220 C$=INPUT$(LOC(1),#1)
230 PRINT C$;
240 GOTO 160
250 CLOSE #1
260 CLS
270 END
```

Listing 3.10 Simple GWBASIC program which can be used to test an asynchronous RS-232 link between two PCs (or PC compatibles)

Miscellaneous faults

Temperature-induced faults

Faults which do not appear until the equipment concerned reaches its normal working temperature (this may typically take fifteen minutes or more) often point to failure within an integrated circuit. Sometimes this is caused by an imperfect internal bond between the metal frame that comprises the pins of the IC and the silicon chip itself. In other cases faults may be attributable to excessive internal temperature causing 'thermal shut-down'.

Temperature-induced faults can invariably be localized to a particular IC device by judicious use of a can of freezer spray. The spray nozzle is simply directed towards each suspect device in turn and a short blast of spray released. Operation will normally be restored when the spray is applied to the faulty device. Freezer spray should, however, be used sparingly as excessive use can damage certain components.

Mechanically induced faults

Faults sometimes occur which can be induced by mechanical shock or vibration. Such faults are almost always attributable to an imperfect electrical contact of some sort. The technique for localizing such faults is gently to tap different areas of the PCB, using the insulated handle of a screwdriver, until the fault appears. This may sound somewhat crude but it is often highly effective! Components that are particularly susceptible to mechanically induced faults are preset resistors, connectors of various types, and quartz crystals.

Supply-borne transients

Another cause of intermittent, and often otherwise inexplicable, data corruption is attributable to switching transients borne on the a.c. mains supply. Most items of electrical apparatus generate transients, which may travel for some considerable distance along the mains wiring, when they are switched on or off. The severity of the transients increases with the rate of change of current or voltage and notable among generators of transient 'spikes' are welding equipment, thyristor or triac power controllers, and motor switch gear.

It is obviously highly desirable to minimize the effects of these transients by means of suitable filtering at source but some transient noise on a domestic or commercial mains supply is unavoidable. One cause, over which we mere mortals have no control, is that of static charges in the atmosphere and lightning in particular. In such cases, amplitudes of several kV have been detected over periods extending from a few microseconds to several tens of milliseconds. With such excessive amplitudes some form of data corruption is almost inevitable!

It is thus good practice to include some form of transient protection on the incoming mains supply to the computer. This usually takes the form of a simple low-pass filter wired in the mains supply input from the power on/off switch, as shown in Figure 3.39. This filter also helps reduce the emission of electrical noise generated by the computer itself, which may otherwise be annoying where a radio receiver is to be used close to the computer. In addition, a good quality mains transformer, incorporating an electrostatic screen between its primary and secondary windings, can also considerably reduce the effects of transient energy. Such components are fitted in better quality equipment as a matter of course.

In severe cases, an a.c. power line monitor should be used to check the cleanliness of a particular mains supply. These instruments are simply plugged into a mains outlet and any transient of greater than a certain amplitude and duration is detected and recorded. It is thus possible to evaluate a supply in order to ascertain whether it is free from transients.

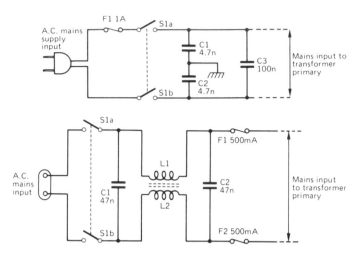

Figure 3.39 Typical mains supply input filters

This consideration is also important when installing and commissioning a computer. It will, of course, be necessary to leave the power line monitor connected for some time and it is also advisable to switch on and off all nearby items of apparatus, particularly any which share the same a.c. outlet.

Several companies now produce mains plugs that incorporate transient suppressors and/or filters. These are relatively inexpensive and are particularly valuable for use with portable equipment that is to be operated from mains supplies of unknown quality. It should also be noted that these plugs can offer a measure of transient protection for equipment operated from a common supply. If, for example, a printer and computer are operated from adjacent mains supplies, it is usually only necessary to fit a filter plug to one of the devices in order to prevent switching transients from the printer reaching the computer.

More elaborate mains filters and suppressors are available for use in situations where transients cannot be eliminated by any other means. In extreme cases, suppressed distribution boxes with four or more separate outlets can be used to provide 'clean' supplies for both the computer and its associated peripherals.

Power supply faults

Power supply faults are usually relatively easily detected using nothing more than straightforward voltage rail checks. In terms of both power dissipation and transient voltages present, the power supply is usually subjected to more electrical stress than any other subsystem within the computer. It is not surprising, therefore, that faults frequently develop in this area.

Before attempting to perform fault diagnosis on the power supply, readers should be aware that potentially lethal voltages and currents exist in this section. The following rules should be observed at all times:

(a)   Always disconnect the mains supply by removing the plug – do not simply rely on the mains switch for isolation and protection.

(b)   Never attempt to dismantle the power supply (or any other part of the equipment) when the mains supply is connected.
(c)   Do not connect the earth lead of an item of test equipment to anything other than the common earth rail of the equipment under test.
(d)   When fault tracing on the high voltage side of 'live' circuits, the insulated probe of the test meter should be transferred from point to point using one hand only. Under no circumstances should the unused hand be left in contact with an earthed conductor – it is better to leave it safely in one's pocket.

Power supplies fitted to personal computers invariably provide several d.c. output rails, including at least one +5 V rail. This latter output supplies the CPU and support circuitry and is normally regulated to within 5 per cent of the nominal +5 V. The current capability of this rail is usually of the order of 1 A or more.

Two types of voltage regulator are commonly employed – monolithic and switched mode. The former type uses a single integrated circuit, either plastic or metal cased, to produce a fixed output voltage of typically +5 V, -5 V or +12 V. Each voltage rail is supplied from its own regulator, bridge rectifier and smoothing. The failure of one rail can thus be attributed to a particular set of components, while those components associated with fully functional rails can be rapidly eliminated.

The regulator fitted to the main +5 V rail is invariably mounted on a substantial heatsink and this often runs noticeably warm after a reasonable period of operation. At least one manufacturer has placed such a heatsink in a small, totally enclosed case in which no ventilation is provided. Such practice is questionable, to say the least, and this item of equipment is known to fail regularly due to an excessive rise in temperature after a prolonged period of operation.

Monolithic voltage regulators usually incorporate fold-back current limiting, which restricts the d.c. output current in the event of a supply rail component failure. Furthermore, such regulators normally tolerate an indefinite short-circuit across their output. This provision should not, however, be relied upon and inadvertent short-circuiting of the supply rails should always be avoided.

A typical single-rail power supply employing a monolithic three-terminal voltage regulator is shown in Figure 3.40. This circuit represents the minimal solution to providing a +5 V supply rail for a CPU and its support circuitry. This arrangement is not, of course, capable of meeting the demands of such ancillary devices as cassette recorders or disk drives.

Switched mode power supplies are, by virtue of their small size and high efficiency, enjoying increased popularity among personal computer manufacturers. Indeed, several manufacturers have adopted this type of power supply exclusively. Unfortunately, this type of supply is somewhat more complex than a simple monolithic regulator and as a result is often misunderstood.

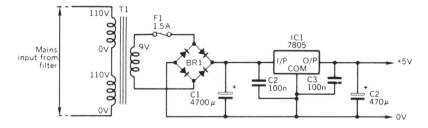

Figure 3.40 Typical mains supply employing a monolithic voltage regulator

The block schematic of a complete switched mode power is shown in Figure 3.41. This supply provides three separate output rails of +5 V for the CPU and support devices (including RAM), +12 V for disk drives and monitor, and -5 V for an RS-232 interface. The incoming mains supply is rectified and smoothed to provide a high voltage d.c. supply for an inverter operating at approximately 50 kHz. The high frequency a.c. output of the inverter is then fed to a transformer, which provides both isolation from the mains supply and the required step-down ratio for each individual secondary winding.

Each transformer secondary is rectified and smoothed and the resulting unstabilized output is fed to a separate regulator. The advantages of switched mode regulators become more significant at high load currents and hence, in this particular unit, the two high current supply rails (+5 V and + 12 V) use switched mode regulators while the low-current supply rail (−5 V) uses a conventional three-terminal monolithic regulator.

Each switched mode regulator consists of a series transistor arrangement similar to that shown in Figure 3.42. This circuit may at first sight resemble that of a conventional series regulator but there are several important differences: notably D1 and L1 and the fact that a pulse waveform, rather than a d.c. level, is applied to the series pass transistors.

In order to provide a sufficiently high current gain at the relatively large value of collector current required, the two transistors are connected in a Darlington configuration. Since the transistors are PNP types, a 'low' at the base of TR2 will cause both transistors to turn on (supplying current to L1) whereas a 'high' at the base of TR2 will cause both transistors to turn 'off'. It should be noted that the 'high' level in question is not a normal TTL level but should be within 1.2 V of the d.c. voltage developed across the reservoir capacitor, C1.

In practice, the base of TR2 is supplied with a rectangular pulse train derived from a pulse width modulated oscillator. The d.c. output voltage produced by the regulator is sensed and used to control the duty cycle (i.e. ratio of 'high' to 'high' plus 'low' times) of the oscillator. When the voltage level of the output exceeds the desired value, the duty cycle is increased and consequently the mean output voltage falls. Conversely, if the rail voltage is less than the desired value, the duty cycle decreases and the mean output voltage rises.

An alternative type of switched mode power supply involves control of the high frequency a.c. delivered to the transformer itself. In this type of circuit mains isolation is usually achieved by one of the following possible methods:

(a) sensing the d.c. output and opto-coupling to an amplitude controlled oscillator on the primary side; or
(b) generating a pulse width modulated signal on the secondary side and feeding this via an isolating pulse transformer to a high voltage driver on the primary side.

Typical block schematics of switched mode supplies using these techniques are shown respectively in Figures 3.43 and 3.44.

Fault diagnosis of switched mode power supplies usually involves using an oscilloscope to monitor the pulse train supplied to the switching device. The oscilloscope should not, however, be connected to any point on the primary side of a switched mode regulator unless a suitable mains isolating transformer is employed. Failure to observe this precaution may not only cause serious damage to the equipment but may also result in a potential shock hazard.

Component removal and replacement

Considerable care must be exercised when removing and replacing components mounted on printed circuit boards since extensive damage can be caused by the use of incorrect or

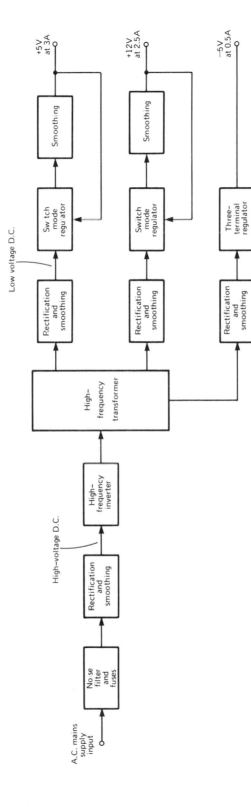

Figure 3.41 Block schematic of a complete switched mode power supply

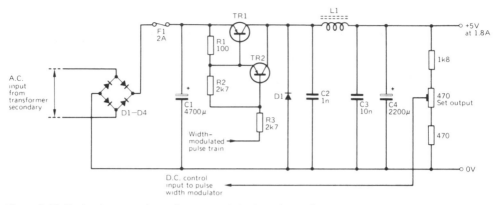

Figure 3.42 Basic elements of a series-pass switched mode regulator

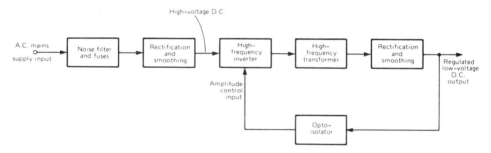

Figure 3.43 Alternative switched mode power supply using an opto-isolator

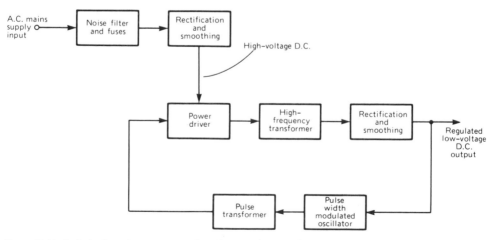

Figure 3.44 Switched mode power supply using a pulse transformer

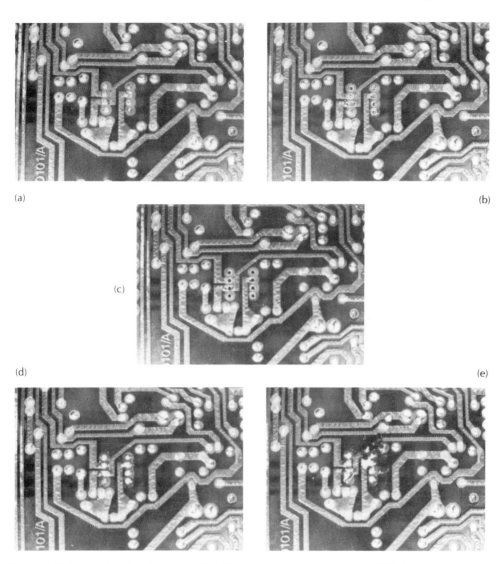

Figure 3.45 Removal and replacement of PCB-mounted components. (a) Carefully locate component pads on the underside of the PCB. (b) Apply soldering iron to each pad in turn and remove molten solder using a desoldering tool. (c) Gently withdraw component from the upper side of the PCB. Check that all holes are cleared of solder. (d) Insert replacement component (fit a DIL socket if the component is an IC), check correct pin orientation and solder in place. (e) Example of incorrectly made joints: excessive solder, excessive flux, and solder bridges between pads

inappropriate techniques. Before attempting to work on the PCB, however, it should ideally be removed from the equipment and placed on an anti-static mat. If this is not possible, it is necessary to ensure that all external leads (including the mains lead) are disconnected.

Before removing a suspect component it is first necessary accurately to locate the component to be removed on the top (component side) of the PCB and then correctly to identify its solder pads on the underside of the PCB. Most good service manuals include PCB layouts viewed from both sides of the board and these can be most useful when locating components.

Once located, the component pads should be gently heated using a soldering iron which should normally have a rating of no more than 20 W and be fitted with a slim pencil bit. The bit should be regularly cleaned using a damp cloth or sponge and a small tin containing such an item is a useful adjunct to any soldering work station. Since excessive heat can easily damage both the PCB and the components fitted to it, temperature controlled soldering irons are much to be preferred. One further point should be made: the bond that exists between the copper track and the PCB itself can be irreversibly damaged by repeated soldering and desoldering at excessive temperature.

Once the solder in the vicinity of the pad in question has become molten (this usually only takes one or two seconds at the most) a desoldering tool should be used to remove the solder. This operation can usually be carried out with a single operation of a desoldering pump. However, where a large amount of solder is present or where the pad covers a considerable area, a second application of the pump may be required.

If the desoldering tool has to be repeatedly applied this usually indicates that either the pump has become clogged or that the iron is not hot enough. With practice only one application of the soldering iron and desoldering tool will be required. Once cleared of solder, the component lead should become free and a similar process should be employed for each of the remaining leads. Special tools are available for the removal of multi-pin IC devices that allow the simultaneous heating of all pins. Removal by any other means can be extremely tedious.

When desoldering is complete, the component should be gently withdrawn from the top (component side) of the board and the replacement component should then be fitted, taking care to observe the correct polarity and orientation where appropriate. The leads should protrude through the PCB to the copper foil side and then be soldered. It is not normally necessary to trim the leads before inserting the component into the PCB since this task can be performed more easily, using a pair of sharp side-cutters, after the component has been soldered in place. Trimming of the component leads will, of course, not be necessary where integrated circuits are concerned. However, in this case, the author strongly advocates the fitting of low-profile sockets to the PCB so that the replacement device need not be soldered. This minimizes the risk of damage to the device through excessive heat or static charges that may be developed in the soldering process, and simplifies replacement in the event of the device failing again.

An alternative method of IC removal, preferred by some technicians, it that of cutting the device away from its pins (on the component side of the PCB) then gently heating each pad (on the underside of the PCB) in turn, while gently pulling the pin away from the board using a pair of long-nosed pliers. This method does, unfortunately, have the disadvantage that not all of the solder is cleared from the pad. Readers will doubtless wish to develop their own technique after trying both methods.

When re-soldering components, care should be taken to ensure that a minimum of solder is used consistent with achieving a sound electrical and mechanical joint. Cleanliness and the correct temperature of the soldering iron bit is extremely important if dry joints are to be avoided. After re-soldering, a careful visual inspection of each joint is essential. This process is greatly assisted by the use of a proprietary bench magnifier. Any solder splashes, or solder bridges between adjacent tracks, should be removed and, if necessary, a sharp-pointed instrument should be used to remove any surplus solder.

In emergency, to prevent damage to the PCB, or when the copper foil side of the PCB may be inaccessible, it is sometimes expedient to remove a component by cutting its leads on the top (component side) of the board. However, care should be taken to ensure that sufficient lead is left to which the replacement component (with its leads suitably trimmed) may be soldered. Furthermore, extra care will be required when the soldering iron bit is placed close to densely packed components on the top side of the PCB. Polystyrene capacitors and other plastic encapsulated components melt very quickly when in contact with a soldering iron. This technique is not, of course, appropriate where IC devices are concerned.

4

Tape and disk drives

The first generation of personal computer users had little choice other than to make use of cassette tapes for data storage. This was slow and unreliable but it was the only means by which users could retain their valuable programs and data. This situation soon changed with the advent of first 8 inch and then 5.25 inch floppy disk drives. These drives were fitted as standard to the early 8080 and Z80 CP/M-based business systems. Hard disk drives, at that time restricted to the mainframe and minicomputer, did not become widely affordable as a personal computer peripheral until the early 1980s, at which point the rapidly growing small business market had moved away from CP/M to PC-DOS and MS-DOS based systems.

Early systems fitted with hard drives were often restricted to 10 or 20 Mbytes of data storage. Although this may sound extremely small by today's standards, it is perfectly adequate for simple DOS-based applications (many first generation business users made use of early versions of packages such as Lotus 1-2-3, dBase, Wordstar, none of which required excessive amounts of disk space). With the advent of graphics oriented shells (such as Windows and OS/2) applications became increasingly demanding on both system memory and hard disk space. A 40 Mbyte hard disk is now barely adequate for one or two simple Windows applications and most users soon realize the need for storage capacities of 80 to 100 Mbytes, or more. Happily, the CD-ROM drive promises to provide storage for vast amounts of data. A single CD-ROM can store over 600 Mbytes of data and hence this method of storage is ideal for CAD, DTP and graphics packages as well as games which use complex graphics, video sequences and digitized sound.

This chapter is devoted to fault finding on cassette tape, floppy and hard disk drives. The basic techniques and characteristics of each form of data storage will be discussed. However it has been assumed that the reader is already conversant with the general principles of magnetic recording. Representative interface circuitry is described together with details of VLSI disk controllers. The chapter is divided into three sections, the first dealing with cassette drives and the other two with floppy and hard disk drives respectively. Each section concludes with a comprehensive list of stock faults and remedies.

Cassette drives

A magnetic storage system based on standard compact cassettes offers mass data storage at the lowest possible cost per bit and is thus ideal for the first-time computer user operating on a restricted budget. Unfortunately such systems have serious shortcomings arising from

Table 4.1 Data storage capacity of some commonly available compact cassettes

Type	Tape length (approx.)	Minutes per side	Data capacity (approx. bytes incl. sync)	
			500 baud	1.2 kbaud
C5	24 ft (7.3 m)	2.5	9.5 K	23 K
C10	47 ft (14.3 m)	5	19 K	46 K
C12	56 ft (17.1 m)	6	22 K	53 K
C15	70 ft (21.3 m)	7.5	28 K	67 K
C30	140 ft (42.7 m)	15	56 K	134 K

both the transport mechanism and the tape medium itself, which not only impose a restriction on the maximum data transfer rate but also make the system prone to data corruption. The compact cassette was originated by Philips and has become universally accepted by audio equipment manufacturers. The take-up and feed spools of the compact cassette are enclosed so that the tape is only exposed at the point at which the erase and read/write heads gain access. The tape transport mechanism applies drive to the tape via a drive spindle and pinch wheel assembly and the motor speed is controlled so that the tape moves at a reasonably constant 1.875 in/sec (4.75 cm/sec). The tape used within the cassette has a width of 0.15 inch and cassettes designed specifically for data storage are invariably of C5, C10, C12, C15, or C30 variety and have the characteristics listed in Table 4.1.

Many personal computers are designed to operate in conjunction with ordinary domestic tape recorders while others either have internally fitted cassette units or require specialized external drives. In the former case, the recording technique usually involves coding the data in the form of audio frequency tones to represent the binary states 0 and 1. In the latter case, various other methods are employed, most popular of which is the double-frequency (f–2f) technique. A number of different standards are employed for cassette drives and many are based upon the Computer User's Tape System (CUTS), which is also known as the Kansas City Standard. In this system the audio tones are 1.2 kHz and 2.4 kHz, a logic 0 being represented by four cycles of 1.2 kHz and a logic 1 by eight cycles of 2.4 kHz. In either case each bit is transmitted in a time interval of 3.3 ms; and thus the data transfer rate is 300 baud (i.e. 300 bits every second). At this point it is worth mentioning that data rates specified in 'baud' and 'bits per second' are not necessarily the same. The difference arises from the additional overhead in bits used for synchronizing and error-checking the serial data stream. The baud rate allows for these additional bits (i.e. it is the total number of bits including data and overhead transmitted in one second) whereas, strictly speaking, the bit rate applies only to the actual data. This may seem a minor point but it often leads to confusion and readers should be aware of the difference. The additional bits required for serial transmission usually comprise start and stop bits and, where relevant, parity and checksum bits. Furthermore, an initial gap (leader) should be provided prior to initial synchronization and gaps should also be provided between data blocks.

The Kansas City Standard, for example, requires that a leader should consist of 30 seconds of 2.4 kHz (logic 1) and that each transmitted character should consist of one stop bit (logic 0), eight data bits (including an optional parity check bit), followed by two stop bits (both logic 1). Furthermore, blocks of data should be separated by five seconds of 2.4 kHz (logic 1). This format is illustrated in Figure 4.1.

Data rates of 300 baud are now considered rather slow and somewhat outdated and there has been a progressive move to faster speeds in recent years; systems using 500, 600, 1200, 1500, and 2400 baud are now common. A system operating at 1200 baud using the same

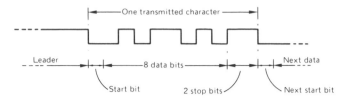

Figure 4.1 Typical format for a character using the Kansas City (CUTS) standard

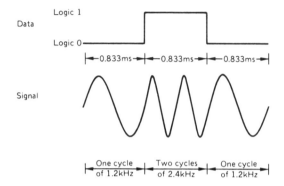

Figure 4.2 Logic level representation using audio tones

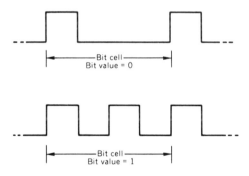

Figure 4.3 Double-frequency (f–2f) technique

tone frequencies as prescribed for the Kansas City Standard would, for example, record a logic 0 using a single cycle of 1.2 kHz and a logic 1 using two cycles of 2.4 kHz, as shown in Figure 4.2.

The most common alternative to the use of frequency-shifted audio tones is the double-frequency (f–2f) technique. This involves recording a saturated pulse train (rather than a sinusoidal tone that is acceptable by most domestic recorders) in which a single pulse in a given time interval (the bit cell) represents a logic 0 whereas two pulses in the same time denote a logic 1, as shown in Figure 4.3. Since synchronizing information can be recovered from the data stream (there is always one pulse present at the start of every bit period), the system is referred to as 'self-clocking'.

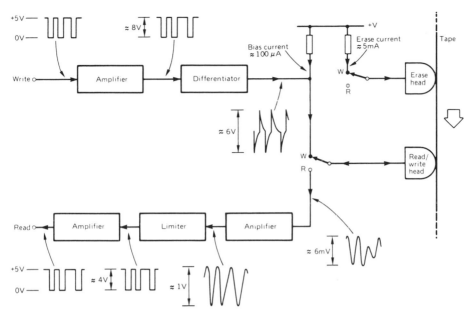

Figure 4.4 Simplified block schematic of a typical internal cassette drive

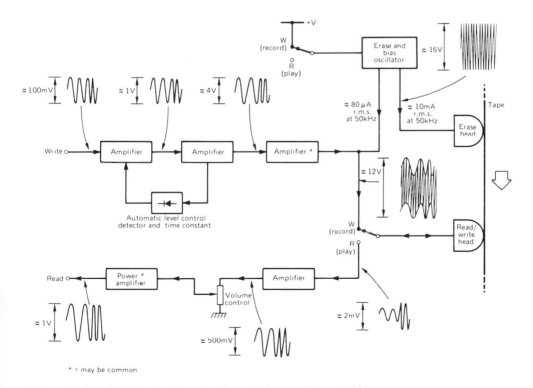

* = may be common

Figure 4.5 Simplified block schematic of a typical external cassette drive

Figure 4.6 Read/write (centre) and erase heads in a typical cassette data recorder

The cassette drive interface ideally consists of a UART (as described in Chapter 1) but may also consist of a PIA/VIA with a somewhat more complex software driver. In such cases, specific PIA/VIA ports are reserved for serial data transfer to and from the cassette recorder. In either case, the serial data stream is assembled in the interface and the required synchronizing and error correcting bits are added at this stage. The composite data and synchronizing stream is then fed to the necessary signal processing circuitry before outputting to the cassette drive electronics.

The signal fed to the cassette recorder is usually in the region of a few hundred milli-volts (rarely is it at TTL levels) and at a medium impedance. Some manufacturers use a bare minimum of electronics within the cassette recorder, sometimes as few as two transistors in the write amplifier together with two or three transistors in the read amplifier.

The simplified block schematic of a typical internal cassette drive is shown in Figure 4.4. The erase line is supplied with a direct current of typically between 4 and 10 mA whenever the unit is operated in the write mode. Read/write and remote-control switching may either be accomplished either purely electronically or with the aid of miniature relays. Electronic motor speed control is usually fitted in better quality equipment.

The simplified block schematic of a typical external cassette arrangement is shown in Figure 4.5. Such equipment may use either d.c. or a.c. erase and recording bias, with the latter preferred for better quality equipment. The interface must be designed so that it is possible to connect as wide a variety of external recorders as possible. Hence, some form of automatic level control is useful and motor control should ideally be provided by means of a relay, which not only provides a high degree of isolation for the interface but also avoids problems associated with the differing supply requirements of d.c. motors used in cassette recorders.

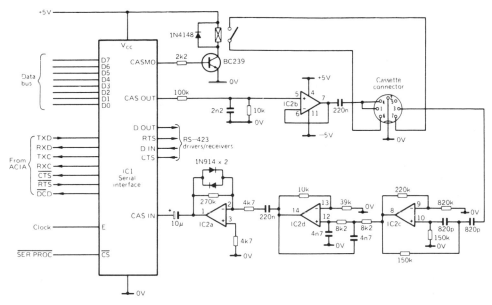

Figure 4.7 Cassette interface for use with an external domestic cassette drive

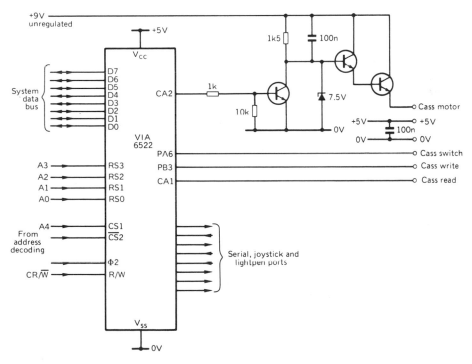

Figure 4.8 Cassette interface for use with a dedicated cassette drive

The read section often comprises two, or more, operational amplifiers configured as filters (invariably of the Sallen-and-Key variety) followed by a limiter/detector stage, as shown in the cassette interface of Figure 4.7. This circuit is designed for use with a wide variety of domestic cassette recorders and uses relay switching of the motor supply. An alternative arrangement, suitable for a dedicated cassette drive and using a VIA, is shown in Figure 4.8. This circuit uses electronic switching of the cassette motor supply and TTL signal levels are fed to and from the read and write amplifiers.

Cassette drive fault location

Many of the faults associated with cassette drives are easily found. Typical examples are failure of the mechanical interlock between controls, broken drive belts, and defective connecting leads. When faults are more obscure, however, it is essential to establish whether or not they lie within the coniputer interface or within the mechanics or electronics of the cassette drive itself. The ideal method of performing this check is by substituting a known working cassette drive for the suspect drive. If this is not possible, readers should first check that the cassette supply is normal (i.e. check the mains or d.c. supply within the cassette drive) and then make checks on the cassette interface to establish (a) whether motor control is normal, (b) whether a write signal is output, and (c) whether a read signal is returned. These checks can be easily performed using nothing more than a logic probe and multi-meter, and measurements can conveniently be made at the cassette connector on the CPU or interface board.

Figure 4.9 Planetary drive mechanism in a typical cassette data recorder

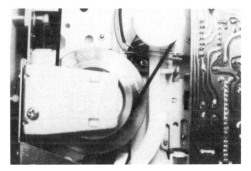

Figure 4.10 Flywheel and belt drive in a typical cassette data recorder

Users of cassette recorders tend to be blissfully unaware of the need for routine maintenance of such units. it is not unusual to encounter a unit which is failing to perform correctly for no other reason than an excessive coating of dirt and oxide on the tape head. Often the user is unaware of the existence of proprietary tape head cleaners which could have prevented such a build-up and avoided an expensive service call. Routine maintenance should follow these guidelines:

1. Check for correct seating of cassette and alignment of heads relative to the tape as the read/write or play key is depressed.
2. Remove cassette and examine heads for wear and oxide deposit.

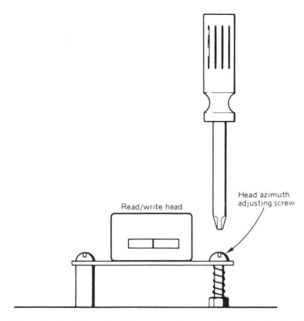

Figure 4.11 Azimuth adjustment of a cassette read/write head

3. Clean heads using cotton bud and alcohol-based cleaning solution.
4. Examine drive spindle, rubber pinch wheel, and all surfaces along the tape path. Clean if necessary.
5. Check that pinch wheel disengages from drive spindle correctly whenever fast forward or fast rewind are selected (this can be a cause of tape spillage).
6. Clean and lubricate mechanical parts according to the manufacturer's recommendations.
7. Check speed using test tape and, if necessary, adjust speed control. If speed is not constant check drive belt, pinch wheel pressure, and flywheel alignment.
8. Check read and write functions using blank tape and diagnostic program (may be loaded from the test tape).

Many readers will already be familiar with the operation of cassette tape recorders, and the servicing of those intended for data storage follows exactly the same principles as those employed for music and speech. Hence, rather than adopt a step-by-step procedure we shall discuss the cause and remedy for a number of typical 'stock faults'.

Cassette drive stock faults

Symptom	Cause	Action
Motor not turning	Power supply defective	Check supply rail
	Motor control relay/series transistor	Replace relay/series transistor
	Defective speed regulator	Check regulator
	Defective cable or connector	Check for d.c. at appropriate points, check continuity with multimeter

Cassette drive stock faults

Symptom	Cause	Action
	Motor defective	Replace motor
Motor turning but tape not moving	Drive belt broken or excessively worn	Replace belt
No read or write	Power supply failure	Check supply rails and regulators
	Read/write head open circuit	Check head for continuity, check head connections to PCB
	I/O failure	Check I/O device, including address decoding and chip select signals
	Defective cable or connector	Check using multimeter or logic probe at appropriate points
	Read/write head dirty or worn	Check read/write head, clean or replace
Read but no write (previous data not erased)	Erase head open-circuit	Check head for continuity, check head connections to PCB
	Erase circuitry not functioning	Check erase oscillator or d.c. feed to erase head
	Erase head dirty or worn	Check erase head, clean or replace
Read but no write (previous data erased)	Write amplifier defective	Check for write signal at the read/write head and work backwards to the I/O device
Write but no read (tape can be read on a similar machine)	Read amplifier defective	Check for read signal at the read/write head and work forwards to the I/O device
Inability to read tapes made on other machines	Speed incorrect	Check motor speed regulator, adjust if possible.
	Worn drive belt	Replace belt
	Incorrect read signal level	Adjust gain control
Intermittent data errors	Speed irregular	Check motor speed regulator
	Worn drive belt	Replace belt
	Worn or eccentric pinch wheel	Replace pinch wheel
	Insufficient pinch wheel pressure	Adjust pinch wheel
	Flywheel defective	Check for excessive play on flywheel
	Insufficient erase current	Check erase signal or d.c. feed to erase head
	Incorrect recording or reading levels	Check levels and, if possible, adjust
	Faulty ALC circuitry	Check ALC detector and time constant
Intermittent data errors with particular media	Inconsistent magnetic oxide coating	Replace cassette
	Tape stretched or creased	Replace cassette
	Cassette pressure pad defective	Adjust or replace pressure pad
Gradual deterioration in performance, increasing number of data errors	Heads contaminated with oxide	Clean heads
	Residual magnetism in read/write head	De-magnetize read/write head
	Incorrect azimuth of read/write head	Adjust head azimuth (see Figure 4.11)

Cassette drive stock faults

Symptom	Cause	Action
Wind or rewind too slow	Cassette defective Friction plate worn Friction lever worn Torque low	Replace cassette Replace or adjust friction plate Replace or adjust lever Check and adjust pulley assembly
Tapes damaged	Excessive take-up torque Excessive pinch wheel pressure	Adjust or replace assembly Adjust pinch wheel pressure
Tape spillage	Pinch wheel not disengaging correctly Friction plates worn	Check pinch wheel assembly Replace or renew friction plates
Pause inoperative	Pinch wheel not disengaging	Check pinch wheel assembly and slider linkage
Eject inoperative	Eject linkage or eject spring faulty	Check linkage or replace spring

Disk drives

Magnetic disk drives are available in various forms, from the hard Winchester types which are suitable for small business applications to the compact floppy which is ideal for the domestic user. The main types are summarized below:

1. *Hard disks.* These units generally employ non-interchangeable disks, are relatively expensive and offer typical storage capacities of 20 Mbyte or more.
2. *8 inch floppy disks.* Now obsolete, these were the forerunners of the 5.25 inch mini-floppy disk. Disks are contained within a protective cardboard sleeve, are inter-changeable and offer typical storage capacities of between 400K and 1 Mbyte.
3. *5.25 inch floppy disks.* Until recently, these were the most popular form of on-line storage for use with personal computers. Typical storage capacities are between 360K and 1.2 Mbyte.
4. *3.5 inch (approx.) compact or micro-floppy disks* The disk is again removable but is often supplied in a rigid plastic cartridge rather than a flexible sleeve. Storage capacities are normally between 360K for a single-sided double-density disk and 1.44 Mbyte for a double-sided high-density disk. Disks are available which will provide storage of up to 2.88 Mbyte (using standard IBM formatting) and even larger capacities can be provided using special drives and formatting.

Floppy disk drives

The standard 8 inch floppy disk was originally developed by IBM as part of the IBM 3740 key-to-disk data-entry system. The IBM format divides the magnetic oxide coated disk surface into a number of concentric tracks. Each track is divided into a number of sectors in which either 128, 256 or 512 bytes are stored depending upon the recording density and technique employed. The IBM 3740 format, which is described more fully later, has been much copied and many of today's 5.25 inch mini-floppy disk drive systems are based upon it. There are, however, one or two notable exceptions to this, including some equipment manufactured by such well-known names as ACT, Apple and Commodore.

Figure 4.12 Atari XC12 program recorder chassis showing erase head, read/write head, pinch-wheel assembly and tape counter drive belt

Figure 4.13 Motor drive belt and flywheel assembly in the XC12 program recorder

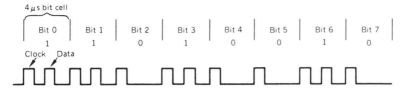

Figure 4.14 Typical FM recording signal for the hex character D2. *Rules*: 1. Write a clock bit at the start of each bit cell. 2. If the data is a 1, write a data bit at the centre of the bit cell.

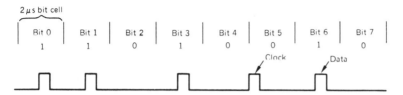

Figure 4.15 Typical MFM recording signal for the hex character D2. *Rules*: 1. If the data is a 1, write a data bit at the centre of the bit cell. 2. Write a clock bit at the start of a bit cell if no data was written in the last bit cell and no data will be written in the current bit cell.

The two most commonly employed recording techniques use either frequency modulation (FM) or modulated frequency modulation (MFM). The former technique is identical to the double frequency (f–2f) method that was described earlier in relation to cassette data recorders. A comparison of FM and MFM techniques can be made from Figures 4.14 and 4.15. Both methods involve writing a serial pulse train (comprising both data and clock pulses) to the disk.

In the case of FM, a clock pulse is present at the start of each bit cell. In the FM method a 1 is written by including a pulse in the centre of the cell (i.e. between consecutive clock pulses). In the MFM method things are a little more complex and, whereas a 1 is again written by placing a pulse in the centre of the bit cell, no regular clock pulse is written. A clock pulse is only written at the start of a cell when a 0 appears in both the preceding cell and in the cell in question.

Standard flexible disks (once referred to as 'mini-floppy' disks) have a diameter of 5.125 inches (130.2 mm) and the disk sleeve is 5.25 inches (133.4 mm) square. Disks are available in both hard- and soft-sectored formats, the latter enjoying by far the greatest popularity.

Hard-sectored disks have a series of index holes to indicate the start of each sector. The sectors on soft-sectored disks have to be written during the formatting process, which effectively writes a framework of tracks and sectors in which the data is subsequently placed.

Mini-floppy disk drives are often categorized by their height in relation to those which first became available (i.e. full-height drives). In recent years there has been a trend towards more compact drives in order to permit a consequent saving of space in the equipment to which they are fitted. This is, of course, particularly important where drives are to be fitted in portable equipment.

A floppy disk drive generally consists of a chassis incorporating the following components:

1. A drive mechanism to rotate the disk at a constant speed.
2. A read/write head mounted on a precision positioning assembly invariably driven by a stepper motor.

3. Control circuitry that interprets inputs from the disk controller and generates signals to:
   (a) start the drive motor;
   (b) implement write protection so that protected disks cannot be overwritten;
   (c) drive the head position actuator, which moves the head from track to track;
   (d) activate the head load solenoid, which moves the head against the disk;
   (e) locate the physical index that indicates the start of each track.
4. Read/write circuitry (invariably mounted on the same PCB as the control circuitry), which interfaces the read/write head to produce/accept TTL-compatible signal levels.

A precision servo-controlled d.c. motor is used to maintain the disk speed at 300 rpm ± 1.5 per cent for a mini-floppy drive, or 360 rpm ±1.5 per cent for a standard floppy drive. Coupling to the disk rotating spindle is normally achieved by means of a rubber drive belt, although some modern units use direct drive from the motor to the spindle/flywheel assembly.

Figure 4.16 Belt drive in an early floppy disk drive (Teac FD-50)

The drive spindle engages with the centre of the disk (which is usually reinforced by means of additional hub rings) so that the disk rotates within its outer sleeve. The material of the sleeve is chosen so that friction between disk and sleeve is minimal.

Unlike larger hard disks, where the read/write heads ride on a thin cushion of air above the disk surface, the read/write head of a floppy disk makes physical contact with the disk surface (i.e. it is permanently 'crashed') through an elongated hole provided in the sleeve. The presence (or absence) of a write protect notch is detected by means of an LED and photo-transistor and, if present, write operation is inhibited. Another photo-detector arrangement is used to locate the start of recorded tracks by means of the physical index hole in the disk.

The read/write head assembly is accurately positioned through the use of a precision spiral cam. This cam has a V-groove with a ball-bearing follower which is attached to the head of carriage assembly. Precise track selection is accomplished as the cam is rotated in small discrete increments by a stepping motor. The read/write heads themselves have straddle erase elements which provide erased areas between adjacent data tracks, hence minimizing the effects of data overlap between adjacent tracks when disks written on one drive are read by another.

To ensure a very high degree of compliance with the read/write head, precise registration of the diskette is essential. This is accomplished, with the diskette held in a plane perpendicular to the read/write head, by a platen located in the base casting. The head is loaded against the disk by means of the head load solenoid and a spring-loaded pressure pad is used to maintain contact between the head and the oxide-coated disk surface.

Figure 4.17 Lead screw and head carriage assembly in a Teac FD-50 drive. (The end-stop microswitch can be seen in the upper right-hand corner)

Figure 4.18 Head stepper motor (left) and flywheel drive motor of an FD-50 drive

Figure 4.19 Head load solenoid in a Teac FD-50 drive

Figure 4.20 720K 3.5 inch disk drive fitted to the Atari 1040STFM

Figure 4.21 Modern 5.25 inch 1.2 Mbyte disk drive

Table 4.2 Characteristics of some older full-height 5.25" floppy drives

Maker	Drive type	Number of tracks per side	Number of sides	Tracks per inch	Compatible drives
Shugart	SA400	35/40	1	48	Teac FD-50A
Shugart	SA450	35/40	2	48	Teac FD-50B
Shugart	SA460	80	2	96	Teac FD-50F
Teac	FD-50A	35/40	1	48	Shugart SA400
Teac	FD-50B	40	2	48	Shugart SA450
Teac	FD-50C	77	1	100	Micropolis 1015 Model II
Teac	FD-50E	70/80	1	96	
Teac	FD-50F	70/80	2	96	

The first mini-floppy disk drive to gain popularity was the SA400 from Shugart Associates. This 35 (or 40) track drive provides an unformatted capacity of 125K bytes in single density (FM) or 250K bytes in double density (MFM), the data transfer rates being respectively 125 Kbit/sec and 250 Kbit/sec. The drive provides an average latency of 100 ms, a stepping time (track to track) of 20 ms and an average access time of 280 ms. The drive requires d.c. supplies of +12 V ± 5 per cent at 0.9 A (typical) and +5 V ± 5 per cent at 0.5 A (typical).

Figure 4.22 Screened head assembly and head positioning mechanism on a modern 5.25 inch disk drive

Figure 4.23 Partially disassembled motor drive assembly on a modern 5.25 inch disk drive

Figure 4.24 Index hole sensor (accessible after dismantling the drive motor assembly - see Figure 4.21)

Table 4.3 Characteristics of some typical half-height 5.25 inch floppy drives

Maker	Drive type	Number of tracks per side	Number of sides	Tracks per inch
Shugart	SA455	40	2	48
Shugart	SA465	80	2	96
Teac	FD-55A	40	1	48
Teac	FD-55B	40	2	48
Teac	FD-55E	80	1	96
Teac	FD-55F	80	2	96
Mitsubishi	M4851	40	2	48
Mitsubishi	M4852	80	2	96
Mitsubishi	M4853	80	2	96
Mitsubishi	M4854	77	2	96
Mitsubishi	M4855	80	2	96
Hitachi	HFD510A	80	2	96
Hitachi	HFD505A	40	2	96
TEC	FB501	40	1	48
TEC	FB502	80	1	96
TEC	FB503	40	2	48
TEC	FB504	80	2	96

In recent years, the FD-50 series of full-height drives from Teac have achieved immense popularity (the FD-50A being compatible with Shugart's SA400). The characteristics of a number of commonly available full-height drives are summarized in Table 4.2.

Table 4.4 Characteristics of some typical 3.5 inch and 3.0 inch floppy drives

Maker	Drive type	Disk diameter (inch)	Number of tracks	Number of sides	Tracks per inch
Shugart	SA300	3.5	80	1	135
Mitsubishi	MF351	3.5	80	1	135
Hitachi	HFD305S	3.0	40	2	100
Teac	FD-30A	3.0	40	1	100
Teac	FD-235F	3.5	80	2	135

Half-height drives have also become increasingly popular, with modern devices by Tandon, Micropolis and Mitsubishi (among others) offering storage capacities well in excess of the SA400 and almost comparable with the smaller hard disks. A number of half-height drives are summarized in Table 4.3.

The first available compact drive was a 3.5 inch unit produced by Sony. This was soon joined by 3.25 inch units from Seagate, Tabor, Mitsubishi and Teac. 3 inch drives were produced by Hitachi, Matsushita, and Maxell (see Table 4.4).

Wisely, manufacturers of 3.5 inch floppy drives retained compatibility with the 5.25 inch industry-standard interface. The Mitsubishi and Teac drives, for example, operate at 300 rpm and use an 80-track format with 135 tracks per inch. The standard data transfer rate is 125 Kbit/sec in single density (FM) and 250 Kbit/sec in double density (MFM) while the unformatted storage capacity is 250 Kbytes and 500 Kbytes respectively.

IBM format summary

In order to understand the operation of the floppy disk controller and the disk interface circuitry, some familiarity with the IBM format is extremely useful. This format applies to the vast majority of 8 inch disk systems and, with minor changes (such as the number of tracks and/or sectors), to many of the mini-floppy systems in current use. The main points are covered below.

Track format.   The disk has 77 concentric tracks, numbered physically from 00 to 76, with track 00 being the outermost track. During initialization, any two tracks (other than track 00) may be designated as 'bad' and the remaining 75 data tracks are numbered in logical sequence, from 00 to 74.

Sector format.   Each track is divided into 26, 15, or eight sectors of 128, 256, or 512 bytes length respectively. The first sector is numbered 01 and is physically the first sector after the index mark. The remaining sectors are not necessarily numbered in physical sequence, the numbering scheme being determined at initialization. Each sector consists of a number of fields separated by gaps. An ID field is used to identify the sector while a data field contains the information stored. The beginning of each field is indicated by six synchronizing bytes of 00H followed by one byte mark. Table 4.5 shows the contents of gaps in the mini-floppy format.

Address marks.   Address marks are unique patterns, one byte in length, which are used to identify the beginning of ID and data fields and to synchronize the de-serializing circuitry with the first byte of each field. Address mark bytes are different from all other data bytes

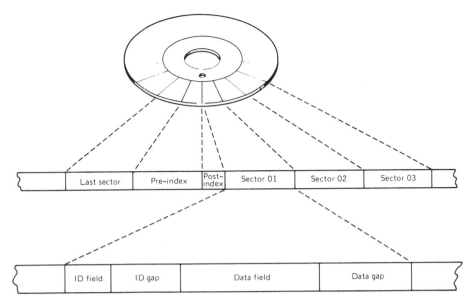

Figure 4.25 IBM format for mini-floppy disks

Table 4.5 Contents of the gaps in the IBM standard mini-floppy format

Gap type	Gap designation	Length (bytes)	Content
1	Post-index	22	16 of FFH followed by 6 of 00H
2	ID	17	11 of FFH followed by 6 of 00H
3	Data	33	26 of FFH followed by 6 of 00H
4	Pre-index	274 (nom)	FF

Note: 00H is sync, FFH is filler

in that certain bit cells do not contain a clock bit (all other data bytes have clock bits in every bit cell).

Four different types of address mark are employed to identify different types of field, as follows:

(a) Index address mark. The index address mark is located at the beginning of each track and is a fixed number of bytes in advance of the first record. (NB: Not used in the 'mini-floppy' format.)

(b) ID address mark. The ID address mark byte is located at the beginning of each ID field on the disk.

(c) Data address mark. The data address mark byte is located at the beginning of each non-deleted data field on the disk.

(d) Deleted data address mark. The deleted data address mark byte is located at the beginning of each deleted data field on the disk.

The clock and data patterns used for the various address marks are shown below:

Address mark type	Clock pattern	Data pattern
Index	D7	FC
ID	C7	FE
Data	C7	FB
Deleted data	C7	F8
Bad track ID	C7	FE

ID field. The ID field is organized as shown in Figure 4.26. The relationship between the sector-length byte and the length of the data field is as follows:

Data field length (bytes)	Sector length byte
128	00
256	01
512	02

One byte

ID address mark	Track number (00—74)	Side number (00—01)	Sector number (01—26)	Sector length (00—02)	CRC (MSB)	CRC (LSB)

Figure 4.26 ID field organization in the IBM format

One byte

Data address mark	Data		CRC (MSB)	CRC (LSB)

Figure 4.27 Data field organization in the IBM format

Data field. The data field is organized as shown in Figure 4.27. The data is either 128, 256, or 512 bytes in length and is followed by two bytes of cyclic redundancy check (CRC) characters.

CRC characters. The 16-bit CRC character is generated using the polynomial $X^{16} + X^{12} + X^5 + 1$, normally initialized to FFH. Its generation includes all characters in the ID or data field except the CRC itself.

Bad track format. The format is the same as that used for good tracks with the exception that the track number, side number, sector number, and sector length are all set to FFH.

Floppy disk controllers

Floppy disk controllers facilitate the storage and retrieval of data in the sectors and tracks which are written on the disk during the formatting process. The disk controller is thus an extremely complex device, being capable of both formatting the disk and then writing/reading the data on it.

Since neither the user nor the programmer is concerned with the actual organization of data in tracks and sectors, an operating system is required to carry out management and housekeeping associated with the maintenance of disk files. The disk operating system (DOS) thus acts as a bridge between the user and the floppy disk controller which, as an absolute minimum:

```
0000    FFFF FFFF FFFF FFFF FFFF FFFF FFFF E3FF
0010    FFFF FFFF FE01 0008 010E CEFF FFFF FFFF
0020    FFFF FFFF FFFF FE00 0000 0000 1FDD DDDD
0030    DDDD DDDD DDDD DDDD DDDD DDDD DDDD DDDD
0040    DDDD DDDD DDDD DDDD DDDD DDDD DDDD DDDD
0050    DDDD DDDD DDDD DDDD DDDD DDDD DDDD DDDD
0060    DDDD DDDD DDDD DDDD DDDD DDDD DDDD DDDD
0070    DDDD DDDD DDDD DDDD DDDD DDDD DDDD DDDD
0080    DDDD DDDD DDDD DDDD DDDD DDDD DDDD DDDD
0090    DDDD DDDD DDDD DDDD DDDD DDDD DDDD DDDD
00A0    DDDD DDDD DDDD DDDD DDDD DDDD DDDD DDDD
00B0    DDDD DDDD DDDD DDDD DDDD DDDD DDDD DDDD
00C0    DDDD DDDD DDDD DDDD DDDD DDDD DDDD DDDD
00D0    DDDD DDDD DDDD DDDD DDDD DDDD DDDD DDDD
00E0    DDDD DDDD DDDD DDDD DDDD DDDD DDDD DDDD
00F0    DDDD DDDD DDDD DDDD DDDD DDDD DDDD DDDD
0100    DDDD DDDD DDDD DDDD DDDD DDDD DDDD DDDD
0110    DDDD DDDD DDDD DDDD DDDD DDDD DDDD DDDD
0120    DDDD DDDD DDDD DDDD DDDD DDDD DD22 7CFF
0130    FFFF FFFF FFFF FFFF FFFF FFFF FFFF F000
0140    0000 0000 FE01 0004 014B A3FF FFFF FFFF
0150    FFFF FFFF FFFF C000 0000 0000 FBDD DDDD
0160    DDDD DDDD DDDD DDDD DDDD DDDD DDDD DDDD
0170    DDDD DDDD DDDD DDDD DDDD DDDD DDDD DDDD
0180    DDDD DDDD DDDD DDDD DDDD DDDD DDDD DDDD
0190    DDDD DDDD DDDD DDDD DDDD DDDD DDDD DDDD
01A0    DDDD DDDD DDDD DDDD DDDD DDDD DDDD DDDD
01B0    DDDD DDDD DDDD DDDD DDDD DDDD DDDD DDDD
01C0    DDDD DDDD DDDD DDDD DDDD DDDD DDDD DDDD
01D0    DDDD DDDD DDDD DDDD DDDD DDDD DDDD DDDD
01E0    DDDD DDDD DDDD DDDD DDDD DDDD DDDD DDDD
01F0    DDDD DDDD DDDD DDDD DDDD DDDD DDDD DDDD
0200    DDDD DDDD DDDD DDDD DDDD DDDD DDDD DDDD
0210    DDDD DDDD DDDD DDDD DDDD DDDD DDDD DDDD
0220    DDDD DDDD DDDD DDDD DDDD DDDD DDDD DDDD
0230    DDDD DDDD DDDD DDDD DDDD DDDD DDDD DDDD
0240    DDDD DDDD DDDD DDDD DDDD DDDD DDDD DDDD
0250    DDDD DDDD DDDD DDDD DDDD DDDD DD22 7CFF
0260    FFFF FFFF FFFF FFFF· FFFF FFFF FFFF 0000
0270    0000 000F FE01 0009 013D FFFF FFFF FFFF
0280    FFFF FFFF FFFF F800 0000 0000 FBDD DDDD
0290    DDDD DDDD DDDD DDDD DDDD DDDD DDDD DDDD
02A0    DDDD DDDD DDDD DDDD DDDD DDDD DDDD DDDD
02B0    DDDD DDDD DDDD DDDD DDDD DDDD DDDD DDDD
02C0    DDDD DDDD DDDD DDDD DDDD DDDD DDDD DDDD
02D0    DDDD DDDD DDDD DDDD DDDD DDDD DDDD DDDD
02E0    DDDD DDDD DDDD DDDD DDDD DDDD DDDD DDDD
02F0    DDDD DDDD DDDD DDDD DDDD DDDD DDDD DDDD
0300    DDDD DDDD DDDD DDDD DDDD DDDD DDDD DDDD
0310    DDDD DDDD DDDD DDDD DDDD DDDD DDDD DDDD
0320    DDDD DDDD DDDD DDDD DDDD DDDD DDDD DDDD
```

Figure 4.28 Part of the contents of a track formatted according to the IBM standard (all bytes of 'DD' are data)

(a) translates requests for logical files into physical tracks and sectors;

(b) provides mechanisms for copying, deleting, renaming, and dumping of files; and

(c) maintains some form of directory, which comprises a list of files together with their physical locations on the disk. This list of files is also stored on the disk and is updated every time a file is added or modified.

Floppy disk controllers are invariably based upon one of several currently available VLSI devices which considerably simplify the hardware requirements of the disk interface and are instrumental in reducing the overall chip count. The disk controller has various functions, which:

1. Format the disk with the required number of tracks and sectors as determined by the DOS.
2. Accept commands issued by the CPU and translate these to appropriate actions within the disk drive, such as positioning the read/write head. Commands are invariably loaded via the data bus into a command register within the floppy disk controller.
3. Maintain various internal registers which:
    (a) reflect the current status of the controller,
    (b) indicate the current track over which the read/write head is positioned, and
    (c) hold the address of the desired sector position.
4. Provide an interface to the CPU bus so that:
    (a) during the write process, incoming parallel data from the bus is converted to a serial self-clocking data stream for writing to the floppy disk, and
    (b) during the read process, incoming serial data from the floppy disk is separated from the accompanying clock, and fed to a serial-to-parallel shift register before outputting to the data bus.
5. Generate the necessary cyclic redundancy check (CRC) characters and append these to the write data stream at the appropriate time.

The floppy disk controller is connected between the CPU interface and disk interface, as shown in Figure 4.29. The CPU interface may consist of a VIA/PIA chip, or simply a bidirectional buffer onto the data bus. However, where the floppy disk controller is housed on the CPU card, a minimum of interfacing is required and the device may be linked directly to the CPU bus and relevant control lines.

Each disk drive contains its own interface to the bus, which links all the drives in a system to the floppy disk controller. The most commonly used bus arrangement is that originated by Shugart and first employed with the Shugart SA400 drive. This bus uses a 34-way connector, the 17 odd-numbered lines of which are common earth. The typical designation and function of the signal lines are shown in Table 4.6. It should be noted that since the drive requires an appreciable current the +12 V and +5 V power lines require a separate connector and often employ a power source separate from that of the CPU.

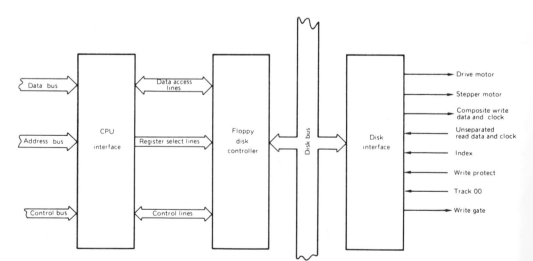

Figure 4.29 Simplified block schematic of a floppy disk interface

Table 4.6 Typical pin assignment for a 34-way mini-floppy disk bus

Pin number	Designation	Function
2	n.c.	
4	HEAD LOAD	Output from FDC, active low, activates the head load solenoid
6	DS4	Drive 4 select, output from FDC, active low
8	INDEX	Input to FDC, active low
10	DS1	Drive 1 select, output from FDC, active low
12	DS2	Drive 2 select, output from FDC, active low
14	DS3	Drive 3 select, output from FDC, active low
16	MOTOR ON	Output from FDC, active low
18	DIRC	Step direction select output from FDC, step out when high, step in when low
20	STEP	Step output from FDC, step on positive-going edge
22	WRITE DATA	Output from FDC, inactive high, pulsed low
24	WRITE GATE	Output from FDC, write when low, read when high
26	TRACK 00	Input to FDC, low when head positioned over track 00
28	WRITE PROTECT	Input to FDC, active low
30	READ DATA	Input to FDC, inactive high, pulsed low
32	SIDE SELECT	Output from FDC, side select (double-sided drives only)
34	READY	Input to FDC, active low

Note: There are some minor variations in the names given to the various lines and, in particular, drive selects are often numbered DS0 to DS3 rather than DS1 to DS4, HEAD LOAD and READY signals are not always provided.

Figure 4.30 Drive select DIP switch fitted to an FD-50 drive (a DIL 150 ohm terminating network is adjacent to the DIP switch)

Figure 4.31 Drive select jumpers (marked 'JP') fitted to the 5.25 inch drive in an Amstrad PC1640

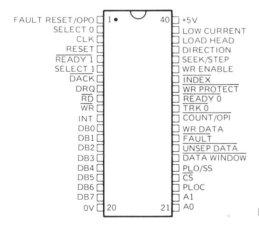

Figure 4.32 8271 pin connections

In order to illustrate the operation of the floppy disk controller, two representative devices will now be discussed. Where necessary, readers should consult the relevant manufacturer's data sheets for further information.

8271 floppy disk controller

Intel's 8271 floppy disk controller, which was originally designed as an 8080 peripheral chip, can interface either two single or one dual floppy drive to an eight-bit microprocessor. The 8271 supports a comprehensive IBM 3740 compatible soft-sectored format which includes provision for the designation and handling of bad tracks.

The 8271 is housed in a 40-pin DIL encapsulation, as shown in Figure 4.32. The functions of the principal signal lines are summarized below:

A0–A1	Register select lines.
DB0–DB7	8-bit tristate, bidirectional data bus.
WR	Input, active low. Signals the control logic that a transfer of data from the data bus to the 8271 is required.
RD	Input, active low. Signals the control logic that a transfer of data from the 8271 to the data bus is required.
INT	Output, active high. Indicates to the CPU that the 8271 requires service.
CS	Input, active low. Enables the 8271 in conjunction with the RD and WR inputs.
RESET	Input, active high. Forces the 8271 into an inactive state. The chip then remains idle until a command is issued by the CPU. The drive interface output signals are all taken low.
CLK	Clock input.
DRQ	Output, active high. The 8271 can transfer data in either DMA or non-DMA mode. The DMA request signal is used to request a transfer of data between the 8271 and system memory.
DACK	Input, active low. The DMA acknowledge signal notifies the 8271 that a DMA transfer cycle has been granted in response to a DRQ signal.
SELECT 0, SELECT 1	Outputs, active high. These lines are used to specify the selected drive.
FAULT	Output, active high. This line may be used to reset an error condition which has been
RESET/OPO	Latched by a drive.
LOW CURRENT	Output, active high. This line notifies the drive that track 43 or greater is selected. This signal may be used to enable compensation for the lower velocity while recording data on the inner tracks by adjusting the current in the head (equivalent to TG43 of the 179X series, of devices).
READY 0, READY 1	Input, active low. These lines indicate that the specified drive is ready.
FAULT	Input, active low. A low on this line indicates that the file is in an unsafe condition.
COUNT/OPI	Input, active low. If the optional seek/direction/count seek mode is selected, the count pin is pulsed to step the head to the desired track.
WR PROTECT	Input, active low. A low on this line indicates that the disk inserted in the selected drive is write protected.
TRK0	Input, active low. This line goes low when the head is positioned over track zero.
INDEX	Input, active low. This line goes low when the physical index hole is detected.
PLO/SS	Input, active high. This input is used to specify the type of data separation employed as follows: (a) if the line is pulled high, a phase-locked oscillator is employed (see Figure 4.33); (b) if the line is taken low, a monostable is employed (see Figure 4.34).

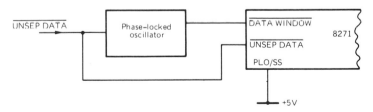

Figure 4.33 Using a phase-locked oscillator data window generator with the 8271

WR DATA	Output. Composite write data.
UNSEP DATA	Input. Inverted signal comprising data and clock.

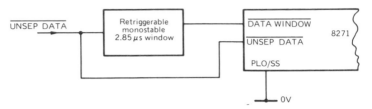

Figure 4.34 Using a monostable data window generator with the 8271

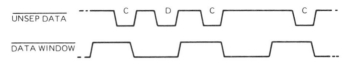

Figure 4.35 Data window timing for Figure 4.33

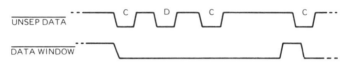

Figure 4.36 Data window timing for Figure 4.34

DATA WINDOW   Input signal derived from either a phase-locked oscillator or a monostable (depending upon the state of the PLO/SS line) and is used in the data separation process, see Figures 4.35 and 4.36.

PLOC   Output. This line goes high when the 8271 has attained data synchronization by detecting two bytes of zero followed by an expected address mark. The line stays high until the end of the ID or data field.

WR ENABLE   Output, active high. This signal enables the write logic of the drive.

SEEK/STEP   Output, active high. Seek control is accomplished in conjunction with the DIRECTION and COUNT lines and can be implemented in two ways:
(a) When the programmed step rate is equal to zero, the 8271 holds the seek line high until the appropriate number of pulses has been counted on the COUNT input.
(b) When the programmed step rate is not equal to zero, the output indicates a STEP in the direction signalled by the DIRECTION line.

DIRECTION   Output. Used to specify the SEEK direction in the following manner:
(a) a high steps the head in (towards the spindle)
(b) a low steps the head out (away from the spindle).

LOAD HEAD   Output, active high. A high on this line causes the head load solenoid to load the head against the disk.

The simplified internal arrangement of the 8271 is shown in Figure 4.37. Where the device is to be capable of DMA operation, a separate DMA controller (such as the Intel 8257) is required. In non-DMA mode, the CPU passes data to the 8271 in response to the non-DMA requests indicated by the status word. Data is passed to and from the chip by asserting the DACK and the RD or WR signals.

The 8271 disk interface supports a high-level command structure and, although the device is primarily suited to the control of two single or one dual drive, with a minimum of software support the device can control four drives by expanding the two drive-select lines using external circuitry.

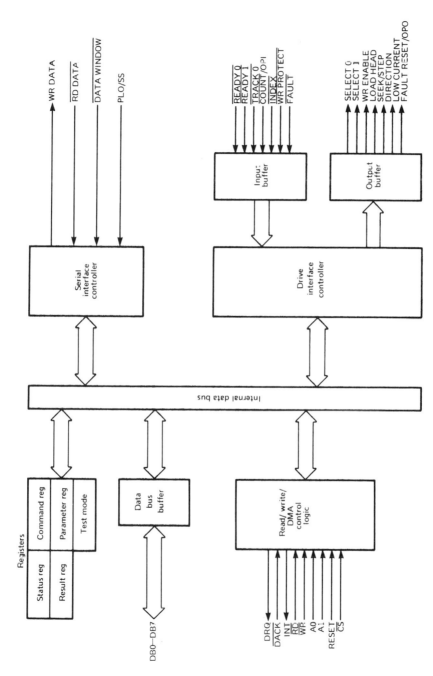

Figure 4.37 Simplified internal arrangement of the 8271

179X floppy disk controllers

In recent years the Western Digital Corporation have produced a range of extremely popular floppy disk controllers. First to become widely used was the 1771 which featured programmable control of such parameters as head loading and track-to-track settling time. Following hard on the success of the 1771 was a family of devices known as the 179X series. The six members of this family are categorized by the final digit (X) and represents a significant improvement on the 1771, incorporating such features as double-density (MFM) operation, write precompensation, and side selection.

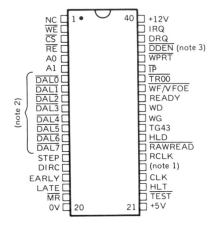

Notes:
1. RG when X = 1,3 SSO when X = 5,7
2. Bus non-inverted when X = 3,7
3. Not connected when X = 2,4

Figure 4.38 179X pin connections

Like the Intel 8271, the 179X family of devices fully support the soft-sector IBM format and are housed in 40-pin DIL packages, as shown in Figure 4.38, The functions of the principal signal lines are summarized below:

A0–A1   Register select lines which operate as follows (Z = don't care):

Address line		CS	Register selected	
A1	A0		RE low	WE low
0	0	0	Status	Command
0	1	0	Track	Track
1	0	0	Sector	Sector
1	1	0	Data	Data
Z	Z	1	Tristate	Tristate

DAL0–DAL7   8-bit, bidirectional data bus (the logical sense of these lines varies according to the particular device, see Figure 4.38).

WE   Active low write enable input, which signals that data is to be written from the bus to the 179X when CS is low.

RE   Active low read enable input, which signals that data is to be read from the 179X to the bus when CS is low.

IRQ	Output, open drain, active high. This interrupt request line goes high at the completion of any task and is low when either the status register is read or the command register is written to. A 10 kohm pull-up resistor is normally used.
CS	Input, active low. Used to enable the 179X in conjunction with the RE and WE inputs.
MR	Input, active high. Master reset which, when held low for 50 μs or more, resets the device and loads 03H into the command register. The 'not ready' status bit (bit 7) of the command register is reset when MR is low. When MR is returned to a high, a restore command is executed and 01H is loaded into the sector register regardless of the state of the READY signal from the drive interface.
CLK	Clock input. This is usually 2 MHz for 8 inch drives and 1 MHz for 5.25 inch drives.
DRQ	Output, open drain, active high. The data request line indicates that during read operations the data register contains assembled data, and that during write operations the data register is empty. A 10 kohm pull-up resistor is normally used.
STEP	Output, pulsed high. A pulse is generated for each step required.
DIRC	Output, active high. The direction output goes high when stepping in and low when stepping out.
EARLY	Output, active high. Indicates that the current write data pulse should be shifted early for write precompensation.
LATE	Output, active high. Indicates that the current write data pulse should be shifted late for write pre-compensation.
TEST	Input, active low. This line is used for testing and is normally either pulled-up or left open.
HLT	Input, active high. When the head load timing input is high, the 179X assumes that the head is engaged. The signal is normally derived from a monostable driven from the head load output.
RG (X = 1,2,3,4)	Output, active high. This read gate output is used to synchronize an external data separator. In single density mode, this line goes high after two bytes of 00H whereas, in double density mode, it goes high after four bytes of either 00H or FFH.
SSO (X = 5,7)	Side select output, which is controlled by the side compare flag, S. A separate flag, U, is used to update the side select output so that the side select output goes high when U = 1 and low when U = 0.
RCLK	Read clock input derived from the incoming composite data stream from the disk interface.
RAW READ	Composite data stream from the disk interface. This input consists of one negative-going pulse for each flux transition.
HLD	Output, active high. When the head load line is high, the read/write head is loaded against the disk.
TG43	Output, active high. The line goes high whenever the head is positioned above tracks 44 to 76. (Equivalent to the LOW CURRENT input of the 8271.)
WG	Output. The write gate line must be high before data is written to the disk.
WD	Output. The write data output comprises a 200 ns pulse in double density (MFM) mode, or a 400 ns pulse in single density (FM) mode. One pulse is produced for each flux transition.
READY	Active high input, which signals that the disk is ready for data to be read or written. If the line is low, read and write operation is inhibited. The state of the READY line may be examined by reference to bit 7 of the status register.
WF/VFOE	This bi-directional signal line is used to signify write faults at the drive and to enable an external phase-locked data separator. When WG is high, the line operates in WRITE FAULT mode and, if the line goes high, a write command is immediately terminated. When WG is low, the line operates as a VFO ENABLE output. In this case, the line goes low during a read operation after the head has loaded and settled (i.e. HLT goes high). An external pull-up resistor of 10 kohm is normally required.
TRK00	Input, active low. This input goes high when the read/write head is positioned over track 00.
IP	Input, pulsed low. The index pulse input goes low whenever the physical index is located.
WPRT	Input, active low. This state of this line is sampled whenever a write command is received. If the line is found to be low, the write command is aborted and the appropriate status bit is set.
DDEN	Input, active low. This line selects double and single-density modes when respectively low and high.

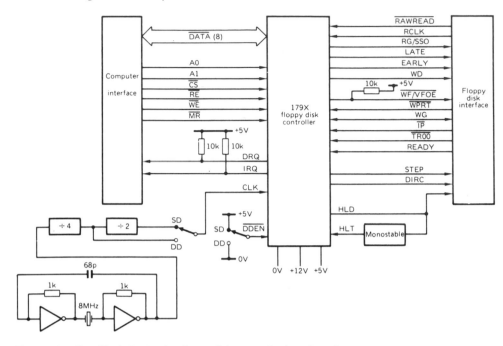

Figure 4.39 Simplified circuit of a floppy disk controller based on the 179X

The basic arrangement of a floppy disk controller using a 179X is shown in Figure 4.39. This circuit can be configured for either single- or double-density operation by means of switches S1 and S2. The head load time delay is produced by a monostable which is optimized for the particular disk drive employed. The output lines to the disk bus are suitably buffered.

Floppy disk drive fault location

Fault diagnosis on disk drives can be just as complex a task as that associated with the CPU and its immediate support circuitry. In addition, it must be recognized that the drive contains highly sophisticated electronic and mechanical components which require both careful and sympathetic handling. Hence it is recommended that, at least for the inexperienced reader, consideration be given to returning drives for overhaul and service by the manufacturer or importer as this may be more cost-effective in the long run. In any event, fault diagnosis within drives should only be carried out when one is certain that the disk interface and controller can be absolved from blame. Thus, whenever the drive in a single-drive system is suspect, it should first be replaced by a unit that is known to be good. In a two-drive system it will, of course, be relatively easy to recognize a failure within one or other of the drives. Even so, it is worth interchanging the two drives before attempting to dismantle the suspect unit.

Great care should be exercised whenever operating on or near the read/write heads. These are the single most expensive component within the drive and are easily damaged. Fortunately, head adjustment is normally only required when either (a) the head itself, or the assembly on which it is mounted, is replaced, or (b) a particular drive is found to be incompatible with others when disks are exchanged.

Alignment invariably requires the use of a special tool in conjunction with an analogue alignment disk and an oscilloscope. The alignment disk usually contains both continuous tones and bursts of tones which are used respectively to adjust radial alignment and azimuth. Alignment disks are normally supplied with full instructions showing typical display patterns and are usually capable of performing the following operations:

1. Locating track 00.
2. Adjusting the index timing and hence motor speed.
3. Checking the skew error of the head positioning mechanism.
4. Aligning the head positioning mechanism with the track centre line.
5. Verifying read output for correct head-to-disk compliance.
6. Checking the head azimuth.

As with cassette drives, the read/write heads of disk units require regular cleaning to ensure trouble-free operation. In use, the disk surface is prone to environmental contaminants such as smoke, airborne dust, oils and fingerprints, and these can be transferred to the read/write heads along with oxide particles from the coating of the disk itself. Periodic cleaning is thus essential and, although this can easily be carried out by untrained personnel using one of several excellent head cleaning kits currently available, head cleaning is rarely given the priority it deserves. Thus, whenever a disk-based system is being serviced, routine cleaning of the heads may be instrumental in avoiding future problems.

The procedure for gaining access to and inspecting a floppy disk drive tends to vary from one manufacturer to another. As usual, one should first switch off and disconnect the mains supply before delving inside the equipment. Drives are normally secured internally by between four and eight machined screws which locate with the diecast chassis of the drive. These screws should be relatively easy to identify and remove but care should be taken when they are replaced since they are sometimes prone to becoming cross-threaded in the diecast material.

Once the drive chassis is free, it can be gently withdrawn from the equipment in order to permit internal inspection. At this stage it may be necessary to release or extend the connecting leads at the rear (34-way ribbon plus 3/4-way power cable). The majority of the drive electronics (read/write amplifiers, bus buffers and drivers) normally occupies a single PCB on the upper side of the drive while the drive motor speed control and stepper motor drivers are consigned to the underside of the unit along with the flywheel and drive belt (if any).

Where the upper PCB occupies the entire area of the drive (as with the original SA400/FD50 series) it will be necessary to remove the PCB retaining screws and raise the board into a vertical position to gain access to the interior of the drive. Provided you are careful it is quite safe for the drive to be operated in this position and thus it is possible to examine the appearance of a loaded disk and check for correct operation of the head load bail arm, head load solenoid, pressure pad, head assembly, and stepping motor.

At this stage, the heads and lead screw assembly may still not be fully visible and, for a complete inspection, it may be necessary to completely or partially remove the head load bail arm. This is accomplished by removing the rear retaining screws and then carefully easing the arm upwards and outwards. It may also be necessary to remove or unclip the head cable during the process. The head load solenoid, pressure pad, head assembly and lead screw should now be clearly visible and can be inspected for signs of damage or wear. Before reassembly, the heads should be thoroughly inspected and cleaned using a cotton bud and proprietary alcohol-based cleaning solvent.

Figure 4.40 Read input circuitry of an FD-50 drive (the head connector is shown in the upper left corner)

```
100 REM ************************************************************
110 REM **                                                        **
120 REM **                  D I S K C H E C K                     **
130 REM **                                                        **
140 REM ************************************************************
150 REM
160 REM                   VERSION 1.2   07/04/84
170 REM
180 REM
190 REM ** INITIALISING **
200 REM
210 CLS
220 S=0: CLEAR 200: DIM B(8)
230 PRINT @0,"DISKCHECK   VERSION 1.2"
240 INPUT "WHICH DRIVE "; DR
250 SS$=STRING$(63,131)
260 REM
270 REM ** INITIAL STATUS CHECK - TEST 1 **
280 REM
290 GOSUB 750
300 GOSUB 900
310 GOSUB 830
320 REM
330 REM ** START DRIVE MOTOR - TEST 2 **
340 REM
350 POKE&H37E0,DR : REM DR = DRIVE NUMBER
360 GOSUB 900
370 GOSUB 830
380 REM
390 REM ** HEAD LOAD - TEST 3 **
```

```
400 REM
410 POKE&H37EC,08 : REM 08 FOR HEAD LOAD
420 GOSUB 900
430 GOSUB 830
440 REM
450 REM ** WRITE DATA - TEST 4 **
460 REM
470 T$="THE QUICK BROWN FOX JUMPS OVER THE LAZY DOG 1234567890"
480 OPEN "O",1,"TESTDAT"
490 PRINT£1,T$
500 PRINT@576,SS$
510 PRINT@640,"W/DATA: ";T$
520 CLOSE 1
530 PRINT@704,SS$
540 GOSUB 900
550 GOSUB 830
560 REM
570 REM ** READ DATA - TEST 5 **
580 REM
590 OPEN "I",1,"TESTDAT"
600 INPUT£1,T$
610 PRINT@768,"R/DATA: ";T$
620 CLOSE 1
630 PRINT@832,SS$
640 GOSUB 900
650 GOSUB 830
660 REM
670 REM ** END ROUTINE **
680 REM
690 PRINT@896, "<E> TO END, <A> TO RUN AGAIN"
700 R$=INKEY$
710 IF R$="" GOTO 700
720 IF R$="E" OR R$="e" CLS: END
730 IF R$="A" OR R$="a" GOTO 190
740 REM
750 REM ** PRINT STATUS REGISTER HEADING **
760 REM
770 PRINT @48,"STATUS REGISTER"
780 PRINT @96,"BIT:      7  6  5  4  3  2  1  0"
790 PRINT @160,"VALUE:"
800 PRINT @224,"TEST:"
810 RETURN
820 REM
830 REM ** PRINT CURRENT STATUS REGISTER **
840 REM
850 S=S+1 : REM UPDATE COUNTER
860 PRINT @(168+(S*64)),B(7);B(6);B(5);B(4);B(3);B(2);B(1);B(0)
870 PRINT @(164+(S*64)),S
880 RETURN
890 REM
900 REM ** GET CURRENT STATUS REGISTER **
910 REM
920 X=PEEK(&H37EC)
930 REM
940 REM ** CONVERT TO BINARY **
950 REM
960 FOR N=0 TO 7: B(N)=X-INT(X/2)*2: X=INT(X/2): NEXT N
970 RETURN
```

Listing 4.1 Simple BASIC program for reading the status register of a floppy disk controller

```
DISKCHECK   VERSION 1.2                         STATUS REGISTER
                             BIT:     7  6  5  4  3  2  1  0
                             VALUE:
                             TEST 1   1  0  0  0  0  0  0  0
                                  2   0  0  0  0  0  0  0  0
                                  3   0  1  1  0  0  0  0  1
                                  4   0  1  1  0  0  0  0  0
                                  5   0  0  0  0  0  0  0  0

W/DATA: THE QUICK BROWN FOX JUMPS OVER THE LAZY DOG 1234567890
--------------------------------------------------------------
R/DATA: THE QUICK BROWN FOX JUMPS OVER THE LAZY DOG 1234567890
--------------------------------------------------------------
<E> TO END, <A> TO RUN AGAIN


DISKCHECK   VERSION 1.2                         STATUS REGISTER
                             BIT:     7  6  5  4  3  2  1  0
                             VALUE:
                             TEST 1   1  0  0  0  0  0  0  0
                                  2   1  0  0  0  0  0  0  0
                                  3   1  0  0  0  0  0  0  1
                                  4   0  1  1  0  0  0  0  0
                                  5   0  0  0  0  0  0  0  0

W/DATA: THE QUICK BROWN FOX JUMPS OVER THE LAZY DOG 1234567890
--------------------------------------------------------------
R/DATA: THE QUICK BROWN FOX JUMPS OVER THE LAZY DOG 1234567890
--------------------------------------------------------------
<E> TO END, <A> TO RUN AGAIN
```

Figure 4.41 Typical screen dump obtained from the program shown in Listing 4.1

Disk controller status

Address (hex)	Byte (hex)	Status 7	6	5	4	3	2	1	0
43E	1	0	0	0	0	0	0	0	1
43F	81	1	0	0	0	0	0	0	1
440	25	0	0	1	0	0	1	0	1
441	0	0	0	0	0	0	0	0	0
442	4	0	0	0	0	0	1	0	0
443	0	0	0	0	0	0	0	0	0

Figure 4.42 Typical output produced by the program of Listing 4.2

For all but the most obvious mechanical faults in disk drives, a software diagnostic test disk is essential. It is rarely possible to make meaningful assessments of the performance of drives without such an aid. Disk diagnostics are available for most quality disk-based systems but these vary widely in sophistication. As a minimum they should be capable of:

(a) Selecting a particular drive and verifying the operation of the disk controller by reading the status register. Simple BASIC programs for displaying the status register of disk

```
DEF  SEG  =  0
CLS
PRINT  "Disk  controller  status"
PRINT  "Address",  "Byte",  "  Status"
PRINT  "(hex)",  "(hex)",  ;
FOR  i  =  7  TO  0  STEP  -1
  PRINT  i;
NEXT  i
PRINT
PRINT
FOR  address  =  &H43E  TO  &H443
  v  =  PEEK(address)
  GOSUB  convert
  PRINT  HEX$(address),  HEX$(v),  ;
  FOR  i  -  7  TO  0  STEP  -1
    PRINT  b(i);
  NEXT  i
  PRINT
NEXT  address
PRINT
END
'
convert:
x  =  v
FOR  n  =  0  TO  7
  b(n)  =  x  -  INT(x  /  2)  *  2
  x  =  INT(x  /  2)
NEXT  n
RETURN
```

Listing 4.2 A simple Microsoft QuickBASIC program that displays the FDC status in an IBM PC or compatible system

controllers are shown in Listings 4.1 and 4.2. Screen dumps obtained from these programs are shown in Figures 4.41 and 4.42 respectively.

(b) Performing step-in and step-out operations and testing for track 00.
(c) Reading and displaying the contents of a selected track.
(d) Writing a particular byte pattern in a selected track (or tracks), then reading and verifying the result. (Figure 4.43 shows the result of carrying out operations (d) and (c) with a typical disk diagnostic.)
(e) Measuring, and displaying, the rotational speed of the disk.

Measurement of the drive motor speed should always be made when disk-based equipment is being serviced since this too can be instrumental in avoiding future problems. Adjustment is invariably provided by means of a small preset potentiometer mounted on the motor speed control PCB. Access to this control is often arranged so that speed adjustment can be carried out without having to dismantle, or even remove, the drive. The drive speed should be within ±3 rpm of 300 rpm and should always be adjusted whenever it is outside this range. With care, it should be possible to adjust the speed to within 0.5 rpm of the nominal 300 rpm.

```
Track  01    Bytes read = 0C31
Sector   TN   SD   SN   SL   CHKSM   DAM   CHKSM
  01     01   00   08   01   CE0E    FB    5C43
  02     01   00   04   01   A34B    FB    5C43
  03     01   00   09   01   FF3D    FB    5C43
  04     01   00   00   01   6787    F8    CAC9
  05     01   00   01   01   56B4    FB    5C43
  06     01   00   06   01   C12D    F8    CAC9
  07     01   00   03   01   34D2    FB    5C43
0000  FFFF FFFF FFFF FFFF FE01 0008 010E CEFF   ~.....N
0010  FFFF FFFF FFFF FFFF FFFF FC00 0000 0000   ¦......
0020  FB00 0102 0304 0506 0708 090A 0B0C 0D0E   (...............
0030  0F10 1112 1314 1516 1718 191A 1B1C 1D1E   ................
0040  1F20 2122 2324 2526 2728 292A 2B2C 2D2E   . !"£$%&' ()*+,-.
0050  2F30 3132 3334 3536 3738 393A 3B3C 3D3E   /0123456789:;<=>
0060  3F40 4142 4344 4546 4748 494A 4B4C 4D4E   ?ƏABCDEFGHIJKLMN
0070  4F50 5152 5354 5556 5758 595A 5B5C 5D5E   OPQRSTUVWXYZ[\]^
0080  5F60 6162 6364 6566 6768 696A 6B6C 6D6E   _'abcdefghijklmn
0090  6F70 7172 7374 7576 7778 797A 7B7C 7D7E   opqrstuvwxyz{¦}~
00A0  7F80 8182 8384 8586 8788 898A 8B8C 8D8E   ................
00B0  8F90 9192 9394 9596 9798 999A 9B9C 9D9E   ................
00C0  9FA0 A1A2 A3A4 A5A6 A7A8 A9AA ABAC ADAE   . !"£$%&' ()*+,-.
00D0  AFB0 B1B2 B3B4 B5B6 B7B8 B9BA BBBC BDBE   /0123456789:;<=>
00E0  BFC0 C1C2 C3C4 C5C6 C7C8 C9CA CBCC CDCE   ?ƏABCDEFGHIJKLMN
00F0  CFD0 D1D2 D3D4 D5D6 D7D8 D9DA DBDC DDDE   OPQRSTUVWXYZ[\]^
0100  DFE0 E1E2 E3E4 E5E6 E7E8 E9EA EBEC EDEE   _'abcdefghijklmn
0110  EFF0 F1F2 F3F4 F5F6 F7F8 F9FA FBFC FDFE   opqrstuvwxyz{¦}~
0120  FF43 5CFF FFFF FFFF FFFF FFFF FFFF FFFF   C\
0130  FFE0 0000 0000 01FE 0100 0401 4BA3 FFFF   '.....~....K£
0140  FFFF FFFF FFFF FFFF FFE0 0000 0000 00FB   '.....(
0150  0001 0203 0405 0607 0809 0A0B 0C0D 0E0F   ................
0160  1011 1213 1415 1617 1819 1A1B 1C1D 1E1F   ................
0170  2021 2223 2425 2627 2829 2A2B 2C2D 2E2F    !"£$%&' ()*+,-./
0180  3031 3233 3435 3637 3839 3A3B 3C3D 3E3F   0123456789:;<=>?
0190  4041 4243 4445 4647 4849 4A4B 4C4D 4E4F   ƏABCDEFGHIJKLMNO
01A0  5051 5253 5455 5657 5859 5A5B 5C5D 5E5F   PQRSTUVWXYZ[\]^_
01B0  6061 6263 6465 6667 6869 6A6B 6C6D 6E6F   'abcdefghijklmno
01C0  7071 7273 7475 7677 7879 7A7B 7C7D 7E7F   pqrstuvwxyz{¦}~
01D0  8081 8283 8485 8687 8889 8A8B 8C8D 8E8F   ................
01E0  9091 9293 9495 9697 9899 9A9B 9C9D 9E9F   ................
01F0  A0A1 A2A3 A4A5 A6A7 A8A9 AAAB ACAD AEAF    !"£$%&' ()*+,-./
0200  B0B1 B2B3 B4B5 B6B7 B8B9 BABB BCBD BEBF   0123456789:;<=>?
0210  C0C1 C2C3 C4C5 C6C7 C8C9 CACB CCCD CECF   ƏABCDEFGHIJKLMNO
0220  D0D1 D2D3 D4D5 D6D7 D8D9 DADB DCDD DEDF   PQRSTUVWXYZ[\]^_
0230  E0E1 E2E3 E4E5 E6E7 E8E9 EAEB ECED EEEF   'abcdefghijklmno
0240  F0F1 F2F3 F4F5 F6F7 F8F9 FAFB FCFD FEFF   pqrstuvwxyz{¦}~
0250  435C FFFF FFFF FFFF FFFF FFFF FFFF FFFF   C\
0260  FF00 0000 0000 0FFE 0100 0901 3DFF FFFF   ......~....=
0270  FFFF FFFF FFFF FFFF FFC0 0000 0000 00FB   Ə.....(
0280  0001 0203 0405 0607 0809 0A0B 0C0D 0E0F   ................
0290  1011 1213 1415 1617 1819 1A1B 1C1D 1E1F   ................
02A0  2021 2223 2425 2627 2829 2A2B 2C2D 2E2F    !"£$%&' ()*+,-./
02B0  3031 3233 3435 3637 3839 3A3B 3C3D 3E3F   0123456789:;<=>?
02C0  4041 4243 4445 4647 4849 4A4B 4C4D 4E4F   ƏABCDEFGHIJKLMNO
02D0  5051 5253 5455 5657 5859 5A5B 5C5D 5E5F   PQRSTUVWXYZ[\]^_
02E0  6061 6263 6465 6667 6869 6A6B 6C6D 6E6F   'abcdefghijklmno
02F0  7071 7273 7475 7677 7879 7A7B 7C7D 7E7F   pqrstuvwxyz{¦}~
0300  8081 8283 8485 8687 8889 8A8B 8C8D 8E8F   ................
0310  9091 9293 9495 9697 9899 9A9B 9C9D 9E9F   ................
```

Figure 4.43 Typical result of diagnostic tests writing and reading a disk track with 256 different bytes in each sector

Figure 4.44 Flywheel of a Teac FD-50 drive showing stroboscopic calibration for 50 Hz (inner) and 60 Hz (outer) neon light sources

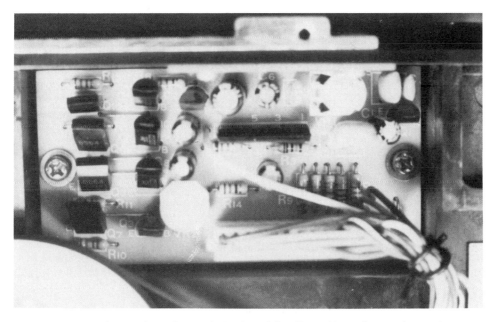

Figure 4.45 Motor drive and speed control circuitry of the FD-50 drive. (The speed control potentiometer, VR1, can be seen in the upper right-hand corner)

Figure 4.46 Typical interior of a modern half-height drive. (The head connecting cable can be clearly seen)

Floppy disk drive stock faults

Symptom	Cause	Action
Drive motor not turning	Power supply defective	Check supply rail
	'Motor on' signal not active	Check disk controller and disk bus (pin 16)
	Defective speed regulator	Check regulator
	Defective cable or connector	Check for d.c. at appropriate points
	Motor defective	Replace motor
Motor turning but disk not moving	Drive belt broken or excessively worn	Replace belt
	Head load bail arm defective	Check arm and adjust or replace
No read or write	Power supply failure	Check supply rails and regulator
	Head not loading	Check head load mechanism and solenoid. Check disk bus (pin 4) and work towards solenoid driver
	Head not stepping	Check stepper motor mechanism. Check disk bus (pin 20) and work towards stepper motor drivers

Floppy disk drive stock faults

Symptom	Cause	Action
	Pressure pad assembly defective	Check pressure pad and spring tension. Renew if necessary
	Index hole not located	Check LED and photo-detector circuitry
	Read amplifier defective	Check read amplifier and move towards disk controller. Check disk bus (pin 30)
	Read/write head open circuit	Check head for continuity, check head connections to PCB
	Drive not selected	Check drive select lines using logic probe
	Read/write head dirty or worn	Check read/write head, clean or replace
Read but no write	Disk write-protected	Remove write-protect tab
	Write-protect circuitry faulty	Check write-protect LED and photo-detector. Check disk bus (pin 26)
	Write amplifier defective	Check for write signal at the read/write head and work backwards to the disk controller. Check disk bus (pin 20)
	Disk controller failure	Check disk bus (pin 24)
Inability to read disks made on other machines	Speed incorrect	Check motor speed and adjust
	Disk format incorrect	Drive and/or DOS incompatible
Intermittent data errors	Speed irregular	Check motor speed regulator
	Worn drive belt (older drives)	Replace belt
	Worn bearing (newer drives)	Replace/lubricate bearing
	Head pressure incorrect	Adjust or renew head load spring mechanism
	Data separation fault	Check data separation circuitry using oscilloscope and test disk
	Flywheel defective	Check for excessive play on flywheel
	Incorrect reading and writing signal levels	Check read/write amplifiers
	Read/write head dirty or worn	Check read/write head, clean or replace
Intermittent data errors with certain disks	Inconsistent magnetic oxide coating	Replace disk
	Disk hub rings damaged or off-centre (5.25" disk)	Replace disk
	Defective disk centre (3.5" disk)	Replace disk
	Excessive internal friction between disk and envelope	Replace disk
Gradual deterioration in performance, increasing number of data errors	Read/write head contaminated with oxide	Clean head
	Read/write head worn	Replace head
	Head assembly out of alignment	Check head azimuth with analogue alignment disk

Floppy disk drive stock faults

Symptom	Cause	Action
	Head carriage worn	Adjust or replace head carriage
	Insufficient head pressure	Adjust pressure pad
	Speed incorrect	Check motor speed and adjust
		Soak test and measure speed
		after drive has reached its
		normal working temperature
Disk damaged	Excessive head pressure	Adjust pressure pad
	Head worn or damaged	Replace head
	Drive spindle and platen out	Re-align
	of alignment	
	Foreign body lodged in	Replace head or pressure pad
	head or pressure pad	

Replacing a floppy disk drive

The procedure for removing and replacing a floppy disk drive is quite straightforward. You should adopt the following procedure:

1. Power-down and gain access to the interior of the system unit or drive enclosure.
2. Locate the drive in question and remove the disk-drive power and floppy disk bus connectors from the rear of the drive.
3. Remove the retaining screws from the sides of the drive (four screws are usually fitted). In the case of the older AT-style system units in which the drives are mounted using plastic guides, you should remove the two retaining screws and metal tabs at the front of the system chassis.
4. Once the drive chassis is free, it can be gently withdrawn from the system unit. Any metal screening can now be removed in order to permit inspection. The majority of the drive electronics (read/write amplifiers, bus buffers and drivers) normally occupies a single PCB on one side of the drive.
5. The head load solenoid, head assembly and mechanical parts should now be clearly visible and can be inspected for signs of damage or wear Before reassembly, the heads should be thoroughly inspected and cleaned using a cotton bud and proprietary alcohol-based cleaning solvent.
6. Re-assemble the system (replacing the drive, if necessary) and ensure that the disk bus and power cables are correctly connected before restoring power to the system.

Take special care when replacing machined screws which locate directly with the diecast chassis of a disk drive. These screws can sometimes become cross-threaded in the relatively soft diecast material. If you are fitting a new drive, you must also ensure that you use screws of the correct length. A screw that is too long can sometimes foul the PCB mounted components.

It is also important to note that a 34-way male PCB header is usually fitted to 3.5" drives and that the matching female IDC connector can easily be attached the wrong way round. You should thus check that the connector has been aligned correctly when replacing drive. Pin-1 (and/or pin-34) is usually clearly marked on the PCB. You should also notice a stripe along one edge of the ribbon cable. This stripe must be aligned with pin-1 on the connector.

Hard disk drives

Like floppy disks, the data stored on a hard disk takes the form of a magnetic pattern stored in the oxide coated surface of a disk. Unlike floppy disks, hard disk drives are sealed in order to prevent the ingress of dust, smoke and dirt particles. This is important since hard disks work to much finer tolerances (track spacing, etc.) than do floppy drives. Furthermore, the read/write heads of a hard disk 'fly' above the surface of the disk when the platters are turning. Due to the high speed of rotation (typically 3600 rev/min) it is essential that none of the read/write heads comes into direct contact with the area of the disk surface used for data storage.

A typical 120 Mbyte IDE drive has two platters which provide four data surfaces. The drive is thus fitted with four read/write heads (one for each data surface). The read/write heads are all operated from the same 'voice coil' actuator so that they step in and out together across the surface of the disk. In addition, the innermost cylinder is designated as a 'landing zone'. No data is stored in this region and thus it provides a safe place for the heads to 'land' and make contact with the disk surface.

When the drive is static or coming up to speed, the heads remain in the landing zone. When sufficient rotational speed has been achieved, the heads leave the surface of the disk and are then stepped across to the active part of the disk surface where reading and writing takes place. Finally, when the disk becomes inactive, the motor ceases to rotate and the heads return to the landing zone where they are 'parked'.

Hard drive types

A variety of different hard disk types are supported by personal computers including ST506 (MFM), RLL, ESDI, and SCSI types. Since they all have different interfacing requirements, it is important to know which type you are dealing with! Typical data transfer rates and capacities for various types of hard disk drive are shown in Table 4.7.

Table 4.7 Typical data transfer rates and capacities for various types of hard disk drive

Drive type	Data transfer rate (bit/sec)	Capacity (Mbyte)
ST506	0.1–1M	10–20
ESDI	1.2–1.8M	40–320
IDE	1–7M	80–340
SCSI	1–2M	80–680
(see page 71)		

The ST506 interface standard

The Shugart ST506 interface standard was popular in the late 1970s and early 1980s and it became the hard disk standard to be used in the first generations of IBM PCs that were supplied with hard disks. The ST506 uses 'modified frequency modulation' (MFM) to digitally encode its data. This method of recording digital information has now been superseded by 'run-length-limited' (RLL) encoding which uses the available disk space more efficiently. Note that MFM ST506 drives are normally formatted with 17 sectors per track whilst RLL drives generally use 26 sectors per track.

When RLL encoding is used, a limit is imposed on the number of consecutive 0 bits that can be recorded before a 1 bit is included. '2,7 RLL' uses strings of between 2 and 7 consecutive 0 bits whilst '3,9 RLL' is based on sequences of between 3 and 9 consecutive 0 bits before a 1 bit is inserted. 2,7 RLL and 3,9 RLL respectively offer a 50% and 100% increase in drive capacity.

ST506 drives, whether MFM or RLL types, require a complex hard disk controller card. Drives are connected to the card by means of two separate ribbon cables; a 34-way cable for control signals and a 20-way cable for data.

ESDI drives

The 'enhanced small device interface' (ESDI) is an updated and improved standard based on the original ST506 interface. ESDI was first introduced by Maxtor in 1983 and its BIOS code is generally software-compatible with the earlier standard. You should note, however, that most ESDI drives are formatted to 32 sectors per track. Like ST506 drives, ESDI units require the services of a separate hard disk controller card. Both the ESDI and ST506 interface standards support up to four physical drives though usually no more than two drives are actually fitted.

IDE drives

'Integrated drive electronics' (IDE) drives are designed to interface very easily with the ISA bus. The interface can either make use of a simple adaptor card (without the complex controller associated with ST506 and ESDI drives) or can be connected directly to the system motherboard where the requisite 40-way IDC connector has been made available by the manufacturer.

In either case, the 40-way ISA bus extension is sometimes known as an 'AT attachment'. This system interface is simply a subset of the standard ISA bus signals and it can support up to two IDE drives in a 'daisy-chain' fashion (i.e., similar to that used for floppy disk drives). This makes IDE drives extremely cost-effective since they dispense with the complex hard disk controller/adaptor card required by their predecessors.

IDE drives are 'low-level formatted' with a pattern of tracks and sectors already in-place when they reach you. This allows them to be formatted much more efficiently; the actual *physical* layout of the disk is hidden from BIOS which only sees the *logical* format presented to it by the integrated electronics. This means that the disk can have a much larger number of sectors on the outer tracks than on the inner tracks. Consequently, a much greater proportion of the disk space is available for data storage.

Formatting a hard disk

Formatting a hard disk is essentially a three-stage process but you don't always have to perform all three stages. The first stage of the process, a 'low-level' or 'physical' format, allows the drive to be configured for a particular hard disk controller card. The low-level format writes tracks and sectors on the magnetic surface and allocates numbers to identify their *physical* position on the disk. At this stage, the sectors may be 'interleaved'.

Interleaving

Although the 17 sectors of an ST-506 compatible hard disk are numbered 1 to 17, there is no reason why the sectors should be numbered *consecutively*. Indeed, there is a very good reason for *not* numbering them in a strict numerical sequence. It is worth attempting to explain this particular point.

A considerable improvement in data transfer rate can be achieved by not attempting to read the sectors of a hard disk in strict physical sequence. This is because the controller transfers a sector at a time and, when it is ready to read the next physical sector it is quite likely that the sector will have already passed under the read/write head. In this case it will be necessary to wait until the disk has completed a further revolution before it is possible to read the next wanted sector. A far better scheme would be to arrange the sectors so that the next wanted sector is one or two sectors further on.

In 1 : 1 interleaving (i.e., no interleaving) the sectors are numbered consecutively around the circumference of the disk. 2 : 1 interleaving numbers the sectors 1,10,2,11,3,12, etc, and 3 : 1 interleaving uses the sequence 1,7,13,2,8, etc.

Performing a low-level format

There are three methods of performing a low-level hard disk format:

(a)   Using formatting software supplied on disk and shipped with a drive and/or controller.
(b)   Using the BIOS set-up program when it includes a 'hard disk' utility.
(c)   Using a formatting program resident within the hard disk controller's ROM.

In the first case, you need only insert the disk in drive A, run the program and follow the on-screen instructions. In the last case, you may have to use a system monitor/debugger (such as Debug) in order to execute the low-level formatting code stored in the disk controller's ROM. In all three cases you must specify information on the drive including its type, number of heads, cylinders, landing zone, etc. You can usually also specify the interleaving that you wish to use.

Partitioning

Once a low-level format has been completed, the disk can be partitioned so that it behaves as several *logical* drives. Partitioning was originally invented to work around one of the early limitations of the DOS provided with IBM PCs and compatibles. These early DOS versions used a 16-bit sector numbering system and thus could only support a hard disk of up to 32 Mbyte.

To put this into context, assume that you have an 80 Mbyte drive in an IBM-compatible system operating under MS-DOS 3.3. The 'primary partition' (C) could have 32 Mbyte with two further 'extended partitions' (D and E) of 24 Mbyte each. Note that, whilst they can be of different sizes, neither of the extended partitions should exceed 32 Mbyte 'in size.

With the advent of MS-DOS 5.0 there is no longer any need to partition a large drive into several smaller logical drives. You can, if you wish, have a single 'primary DOS partition' and no 'extended DOS partitions' (note that MS-DOS 5.0 provides for up to 23 logical drives within the extended DOS partition). The primary DOS partition can occupy the entire drive.

Table 4.8 MS-DOS hard drive partition table

Offset	Size	Field	Purpose
+0	1	Boot indicator	Indicates if partition is startable, as follows:
		Contents (hex)	*Meaning*
		00	Non-startable partition
		80	Startable partition
+1	1	Begin head	Side on which partition starts
+2	1	Begin sector	Sector at which partition starts
+3	1	Begin cylinder	Cylinder at which partition starts
+4	1	System ID	Identifies partition type, as follows:
		Contents (hex)	*Meaning*
		00	Empty partition entry
		01	DOS FAT-12
		02	XENIX
		04	DOS FAT-16
		05	Extended partition
		06	DOS > 32M
		07	HPFS
		64	Novell
		75	PCIX
		DB	CP/M
		FF	BBT
+5	1	End head	Side on which partition ends
+6	1	End sector	Sector at which partition ends
+7	1	End cylinder	Cylinder at which partition ends
+8	4	Relative sectors	Number of sectors before start of partition
+12	4	Number sectors	Number of sectors in partition

Using FDISK in IBM compatible systems

The DOS FDISK utility creates and displays information about partitions and logical drives. It also sets the active partition and allows you to delete partitions and logical drives. FDISK provides simple on-screen instructions. If the drive has been used before, it is worth display-ing the existing partition information before you make any changes.

When you exit FDISK the system will restart and the new options will then take effect. If you have changed the size of the primary DOS partition, FDISK will prompt you to insert an MS-DOS system disk in drive A. After using FDISK you should use the DOS FORMAT command to format any partition that you have created or changed. If you fail to do this DOS will display an 'invalid media' error message.

It is important to note that FDISK destroys all existing files in the partitions that you modify. Thus, if you intend to use FDISK to change the partitions on the hard disk it is vital to backup the user's data to floppy disk.

Lastly, when formatting the primary DOS partition of the hard disk, it is essential to trans-fer the DOS system files by using the /S switch within the FORMAT command. If, for example, you have created a primary DOS partition (C) with two logical drives (D and E) in the extended partition, you should use the following three DOS commands:

```
FORMAT C: /S
FORMAT D:
FORMAT E:
```

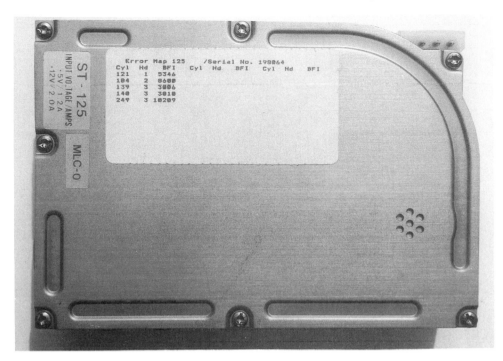

Figure 4.47 Exterior view of the ST-125 hard disk drive

Figure 4.48 Drive electronics of the ST-125 hard disk drive

Figure 4.49 Exterior view of the ST-251 hard disk drive

Figure 4.50 Drive electronics of the ST-251 hard disk drive

Figure 4.51 Interior view of the ST-251 hard disk drive showing the head arm and actuator mechanism

Figure 4.52 Interior view of the ST-251 hard disk drive showing the head arm counterweight

Figure 4.53 Interior view of the ST-251 hard disk drive showing the head actuator

The master boot record

Hard disk drives, like floppy disks, have a boot record which occupies the very first sector of the disk. On hard disks, this is known as the 'master boot record'. Apart from the basic parameter table, the structure of the boot sector is somewhat different from that used for a floppy disk.

The master boot program (starting at byte 0) copies itself to a different location in memory and then inspects the partition table looking for a startable partition. If more than one startable partition exists or any Boot Indicator is not 80 or 0 then DOS will display an 'Invalid Partition Table' error message.

When the partition table has been successfully validated, the boot program obtains the Begin Head, Sector, and Cylinder for the startable partition and reads it from the hard disk to absolute memory location 0000:7C00 in a PC or PC-compatible machine. The last two bytes of the master boot record (55 AA) are then checked before program execution jumps to location 0000:7C00. From this point on startup is identical to booting from a floppy disk on which the operating system has been placed.

Hard drive fault location

Failure of one or more of the read/write heads, the drive electronics, the voice coil actuator, or a major problem with one or more of the disk surfaces can render a hard disk drive inoperable. Furthermore, whilst many of these faults are actually quite simple, specialist tools, test facilities and a 'clean area' are essential if a hard drive is to be successfully repaired.

For this reason, it is wise not to attempt to carry out an internal repair unless you are completely confident that you can dismantle, inspect, repair, align and reassemble the unit without a hitch. If you have any doubts about this it is better to return the unit for special-ist attention. Furthermore, modern drives offer significantly greater amounts of data storage and better overall performance than their predecessors and thus, in many cases, you will not wish to replace an older hard drive with an identical unit. On a 'cost-per-kbyte' basis, modern drives are considerably cheaper than their predecessors.

Hard disk drive stock faults

Symptom	Cause	Action
System will not boot	Boot sector corrupt	Insert system floppy disk and re-boot, check boot sector
No read or write	Power supply failure	Check supply rails and regulator
	Drive not selected	Check drive select lines using logic probe
	Disk controller failure	Check hard disk bus. Replace controller card
Drive access light becomes illuminated but system hangs or reports an error	Voice coil, actuator or drive motor failed	Check hard drive electronics, voice coil and motor drivers
Slow access time	Disk files severely fragmented	Use disk optimiser program to de-fragment disk
	Disk full	Delete unwanted files to create more hard disk space
Disk space progressively reduces for no reason	Boot sector virus	Run virus scan software. Clean all affected files
DOS reports errors on certain files	Run CHKDSK (or equivalent hard disk utility) to check the hard disk for logical errors	Convert any lost chains to files. View files and attempt to recover any lost data
Hard drive noisy	Mechanical problem inside drive	Back-up all important files. Dismantle and inspect drive. If necessary, replace drive
	Worn bearing	As above
Increasing DOS errors as system warms up	Drive low-level formatted when 'cold'	Back-up all important files. Allow system to reach normal working temperature before performing another low-level format
Inability to find/read files previously made	Drive surface and/or heads damaged	Back-up all important files. Perform low-level format (to lock-out damaged sectors). Replace hard drive if low-level format fails.
Directory contains nonsense (including unreasonably large or small file sizes)	Directory or FAT corrupted	Use hard disk recovery program to remake corrupt directory or FAT
Irregular data errors	Speed irregular	Check motor speed regulator

Replacing a hard disk drive

The procedure for removing and replacing a hard disk is very similar to that which applies to a floppy disk drive. The following procedure is recommended:

1. Power-down and gain access to the interior of the system unit.
2. Remove the hard disk's power and data connectors from the rear of the drive.
3. Remove the retaining screws from the sides of the drive (four screws are usually fitted).
4. Once the drive chassis is free, it can be gently withdrawn from the system unit.
5. Re-assemble the system (replacing the drive and, if necessary also the controller card). Ensure that the data and power cables are correctly connected before restoring power to the system.
6. If the drive is new and has not been formatted by the manufacturer or supplier, you will have to perform a 'low-level' format (see page 201). You must then use the DOS FDISK utility (or equivalent) to set-up the partitions and prepare the disk for DOS. Finally you should use the DOS FORMAT command to prepare the disk for data.

It is important to note that, apart from mechanical shock, one of the most common problems with hard disks is related to temperature; drives will often not operate correctly at very low or very high temperatures. This problem can, however, be greatly reduced by ensuring that the hard disk is formatted at the normal working temperature of the machine. Thus, before you attempt to carry out a low-level format, you should wait for between 15 and 20 minutes for the machine's internal temperature to stabilize.

5
Printers

For the serious personal computer user an ability to produce hard copy soon becomes highly desirable and, while the quality of the print produced may be less critical for such applications as program listings or household accounts, any printer worth its salt should be capable of producing near letter-quality copy. Fortunately, a vast range of printers is available to fulfil a wide variety of applications and at costs which currently range from a little more than £100 to well over £2000.

Various techniques are employed for generating printed output ranging from those closely related to the electronic office typewriter using single-sheet paper and impact daisywheels to those requiring rolls of specially coated thermally sensitive paper. Most modern printers are capable of reproducing graphic images as well as producing straightforward text output and recent developments in printers have centred around the introduction of ink-jet and bubble-jet printers as well as those using high-resolution laser, LCD and LED technology.

Despite the emergence of many new printing technologies, the impact dot matrix printer has steadfastly retained a very significant proportion of the market for personal computer printers. These units offer reasonable print quality with a variety of print styles (which may be modified under software control) coupled with an ability to support proportional spacing of the printed characters as well as reproduction of graphic images. Impact dot matrix printers are relatively fast (typically printing at between 50 and 200 characters per second) and are very reasonably priced. To date, sales of dot matrix printers have undoubtedly exceeded sales of all other types of printer. Recently, however, low-cost ink-jet and laser printers have begun to provide a cost-effective alternative to their impact dot matrix counterparts.

Colour printing

Various methods are used to provide colour printing. These include dye sublimation, coloured ribbons, coloured ink cartridges, and wax transfer. This latter technique uses a sheet of thin plastic film coated with panels alternately of yellow, magenta and cyan wax. As the paper passes through the printer, it comes into contact with a matrix of heater elements in the print head which melt pixels of wax from the plastic film. The paper passes three times through the printer, once for each of the colours.

An alternative to this three-colour process (in which black has to be built-up additively) employs an additional panel of black wax coated film. Wax transfer offers cleaner, more vivid colour printing than colour ink-jets or impact dot-matrix printers. Unfortunately, the process is somewhat more complex and more expensive than the two other methods.

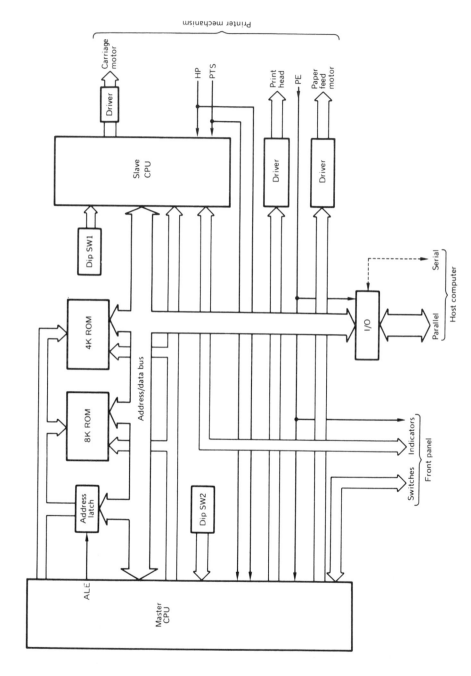

Figure 5.1 Simplified block schematic of a typical printer electronic system

Printer emulation

Printers use a variety of different control character sequences in order to select different printing formats and styles. Regardless of the technology employed for printing, most modern printers will emulate one or more of the most popular types of printer including the IBM Proprinter, HP DeskJet, Epson LQ series, or HP LaserJet 2, 3 or 4.

Dot-matrix printers

Impact dot-matrix printer electronics

The electronics of a dot matrix printer are necessarily complex. So much so, in fact, that it is an ideal application for dedicated microprocesser control! The simplified block schematic of a typical printer electronic system is shown in Figure 5.1. This particular arrangement uses two processors: a master which executes the main control program (including initializing the system, providing hex dump and self-print facilities, generating requests for data input, and controlling the print head) and a slave which controls the position and speed of the head carriage motor.

The control program and character set are contained in two ROMs having capacities of 8K and 4K respectively. Thus, to modify the control program or to change the character set it is only a matter of changing the relevant ROM.

Since the CPU output current is limited, buffers, high-current drivers and power transistor switches are used to interface the print head actuator solenoids and the carriage and

Figure 5.2 Control program and character set ROMs in an Epson MX80 dot matrix printer

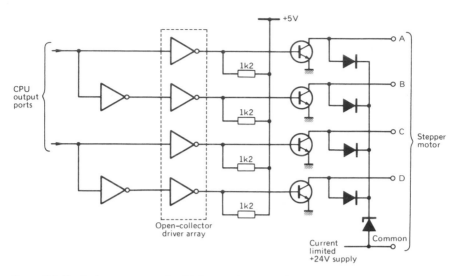

Figure 5.3 Typical arrangement for driving a printer stepping motor

Figure 5.4 8039 master CPU in an Epson MX80 dot matrix printer

Figure 5.5 Switching transistors used for driving stepper motors (left) and print head solenoids (centre) in an Epson MX80 dot matrix printer

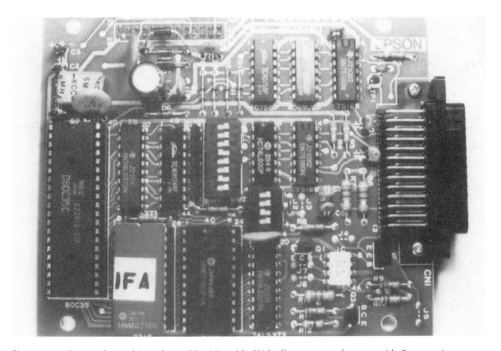

Figure 5.6 Optional serial interface (RS-232) with 2K buffer memory for use with Epson printers

Table 5.1 Pin assignment and typical nomenclature used for a parallel printer interface

Signal pin no.	Return pin no.	Signal	Function
1	19	STROBE	Active low strobe pulse input to read data. Pulse width must be >0.5 μs
2–9	20–27	DATA	Eight TTL-compatible data lines. Each has its own signal ground return for use with twisted pair cables. D0 is connected to pin 2, D1 to pin 3, and so on
10	28	ACKNLG	Output pulsed low for approx. 0.5 μs which signals that data has been received and that the printer is ready to accept more data
	29	BUSY	Output, active high. This line goes high under the following conditions: (a) during data entry (b) during a printing operation (c) in the OFF-LINE state (d) during print error status
12	10	PE	Output, active high. Signals that the printer is out of paper
		SLCT	Output, active high. Signals that the printer is in the selected state.
14	–	AUTO-FEED XT	When this input is low, the paper is automatically fed one line after printing
15	–	n.c.	
16		0V	Logical common
17	–	GND	Chassis ground (normally isolated from the logical common)
18	–	n.c.	
31	–	RESET	When this input is low, the printer controller is reset to its initial state and the print buffer is cleared. A pulse of >50 μs is required
12	–	ERROR	Output, active low. This line goes low under the following conditions: (a) in the PAPER-END state (b) in the OFF-LINE state (c) when a print error has occurred
33	–	GND	Return signal ground
34	–	n.c.	
35	–	0V	Pulled high to indicate the +5 V supply
36	–	SLCT IN	Active low input. Data entry to the printer is only possible when this signal is taken low

line feed stepper motors. DIL switches are used to provide various print options but their functions can often be duplicated under software control from the host computer. Figure 5.3 shows one arrangement for driving a printer stepping motor.

The interface to the host computer generally conforms to the Centronics parallel standard. This interface normally employs a 36-pin Amphenol connector (part number 57-30360) or its equivalent. The pin assignment and typical signal nomenclature for this connector is shown in Table 5.1.

Where a serial interface is provided, it invariably conforms to the RS-232 standard described in Chapter 1. Since such an interface is more complex (both in terms of circuitry and the necessary software driver) than a parallel interface, it is often supplied as an optional accessory. Furthermore, since printing is executed at a relatively slow speed many manufacturers provide internal buffer memories that permit fast downloading of data so that printing can continue while the computer is freed for other work.

Internal control signals of particular note are the home position (HP), position timing signal (PTS), and paper end signal (PE). These are discussed more fully in the next section.

Impact dot-matrix printer mechanics

The printer mechanism generally consists of the following principal components:

1. Head carriage.   The head is mounted on a carriage which travels laterally along two guide shafts. Power is transmitted to the head carriage by means of a toothed belt driven by a stepping motor.

Figure 5.7 Print head (in the extreme right-hand printing position) and carriage motor in an Epson MX80 printer

2. Print head.   The print head is arguably the single most crucial component within the printer. It consists of a set of 5, 7, 9 or 24 pins which are individually fired against a ribbon by means of a solenoid arrangement as shown in Figure 5.8. The needles protrude by about 0.6 mm when actuated, thus striking the inked ribbon and leaving a dot on the surface of the paper. The pin returns to its rest position as a result of the reaction of its impact on the paper and platen and is aided by a return spring within the print head. During printing, the column of dots produced by the head are organized on a matrix basis with 5 × 7, 7 × 9 and 9 × 14 being popular. The formation of a printed character on a simple 5 × 7 matrix is shown in Figure 5.11.

Figure 5.8 Head carriage with print head removed (the head lock lever is clearly visible in its released position)

Figure 5.9 Head carriage stepper motor (left) and paper feed stepper motor on an Epson MX80 dot matrix printer. (The head position timing sensor is located on the small printed circuit board beneath the head carriage stepper motor)

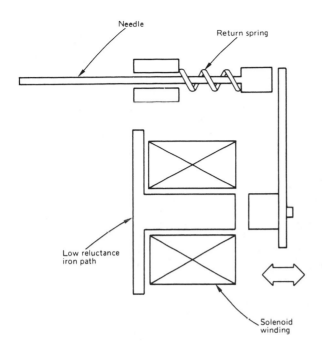

Figure 5.10 Head actuator mechanism

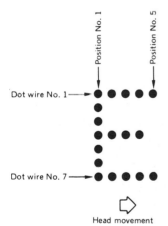

Figure 5.11 Formation of a typical printed character using a 5 × matrix

3. Paper feed mechanism. A stepping motor drives a friction/sprocket wheel assembly, which feeds paper through the printer.

4. Ribbon feed mechanism. When the head carriage timing belt rotates, a train of planetary pinions are rotated causing the ribbon driving gear to feed the inked ribbon, which is normally contained in a cartridge case. The ribbon therefore only feeds when the head carriage is in motion. On most popular types of printer, the ribbon is an endless loop contained in a replaceable cartridge. This has a normal life expectancy of between five and 10 cycles (ribbon revolutions) depending upon the ribbon quality and age.

5. Sensors.   Various sensors are vital to the operation of the printer. These include:
(a) the home position sensor, which is mounted at the extreme left-hand travel of the carriage and generates the HP signal;
(b) the head position sensor, which indicates the current position of the print head and produces the PTS signal; and
(c) the paper sensor which indicates that the supply of paper has become exhausted and provides the PE signal.

Sensors (a) and (b) invariably consist of an LED and photo-detector while sensor (c) is often nothing more than a magnet and a reed-relay.

Figure 5.12 Home position sensor (centre) and planetary ribbon driving gears of an Epson MX80 dot matrix printer

6. Chassis.   A rigid exterior frame to which the carriage assembly, platen, paper feed mechanism, ribbon feed mechanism, etc. are mounted. The chassis is invariably of pressed steel construction.

Routine maintenance of impact dot-matrix printers

As with disk drives, periodic maintenance can be instrumental in preventing faults and optimizing the performance of printers. Routine inspection and cleaning should be performed at intervals of 100 hours or so of operation and should consist of:

1. Removal of paper, dust and any other foreign matter which has accumulated within the printer.
2. A check that the ribbon cartridge is properly seated and that the ribbon itself is in a satisfactory condition.

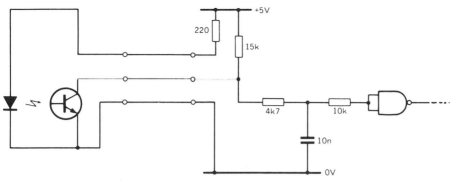

Figure 5.13 Typical arrangement used for generating the home position (HP) and position timing (PTS) signals

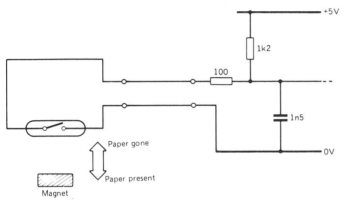

Figure 5.14 Typical arrangement used for generating the paper end (PE) signal

Figure 5.15 Paper end sensor on an Epson MX80 dot matrix printer

3. A check that the paper feed is correctly aligned and that the paper path is unobstructed.
4. An examination of the carriage shafts checking that they are not dry and in need of lubrication.
5. A check that the head gap adjustment is correct and that the printing pressure is normal.

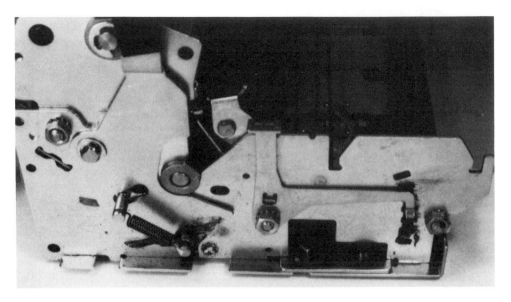

Figure 5.16 Head gap adjusting lever shown in mid-position. (The lever is moved forwards to reduce the head gap and vice versa)

A more rigorous inspection and lubrication should be performed at 600 to 900 hour intervals. This should consist of:

1. Disassembly of the outer case for:
   (a) removal of dust, fluff, and other foreign matter which may have accumulated in the main body of the printer. This is best accomplished by means of a vacuum cleaner fitted with a small nozzle;
   (b) cleaning of the carriage shafts, ribbon driving gear, and planetary pinion using a soft cloth lightly moistened with an isopropyl alcohol or trichloro-trifluoroethane-based cleaning solution. (Note that some solvent-based cleansers are unsuitable for use on plastics and they should therefore not be used on printers. If in doubt, or where the solvent is not clearly identified or labelled, a few drops should be sparingly applied to a point on the inside of the plastic case and any reaction noted. If, after a minute or two, no reaction is apparent, the surface should be wiped clean and, if there is still no adverse effect, the solvent may be considered safe to use.)

2. A thorough internal examination with particular emphasis on:
   (a) alignment of the print head and distance of the print head from the platen;
   (b) condition of the platen, carriage shafts, and ribbon feed mechanism;
   (c) condition of the teeth of the planetary pinions and sprocket transmission gear.

3. Running a 'self-test' (or alternative diagnostic routine) and carefully examining printed characters for such faults as deformation of the print head, missing or jammed needles, etc. Adjusting the gap between the head nose and platen to ensure satisfactory printing. (Note that this adjustment must be carried out using the type of paper normally used in conjunction with the printer in question.)

4. Lubrication of moving parts and, in particular:
    (a) carriage shafts,
    (b) moving parts associated with the head-lock lever,
    (c) hooked part of the head-lock lever spring,
    (d) sliding parts of the head adjusting lever,
    (e) toothed parts of the belt driving pulley,
    (f) gear teeth of the paper feeding motor assembly,
    (g) teeth of the ribbon driving gear and drive gear securing shaft,
    (h) teeth of the planetary pinion and contact point of the planetary pinion, leaf spring, and securing shaft,
    (i) teeth of the sprocket transmission gear,
    (j) contact point between belt-driven pulley flange and plain washer,
    (k) sliding part between paper holding lever and frame,
    (l) sliding parts between release and auxiliary levers,
    (m) contact points between paper feed rollers and roller support shafts.
    Care must be taken not to over-lubricate and any excess lubricant must be removed since this will tend to accumulate dust and dirt and may contaminate the paper, ribbon, and platen.
    Note that, wherever possible, it is advisable to follow the individual manufacturer's recommendations concerning lubrication since different grades of lubricant are often required at various points. If no such information is available, a multi-purpose hydro-carbon-based grease is usually suitable for all sliding components, pivots, and gears. This grease is normally available in tubes of about 50 ml which have an integral applicator nozzle. A lighter machine oil is often preferred for the carriage shafts and this should be applied through the flexible spout fitted to the 50, 100 or 250 ml tin in which the product is supplied.

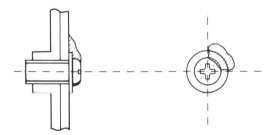

Figure 5.17 Appearance of a correctly bonded screw head

5. A check that sealed and bonded components (such as bolt heads and nuts) are secure. Such bonds have been known to deteriorate when subjected to mechanical shock or may have become broken due to adjustment or component replacement. In either case, a few drops of screw-locking adhesive should be sparingly applied (taking care to avoid blocking the screw head) as shown in Figure 5.17. Bonding points normally include:

(a) platen securing screws
(b) base frame securing screws
(c) head adjusting lever securing nut
(d) paper end sensor securing screws
(e) position timing sensor securing screws
(f) home position sensor securing screws
(g) ribbon mask securing screws
(h) belt tension plate securing screws
(i) terminal board assembly securing screws.

6. Removal of the print head (it is not normally necessary to disconnect the head ribbon cable) and inspection of the nose. The nose should be carefully cleaned using a soft brush and any foreign matter lodged in the gap should be gently removed.

Dismantling impact dot-matrix printers

The typical procedure for dismantling a printer is as follows:

1. Switch 'off' and disconnect the printer from the mains supply.
2. Disconnect the printer from the host computer.
3. Remove the Perspex dust cover.
4. Completely remove the paper from the machine together with the separator (if fitted).
5. Remove the manual paper feed knob. (This is usually accomplished by gripping the knob firmly and pulling away from the printer. If necessary, the process can be aided by inserting the blade of a flat-bladed screwdriver between the knob and the outer case.)
6. Remove the case securing screws (usually four) which are invariably located in wells in either the base or the top-side of the unit. Store the screws in a safe place.
7. Separate the two halves of the outer case moulding, exposing the print mechanism and main printed circuit board. (Note that it may be necessary temporarily to disconnect the control panel to facilitate separation of the two case halves.)

Replacing an impact dot-matrix print head

The print head is a particularly vulnerable component and one which often requires attention. Removal and replacement of the print head is therefore made relatively simple and does not normally require the complete disassembly of the printer. The usual procedure is:

1. Perform stages 1 to 4 of the dismantling procedure above.
2. Manually move the print head to the extreme right-hand end to permit access to the head ribbon cable and head lock lever.
3. Remove the head ribbon cable from the connector on the terminal board below.
4. Turn the head lock lever (usually mounted on the head carriage below and on the left-hand side of the head) clockwise. Carefully remove the print head assembly by pulling gently upwards, and away from the printer.
5. The replacement print head can now be fitted by adopting the reverse of the above procedure.

Impact dot-matrix printer fault location

Faults arising within printers may be either electronic or mechanical in nature. In either case, one should first refer to the 'self-test' facility found on most printers, which is often selected by applying power with the line feed button depressed. Some printers also provide audible warning indications of certain types of fault, which usually include abnormalities of the print head or failure of one or more of the print head driver transistors.

The following stock faults cover the majority of problems associated with dot matrix printers together with some which are also appropriate to daisywheel and ink-jet types. A typical printer test routine written in BASIC is shown in Listing 5.1. This program provides the user with the option of sending to the printer either the normal ASCII character set or a string entered from the keyboard. Various print options are also incorporated, as is a continuous test facility. The control codes are relevant to the popular Epson MX80 series of printers but may be easily modified to suit other printers. Typical printout from the program is shown in Figures 5.18 and 5.19.

```
100 REM ******************************************
110 REM **                                      **
120 REM **      P R I N T E R    C H E C K       **
130 REM **                                      **
140 REM ******************************************
150 REM
160 REM              VERSION  1.0   27/04/84
170 REM
180 REM ** INITIALISING **
190 REM
200 CLS: CLEAR 5000
210 REM
220 REM ** DISPLAY MENU **
230 REM
240 CLS: PRINT TAB(22) "PRINTER CHECK"
250 PRINT TAB(22) "-------------"
260 PRINT: PRINT TAB(26) "MENU"
270 PRINT TAB(16) "<1>    PRINT ASCII CHARACTER SET"
280 PRINT TAB(16) "<2>    PRINT FROM KEYBOARD"
290 PRINT TAB(16) "<3>    PRINT CONTINUOUSLY"
300 PRINT TAB(16) "<4>    EXIT THE PROGRAM"
310 PRINT: PRINT TAB(16) "ENTER YOUR CHOICE...."
320 C$=INKEY$
330 IF C$="" GOTO 320
340 IF ASC(C$)<48 OR ASC(C$)>53 THEN 320
350 C=ASC(C$)-48
360 ON C GOTO 370,490,600,680
370 REM
380 REM ** ASCII CHARACTER SET ROUTINE **
390 REM
400 GOSUB 730
410 CLS: PRINT "ASCII CHARACTER SET"
420 FOR D=32 TO 63
430 FOR I=0 TO 64 STEP 32
440 LPRINT D+I;CHR$(D+I),
450 NEXT I
460 LPRINT
470 NEXT D
480 GOTO 210
490 REM
500 REM ** KEYBOARD PRINT ROUTINE **
510 REM
520 GOSUB 730
530 CLS: PRINT "KEYBOARD PRINT ROUTINE"
540 PRINT: PRINT "ENTER THE STRING TO BE PRINTED"
550 PRINT "USING NOT MORE THAN 32 CHARACTERS"
560 INPUT SP$
570 IF LEN(SP$)>32 THEN SP$=LEFT$(SP$,32)
580 FOR N=1 TO 8: LPRINT SP$: NEXT N
590 GOTO 220
600 REM
610 REM ** CONTINUOUS PRINT ROUTINE **
```

```
620 REM
630 GOSUB 730
640 CLS: PRINT "CONTINUOUS PRINT ROUTINE"
650 PRINT: PRINT "PRESS <BREAK> TO ABORT"
660 FOR PC=64 TO 127: P$=STRING$(64,PC): LPRINT P$: NEXT PC
670 GOTO 660
680 REM
690 REM ** EXIT PROGRAM **
700 REM
710 LPRINT CHR$(27); CHR$(70): LPRINT CHR$(18)
720 CLS: END
730 REM
740 REM ** SET PRINTER SUBROUTINE **
750 REM
760 CLS: PRINT "SET PRINTER ROUTINE"
770 PRINT: PRINT "TYPE:-"
780 PRINT "      <C> FOR CONDENSED"
790 PRINT "      <E> FOR EMPHASIZED"
800 PRINT "      <N> FOR NORMAL"
810 PRINT "ENTER YOUR CHOICE...."
820 R$=INKEY$
830 IF R$="" GOTO 820
840 IF R$="C" OR R$="c" LPRINT CHR$(15): RETURN
850 IF R$="E" OR R$="e" LPRINT CHR$(27);CHR$(69): RETURN
860 IF R$="N" OR R$="n" LPRINT CHR$(27);CHR$(70): LPRINT CHR$(18): RETURN
870 GOTO 820
```

Listing 5.1 BASIC program for checking a printer (control codes are relevant to the MX80 series of printers)

32	64 @	96 `
33 !	65 A	97 a
34 "	66 B	98 b
35 £	67 C	99 c
36 $	68 D	100 d
37 %	69 E	101 e
38 &	70 F	102 f
39 '	71 G	103 g
40 (	72 H	104 h
41)	73 I	105 i
42 *	74 J	106 j
43 +	75 K	107 k
44 ,	76 L	108 l
45 -	77 M	109 m
46 .	78 N	110 n
47 /	79 O	111 o
48 0	80 P	112 p
49 1	81 Q	113 q
50 2	82 R	114 r
51 3	83 S	115 s
52 4	84 T	116 t
53 5	85 U	117 u
54 6	86 V	118 v
55 7	87 W	119 w
56 8	88 X	120 x
57 9	89 Y	121 y
58 :	90 Z	122 z
59 ;	91 [	123 {
60 <	92 \	124 ¦
61 =	93]	125 }
62 >	94 ^	126 ~
63 ?	95 _	127

Figure 5.18 Typical print-out obtained from the program of Listing 5.1 when emphasized printing of the ASCII character set is selected

```
ɑɑɑɑɑɑɑɑɑɑɑɑɑɑɑɑɑɑɑɑɑɑɑɑɑɑɑɑɑɑɑɑɑɑɑɑɑɑɑɑɑɑɑɑɑɑɑɑɑɑɑɑɑɑɑɑɑɑɑ
AAAAAAAAAAAAAAAAAAAAAAAAAAAAAAAAAAAAAAAAAAAAAAAAAAAAAAAAAAAAA
BBBBBBBBBBBBBBBBBBBBBBBBBBBBBBBBBBBBBBBBBBBBBBBBBBBBBBBBBBBBBB
CCCCCCCCCCCCCCCCCCCCCCCCCCCCCCCCCCCCCCCCCCCCCCCCCCCCCCCCCCCCC
DDDDDDDDDDDDDDDDDDDDDDDDDDDDDDDDDDDDDDDDDDDDDDDDDDDDDDDDDDDDDD
EEEEEEEEEEEEEEEEEEEEEEEEEEEEEEEEEEEEEEEEEEEEEEEEEEEEEEEEEEEEE
FFFFFFFFFFFFFFFFFFFFFFFFFFFFFFFFFFFFFFFFFFFFFFFFFFFFFFFFFFFFF
GGGGGGGGGGGGGGGGGGGGGGGGGGGGGGGGGGGGGGGGGGGGGGGGGGGGGGGGGGGGG
HHHHHHHHHHHHHHHHHHHHHHHHHHHHHHHHHHHHHHHHHHHHHHHHHHHHHHHHHHHHH
IIIIIIIIIIIIIIIIIIIIIIIIIIIIIIIIIIIIIIIIIIIIIIIIIIIIIIIIIIIII
JJJJJJJJJJJJJJJJJJJJJJJJJJJJJJJJJJJJJJJJJJJJJJJJJJJJJJJJJJJJJJ
KKKKKKKKKKKKKKKKKKKKKKKKKKKKKKKKKKKKKKKKKKKKKKKKKKKKKKKKKKKKKK
LLLLLLLLLLLLLLLLLLLLLLLLLLLLLLLLLLLLLLLLLLLLLLLLLLLLLLLLLLLLL
MMMMMMMMMMMMMMMMMMMMMMMMMMMMMMMMMMMMMMMMMMMMMMMMMMMMMMMMMMMMMM
NNNNNNNNNNNNNNNNNNNNNNNNNNNNNNNNNNNNNNNNNNNNNNNNNNNNNNNNNNNNNN
OOOOOOOOOOOOOOOOOOOOOOOOOOOOOOOOOOOOOOOOOOOOOOOOOOOOOOOOOOOOOO
PPPPPPPPPPPPPPPPPPPPPPPPPPPPPPPPPPPPPPPPPPPPPPPPPPPPPPPPPPPPPP
QQQQQQQQQQQQQQQQQQQQQQQQQQQQQQQQQQQQQQQQQQQQQQQQQQQQQQQQQQQQQQ
RRRRRRRRRRRRRRRRRRRRRRRRRRRRRRRRRRRRRRRRRRRRRRRRRRRRRRRRRRRRRR
SSSSSSSSSSSSSSSSSSSSSSSSSSSSSSSSSSSSSSSSSSSSSSSSSSSSSSSSSSSSSS
TTTTTTTTTTTTTTTTTTTTTTTTTTTTTTTTTTTTTTTTTTTTTTTTTTTTTTTTTTTTTT
UUUUUUUUUUUUUUUUUUUUUUUUUUUUUUUUUUUUUUUUUUUUUUUUUUUUUUUUUUUUUU
VVVVVVVVVVVVVVVVVVVVVVVVVVVVVVVVVVVVVVVVVVVVVVVVVVVVVVVVVVVVVV
WWWWWWWWWWWWWWWWWWWWWWWWWWWWWWWWWWWWWWWWWWWWWWWWWWWWWWWWWWWWWW
XXXXXXXXXXXXXXXXXXXXXXXXXXXXXXXXXXXXXXXXXXXXXXXXXXXXXXXXXXXXXX
YYYYYYYYYYYYYYYYYYYYYYYYYYYYYYYYYYYYYYYYYYYYYYYYYYYYYYYYYYYYYY
ZZZZZZZZZZZZZZZZZZZZZZZZZZZZZZZZZZZZZZZZZZZZZZZZZZZZZZZZZZZZZZ
ɛɛɛɛɛɛɛɛɛɛɛɛɛɛɛɛɛɛɛɛɛɛɛɛɛɛɛɛɛɛɛɛɛɛɛɛɛɛɛɛɛɛɛɛɛɛɛɛɛɛɛɛɛɛɛɛɛɛɛɛ
\\\\\\\\\\\\\\\\\\\\\\\\\\\\\\\\\\\\\\\\\\\\\\\\\\\\\\\\\\\\\\
```

Figure 5.19 Typical print-out obtained from the program of Listing 5.1 when emphasized continuous printing is selected

As a further example, the Microsoft QuickBASIC program shown in Listing 5.2 can be used in conjunction with an IBM PC or compatible system. The program has been designed for an Epson printer (or one which supports Epson emulation) and it prints both the standard (ASCII) and extended (non-ASCII) character sets (characters corresponding to codes from 32 to 127 and 128 to 255 respectively). In addition, the program will print directly from the keyboard, send line feed and form feed characters, exercise the printer continuously, and print 'style sheets' for the printer concerned.

The 'setup' option (press <S>) allows users to select the required print style and repeat any of the main menu tests, as required. The 'setup' option provides a number of options including condensed, double strike, emphasized, italic, normal, subscript, and superscript print modes (and allowable combinations of these basic styles).

```
'*****************************************************
'**                                               **
'**  Name:      PRINTER.BAS     Version: 0.15      **
'**  Function: Checks Epson compatible printers    **
'**  Language: Microsoft QuickBASIC                **
'**  Notes:    Use parallel printer port LPT1      **
'*****************************************************
'
' Initialise
'
ON ERROR GOTO warning
SCREEN 0
COLOR 15, 1
ul$ = STRING$(31, CHR$(205))
'
' Check printer is on-line and ready
```

```
DEF SEG = &H40
status& = PEEK(9) * 256 + PEEK(8) + 1
IF INP(status&) <> 223 THEN
  CLS
  PRINT " Printer not ready!"
  DO
  LOOP UNTIL INP(status&) = 223
END IF
DEF SEG
' Reset printer to start
GOSUB cancel
' Set up print style flags
nf$ = "*": cf$ = "": bf$ = "": ef$ = ""
if$ = "": sbf$ = "": spf$ = ""
'
' Display main menu
'
DO
main:
CLS
PRINT ul$
PRINT " PRINTER CHECK"
PRINT ul$; ""
PRINT " Select option..."
PRINT " [A] = print standard ASCII character set"
PRINT " [E] = print extended character set"
PRINT " [K] = print from keyboard"
PRINT " [L] = send line feed"
PRINT " [F] = send form feed"
PRINT " [C] = continuous printing"
PRINT " [P] = print style check sheet"
PRINT " [S] = setup printer"
PRINT " [Q] = quit"
DO
  r$ = UCASE$(INKEY$)
LOOP UNTIL r$   "" AND INSTR("AEKLFCPSQ", r$)
IF r$ = "Q" THEN GOSUB cancel: CLS : END
'
PRINT ul$
IF r$ = "A" THEN GOSUB standard
IF r$ = "E" THEN GOSUB extended
IF r$ = "K" THEN GOSUB keyboard
IF r$ = "L" THEN GOSUB linefeed
IF r$ = "F" THEN GOSUB formfeed
IF r$ = "C" THEN GOSUB continuous
IF r$ = "P" THEN GOSUB style
IF r$ = "S" THEN GOTO setup
LOOP
'
standard:
PRINT " Standard ASCII character set..."
LPRINT
LPRINT "Standard ASCII character set..."
LPRINT
FOR char = 32 TO 79
  LPRINT CHR$(char);
NEXT char
LPRINT
FOR char = 80 TO 127
  LPRINT CHR$(char);
```

```
NEXT char
LPRINT
RETURN
'
extended:
PRINT " Extended character set..."
LPRINT
LPRINT "Extended character set (non-ASCII)..."
LPRINT
FOR char = 128 TO 191
  LPRINT CHR$(char);
NEXT char
LPRINT
FOR char = 192 TO 255
  LPRINT CHR$(char);
NEXT char
LPRINT
RETURN
'
keyboard:
PRINT " Printing from keyboard."
PRINT " Press [#] to quit..."
PRINT ul$
LPRINT
DO
  LOCATE , , 1   'turn cursor on for text entry
  r$ = INPUT$(1)
  IF r$ = "#" THEN
    LOCATE , , 0
    LPRINT
    GOSUB waitkey
    RETURN
  END IF
  PRINT r$;
  LPRINT r$;
LOOP
'
linefeed:
PRINT " Sending line feed..."
LPRINT CHR$(13);
RETURN
'
formfeed:
PRINT " Sending form feed..."
LPRINT CHR$(12);
RETURN
'
continuous:
PRINT " Continuous printing."
PRINT " Press [#] to quit..."
PRINT ul$
LPRINT
DO
  r$ = INKEY$
  LPRINT "H";
LOOP WHILE r$ <> "#"
LPRINT
RETURN
'
style:
PRINT " Printing style check sheet..."
```

```
GOSUB cancel
LPRINT CHR$(12);
FOR lin% = 1 TO 4
  LPRINT
NEXT
LPRINT STRING$(64, "_")
LPRINT
LPRINT "Style check sheet: "; TIME$; "   "; DATE$
LPRINT
LPRINT STRING$(64, "_")
LPRINT
test$ = ""
FOR char = 1 TO 40
  test$ = test$ + CHR$(char + 64)
NEXT char
' normal mode
GOSUB cancel
LPRINT "Normal:       "; test$
LPRINT
' condensed mode
LPRINT CHR$(15);
LPRINT "Condensed:    "; test$
LPRINT
GOSUB cancel
' double-strike mode
LPRINT CHR$(27); "G";
LPRINT "Double-strike: ";    test$
LPRINT
GOSUB cancel
' italic mode
LPRINT CHR$(27); "4";
LPRINT "Italic:       "; test$
LPRINT
GOSUB cancel
' emphasized mode
LPRINT CHR$(27); "E"
LPRINT "Emphasized:   "; test$
LPRINT
GOSUB cancel
' superscript mode
LPRINT CHR$(27); "S"; "0";
LPRINT "Superscript:  "; test$
LPRINT
GOSUB cancel
' subscript mode
LPRINT CHR$(27); "S"; "1";
LPRINT "Subscript:    "; test$
LPRINT
GOSUB cancel
LPRINT
LPRINT STRING$(64, "_")
LPRINT CHR$(12);
RETURN
'
setup:
DO
  '
  '  Display setup menu
  '
  CLSPRINT ul$
  PRINT" PRINTER SETUP"
```

```
      PRINT  ul$;  ""
      PRINT  " Select  option..."
      PRINT  " [C]  =  condensed  print       ";  cf$
      PRINT  " [B]  =  double  strike ";  bf$
      PRINT  " [E]  =  emphasized        ";  ef$
      PRINT  " [I]  =  italic  print    ";  if$
      PRINT  " [N]  =  normal  print    ";  nf$
      PRINT  " [S]  =  subscript        ";  sbf$
      PRINT  " [T]  =  superscript      ";  spf$
      PRINT  " [X]  =  exit  to  main  menu"
   DO
      r$  =  UCASE$(INKEY$)
   LOOP  UNTIL  r$  <>  ""  AND  INSTR("CBENISTX",  r$)
   IF  r$  =  "X"  THEN  GOTO  main
   '
   PRINT  ul$
   IF  r$  =  "C"  THEN  LPRINT  CHR$(15);  :  cf$  =  "*":  nf$  =  ""
   IF  r$  =  "B"  THEN  LPRINT  CHR$(27);  "G";  :  bf$  =  "*":  nf$  =  ""
   IF  r$  =  "E"  THEN  LPRINT  CHR$(27);  "E";  :  ef$  =  "*":  nf$  =  ""
   IF  r$  =  "I"  THEN  LPRINT  CHR$(27);  "4";  :  if$  =  "*":  nf$  =  ""
   IF  r$  =  "N"  THEN
      GOSUB  cancel
      nf$  =  "*"
      cf$  =  "":  bf$  =  "":  ef$  =  "":  if$  =  "":  sbf$  =  "":  spf$  =  ""
   END  IF
   IF  r$  =  "S"  THEN
      LPRINT  CHR$(27);  "S";  "0";
      sbf$  =  "*":  spf$  =  "":  nf$  =  ""
   END  IF
   IF  r$  =  "T"  THEN
      LPRINT  CHR$(27);  "S";  "1";
      spf$  =  "*":  sbf$  =  "":  nf$  =  ""
      END  IF
   LOOP
   '
   cancel:
   LPRINT  CHR$(18);  :  cf$  =  ""  ' cancel  condensed  mode
   LPRINT  CHR$(27);  "F";  :  ef$  =  ""    ' cancel  emphasized  mode
   LPRINT  CHR$(27);  "H";  :  bf$  =  ""    ' cancel  double  strike  mode
   LPRINT  CHR$(27);  "5";  :  if$  =  ""    ' cancel  italic  mode
   LPRINT  CHR$(27);  "T";  :  sbf$  =  "":  spf$  =  "":  ' cancel  sub/super
   RETURN
   '
   waitkey:
   PRINT  ul$
   PRINT  " Press  any  key  to  continue..."
   DO
      r$  =  INKEY$
   LOOP  UNTIL  r$  <>  ""
   RETURN
   '
   warning:
   PRINT  ul$
   PRINT  " An  error  has  occurred!"
   GOSUB  waitkey
   RESUME  main
```

Listing 5.2 Microsoft QuickBASIC program for testing an Epson-compatible printer used in conjunction with an IBM PC or compatible system

Impact dot-matrix printer stock faults

Symptom	Cause	Action
Printer non-functional. Controls and indicators inoperative	Mains input fuse blown	Check and replace. If fuse still blows check input filter, mains transformer, and power supply
	Mains switch defective	Disconnect from mains supply and test mains switch for continuity
	Input filter defective	Check filter inductors for continuity
	Mains transformer open circuit	Check resistance of winding with an ohmmeter. (Typical values of primary and secondary winding resistance are 40 ohm and 1 ohm respectively)
	Power supply defective	Check individual raw d.c. rails. Check rectifiers and regulators
Head carriage moves but no characters are printed	Head activating pulse absent or too narrow	Check the head driving pulse using an oscilloscope (see Figure 5.20). Check the head pulse monostable and/or the head trigger from the master CPU (see Figure 5.20). Check positive supply rail to head driver transistors
	Incorrect head gap	Check and adjust
Head carriage moves but printing is faint or inconsistent	Incorrect head gap	Check and adjust
	Worn ribbon	Replace ribbon
Head carriage moves but one or more of the dot positions is missing	Defective head driver or open circuit print head	Check the waveform at the collector and base of each driver transistor (see Figure 5.20). If any collector waveform is found to be permanently high while the base is normal, remove the transistor, test and replace. If any collector waveform is found to be permanently low while the base is normal, disconnect the print head ribbon cable and measure the resistance of the actuator solenoid in question (typically 22 ohm). Replace the print head if the actuator solenoid is found to be open circuit, otherwise remove the driver transistor, test and replace .
	Defective print head	If all waveforms are normal and all actuator solenoids measure approximately 22 ohm, it is possible that one or more of the needles has become seized or broken. It will then be necessary to remove and replace the print head. A substitution test should thus be carried out
	Defective driver or buffer	If one or more of the base waveforms is incorrect, check the driver using an oscilloscope and work backwards to the master CPU

Impact dot-matrix printer stock faults *continued*

Symptom	Cause	Action
Head carriage does not move, 'out of paper' indicator is illuminated	Paper end detector faulty	Check PE signal and paper end sensor
Head carriage does not move or moves erratically	Timing belt broken or worn Timing belt tension incorrect Timing sensor defective	Check and replace Adjust tension plate assembly Check PTS signal. Check position timing sensor
	Defective carriage motor or driver transistor	Check waveforms at the collector of the four carriage motor driver transistors and verify the correct phase relationship (see Figure 5.21). If one of the collector waveforms is permanently high whilst the base waveform is normal, remove, test and replace the transistor in question. If one of the collector waveforms is permanently low while the base waveform is normal, check the resistance of the relevant winding on the stepper motor (typically 40 to 50 ohm). If necessary compare with values obtained from the other windings. Remove and replace the carriage motor if any one of the windings is found to be abnormal, otherwise check the driver transistor for a collector-emitter short-circuit
	Defective driver or buffer	If one or more of the base waveforms is incorrect, check the driver using an oscilloscope and work backwards to the slave CPU
Paper feed abnormal or not feeding at all	Defective paper release mechanism or sprocket drive Defective line feed motor or driver transistor	Check friction feed and sprocket drive assembly. Adjust or replace. Check waveforms at the collector and base of each of the four line feed motor driver transistors and verify the correct phase relationship (see Figure 5.21). If one of the collector waveforms is permanently high while the base waveform is normal, remove, test and replace the transistor in question. If one of the collector waveforms is permanently low while the base is normal, check the resistance of the relevant winding on the line feed stepper motor (typically 40 to 50 ohm). If necessary, compare with values obtained from the other windings. Remove and replace the line feed motor if any of the windings is found to be abnormal, otherwise check the

Impact dot-matrix printer stock faults *continued*

Symptom	Cause	Action
	Defective driver or buffer	driver transistor for a collector-emitter short-circuit
		If one or more of the base waveforms is incorrect, check the driver with an oscilloscope and work backwards to the CPU
Printer executes 'self-test' but will not accept printing instructions from the host computer	Interface faulty	Check interface cable and connectors. Check interface circuitry and, in particular, the BUSY (pin 11) and ERROR (pin 32) status signal lines
Abnormal indication on switch panel (e.g. 'LF', 'FF' or 'OFF-LINE' switches inoperative)	Control switch or indicator defective	Remove and check switch panel. Check switch panel connector and interconnecting cable to main PCB. Clean or replace any defective switch. Test and replace any defective switch or indicator.

Laser printers

In recent years laser printers have become increasingly attractive as a cost-effective means of producing high quality printed output. Most modern laser printers will provide printing resolutions of 300 dots per inch (d.p.i.) whilst some can operate at 600 and even 1200 d.p.i.

Cut sheet paper is fed into the printer by means of rollers which operate on a paper input tray. Within the printer, a focused laser beam and a rotating mirror are used to draw, line by line, an image of the page on a photosensitive drum. The drum usually rotates by 1/300th of an inch as each line of the image is built up.

The image present on the drum comprises a pattern of electrostatic charges which attracts and retains the fine particles of black toner. A piece of electrostatically charged paper (charged by passing against a fine wire to which a high voltage is applied) is then rolled against the drum. In this process, toner is transferred from the OPC drum to the paper. It is then fused into place by heated rollers.

The rotation of the drum then brings its surface next to a thin wire called the corona wire, which creates a positive field that returns the entire surface of the drum to its original negative charge before the next revolution begins. The paper, with its fused image, then exits from the printer into a paper collection tray. The principal internal and external features of a modern laser printer are shown in Figures 5.22 and 5.23.

Laser printer fault location

Like their impact dot matrix counterparts, faults arising within laser printers may be either electronic or mechanical in nature. In either case, one should first refer to the 'self-test' facility or to the error messages provided on the front-panel display.

The following stock faults cover the majority of problems associated with laser printers. The printer test routines described earlier (e.g. that shown in Listing 5.2) may be used to

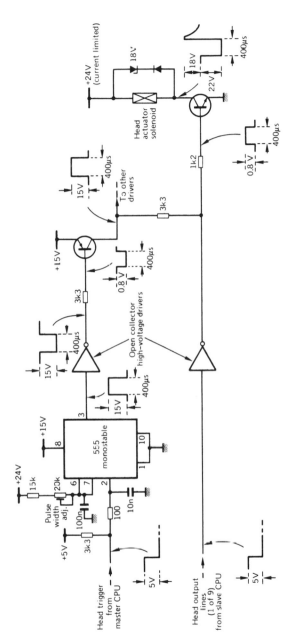

Figure 5.20 Typical arrangement used for driving the head actuator solenoids

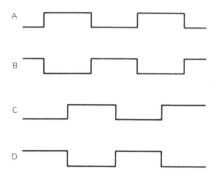

Figure 5.21 Typical phase relationship between the waveforms provided by the head carriage and line feed stepper motors

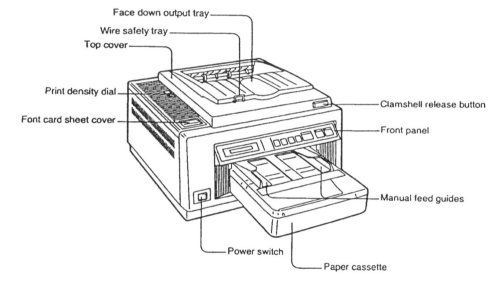

Figure 5.22 Principal external features of a modern laser printer

test a laser printer provided Epson emulation is first selected using the front-panel controls.

Laser printers (particularly those used relatively heavily) need regular maintenance if they are to continue to operate reliably. Most manufacturers recommend a routine service and thorough cleaning of the paper feed path and transfer surfaces at intervals ranging from 15 000 to 20 000 printed pages. Ozone filters and transfer units (corona wires and fusers) should also be inspected (and, if necessary replaced) at this time. Routine maintenance procedures (such as cleaning the corona wire) should, of course, be carried out with reference to the manufacturer's operation and/or service manuals.

Routine maintenance of laser printers

Routine laser printer maintenance usually involves the following steps:
1. Remove power from the printer, disconnect from the host computer and open the clam

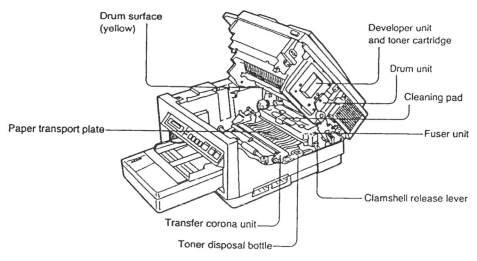

Figure 5.23 Principal internal features of a modern laser printer

---

Style check sheet: 18:41:42   09-11-1993

Normal: ABCDEFGHIJKLMNOPQRSTUVWXYZ[\]^_`abcdefgh

Condensed: ABCDEFGHIJKLMNOPQRSTUVWXYZ[\]^_`abcdefgh

Double-strike: ABCDEFGHIJKLMNOPQRSTUVWXYZ[\]^_`abcdefgh

Italic: *ABCDEFGHIJKLMNOPQRSTUVWXYZ[\]^_`abcdefgh*

Emphasized: ABCDEFGHIJKLMNOPQRSTUVWXYZ[\]^_`abcdefgh

Superscript: ABCDEFGHIJKLMNOPQRSTUVWXYZ[\]^_`abcdefgh

Subscript: ABCDEFGHIJKLMNOPQRSTUVWXYZ[\]^_`abcdefgh

Figure 5.24 Laser printed output from the program of Listing 5

---

shell.
2.   Remove all paper, dust, toner and any other foreign matter which has accumulated within the printer.
3.   Replace the ozone filter.
4.   Wipe all surfaces (including rollers) along the paper path with a soft, dry cloth.

5. Check that the OPC drum and toner cartridges are correctly seated.
6. Examine rollers, drive wheels and gear teeth for damage or wear.
7. Carefully clean the corona wire using a cotton swab.
8. Reassemble the printer and perform a printer self-test to check operation.

Laser printer stock faults

Symptom	Cause	Action
Printer non-functional. Controls and indicators inoperative	Mains input fuse blown	Check and replace. If fuse still blows check input filter, mains transformer, and power supply
	Mains switch defective	Disconnect from mains supply and test mains switch for continuity
	Input filter defective	Check filter inductors for continuity
	Power supply defective	Check individual raw d.c. rails Check rectifiers and regulators
Printer non-functional 'Not Ready' message appears	Clam shell not closed	Check clam shell is closed
	Toner cartridge empty or not fitted correctly	Check toner cartridge
	OPC drum not fitted correctly	Check OPC drum
	Input paper tray not present	Check input paper tray
Printer non-functional 'Paper Jam' message displayed	Output paper tray full	Check output paper tray
	Paper feed path blocked	Check paper feed path and remove blockage
Printer non-functional 'Toner Out' message displayed	Toner cartridge empty	Replace toner cartridge
Printer non-functional 'Paper Out' message displayed	Input paper tray empty	Place paper in input tray
Printer non-functional 'Invalid Font' message displayed	Font card missing or faulty	Check font card is correctly located
Paper will not feed	Input paper tray not located correctly	Check position of paper tray Push tray fully home
	Incorrect paper source	Select correct paper source
Paper jams frequently	Incorrect roller pressure	Check paper feed path and roller pressure.
	Paper still present in feed path	Check paper feed path and remove any paper or debris blocking the feed path
Printer 'hangs'	Defective interface, connector or cable	Check interface, connector and printer cable
Nonsensical printed output (hex. codes printed)	Incorrect emulation selected	Check that emulation and printer driver selected on host computer are compatible with one another
Printing terminates before graphic images are completed	Insufficient memory	Upgrade printer memory
Printer executes 'self-test' but will not accept printing instructions from the host computer	Interface faulty	Check interface cable and connectors Check interface circuitry and, in particular, the BUSY (pin 11) and ERROR (pin 32) status signal lines

Symptom	Cause	Action
Abnormal indication on control panel (e.g. all display lights illuminated simultaneously)	Printer electronic fault	Refer to printer manual. Replace printer electronic card
Randomly distributed marks appear on paper	Dirt/toner present in paper	Inspect and clean the paper path
Vertical streaks appear on paper	Scratched drum Damaged fuser roller	Inspect and replace drum Inspect and replace fuser roller

6
Displays

Various different display technologies have emerged for use in personal computers, however the most popular (and longest lasting) display technology is based on the cathode ray tube (CRT) where a rectangular raster is scanned by means of a moving electron beam. This technology is well established yet has been refined over a number of years as a result of continuous developments in the production of television receivers.

Unfortunately, television receivers have severe limitations when used to display the output of personal computers. This is particularly true when 80 or 132 column text, or high-resolution graphics are to be displayed. Generally, monochrome (black and white) receivers perform somewhat better than colour receivers (unless the latter are fitted with separate R-G-B sync inputs and high quality CRT) but bandwidth limitations associated with the IF and detector circuitry usually render even these unsuitable for critical applications.

For example, 80-column text is composed of characters which have a width of 8 pixels. Each line therefore consists of 640 individual pixels and the bandwidth of the monitor must be in excess of 10 MHz in order to produce an acceptable display. Unfortunately, few television receivers are capable of bandwidths much in excess of 6 MHz. The solution, of course, is the use of a purpose-designed monitor. These are available in monochrome (with a choice of screen phosphor) or colour, and normally accept either composite video and sync (at a nominal 1 V into 75 ohm) or R-G-B sync (usually at TTL levels) respectively.

The simplified block schematic of a monochrome raster scan display is shown in Figure 6.1. The data to be displayed is fed in in serial form, line by line, to the video circuits where it is used to modulate the brightness of the electron beam on the face of the CRT. Colour displays are essentially the same, but three separate video channels are provided for the red, green, and blue signals.

Deflection of the electron beam across the face of the CRT follows the principles of raster scan displays, which were discussed in Chapter 1. Separate oscillators are used to generate the horizontal and vertical scanning signals and the beam is deflected by virtue of the instantaneous magnetic field generated by the deflection coils which form a yoke around the neck of the CRT. Note that because of the inductive nature of the scanning yoke, the output voltage from the deflection amplifiers will not be a perfect ramp (sawtooth). The current following in the deflection coils should, however, rise linearly as the scan proceeds. This simple point often confuses the newcomer!

The vertical (frame) oscillator usually operates at 50 Hz to 70 Hz and the horizontal (line) oscillator at 15.625 kHz to 25 kHz. The lower set of figures (50 Hz and 16.625 kHz for frame and line respectively) produce a 625-line TV-compatible display. However, note that not all of the 625 lines are actually scanned since the vertical flyback occupies several line periods.

The high voltages required for the cathode ray tube (8 to 12 kV for the final anode and 300 to 500 V for the focus and accelerating anodes) are invariably derived from the horizontal (line) flyback signal by means of a transformer arrangement and a diode multiplier. This circuitry is usually fully encapsulated for reasons which should be obvious!

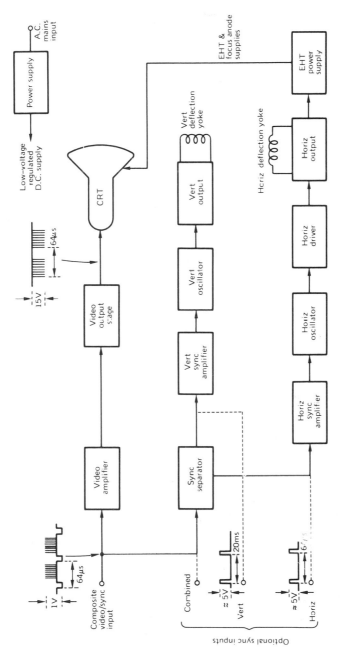

Figure 6.1 Simplified block schematic of a monochrome raster scan display

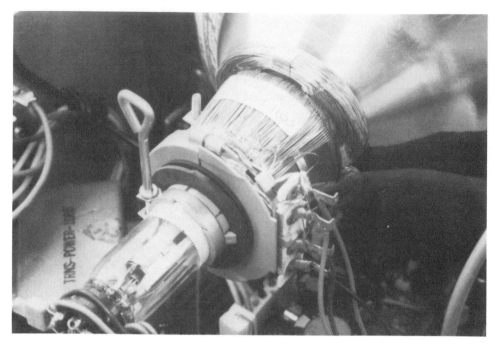

Figure 6.2 Deflection yoke assembly fitted to the neck of the CRT of a typical monochrome raster

Figure 6.3 Line flyback EHT generator. (The line flyback transformer is fully encapsulated and the EHT lead connects to the final anode near the screen of the CRT. Horizontal linearity and width adjustments can also be seen)

Colour displays

The screen of a colour CRT contains three types of phosphor which emit respectively red, green and blue light when struck by an electron beam. These three primary colours can be combined at various intensities to produce a virtually infinite set of colours (see Table 6.1).

Table 6.1 Colours resulting from the illumination of adjacent differently coloured phosphor dots

Phosphor dots illuminated	Color perceived on the CRT screen
Red	Red
Green	Green
Blue	Blue
Red and green	Yellow
Red and blue	Magenta/violet/pink
Green and blue	Cyan/turquoise/light blue
Red, green and blue	White/grey

Each primary colour has a separate electron gun, with a separate grid to control its brightness. The three electron beams are accelerated and focused by a single anode assembly and deflected across the screen by a single set of deflection coils. The three beams arrive at the screen at slightly different angles. A mask (see Figure 6.4) which is at EHT voltage is located a few millimetres from the screen phosphor. The small holes in the mask break each beam into six or seven smaller beams before they hit the screen phosphor. The angle of the beam at the mask directs the beam to the correctly coloured phosphor dots.

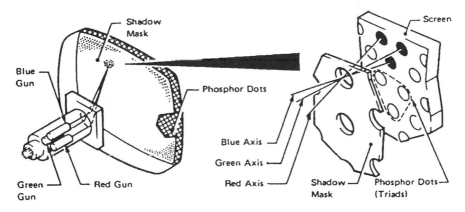

Figure 6.4 Principle of the shadow mask colour CRT

Another group of coils is arranged around the neck of the CRT between the cathodes and the common anode. These are used to improve purity and convergence. The purity coils move the three beams together under horizontal and vertical controls to strike the shadow mask at the correct angles.

The static convergence assembly comprises three thumbwheels or coaxial sets of levers mounted on the CRT neck. These, together with the blue lateral static convergence potentiometer, allow the three colour beams to be individually aligned at the centre of the screen.

The overall deflection distortion is corrected by pincushion correction magnets mounted on the CRT neck assembly. The distortion of each beam is, however, slightly different but these differences may be corrected for electronically by means of the dynamic convergence circuits.

Dismantling

Dismantling a raster scan display usually involves removing the rear panel and/or plastic outer casing secured by means of self-tapping screws. Alternatively, in some displays, the chassis may be withdrawn from the rear of the casing (leaving the CRT and deflection assembly in place) in order to permit access to the PCB and adjustment points. Note that with the exception of the main PCB it is not usually necessary to remove the CRT and deflection assembly in order to undertake normal service work. Indeed, one should avoid disturbing the adjustments on the deflection assembly (particularly where colour monitors are concerned). This assembly should only be removed when either the CRT or the scanning yoke itself has to be replaced.

Display adjustment

Some adjustment of the pre-set controls of a raster scan display will almost certainly be required whenever a major component replacement or substitution is made. The procedure varies greatly according to the complexity of the display concerned.

In all cases and before attempting to make any adjustments, it is essential to ensure that the display is operating correctly and that no component fault is present. A raster should be displayed that fills the entire screen area with a fine rectangular grid of lines (preferably white on a black background). If such a display is difficult to arrange, the entire screen area can be filled with a suitable graphics block or, alternatively, rows of text characters can be employed. In this case the letters H or M should be used as these are quite critical on bandwidth.

The adjustments shown in Table 6.2 are typical of those required for a high-quality monochrome or colour raster scan display. It is important that where a particular adjustment has no obvious effect it should be returned to its initial position. For this reason it is useful to make a mental note of the initial position of the control before starting to make any adjustments. A small bench mirror can be extremely useful in avoiding the usual contortions associated with craning one's head over the monitor to examine the effect of making an adjustment!

Colour adjustments

When making colour adjustments, the controls should be adjusted in the following sequence:

1. Coarse raster adjustment (H and V position)
2. Static convergence

Table 6.2 Typical adjustment procedure for a raster scan display

Adjustment	Preset control	Procedure
Horizontal sync	H-hold preset resistor; H-osc. inductor	Adjust H-hold preset to mid-position; adjust H-osc. inductor to centre of range over which picture achieves sync
Horizontal linearity	H-lin. inductor	Adjust for equal width character 'H' at the left, right, and centre of the display
Horizontal width	Width inductor	Adjust for correct width of display. (Note that this adjustment interacts with the linearity and it will be necessary to repeat the previous adjustment.)
Vertical sync	V-hold preset resistor	Adjust to the centre of the range over which picture achieves sync
Vertical linearity and vertical height	V-lin. preset resistor; V-height preset resistor	Adjust V-height preset to obtain a display of approximately 70 per cent of the normal height. Use V-lin. preset to obtain equal height characters at the bottom, middle, and top of the display. Adjust V-height preset to obtain a full height display
Contrast	Contrast preset resistor	Adjust for satisfactory display contrast
Brightness	Brightness preset resistor	Adjust external brightness control to maximum (at which point the display raster should be clearly visible). Adjust brightness preset to the point where the background raster just disappears
Focus	Dynamic focus preset resistor; focus preset resistor	Adjust dynamic focus preset to minimum. Adjust focus preset to ensure that the display is focused uniformly. Adjust the dynamic focus preset for uniform focus at the edges of the display. Repeat the two previous adjustments for optimum focusing
Screen centring	Centring magnet	Adjust the magnet to provide a display which has the same periphery at the bottom and top, and at the left and right
Image deformation	Correction magnet	Rotate the four correction magnets to gradually correct any deformation of the display

Table 6.2 Typical adjustment procedure for a raster scan display

Adjustment	Preset control	Procedure
Static convergence	Pre-set adjustments (R and G) and blue lateral preset	Display convergence test pattern and adjust for correct convergence at the centre of the screen. Adjust the blue lateral control until the patterns align horizontally and vertically
Colour purity	Pre-set potentiometers	Display red pattern or red characters across entire screen. Adjust pre-set controls until all characters appear in red
Dynamic convergence	Pre-set potentiometers fitted to the convergence amplifier circuits	Display convergence test pattern and adjust for correct convergence first at the centre of the screen, then at each of the screen edges and finally at the four corners of the screen. Repeat as necessary
Colour balance	Pre-set R, G and B potentiometers usually fitted to the small PCB on the CRT base	Set all three to maximum position then reduce each one in turn to obtain correct colour balance (start with no more than about 15 per cent reduction of each control)

Figure 6.5 Convergence adjustments fitted to the neck of the CRT in an IBM colour display

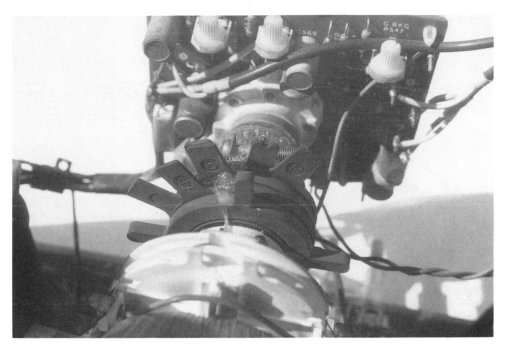

Figure 6.6 Convergence adjustments viewed from the front of the CRT in an IBM colour display

Figure 6.7 Red, green and blue preset adjustments fitted to the rear CRT connector PCB in an IBM colour display

Figure 6.8 Focus and correction preset adjustments fitted to the line flyback transformer assembly in an IBM colour display

Figure 6.9 Horizontal width adjustment in an IBM colour display

3. Colour purity
4. Repeat steps 1 to 3 (as necessary)
5. Dynamic convergence
6. Focus
7. Colour balance
8. Fine raster adjustment (H and V position)
9. Repeat steps 1 to 8 (as necessary).

Alignment software

Adjustments to a raster scan display are greatly aided by means of a video pattern generator which provides signals for colour purity, focus and convergence adjustment. If such an
item is unavailable, some simple software can greatly assist the adjustment process by
displaying simple grid, circle, and dot patterns on the display screen. A representative
display alignment program written in Microsoft QuickBASIC and designed for the IBM PC
(or compatible systems) is shown in Listing 6.1. This program will allow you to carry out
various checks and adjustments on a variety of PC displays including basic text mode
displays (80 × 25 monochrome), CGA, EGA, and VGA colour types.

The program has two menu screens and it initializes in 'Text' mode. You can then either
display a chequerboard (80 × 25 grid) by pressing <T> or move to the 'setup display' sub-
menu by pressing <S>. Here you have a choice of a 'Text Mode', 'CGA' (320 × 200, 4
colours), 'EGA' (640 × 200, 16 colours), and 'VGA' (640 × 350, 16 colours).

Once the required display mode has been selected, you should exit to the main menu
and continue with one or more of the checks. Assuming that you have selected a graphics
mode (CGA, EGA, or VGA) you can select from:

1. *Alignment test*   This test displays a series of concentric circles and it is used for adjusting height, width, vertical linearity, and horizontal linearity.
2. *Grid test.*   This test displays a grid (horizontal and vertical lines) and is used to
check colour convergence.
3. *Dot test.*   This test displays a matrix of single-pixel dots. It can be used to check
dynamic focus (all dots should be the same size) and convergence.
4. *Colour bars.*   This test displays 16 colours bars (4 in CGA mode) and can be used
for performing colour adjustments.
5. *Text display.*   This test displays a chequerboard of text characters (ASCII 32 and 219
respectively). You should check that the 80 × 25 display fills the display
with an adequate margin all round.

Display fault location

Fault location on raster scan displays will be relatively easy for anyone with some experience of TV servicing, but it can be somewhat daunting for those who are only acquainted
with trouble-shooting on digital circuits. It is also important to note that high voltages are
present in monitors and, while it is unlikely that shocks from the EHT circuits of a monitor
will be fatal, great care should always be taken to avoid contact with live high voltage
circuits. Indeed, it is usually wise to allow such circuits several minutes to discharge before
making any direct connection to them. Those with TV experience will know that a healthy
respect for high voltage circuits will pay dividends in the end!

```
' *******************************************************
' **  Name:       DISPLAY.BAS                         **
' **  Function:   Checks Text/CGA/EGA/VGA displays    **
' **  Language:   Microsoft QuickBASIC                **
' **  Notes:      Requires appropriate display        **
' **              adapter card                        **
' *******************************************************
'
' Initialise
'
ON ERROR GOTO warning
'
Initialise in text mode
SCREEN 0
COLOR 15, 1
xc = 0
mode$ = "Text"
ul$ = STRING$(40, CHR$(205))
' Display main menu
DO
main:
CLS
PRINT ul$
PRINT " DISPLAY CHECK   Current mode = "; mode$
PRINT ul$; ""
PRINT " Select option..."
IF xc <> 0 THEN
  PRINT "  [A] = alignment test"
  PRINT "  [G] = grid test"
  PRINT "  [D] = dot test"
  PRINT "  [C] = colour bars"
END IF
PRINT "  [T] = text display"
PRINT "  [S] = setup display mode"
PRINT "  [Q] = quit"
DO
  r$ = UCASE$(INKEY$)
LOOP UNTIL r$ <> "" AND INSTR("AGDTCSQ", r$)
IF r$ = "Q" THEN CLS : SCREEN 0: END
'
PRINT ul$
IF xc <> 0 THEN
  IF r$ = "A" THEN GOSUB alignment
  IF r$ = "G" THEN GOSUB grid
  IF r$ = "D" THEN GOSUB dot
  IF r$ = "C" THEN GOSUB colours
END IF
IF r$ = "T" THEN GOSUB text
IF r$ = "S" THEN GOTO setup
LOOP
'
alignment:
CLS
FOR x = xc / 4 TO xc STEP xc / 4
  CIRCLE (xc, yc), x
NEXT x
LINE (0, yc)-(2 * xc, yc)
LINE (xc, 0)-(xc, 2 * yc)
GOSUB keywait
```

```
RETURN
`
grid:
CLS
FOR y = 0 TO 2 * yc STEP yc / 10
  LINE (0, y)-(2 * xc, y)
NEXT y
FOR x = 0 TO 2 * xc STEP xc / 15
  LINE (x, 0)-(x, 2 * yc)
NEXT x
GOSUB keywait
RETURN
`
dot:
CLS
FOR y = 0 TO 2 * yc STEP yc / 10
  FOR x = 0 TO 2 * xc STEP xc / 15
    PSET (x, y)
    NEXT x
 NEXT y
GOSUB keywait
RETURN
`
text:
CLS
IF mode$<> "CGA" THEN xlim = 80 ELSE xlim = 40
FOR x = 1 TO xlim STEP 2
  FOR y = 1 TO 25 STEP 2
    LOCATE y, x
    PRINT CHR$(219);
  NEXT y
NEXT x
FOR x = 2 TO xlim STEP 2
  FOR y - 2 TO 25 STEP 2
    LOCATE y, x
    PRINT CHR$(219);
  NEXT y
NEXT x
GOSUB keywait
RETURN
`
colours:
IF mode$ <> "CGA" THEN
  COLOR 0, 0
  CLS
  x = 0
  xold = 0
  inc = xc / 8
  FOR colour = 0 TO 15
    x = x + inc
    LINE (xold, 0)-STEP(x, 2 * yc), colour, BF
    xold = x
  NEXT colour
ELSE
` CGA uses 4 colours...
  COLOR 0, 0, 1
  CLS
  x = 0
```

```
   xold = 0
   inc = xc / 2
   FOR colour = 0 TO 3
     x = x + inc
     LINE (xold, 0)-STEP(x, 2 * yc), colour, BF
     xold = x
   NEXT colour
END IF
GOSUB keywait
IF mode$ <> "CGA" THEN COLOR 15, 1 ELSE COLOR 1, 2, 1
RETURN
'
setup:
DO
' Display setup menu
CLS
PRINT ul$
PRINT " DISPLAY SETUP   Current mode = "; mode$
PRINT ul$; ""
PRINT " Select option..."
PRINT " [T] = Text Mode (80 col., 16 colours)"
PRINT " [C] = CGA (320 x 200, 4 colours)"
PRINT " [E] = EGA (640 x 200, 16 colours)"
PRINT " [V] = VGA (640 x 350, 16 colours)"
PRINT " [X] = exit to main menu"
DO
  r$ = UCASE$(INKEY$)
LOOP UNTIL r$ <> "" AND INSTR("TCEVX", r$)
IF r$ = "X" THEN GOTO main
PRINT ul$
IF r$ = "T" THEN
  SCREEN 2: SCREEN 0: COLOR 15, 1: xc = 0: yc = 0: mode$ = "Text"
END IF
IF r$ = "C" THEN SCREEN 1: COLOR 1, 2, 1: xc = 160: yc = 100: mode$ = "CGA"
IF r$ = "E" THEN SCREEN 8: COLOR 15, 1: xc = 320: yc = 100: mode$ = "EGA"
IF r$ = "V" THEN SCREEN 9: COLOR 15, 1: xc = 320: yc = 175: mode$ = "VGA"
LOOP
'
waitkey:
PRINT ul$
PRINT " Press any key to continue..."
GOSUB keywait
RETURN
'
keywait:
DO
  r$ = INKEY
LOOP UNTIL r$ <> ""
RETURN
'
warning:
PRINT ul$
PRINT " An error has occurred!"
GOSUB waitkey
RESUME main
```

Listing 6.1 Microsoft QuickBASIC program for alignment of a display in conjunction with an IBM PC or compatible system

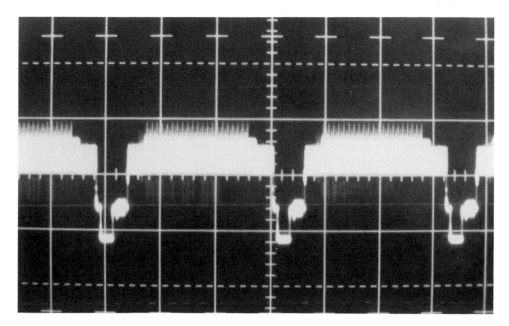

Figure 6.10 Typical video signal waveform showing two complete lines of the display. The line sync pulse is negative-going while the brightness information is positive-going. (Horizontal scale 20 μs/cm, vertical scale 500 mV/cm)

Apart from a multimeter and a high voltage probe, the most useful tool in servicing monitors is an oscilloscope. Nearly all faults can be located easily with these two instruments and more complex video test equipment (such as pattern and colour bar generators) is not required unless one needs to replace tubes and deflection yoke assemblies. Even then, it is quite possible to align the display with reasonable accuracy using the host computer to generate the necessary test patterns.

Before an internal examination of a display is undertaken, it is important to confirm that the fault lies within the monitor and not within the host computer. To this end a known working display should be substituted for the suspect unit. If this is not possible and the host computer provides a modulated RF output, a conventional TV receiver can be used instead. The stock faults that follow cover the vast majority of problems associated with monitors. However, where detailed information is required, readers should consult the individual manufacturer's service manual.

Display stock faults

Symptom	Cause	Action
No raster displayed, controls inoperative	Power supply failure	Check fuses, d.c. supply rails, mains transformer windings for continuity, rectifiers and regulators

Display stock faults *continued*

Symptom	Cause	Action
	Horizontal output stage failure	Check supply rail to horizontal output stage. Check waveform at the collector of the driver stage (see Figure 6.11) and at the collector of the horizontal output stage. If the former is normal while the latter is abnormal, remove and test the output transistor. Replace if defective, otherwise check the windings of the flyback transformer for continuity
	Horizontal oscillator or driver faulty	If, in the above procedure, the signal at the collector of the driver stage is abnormal, check the driver stage and work backwards to the oscillator (see Figure 6.11)
	CRT defective	Check CRT heaters for continuity. Check d.c. voltages at the CRT electrodes (see Figure 6.12). Note that a high voltage probe will be needed to measure the final anode supply. If the d.c. voltages are abnormal, and particularly if any two of the voltages are identical, remove the CRT connector and check for shorts or leakage between the electrodes. Remove and replace the CRT if found to be defective. Take great care when handling the CRT since there is a risk of implosion if subjected to a mechanical shock
Raster is displayed but no video information is present	Video amplifier stage faulty	Check d.c. supply voltage to video amplifier stage. Check input connector. Check video waveform at input and work towards video output stage
Data is displayed but focus is poor	Focus control adjustment	Adjust focus control
	Focus anode supply defective	Check d.c. supply to focus anode (see Figure 6.12)
	CRT defective	Check for internal short between first anode and focus anode
Data is displayed but brightness is low. Display size may increase and focus worsen as brightness is increased	Poor EHT regulation, horizontal output stage defective	Check d.c. supply voltage to horizontal output stage. Check d.c. voltages at CRT electrodes using a high voltage probe for the final anode measurement (see Figure 6.12). Check horizontal flyback transformer for short-circuited turns. Check EHT rectifier arrangement

Display stock faults *continued*

Symptom	Cause	Action
Data is displayed but contrast is poor	Video amplifier or video output stage faulty	Check d.c. voltages on video amplifier stages. Check video waveform at input connector and work forwards to the video output stage
	Contrast control out of adjustment	Adjust contrast control
Data is displayed but brightness is low. Display size remains constant and focus correct as brightness control is varied	Incorrect bias voltage on CRT	Adjust preset brightness control. Check d.c. supply to video output stage
No horizontal sync, display contains a number of near horizontal bars	Horizontal sync stage defective	Check waveforms at sync input and work towards the horizontal oscillator (see Figure 6.11)
No horizontal or vertical sync, display consists of rolling horizontal bars	Sync separator defective	Check waveform at sync input and work towards horizontal and vertical oscillators. Check d.c. voltages on sync separator stage
Reduced height, good vertical linearity	Height control out of adjustment	Adjust height control
Poor vertical linearity, height normal	Vertical linearity out of adjustment	Adjust vertical linearity
Vertical foldover, abnormal height accompanied by poor linearity	Vertical oscillator, driver or output stage defective	Adjust vertical linearity. Check d.c. supply to vertical stages. Check waveforms on vertical stages (see Figures 6.13 and 6.14).
	Vertical yoke defective	Check inductance of vertical yoke (typically 5 to 15 mH)
No vertical scan, display consists of a bright horizontal line	Vertical oscillator, driver or output stage defective	Check d.c. supply to vertical stages. Check waveforms and d.c. voltages
	Vertical yoke defective	Check vertical yoke for continuity (typically 2 to 10 ohm)
Reduced width, good horizontal linearity	Width control out of adjustment	Adjust width control
No horizontal scan, display consists of a bright vertical line	Horizontal yoke defective, linearity or width coil open circuit	Check horizontal yoke for continuity (typically 0.5 to 1.5 ohm). Check width and linearity coils for continuity (typically 0.5 to 2 ohm)
Horizontal linearity poor, width normal	Linearity control out of adjustment	Adjust linearity control
Horizontal linearity poor, width and brightness may be reduced	Horizontal flyback transformer defective, horizontal yoke defective	Check horizontal flyback transformer and horizontal yoke for shorted turns (typical horizontal yoke inductance is 100 to 300 μH).

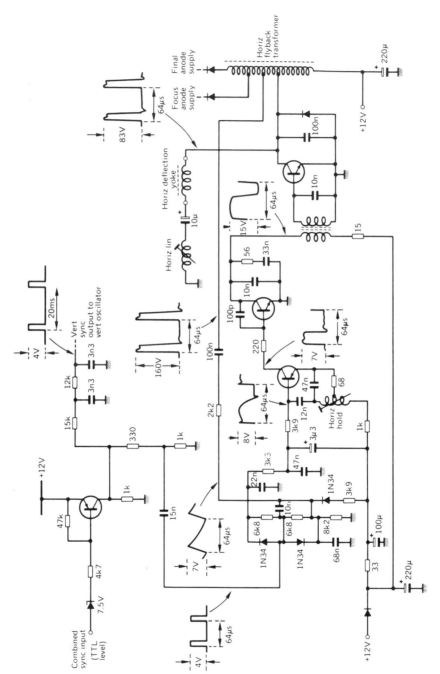

Figure 6.11 Typical waveforms in the horizortal deflection circuits

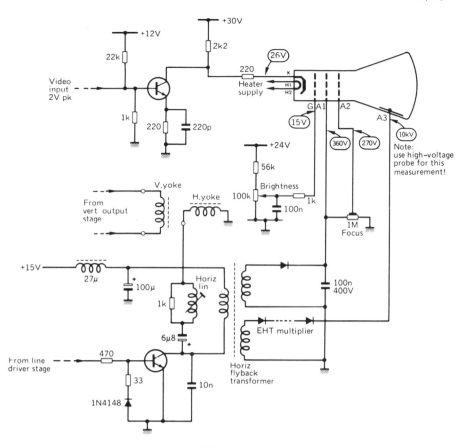

Figure 6.12 Typical circuitry around the CRT showing d.c. voltages

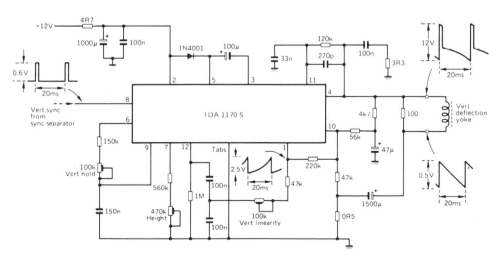

Figure 6.13 Typical vertical deflection system using an integrated circuit

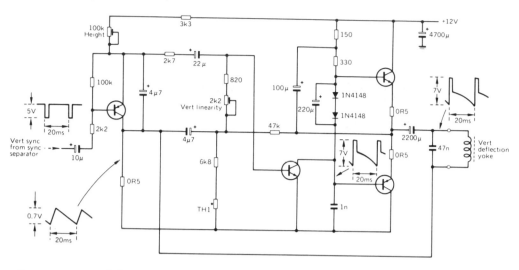

Figure 6.14 Typical discrete vertical deflection circuitry

7

Servicing 68000-based microcomputers

The 68000 family of microprocessors was first officially announced in July 1979. At its launch, the 68000 was heralded as 'a break away from the past!'. Since then, over 30 million processors from the 68000 series have found their way into such diverse equipment as home computers, scientific workstations, laserprinters, CAD/CAM systems, process controllers, and UNIX-based super-microcomputers. The 68000 offers the system designer a sleek and uncluttered architecture with a vast linear address range (the 68000 does not have to resort to the somewhat messy segmented addressing employed with the Intel family of processors).

Origins

The 68000 microprocessor was originally conceived in 1977 by a project team at Motorola, of which the principal architect was Tom Gunter. The project was known as 'Motorola's Advanced Computer System on Silicon' (MACSS). At the time, Motorola was considering what direction to take in the development of their existing 8-bit microprocessors. Gunter proposed a 16-bit microprocessor with extensibility to a full 32 bits. At the time, this was a radical departure from the current 'state of the art' which centred around 8-bit microprocessors employed in systems with a somewhat limited memory capacity (64K bytes maximum).

Tom Gunter proved to be a visionary with his proposal for a highly complex microprocessor (containing the equivalent of approximately 68000 transistors). Gunter's device could only be manufactured in 3 micron HMOS (a process which had not, at the time, been perfected). It would employ 32-bit data paths and two separate arithmetic logic units. Furthermore, the microprocessor would require a massive 64-pin package (only 40-pin packages had been used at that time) and the die used in the production of the semiconductor chip would have to be very much larger than anything that had ever been used before.

It was also proposed that the device would be programmed internally by means of microcode (rather than hard-wiring instructions into the instruction decoder). This technique had been used before in mainframe computers but was somewhat revolutionary in a microprocessor CPU. A split-level microstore was proposed in which a first (narrow) half would control the subsequent sequence of instruction microaddresses. A second (wider) half would actually control the device. The sharing of control states between many micro-addresses would result in significant savings in silicon.

It was something of a testimonial to Motorola's faith in its development team (which included development, software and fabrication engineers) that the project to develop the

68000 actually went ahead! The concept was to create a new family of super-micropro-cessors which would provide increasing levels of functionality and performance.

At the time, it was felt that the majority of future software development would be in high-level languages and that this should be reflected in both the internal architecture and instruction set of the 68000. Thus the chip had a particularly sleek and uncluttered archi-tecture coupled with a straightforward instruction set which employs orthogonal address-ing modes. It is not surprising, therefore, that the 68000 more closely resembled contemporary minicomputers (such as the DEC PDP-11) rather than the 8-bit micro-processors of that time!

68000 compatibility

Unlike its principal rival (Intel) who decided to include a measure of upward instruction set compatibility between its 8 and 16-bit microprocessors, Motorola decided to abandon upward instruction set capability between the 8-bit 6800 and the 16/32-bit 68000. This was a bold decision on the part of Motorola and was one which, at the time, raised many eyebrows in the microcomputer world. With hindsight it was, however, undoubtedly the right decision since it was instrumental in freeing the designers from the constraints of an instruction set which would inevitably become outdated.

Despite its decision not to support the 6800 instruction set, Motorola's 68000 device was made compatible with the standard range of 6800 peripheral devices. The thinking behind this particular was that this new microprocessor would have a ready-made family of well tried and tested peripheral devices rather than wait for a whole new range of peripheral devices to be developed.

At the code level, the 68000 introduced a number of new concepts in the design of microprocessors. Notable amongst these were the separation of user and supervisor code and data areas, the integration of a seven-level interrupt controller with automatic masking of interrupts, on-chip execution processing with 256 exception vectors, and a fully trapped operation code map. By separating user code from supervisor code, it was possible to provide the system with extra resources and instruction which applications could not access. These 'privileged' resources could be enhanced for later (and more powerful) members of the 68000 family whilst the user-level object code could be ported across without the need for any modification.

The 68030 and 68040

More recent developments in 68000 family architecture have seen the introduction of virtual memory (and support for a virtual machine environment) as well as cache memories, dynamic bus sizing, and increasingly faster clock speeds. The original 68000 CPU was designed for operation with a 4 MHz single-phase clock and this configuration provided a mere 0.35 MIPS. Today, a 68030 CPU operating with a 33 MHz clock can provide a staggering 12 MIPS!

The latest member of the 68000 family, the 68040, provides 20 MIPS and contains the equivalent of approximately 1.2 million transistors. Instruction and data caches on this device are sixteen times bigger than those on the 68030 (4K bytes each). The 68040 employs extensive pipelining and 'hard wiring' of key operations and addressing modes and offers an average execution time of 1.25 cycles. The 68040 also contains its own floating point processing unit.

User and supervisor modes

In the design of the 68000, Motorola attempted to address a number of problems which had previously beset 8-bit microprocessors. In particular, it was felt that there could be significant advantages in separating the operating system from an application program running under it.

The separation of the operating system and any applications program which would run under it, is provided by allowing for two basic modes of operation; 'user mode' and 'supervisor mode'.

User mode refers to CPU operations which relate to the applications program whilst supervisor mode is reserved for sole use by the operating system. The distinction is vitally important since it essentially protects the operating system from the ravages of a misbehaved applications program; in supervisor mode, the system enjoys a set of privileged instructions which are not available when running under user mode.

Exceptions

Exceptions act rather like interrupts and can be generated in several ways, both internally and externally. External exceptions are associated with interrupts, the 68000's bus error signal and the reset request line.

The process of executing an exception occurs in four distinct steps, with variations for different exception causes. The first step involves making a temporary copy of the status register and then setting the status register for exception processing. The second step involves determining the exception vector, whilst the third step involves saving the current processor context. The fourth and last step involves obtaining a new context and the processor switching to instruction processing.

The addresses of the routines which actually handle the execution of an exception are held in a table of execution vectors. With the exception of the reset vector (which occupies four words) all of the other 255 exception vectors comprise two words.

The vectors are given numbers (0 to 255) which, when multiplied by four, give the address offset for the corresponding vector within the vector table. As an example, vector number 9 (the trace vector) is at decimal address offset 36 (hexadecimal 024).

The vector numbers (a byte value) may be generated internally or externally depending upon the cause of the exception. In the case of interrupts (vector numbers 25 to 31 inclusive) the peripheral requiring service places the appropriate vector number on the lower half of the data bus (D0 to D7) bus during the interrupt acknowledge bus cycle. By this means the CPU is able to identify which of the peripheral devices is requiring attention.

The CPU forms the vector offset by multiplying the vector number by four. It does this by left-shifting the vector number by two bits and filling the remaining bits with zeros. The result is a 32-bit long word offset. In the case of the 68000 and 68008 this offset is used as the absolute address to obtain the exception vector itself.

The exception vector table occupies 512 words (1K bytes) of low memory, as shown on p.260.

Types of exception

Exceptions may be divided into two principal categories; internally generated and externally generated. Examples of the latter are interrupts, bus error and reset requests. Internally generated exceptions can be originated by instructions (such as TRAP, TRAPV, CHK and DIV), address errors, or tracing (in which an exception is generated after execution of each

Vector	Address		Assignment
	Dec.	Hex.	
0	0	000	Reset: Initial SSP
1	4	004	Reset: Initial PC
2	8	008	Bus Error
3	12	00C	Address Error
4	16	010	Illegal Instruction
5	20	014	Zero Divide
6	24	018	CHK Instruction
7	28	01C	TRAPV Instruction
8	32	020	Privilege Violation
9	36	024	Trace
10	40	028	Line A Emulator
11	44	02C	Line F Emulator
12	48	030	Unassigned, reserved
13	52	034	Unassigned, reserved
14	56	038	Format Error
15	60	03C	Uninitialized Interrupt Vector
16	64	040	Unassigned, reserved
17	68	044	Unassigned, reserved
19	76	04C	Unassigned, reserved
20	80	050	Unassigned, reserved
21	84	054	Unassigned, reserved
22	88	058	Unassigned, reserved
23	92	05C	Unassigned, reserved
24	96	060	Spurious interest
25	100	064	Level 1 Interrupt Vector
26	104	068	Level 2 Interrupt Vector
27	108	06C	Level 3 Interrupt Vector
28	112	070	Level 4 Interrupt Vector
29	116	074	Level 5 Interrupt Vector
30	120	078	Level 6 Interrupt Vector
31	124	07C	Level 7 Interrupt Vector
32 to 47	128 to 191	080 0BF	TRAP Instruction Vectors
48 to 63	192 to 255	0C0 0FF	Unassigned, reserved
64 to 255	256 to 1023	100 3FF	User Interrupt Vectors

Notes: 1. Vector numbers 0 and 1 relate to supervisor program space all other vectors relate to supervisor data space.
2. Vector numbers 12, 13, 16 to 23, and 48 to 63 are reserved for future enhancements.
3. The spurious interrupt vector is taken when a bus error occurs during interrupt processing.
4. Vector numbers 32 to 47 are assigned to the TRAP instruction. TRAP # 1 is assigned to vector number 32, TRAP #2 to vector number 33, and so on.
5. Vector number 14 is unassigned on the 68000 and 68008.

instruction). Exceptions are also generated by illegal instructions, privilege violations, and word fetches from odd addresses.

For convenience, exceptions are grouped into various categories according to relative priority and frequency of occurrence. Group 0 exceptions consist of reset, bus error, and address error. Group 1 exceptions comprise interrupt, trace, privilege violation, and illegal instructions. Group 2 exceptions are those which are associated with the 'normal' processing of instructions (such as TRAP, TRAPV, etc.).

Group 0 exceptions cause the currently executing instruction to be aborted and this allows exception processing to start within two clock cycles. Response to a Group 0 exception is thus virtually immediate.

Group 1 exceptions allow the execution of the current instruction to be completed. Thereafter, exception processing begins before the next instruction. Note that privilege violations and illegal instructions are detected when they are the next instruction to be executed.

Since more than one exception may arise at the same time, some mechanism for determining exception priority is required. This mechanism will determine which one of two (or more) simultaneously occurring exceptions will be dealt with. As an example, if a bus error occurs during the execution of a TRAP instruction, the bus error must take precedence.

Group 0 exceptions have the highest priority whilst Group 2 have the lowest priority. Within Group 0, Reset takes the highest priority, followed by bus error, and address error. Within Group 1, trace has priority over external interrupts, followed by illegal instruction, and privilege violation. In the case of Group 2 exceptions, and since only one instruction can be executed at any given time, there is no need for the allocation of priority levels within the group.

Exception priorities may be summarized in the following table:

Priority	Group	Exception
Highest	0	Reset
	0	Bus error
	0	Address error
	1	Trace
	1	Interrupt
	1	Illegal instruction
	1	Privilege violation
Lowest	2	Instructions (various, having equal priority)

In order that the main program can be resumed from the point at which it was left, it is necessary to preserve the processor context during exception processing. This is achieved by means of a structure known as an 'exception stack frame'. As an absolute minimum, this stack frame must normally contain the contents of the status register and program counter. Note that the composition of an exception stack frame varies according to the processor type and exception group.

68000 based systems

Given its power, and the elegance of its internal architecture, the 68000 has, not surprisingly, proved to be popular with a number of microcomputer manufacturers in the past few years. Indeed, the 68000 (or one of its close relations) is the workhorse of a number of the more powerful second and third generation personal computers. First amongst those to recognize the virtues of Motorola's 16/32-bit technology was Apple with its Lisa and Macintosh machines, followed by Sinclair with its ill-fated QL, Atari with the ST and TT series of microcomputers, and Commodore with its immensely popular Amiga. These machines were all designed for the discerning 'power user', whether games player, student, programmer, or business person.

The Apple Macintosh

First to exploit the potential of the Motorola 16/32-bit processors was Apple with the innovative and imaginative Macintosh. This machine represented a major departure from the direction in which the majority of the industry was moving at that time. The Apple Macintosh followed on from an earlier machine, the Apple Lisa. This machine was revolutionary in that it incorporated the first mouse/window interface which was both hailed as a 'major breakthrough' and scorned as a 'mere gimmick' by computer pundits of the time!

The Apple Macintosh first became widely available in 1984. The 'Mac' operates with a clock speed of 7.83 MHz (compared with the Lisa's 5 MHz clock). The original Macintosh was, however, fitted with less RAM than its more expensive predecessor. In order to compensate for this reduction in available memory, the Macintosh makes somewhat more efficient use of RAM by virtue of code written in 68000 assembly language rather than machine code compiled from Pascal high-level source code.

The specifications for the original Macintosh (1984) included 128K bytes of RAM, 64K bytes of ROM, integral Sony 400K byte 3.5 inch disk drive, 9 inch video monitor offering 512 x 342 pixel resolution, and two serial ports. Later versions were expandable to 512K bytes of RAM by simply substituting 256K bit dynamic RAM devices for the 64K bit devices employed in the original version.

Much of the Macintosh's time critical low-level graphics primitives contained in ROM are called through the group of 68000 'line-A' instructions. These instructions take one of the 480, or so, addresses from the address table stored in low memory and thus provide a set of instructions which essentially function as extensions to the basic instruction set. Access to the Mac's ROM takes place at 7.83 MHz regardless of the screen display. RAM, however, is accessed at a more leisurely 3.92 MHz during screen display periods and at the full 7.83 MHz at other times. The average speed of the system was thus in the region of 6 MHz, or so.

The Macintosh video display (512 x 342 pixels) appears in memory as an array of 10 944 16-bit data words occupying a total of 21 888 bytes of RAM. The most significant bit of each data word represents the left-most displayed pixel. Each horizontal line (comprising 512 pixels) thus consists of 32 words of data shifted out at 15.67 MHz (322.68 µs per 512 pixel line). The last memory bus cycle of each horizontal line is used for sound DMA. During this particular period, a byte of sound data is fetched from the sound buffer and sent to the 8-bit digital to analogue converter (DAC) for conversion into a corresponding analogue voltage level. The update rate for the sound channel is thus equal to the horizontal video rate (22.25455 kHz). The vertical scan of 342 lines is followed by 28 inactive lines during the field flyback period (1.258 ms).

Access to system RAM is divided into synchronous time slots such that the CPU and video circuits share alternate word accesses during the active portion of the horizontal scan. The sound circuits make use of the video time slot during the last memory bus cycle of the horizontal scan. The CPU access to RAM is maximized by allowing it to make use of the unused cycles during horizontal and vertical blanking periods.

Sound generation is available either by means of a timer within the versatile interface adaptor (VIA) or by means of high-speed sampling routines which generate 370 samples of sound data and then places them into a sound buffer after each vertical retrace interrupt. Pitch is controllable (to 24 bits of precision) by means of the 68000's 32-bit data registers. Four voices are available with 1 67 77 216 possible frequencies. A programmable eight-step attenuator provides approximately 20 dB of volume control.

The Macintosh LSI disk controller is based on the earlier disk controller circuitry (designed by Steve Wozniak) fitted to the Apple II. This LSI device was given the unusual name, 'integrated Wozniak machine' (IWM). The IWM provided a maximum data throughput of

500K bits per second. An unusual (and somewhat non-standard) feature of the Macintosh disk system is that the drive motor speed is variable. This is achieved by means of a pulse width modulator circuit which is driven from a look-up data table stored in memory. This arrangement was designed to increase reliability of data transfer and also to maximize use of the available disk space.

Parallel I/O for selecting various system functions is provided by means of a 6522 versatile interface adaptor (VIA). This device also provides basic system timing facilities and supports the mouse and keyboard interface.

Serial communications is provided by a Zilog 8530 serial communications controller (SCC). This device supports data transfer (both synchronous and asynchronous) at rates up to 230.4K bits per second in self-clocking format and up to 1 M bit per second using an external clock. Both of the Mac's serial ports provide single-ended or differential signalling and multi-drop capability.

The Macintosh hardware is based on two circuit boards. One of these boards deals with analogue circuitry (including the video display and power supply) whilst the other contains the digital circuitry (CPU, RAM, ROM and other LSI support devices). The power supply unit fitted in the first production (US) models of the Macintosh employed simple linear circuitry. This power supply unit was later superseded by a more efficient switched-mode power supply.

Macintosh memory map

The Macintosh memory map contains areas dedicated to RAM, ROM and I/O. During system initialization, the 64K byte ROM is mapped into the first 64K byte page of memory (hexadecimal addresses 000000 to 00FFFF). After initialization, the positions of RAM and ROM are changed so that the 128K byte block of RAM occupies the first two pages of memory (hexadecimal addresses 000000 to 01FFFF).

The Phase Read area of memory (mapped into the memory block which extends from F00000 to F7FFFF hexadecimal) is used to synchronize the system's timing signals (this is usually accomplished during initialization by means of appropriate ROM routines).

The VIA is accessed by means of addresses which are mapped into the memory block which extend from E80000 to EFFFFF hexadecimal) whilst the floppy disk controller (IWM) appears within the block extending from D00000 to DFFFFF hexadecimal.

The serial communications controller (SCC) appears within two non-contiguous blocks of memory; 900000 to 9FFFFF hex. for read and B00000 to BFFFFF hex. for write.

The 128K bytes of RAM in low-memory (after system initialization) is divided into a number of blocks which contain:

(a) hardware exception vectors (from 00000 to 000FF hex.)
(b) user memory (from 00100 to 1A6FF hex.)
(c) screen memory (from 1A700 to 1FC7E hex.)
(d) disk speed and sound data (from 1FD00 to 1FFE2 hex.)

Macintosh firmware

The 64K ROM within the Macintosh contains the majority of the Mac's operating system together with a set of optimized 68000 routines which constitute the Macintosh User-Interface Toolbox. The operating system interacts with the system hardware at the lowest level and incorporates such items as device drivers and memory/file management routines.

The toolbox contains the requisite routines for window manipulation, pull-down menu generation, dialogue boxes, fonts, and other facilities provided by the Mac's graphically orientated user-interface. Routines within the toolbox may be accessed via the 68000's line-A instructions.

The original Macintosh was supplied without any bundled application software. Users had to purchase the necessary applications software to meet their needs. Several packages were written to exploit the Mac's WIMP environment. These included MacPaint (a drawing program) and MacWrite (a word processor). Apple also provided various programming languages, including MacPascal and MacBASIC. Both of these languages compile their source code on a line by line basis into an intermediate pseudocode. They thus combine the speed advantages of compiled code with the interactive nature of interpreted code.

A great deal of Macintosh third-party software has since appeared. Such software tends to be directed towards the professional, scientific, and academic markets where the Macintosh has found a particular niche despite increasing competition from its mainstream rival, the IBM PC.

The Sinclair QL

Sinclair's 'Quantum Leap' computer (the QL) first appeared in 1984. The QL was intended to be an affordable machine which would appeal to both the business user and to the hobbyist..It was the first computer to be supplied with in-built Sinclair Microdrives. These units employed cartridges which contain a 200 inch loop of magnetic tape moving at 28 inches per second providing a low-cost (but somewhat slow, inflexible and unreliable) alternative to mass storage based on floppy disk drives.

In order to simplify the system architecture (and permit the use of low-cost 8-bit bus support chips) the QL was based upon the 68008 (8-bit data bus version of the 68000). Early versions of the QL were notoriously unreliable and the operating system ROMs contained some serious bugs. However, many of these problems were corrected in the later production versions.

The QL was also to form the basis for ICL's intelligent workstation ('One-per-desk'). This project was short-lived and was overshadowed by the advent of the PC-compatible which provided ICL with an alternative (and somewhat more acceptable) solution to the need to provide executives with personal computing power.

System architecture

The 68008 CPU (IC18) is supported by two ULA devices; IC23 (associated with real-time clock generation, microdrive and serial data I/O) and IC22 (associated with system clock generation, RAM control and video processing). The main read/write memory comprises two banks of eight 4164 (64K x 1 bit) devices (IC1 to IC16) whilst the system ROM comprises one 32K byte 23256 device (IC33) and one 16K byte 23128 device (IC34). A separate 804Y microprocessor (IC24) handles keyboard input, sound output and handshaking control signals for the two serial ports.

Each microdrive chassis is fitted with its own dedicated 2G007 ULA controller (IC29 for MDV1 and IC30 for MDV2). Separate on-board 5 V regulators are fitted to each microdrive chassis whilst a separate (heatsink mounted) 7805 regulator (IC35) provides the main +5 V system power rail. Two small plastic regulators, IC37 and IC36, respectively provide the +12V and -12V power rails.

PAL-compatible colour video signal processing is achieved by means of IC28 and associated components whilst emitter-follower TR7 sums the RGB and sync. signals to produce a composite video output.

Versions

The 'Build Standard' of the production versions of the QL can be determined with reference to the serial number which appears on the underside of the computer. The prefix of this number gives the Build Standard whilst the remaining figures constitute the individual serial number for the machine. As an example, a machine coded 'D16-109609' conforms to Build Standard D16 and its serial number is 109609.

The Build Standard reflects both modifications to the hardware and changes to the software contained in the system ROM. The following standards may be encountered:

Build Standard	IC33 (0000 hex.)	IC34 (80000 hex.)	ROM version
D6	2 × 16K EPROM	16k EPROM	AH
D7	2 × 16K EPROM	16k EPROM	JM
D8	32K ROM	16k EPROM	AH
D9	32K ROM	16K ROM	AH
D10	32K EPROM	16k EPROM	JM
D11–D14	32K ROM	16K ROM	JM
D15	32K ROM	16K ROM	JM
D16	32K ROM	16K ROM	JS

Note that later Build Standards employ the MG series of ROMs (IC33) together with a separate language ROM (IC34) which may be French, German or Spanish. Build Standard D12 introduced some modifications to the microdrive chassis followed by a new microdrive chassis at Build Standard D13. Build Standard D15 included some further microdrive improvements.

Modifications

Sinclair recommended that the following modifications should be carried out to all pre-Build Standard 12 QL machines when returned for repair:

(a) R104 (82 ohm) inserted in TR1 collector circuit (reduces the dissipation in TR1 and protects the speaker in the event that TR1 becomes short-circuit).
(b) R92 (formerly 220 ohm) increased to 390 ohm.
(c) R105/R106 (1k ohm) introduced across C19, D17.
(d) D22/D23 (1N4148) introduced in series with R100/R101.
(e) R102/R103 (33k ohm) introduced between IC23 pins 21 and 19 and VM12 (-12V rail). (These resistors can be soldered directly to the relevant pins of IC23 and the common connection taken by a short flying lead to pin-1 of IC25.) R102 and R103 pull-down the RAW1 and RAW2 microdrive signals.
(f) IC33 and IC34 upgraded to build standard D11 (or later).

Address (Hex)

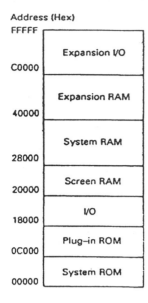

Figure 7.1 Sinclair QL memory map

QL memory map

The QL's system ROM occupies the lower 48K of memory (addresses 00000 to 0BFFF hex. inclusive), as shown in Figure 7.1. The space from 0C000 to 17FFF hex. is available for plug-in expansion ROM. The screen RAM occupies 32K bytes of memory from 20000 to 27FFF hex. whilst the remaining 96K bytes of internally fitted system board RAM extends from 28000 to 3FFFF hex. Expansion RAM (in the form of plug-in cards from third-party manufacturers and vendors) can extend the RAM above 40000 hex. Finally, the region above C0000 is reserved for expansion I/O.

QL firmware

The software contained within the two QL system ROMs includes Tony Tebby's excellent QDOS and the QL's resident SuperBASIC interpreter. This firmware provided the user with a remarkably flexible and powerful environment. Furthermore, the four Psion bundled software packages (Abacus, Archive, Easel and Quill) were of such an exceptional standard that many QL users have been very reluctant to abandon their machines. The QL has now been out of production for several years. Despite this, it is heartening for the dedicated band of QL users to know that the machine is still well supported and lives on in the shape of the powerful and elegant CST Thor computer.

The Atari ST

The Atari ST series first appeared in 1985 and was quick to capture the largest share of the UK market for 16-bit home computers. Since then, the machine has become immensely popular in Europe (notably in Germany). The letters 'ST' stand for 'sixteen/thirty-two' (a reference to the internal architecture of the 68000 chip).

The ST has earned an enviable reputation as a machine for 'serious' users as well as those who would rather play games. Indeed, the original design philosophy expounded by Atari's Chairman, Sam Tramiel, was that the machine would offer 'power without the price'. True to this promise, Atari produced a machine with an unprecedentedly low price and offering a power which had hitherto been seen only in machines costing at least four times as much! It is, therefore, not surprising that the ST has received so many accolades and is now in use in millions of homes and small businesses.

The ST pre-dated its nearest rival, the Commodore Amiga by nearly twelve months. This gave Atari a considerable edge over the opposition and it also enabled software developers to produce a range of titles well in advance of those for the Amiga.

At the outset, the ST found a particular niche in the market for reasonably priced yet powerful systems capable of running graphically orientated software (such as desk-top publishing, CAD, etc.). In this particular market (and especially in academic circles and in the publishing world) the Apple Macintosh had already established itself as a market leader. The ST, however, could offer the same GEM (Graphics Environment Manager) operating system shell coupled with an improved graphics capability at a considerably lower price. Many new computer users (particularly those on limited budgets) were, therefore, tempted away from the Macintosh.

Another area in which the ST found favour was with existing users of the Sinclair QL. The QL was based on the Motorola 68008 and this machine provided an introduction to 18-bit computing for several hundred thousand students and home computer enthusiasts. With the demise of the QL, many users upgraded to the ST which provided a more powerful (and reliable) environment for software development.

Atari have not been content to sit back on the huge success of the basic ST machine. Indeed, a policy of continuous product development at Atari has seen the emergence of the STE and Mega range not to mention Stacey (a portable ST), the Atari TT and the Atari Transputer Workstation!

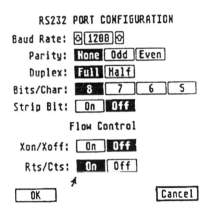

Figure 7.2 A GEM-based selection box (this example is taken from the ST's RS-232 configuration accessory)

Variants of the ST

ST architecture

The main internal components of an ST microcomputer are as follows:
(a) main system board (with or without modulator fitted depending upon the version)
(b) keyboard assembly (with separate processor)

(c) RF shielding (comprising upper and lower parts)

(d) enclosure

(e) mouse

(f) power supply (external or internal depending upon model)

(g) disk drive

(h) phase-locked loop daughter board (units fitted with a modulator)

The ST exists in a number of variants. These are as follows:

Version	Characteristrics
520ST	Early ST model; 512K byte RAM, no modulator fitted; no internal floppy disk drive
520STM	As above but with an internal modulator fitted
1040ST	Later model woth 1024K byte RAM, no modulator fitted, but with internal 3.5 inch floppy disk drive
1040STF	As above
1040STFM	As above but with an internal modulator fitted
1040STE	Enhanced STE (more colours, improved sound, etc.)
Mega ST1	Mega series ST with 1 Mbyte RAM and internal floppy disk drive
Mega ST2	As above but with 2 Mbyte RAM
Mega ST4	As above but with 4 Mbyte RAM

The 68000 CPU is fitted to the main system board and operates at 8 MHz. The system is fitted with 192K bytes of ROM (in six mask programmed VLSI devices) and up to 1 Mbyte of RAM. The system is provided with direct memory access (DMA) facilities via a dedicated DMA controller chip.

The ST offers both serial (RS-232C) and parallel (Centronics compatible) ports and is fitted with connections for an external cartridge ROM and a hard disk interface. The unit also provides analogue RGB and monochrome video outputs and incorporates MIDI facilities.

A separate intelligent keyboard processor is located on the keyboard PCB. This device also provides an interface for the mouse and joystick ports.

The ST employs a bit-mapped video display using 32K bytes of RAM which is fully relocatable within memory. Three display modes are provided:

Low resolution	320 x 200 pixels with 16 colours displayable selected from a palette of 512
Medium resolution	640 x 200 pixels with 4 colours displayable selected from a palette of 512
High resolution	640 x 400 pixels, monochrome only

System hardware

The complete ST hardware is shown (in block schematic form) in Figure 7.3. Three bus systems (data, address and control) link the CPU, ROM, RAM and major VLSI support devices. The keyboard (with its own processor) is linked serially (by means of a 6850 ACIA) to the system. Note that this interface also caters for the mouse and joystick (where fitted).

The 68000 CPU is supported by a number of VLSI devices, foremost amongst which is a chip which is aptly called 'glue'. This device provides the following functions:

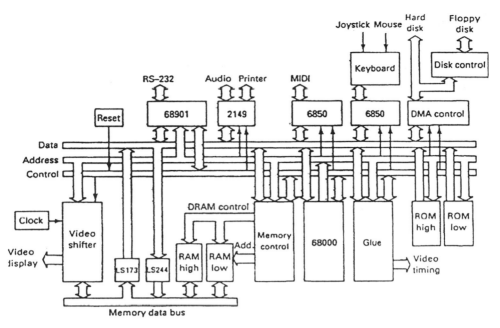

Figure 7.3 Simplified block diagram of the Atari ST

Clock division	Glue accepts the 8MHz CPU clock and divides it in order to produce further clock signals at 2 MHz and 500 kHz.
Video timing	The vertical and horizontal synchronizing signals are generated by glue as are the display enable signals. Glue can be programmed for 50Hz or 60 Hz operation.
Address decoding	Glue provides address decoding to generate the chip select signals for the ACIA, MFP, DMAC, PSG and ROM devices.
Bus arbitration	Glue arbitrates the bus during DMA transfers.
Error detection	Glue detects errors and asserts the CPU bus error (BERR) signal whenever certain illegal conditions are detected (e.g. when data is written to read-only memory).

A Motorola 68901 MFP chip provides interrupt control for up to sixteen inputs. Each input can be individually masked, enabled or disabled by appropriate programming of the MFP. The following interrupts are controlled by the 68901:

(a) disk (FDINT and HDINT for the floppy and hard disk interface respectively)
(b) RS-232C (for the CTS, DCD and RI signals)
(c) monochrome monitor detect (MONOMON)
(d) parallel printer port (BUSY)
(e) display enable (DE)
(f) keyboard interrupt request
(g) MIDI interrupts
(h) MFP timer interrupts

The ST supports DMA transfers at both low and high data rates. The low rates (250K or 500K bits per second) relate to the floppy disk controller whilst the high data rates are employed in conjunction with hard disk drives, laser printers, etc.

The DMA controller organizes the transfer of an entire block of memory at a time and without CPU intervention. The DMA controller works with glue and memory controller to handle this complex task. The DMA controller has an internal 32-byte data buffer.

Memory control

The ST's RAM extends from 00000 to FFFFF hexadecimal (note that the region from 00000 to 00800 hex. is reserved for system use). On the 520ST, the RAM comprises 16 256K bit x 1 chips. On the l040ST, an additional 16256K bit devices are provided in order to extend the memory capacity from 512K bytes to 1 Mbyte (see Figure 7.4).

The operating system (comprising the TOS and GEM code) is contained within the six ROM devices which occupy the following address ranges:

High	Low	Address range
U4	U7	FC0000 to FCFFFF
U3	U6	FD0000 to FDFFFF
U2	U5	FE0000 to FEFFFF

The memory controller accepts addresses from the address bus and produces the corresponding row address and column address strobe signals (RAS and CAS respectively). The memory controller can cope with up to 4 Mbytes of RAM (the operating system ascertains the extent of RAM present in a system during system initialization). The memory controller is responsible for refreshing for the dynamic RAM chips and also loads the video shifter with display data. The ST memory map is shown in Figure 7.4.

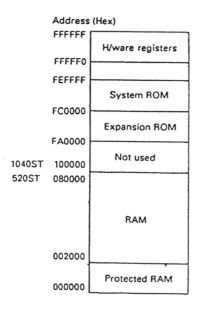

Figure 7.4 Atari ST memory map

Disk interface

The ST series of computers employ the popular Western Digital 1772 floppy disk controller. The ST configuration can cope with either:

(a) one internal and one external floppy disk drive (e.g. 1040STFM); or
(b) two external floppy disk drives (e.g. 520ST).

It is important to note that, whilst most of the floppy disk signals are produced by the 1772 FDC, drive and side selection signals are provided by the programmable sound synthesizer chip (the Yamaha YM1249 PSG).

The 68000 CPU reads and writes to the 1772 FDC by means of the DMA controller. The FDC interrupts the CPU by means of the INTR line via the MFP controller.

The 1772 FDC accepts high level commands from the CPU (such as seek, format track, write sector, read sector, etc.) and passes data to and from the DMA controller.

Parallel and serial I/O

The parallel printer interface is based on the Yamaha YM2149 PSG. The STROBE and data lines are connected to the PSG whilst the BUSY signal is produced by the MFP.

The MFP contains a USART (universal synchronous/asynchronous receiver/transmitter) which handles data transmission and reception. The 2.4576 MHz clock to the MFP is divided by the timer D (pin 16) output of the MFP to provide the basic clock for the asynchronous port. Data rates of between 50 and 19200 bits per second are supported. 1488 line drivers and 1489 line receivers are fitted in order to convert the TTL levels to/from the MFP and PSG in order to make the serial interface compatible with the electrical specification for the ES-232C standard .

Sound and MIDI

The MIDI interface employs a 6850 ACIA (asynchronous communications interface adaptor). This device is buffered from the outside world via two inverters on the transmit side and an optical isolator on the receive side. The input signal is also routed through two inverters to the MIDI OUT connector to provide a MIDI THRU signal.

A Yamaha YM2149 programmable sound generator (PSG) is used to provide three sound channels which are mixed to produce the audio signal which appears at the monitor connector. The PSG is capable of producing sounds with frequencies in the range 30 Hz to 125 kHz. The PSG requires a 2 MHz clock (generated from the system clock by glue).

The Commodore Amiga

The Amiga is Commodore's answer to the Apple Macintosh and Atari ST. The first production models were announced late in 1985, however volume production lagged behind its principal rival, the Atari ST.

Amiga architecture

The Amiga employs a 68000 CPU running at 7.15909 MHz. The original entry-level machine was fitted with 256K bytes of RAM (user-expandable to 512K bytes) but the entry level model (A500) is now provided with 512K bytes of memory as standard (internally upgradable to 1 Mbyte with the aid of the A501 RAM Expansion module). The Amiga is fitted with 128K bytes of ROM.

The Amiga provides no less than five graphics modes:

(a) 320 x 200 pixels in 32 colours
(b) 320 x 400 pixels in 32 colours
(c) 640 x 200 pixels in 16 colours
(d) 640 x 400 pixels in 16 colours
(e) sample-and-hold mode

The graphics are produced by an 8362 custom chip (Denise) which also copes with mouse input. The chip caters for up to two independent bit-mapped images and eight 'sprites' (images that can be rapidly moved around the screen).

An 8370 custom animation chip (Fat Angus) provides the bit blitter functions which are used to move blocks of display data around very rapidly and without CPU intervention (the CPU is then available for other concurrent tasks). Fat Angus also generates all of the necessary system clocks from an external 28 MHz oscillator (Q701 and associated components).

The Amiga has four independent sound channels which are generated by the 8364 custom sound/peripherals chip (Paula). Again, there is no need for the direct intervention of the 68000 CPU .

A custom control chip (Gary) provides the necessary bus control signals and address decoding functions. It also generates the 68000's VPA signal and handles some of the floppy disk control. One of Gary's most crucial functions is display bus arbitration between the 68000 CPU and Fat Angus. (Note that the display RAM bus can be completely isolated from the 68000 bus, thus Fat Angus can be performing a bus cycle on the display buses whilst the 68000 can be simultaneously performing a bus cycle on its buses.)

The Amiga's built-in 3.5 inch double-sided double-density floppy disk drive provides a maximum of 880K bytes of storage. The disk format employs 80 cylinders with eleven 512 byte sectors per track. The disk controller can read an entire track at a time (rather than just one sector).

Amiga hardware

The principal chip functions of the Amiga are as follows:

Reference	Device	Function
U1	68000	CPU
U2	8370	Fat Angus (animation, etc.)
U3	8364	Paula (sound and peripheral control)
U4	8362	Denise (graphics)
U5	–	Gary (bus and floppy disk control)
U6	62402	System ROM (128k × 16 bit)
U7	8520	I/O (Centronics parallel, joystick fire and floppy disk control)
U8	8520	I/O (RS-232 serial and floppy disk control)
U9	6242	Real-time clock
U16–U31	xx256–15	256k × 1 bit RAM (system board)
U42	555	Monostable timer (reset generator)
U48–U63	xx256–15	256k × 1 bit RAM (expansion)
HY1	–	Video hybrid (provides RGB, sync. and composite video signals)

Amiga memory map

The first 512K bytes of memory space is referred to as the 'chip memory' since any function performed by any of the three custom chips must relate to this region of memory. The first Amiga models only used the first 256K bytes of chip memory (addresses 000000 to 03FFFF hexadecimal) whilst in later (and expanded) models this memory extends from 000000 to 07FFFF hex. 8M bytes of memory (from address 200000 to 9FFFFF hex.) is reserved for external expansion. The Amiga's memory map is shown (in simplified form) in Figure 7.5.

Address (Hex)

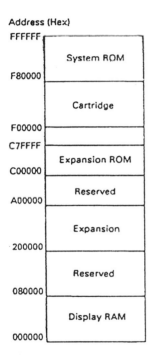

Figure 7.5 Commodore Amiga memory map

The two serial I/O chips (8520) are addressed within the space BFD000 to BFFFFF hex. whilst the three custom chips are accessible within the address range DFF000 to E00000 hex. The system ROM occupies high memory from FD0000 to FFFFFF hex.

Fault finding 68000-based microcomputers

The following information, which relates specifically to the Atari 1040STFM, gives the basic steps in dismantling a modern 68000-based microcomputer. Obvious minor differences exist in the case of units which do not have internal disk drives (such as the Atari 520ST and Sinclair QL) but the steps given should more than adequately describe the process.

1. Before doing anything else, switch the equipment off and disconnect the mains lead.
2. Disconnect the monitor or TV lead from the rear of the computer.
3. Disconnect any remaining devices connected to the rear of the computer (e.g. printer, hard disk drive and/or modem).
4. Disconnect the mouse (and/or joystick) connected to the underside (or rear) of the unit and any item of peripheral hardware connected to the cartridge or expansion ports.
5. Place a soft mat on the work surface and invert the computer so that the bottom of the enclosure is uppermost.
6. Locate and remove the case retaining screws fitted in the base of the unit (take care not to remove screws which retain the disk drive or microdrive chassis, as approppri- ate). (Note that, on the Atari ST the screws that should be removed are located in square recesses not the round recessed holes which secure the disk drive!)
7. Invert the unit so that it is once again the correct way up. Gently prize up the upper half of the case (starting from the left-hand side near the cartridge port in the case of the Atari ST) .
8. Carefully remove the upper case half (push gently to the right in order to clear the disk drive escutcheon, etc.).
9. Lift off the keyboard and disconnect the keyboard cable by removing the connector from the aperture in the screening located just above the joystick port (in the case of the Atari ST 1040) or by gently pulling upwards on the connector marked 'CN13' (in the case of the Commodore Amiga A500).

The following steps apply specifically to the Atari ST:

10. To gain access to the ST's internally fitted switched mode power supply, remove the two cross-point machined screws which retain the power supply screening fitted to the left rear of the unit. Untwist the two retaining lugs and pull the screening upwards from the rear.
11. To gain access to the disk drive, remove the two cross-point machined screws which retain the screening cover fitted at the rear of the disk drive.
12. To remove the disk drive, invert the unit once again and this time remove the three remaining cross-point screws (these are located in round recesses). Unlike the other screws fitted to the base of the unit, these three screws are machined and are approx- imately 25 mm long.
   Re-invert the unit, disconnect the two disk drive connectors from the rear of the drive, and remove the drive. (Note that the power connector may be fitted with a locking tab which must be pulled upwards in order to release the connector for removal.)
13. To remove the switched mode power supply, locate and remove the two cross-point self-tapping screws fitted at the base of the two front retaining brackets (one at the extreme left front of the power supply and one at the extreme right front of the power supply). Do not remove the upper two screws which retain PCB at the top of each bracket! Gently release the unit (complete with mains connector and switch) by prizing it upwards and forwards. The main power connector should then be disconnected (the locking tab must be released before pulling the connector away from the main PCB).
14. To remove the upper shielding (and gain access to the main PCB), remove the four further cross-point screws, twist the eleven remaining lugs, and carefully lift the metal screening clear of the PCB.
15. Access to the clock and video processing circuitry requires the removal of the metal lid of the screened box in the centre of the PCB. This lid is secured by two twisted lugs and may be 'hinged' backwards to reveal its contents (U31, Q3, Q4, Q5, Q6, Q7, Q9, Q10, and associated circuitry).

The following steps refer specifically to the Amiga 500:

16. After removing the keyboard connector (CN13), lift off the keyboard and remove the four screws which retain the upper system board screening (this will require the use of a star-bladed screwdriver, however, an Allen key of appropriate size can also be used to perform this task).
17. Undo the tabs which lock the various sections of screening together and lift off the main upper section to reveal the system board.
18. To remove the disk drive, it is necessary to release the three remaining screws in the base of the Amiga's enclosure and one screw facing forwards (inside the enclosure). The power and data cables can be most easily disconnected from the rear of the disk drive chassis.

After following the preceding steps (or the equivalent steps for a different computer) full access will have been gained to the entire system board. If necessary, the board may be removed from the lower half of the case, however, this is not always necessary since the majority of stock faults relate to items such as the power supply, floppy disk drive, keyboard, etc.

Re-assembly is simply the reverse of disassembly (note, however, that it is important to avoid confusing the self-tapping screws with the machined screws!).

The following general procedure is recommended:

1. Switch on and check that the indicator light is illuminated.
2. Insert a floppy disk into the internal drive (or microdrive cartridge into MDV1 in the case of the QL computer) and reset the system.
3. Check that the disk access light becomes illuminated and that the disk (or microdrive) starts. The initial screen or 'desktop' should normally appear within a few seconds. If this is not the case, and the drive rotates for some time before the desktop appears, this can be caused by a faulty disk drive or defective disk.
4. If the initial screen appears, the CPU, major VLSI support devices, RAM and ROM will normally be functional. In such cases the fault may be attributable to the keyboard, disk interface, or one of the other I/O systems present.
5. Where no initial screen appears (i.e. the monitor or TV remains blank) or if the video display is abnormal, the fault will generally be associated with one of the VLSI support devices, the video processing chip(s), CPU or power supply.
   In such cases it is worth dismantling the system and checking each of the power supply rails before proceeding further. If, however, no initial screen appears but the drive starts up, rotates for a short while and then stops, it is first worth checking the TV or monitor cable and connector since a fault here may result in the loss of a video display.
6. If the power supply voltages all appear to be normal, it is worth checking the clock signal at pin 15 of the 68000 CPU. This signal should comprise square wave of appropriate frequency (e.g. 8 MHz in the case of the Atari ST). Having checked that the clock signal is correct, check the HALT signal at pin 17. This signal should be permanently high. If either of these signals are not correct, check the clock circuitry, CPU and reset circuitry respectively. If the HALT line is held low, check the bus error (BERR) signal at pin 22 of the CPU as the unit is powered on. This signal should be permanently high –if it's pulsing low, this will indicate a fault within a support chip (e.g. GLUE). Note that socketed support chips can be easily tested by replacing them, in turn, with known functional devices.
7. If the clock, HALT, and BERR lines are all correct but the system still appears to be dead, check that the CPU is reading from, and writing to, memory. If the read and write signals appear normal and the data and address lines appear to be pulsing, check the video shifter.

The following symptoms and probable causes should assist readers in fault location:

Symptom	Probable causes
Black screen	Power supply failure, failed video processing, ULA, clock or bus control chips
White screen	Video shifter, ULA, memory controller, DMA controller, CPU
Vertical bars	RAM, memory controller, video processing
One colour missing	Video summer, buffer, video processing
Random screen data	ULA, memory controller
No TV output	Failed modulator
Disk refuses to boot	Disk drive faulty, power supply, FDC, DMA controller or ULA failed
Disk cannot be formatted	FDC, DMA controller, ULA or disk drive failed
Printer port inoperable	ULA, parallel I/O or custom peripheral chip failed
Keyboard inoperable	Keyboard processor failed, ULA faulty (faulty keyboard membrane in the case of the Sinclair QL)
RS-232C inoperable	ULA or serial I/O chip failed, line receiver/driver faulty, +12V or –12V power supply rails missing

Stock faults

The following information relates to some of the most common problems that occur with 68000-based micros:

Power supply

By virtue of the relatively high levels of current and voltage present within the power supply, this area is relatively prone to failure. Fortunately, since modern switched mode power supplies can be very easily removed and replaced as a complete unit, this area is relatively easy to check and service without having to resort to component level fault finding. However, where necessary, fault finding to component level can be carried out with the power supply removed from the computer along the lines suggested in Chapter 3. The usual checks should be made including switching transistor and diodes. If the fuse repeatedly fails, check the components in the primary input for short-circuits.

Disk drives

Like power supplies, disk drives are also somewhat prone to failure. Faults can develop from a number of causes (including misuse) and often caused by failure of mechanical rather than electrical component. Some disk drives will become very noisy either immediately before or immediately after failure. Grinding sounds from a drive should be investigated immediately as continued use may result in irreversible damage to disks!

Many of the early Atari 520ST machines (and some which were upgraded to 1 Mbyte RAM to conform to the 1040 standard) were only fitted with a single-sided internal floppy disk drive (formatted capacity 360K bytes) and thus it is worth replacing a failed drive with a double-sided unit.

The recommended Atari replacement drives are, however, somewhat difficult to obtain and may also be rather expensive in comparison with the low-cost 3.5 inch drives currently available. Hence, it may be worth fitting a substitute drive using one of the many 'upgrade kits' currently available. Such kits tend to be based on more modern (and quieter!) double-sided 3.5 inch drives and several companies provide complete upgrading kits at moderate cost. Note that almost any standard type of 3.5 inch double-sided floppy disk mechanism will make a suitable replacement for the original Atari unit, however, it is important to check the orientation of the 34-way disk bus connector (some may require the disk drive cable to be twisted through 180 degrees). In any event, it is always worth checking the position of pin-1 (marked with a stripe on the disk-drive cable) with respect to the male connector fitted to the disk drive chassis (where pins 1 and 34 are invariably clearly marked on the PCB silk screen).

Before fitting the drive, it is important to check that the drive has been correctly configured by means of PCB links (or track connections) to the DS0 position (i.e. the drive should appear as physical drive A). For further information see Chapter 4.

Mouse and joystick problems

Mouse and joystick ports fitted are susceptible to damage due to repeated insertion and removal of connectors. In some cases, PCB mounted D-type plugs can become deformed or may even become detached from the PCB. Alternatively, PCB tracks may fracture due to excessive strain and repeated mechanical stress. In such cases, it may be necessary to replace the damaged socket(s) and make good the connections to the PCB.

Damage also frequently occurs to mouse or joystick cables which are repeatedly flexed close to the point of entry to the body of a connector. Since most connectors are of the moulded variety, such a fault may necessitate complete replacement of the mouse or joystick.

Defective chip seating

Defective chip seating has been a particular problem with early versions of some of the 68000-based microcomputers. More modern equipment tends not to be fitted with socketed chips and thus this particular fault is less prevalent. Where faulty chip seating is suspected (intermittent faults and crashes after the equipment has been operating for some time) the problem can usually be overcome by removing each VLSI chip in turn and re-seating it into its socket. This process will result in breaking any oxide film that may have accumulated and will generally restore operation successfully. If you have to resort to removing chips in this way it is absolutely essential to follow the usual static avoidance procedures.

RAM failure

RAM failure is, in the author's experience, quite rare in the case of the modern 16- and 32-bit computers. If a failure does occur, it can often be traced to an individual device by means of a 'diagnostic cartridge'. If this item is unavailable, the temperature of each of the RAM chips should be tested in turn (using the usual 'finger test'!) and any chip which is noticeably hotter (or cooler) than the rest should be considered suspect.

Keyboard faults

Keyboards will often give problems when they have been very heavily used. Failure of an individual key is usually associated with an ineffective contact between the carbon pellet and the tracks of the keyboard PCB below it. The carbon pellets are typically mounted within rubber domes (one for each key) which collapse when a key is depressed. The carbon pellet then makes contact between the two tracks on the PCB.

Repairs usually involve disassembly of the keyboard, and careful removal of the keyboard to reveal the rubber domes and carbon pellets. Provided one is careful (and prepared to improvise!) most mechanical keyboard faults can be cured without having to resort to the purchase of a replacement unit.

Interface problems

The serial and parallel interfaces can also sometimes give problems due to non-standard implementation (e.g. the absence of a PAPER END signal in the Atari ST, or the presence of unexpected power rails in the case of the Amiga's RS-232 connector!). If problems are experienced interfacing particular items of peripheral equipment (such as printers, modems, etc.) it is well worth consulting a dealer or making enquiries via a user group.

8
Servicing the IBM PC and compatibles

Of the twelve million personal computers regularly in use in Western Europe, a very significant proportion is accounted for by the IBM PC, PC-XT, PC-AT and numerous clones and compatibles. These machines, more than any other, have set the standard for personal computers in the last decade and have attracted a software base which significantly outstrips all other machines. This chapter is devoted specifically to servicing the IBM range of machines but the techniques are applicable to a wide variety of other 'industry standard' personal computers.

The PC family

Ever since IBM entered the personal computer scene, it was clear that the PC and its successors would gain an immense following. IBM's first effort, the original PC, was announced in 1981 and first appeared in 1982. The PC had an 8088 processor, 64K to 256K of system board RAM (expandable to 640K with 384K fitted in expansion slots). The PC supported

Figure 8.1 IBM PC-XT system board

two 360K floppy disk drives, an 80 column × 25 line display, and 16 colours with an IBM colour graphics adaptor (CGA).

The original PC was quickly followed by the PC-XT. This machine, an improved PC with a single 360K floppy disk drive and a 10M hard disk, was introduced in 1983. The PC-XT was followed in 1984 by a much enhanced machine, the PC-AT. This machine used an 80286 microprocessor (rather than the 8-bit data bus 8088 used in its predecessors). The standard AT provides 1.2M and 20M of floppy and hard disk storage respectively.

While IBM were blazing a trail, many other manufacturers were close behind. The standards set by IBM attracted much interest from other manufacturers, notable among which were Compaq and Olivetti, who were not merely content to produce machines with an identical specification but went on to make significant improvements. Other manufacturers were happy to 'clone' the PC; indeed, one could be excused for thinking that the highest accolade that could be offered by the computer press was that a machine was 'IBM compatible'.

IBM PS/2

IBM's second generation of personal computers, Personal System/2, is based on four machines: Models 30, 50, 60 and 80. The smallest of these (Model 30) is based on an 8086 CPU and has dual 720/1.4M 3.5 inch floppy disk drives and 640K of RAM. Models 50 and 60 use the 80286 CPU with 1M of RAM (expandable) and fixed disk drives of 20M (Model 50), 44M or 70M (Model 60).

IBM's top-of-the-range machine, the Model 80, employs an 80386 CPU and a 1.4M 3.5 inch floppy disk drive. Three different fixed disk/RAM configurations are available for the Model 80 and these are based on 44M fixed disk/1M RAM, 70M fixed disk/2M RAM, and 115M fixed disk/2M RAM. Models 30 and 50 are designed for conventional desk-top operation whilst Models 60 and 80 both feature 'vertical' floor-standing systems units with front access panels for the fixed disk tray. PS/2 family has an impressive expansion capability and the following devices are supported by Models 50, 60 and 80:

- Monochrome display (8503)
- Colour display (8512)
- Colour display (8513) (medium-resolution)
- Colour display (8514) (high resolution)
- Memory expansion kits/cards
- Second fixed disk (44M/70M/115 Mbyte)
- External 5.25 inch floppy disk drive
- Tape streamer (6157)
- Optical disk (internal or external 3363)
- Dual asynchronous communications adaptor
- Internal modem (300/1200 baud)
- IBM PC network (LAN) adaptor
- IBM token-ring (LAN) adaptor
- Multi-protocol adaptor (asynchronous/BSC/SDLC/HDLC)
- System 36/38 workstation emulator adaptor

PC architecture

The term 'PC' now applies to such a wide range of equipment that it is difficult to pin down the essential ingredients of such a machine. However, at the risk of over-simplifying matters, a 'PC' need only satisfy two essential criteria:

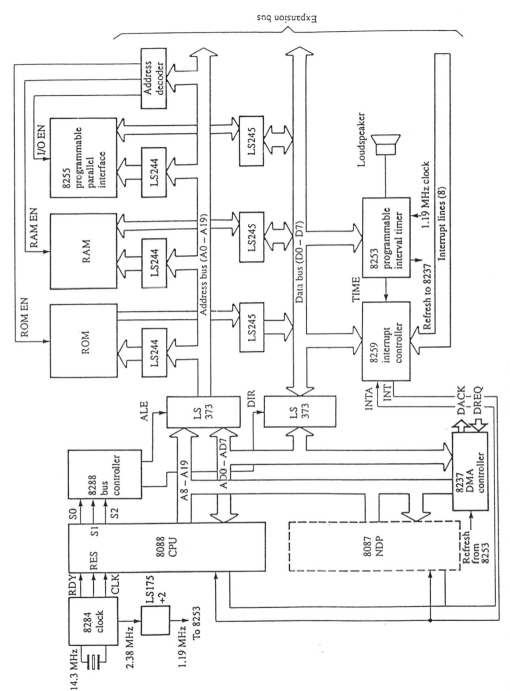

Figure 8.2 System architecture for a generic 8088 (or 8086-based) PC

(a) be based upon an Intel 16 or 32-bit processor (such as an 80 x 86, Pentium, or an equivalent device);

(b) be able to support the MS-DOS, PC-DOS, DR-DOS or a compatible operating system.

Other factors, such as available memory size, display technology, and disk storage, remain secondary.

The generic PC, whether a 'desktop' or 'tower' system, comprises three units; System Unit, Keyboard, and Display. The System Unit itself comprises three items; System Board, Power Supply, and Floppy/Hard Disk Drives.

The original IBM PC System Board employed approximately 100 IC devices including an 8088 CPU, an 8259A Interrupt Controller, an optional 8087 Maths Coprocessor, an 8288 Bus Controller, an 8284A Clock Generator, an 8253 Timer/Counter, an 8237A DMA Controller, and an 8255A Parallel Interface together with a host of discrete logic (including bus buffers, latches and transceivers). Figure 8.2 shows the simplified bus architecture of the system.

Much of this architecture was carried forward to the PC-XT and the PC-AT. This latter machine employed an 80286 CPU, 80287 Maths Coprocessor, two 8237A DMA Controllers, 8254-2 Programmable Timer, 8284A Clock Generator, two 8259A Interrupt Controllers, and a 74LS612N Memory Mapper.

In order to significantly reduce manufacturing costs as well as to save on space and increase reliability, more recent XT and AT-compatible microcomputers are based on a significantly smaller number of devices (many of which may be surface mounted types).

This trend has been continued with today's powerful '386 and '486-based systems. However, the functions provided by the highly integrated chipsets are merely a superset of those provided by the much large number of devices found in their predecessors.

PC specifications

PCs tend to conform to one of the basic specifications shown in Table 8.1.

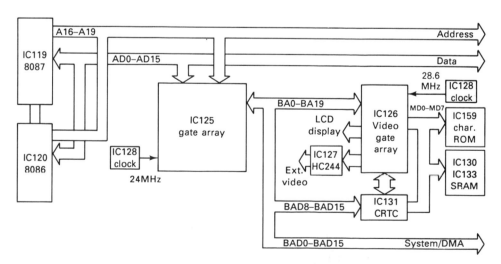

Figure 8.3 Amstrad PPC512/640 processors, gate array and video processing

The 'generic' PC

The system architecture of a generic 8088-based PC was shown in Figure 8.2. There is more to this diagram than mere historical interest as all modern PCs can trace their origins to this particular arrangement. It is, therefore, worth spending a few moments developing an understanding of the configuration.

The 'CPU bus' (comprising lines A8 to A19 and AD0 to AD7 on the left side of Figure 8.2) is separated from the 'system bus' which links the support devices and expansion cards.

The eight least significant address and all eight of the data bus lines share a common set of eight CPU pins. These lines are labelled AD0 to AD7. The term used to describe this form of bus (where data and address information take turns to be present on a shared set of bus lines) is known as 'multiplexing'. This saves pins on the CPU package and it allowed Intel to make use of standard 40-pin packages for the 8088 and 8086 processors.

The system address bus (available on each of the expansion connectors) comprises twenty address lines, A0 to A19. The system data bus comprises eight lines, D0 to D7. Address and data information is alternately latched onto the appropriate set of bus lines by means of the four 74LS373 8-bit data latches. The control signals, ALE (address latch enable) and DIR (direction) derived from the 8288 bus controls are used to activate the two pairs of data latches.

The CPU bus is extended to the 8087 numeric data processor (maths coprocessor). This device is physically located in close proximity to the CPU in order to simplify the PCB layout.

Table 8.1 Typical PC specifications

Standard	Processor	RAM	Floppy disk	Hard disk	Graphics	Parallel port(s)	Serial port(s)	Clock speed
PC	8088	256K	1 or 2 360K	none	Text or CGA	1 or 2	1 or 2	8 MHz
XT	8088 or 80286	640K	1 or 2 5.25" 360K	10M	Text and CGA	1 or 2	1 or 2	8 or 10 MHz
AT	80286	1M	1 or 2 5.25" 1.2M	20M	Text, CGA or EGA	1 or 2	1 or 2	12 or 16 MHz
386SX-based	80386SX	1M to 8M	1 or 2 3.5" 1.44M or 5.25" 1.2M	40M	Text, VGA or SVGA	1 or 2	1 or 2	16 or 20 MHz
386DX-based	80386DX	1M to 16M	1 or 2 3.5" or 1.44M or 5.25" 1.2M	60M	Text, VGA or SVGA	1 or 2	1 or 2	25, 33 or 40 MHz
486DX-based	80486DX	4M to 64M	1 or 2 3.5" 1.44M	100M	Text, VGA or SVGA	1 or 2	1 or 2	25, 33 or 50 MHz
PS/2	80286 or 80386	1M to 16M	1 3.5" 720K or 1.44M	44M, 70M or 117M	Text, EGA or VGA	1 or 2	1 or 2	8, 10, 16 or 20 MHz

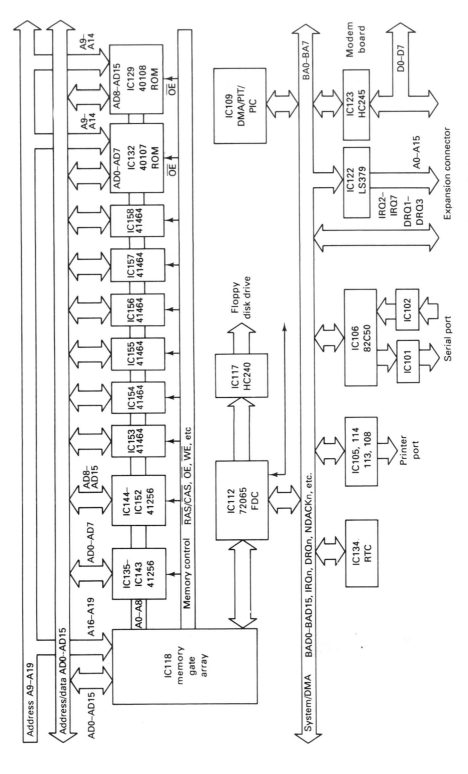

Figure 8.4 Amstrad PPC512/640 memory and I/O. The sophisticated gate array is instrumental in minimizing the overall chip count

Figure 8.5 Amstrad PPC512 processor board

Figure 8.6 Amstrad PPC512 memory board

The original PC required a CPU clock signal of 4.773 MHz from a dedicated Intel clock generator chip. The basic timing element for this device is a quartz crystal which oscillates at a fundamental frequency of 14.318 MHz. This frequency is internally divided by three in order to produce the CPU clock.

The CPU clock frequency is also further divided by two internally and again by two externally in order to produce a clock signal for the 8253 programmable interrupt timer. This device provides three important timing signals used by the system. One (known appropriately as TIME) controls the 8259 programmable interrupt controller, another (known as REFRESH) provides a timing input for the 8237 DMA controller, whilst the third is used (in conjunction with some extra logic) to produce an audible signal at the loudspeaker.

74LS244 8-bit bus drivers and 74LS245 8-bit bus transceivers link each of the major support devices with the 'system address bus' and 'system data bus' respectively. Address decoding logic (with input signals derived from the system address bus) generates the chip enable lines which activate the respective ROM, RAM and I/O chip select lines.

The basic system board incorporates a CPU, provides a connector for the addition of a maths coprocessor, incorporates bus and DMA control, and provides the system clock and timing signals. The system board also houses the BIOS ROM, main system RAM, and offers some limited parallel I/O. It does not, however, provide a number of other essential facilities including a video interface, disk and serial I/O. These important functions must normally be provided by means of adaptor cards (note that some systems which offer only limited expansion may have some or all of these facilities integrated into the system board).

Adaptor cards are connected to the expansion bus by means of a number of expansion slots. The adaptor cards are physically placed so that any external connections required are available at the rear (or side) of the unit. Connections to internal sub-systems (such as hard and floppy disk drives) are usually made using lengths of ribbon cables and PCB connectors.

Typical system board layout

Figure 8.7 shows the system board layout of a generic 8088-based PC-XT. This general layout started with the original PC and has been carried forward with improvements and enhancements into a wide range of PCs (including XT, XT-286, AT and compatible equipment).

The original PC's system board RAM was arranged in four banks, each of which provides 64K of memory. This memory is supplied using up to 36 conventional dual-in-line RAM chips. Bank 0 is the lowest 64K of RAM (addresses 00000 to 0FFFF), Bank 1 the next 64K (addresses 10000 to 1FFFF), and so on. The XT uses a similar RAM layout to the original PC but with larger capacity RAM chips (a total of 512K on the system board). Additional memory can only be provided by means of an appropriate adaptor card.

The original AT motherboard ('AT Type 1') had its RAM organized in two banks (Bank 0 and Bank 1). These accommodate up to 36 128K × 1 bit dual-in-line RAM chips. The later AT motherboard ('AT Type 2') and XT-286 machines both use 'memory modules' (rather than individual RAM chips).

The major support devices (8288 bus controller, 8237A direct memory access controller, etc) on all three basic specification machines (PC, XT and AT) are clustered together on the right of the PCB (as viewed from above). More modern machines use integrated support chips and thus there are less (but more complex) devices present on the motherboard.

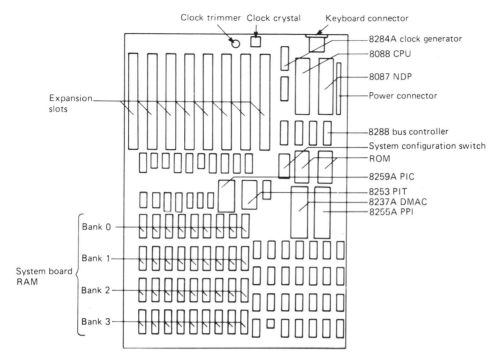

Figure 8.7 Typical generic system motherboard layout

Furthermore, modern system boards invariably use surface mounted components and pin-grid array (PGA) chips (rather than the conventionally soldered dual-in-line chips used in the original specification machines).

Cooling

All PC systems produce heat and some systems produce more heat than others. Adequate ventilation is thus an essential consideration and fans are included within the system unit to ensure that there is adequate air flow. Furthermore, internal air flow must be arranged so that it is unrestricted as modern processors and support chips run at high temperatures. These devices are much more prone to failure when they run excessively hot than when they run cool or merely warm.

If the system unit fan fails to operate (and it is not thermostatically controlled) check the supply to it. If necessary replace the fan. If the unit runs slow or intermittently it should similarly be replaced.

Dismantling a PC system

The procedure for dismantling a system depends upon the type of enclosure. The three examples that follow should at least give you some idea of the main points.

Figure 8.8 Intel '486DX CPU chip in a PGA connector

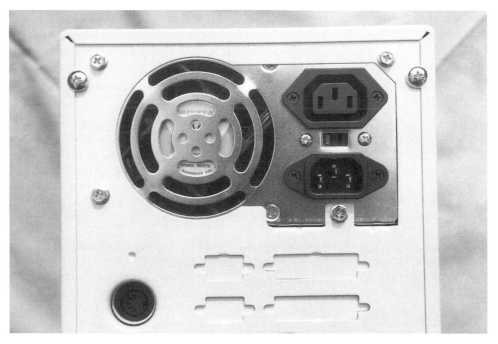

Figure 8.9 Rear view of modern tower system showing power supply, fan, display power and 5-pin DIN keyboard connector

Standard IBM PC, XT and AT system units

1. Exit from any program that may be running.
2. Type PARK to park the hard disk heads (if appropriate).
3. Remove the floppy disk(s) from the drive(s).
4. Switch the system unit power off (using the power switch at the rear of the system unit case).
5. Switch off at the mains outlet and disconnect the mains power lead.
6. Switch off and disconnect any peripherals that may be attached (including keyboard, mouse, printer, etc).
7. Disconnect the display power lead and video signal cable from the rear of the system unit. Remove the display and place safely on one side.
8. Remove the cover retaining screws from the rear of the system unit.
9. Carefully slide the system unit cover away from the rear and towards the front. When the cover will slide no further, tilt the cover upwards, remove the cover from the base and set aside.
10. You will now have access to the system board, power supply, disk drives, and adaptor cards.

Tower units

As steps 1 to 6 for a standard system plus:

7. Disconnect the display power lead and video signal cable from the rear of the system unit.
8. Remove the cover retaining screws from the rear of the system unit.
9. Carefully slide the system unit cover towards the rear until it is clear of the front fascia. Then lift the cover clear of the system unit. It is not usually necessary to remove the fascia.
10. You will now have access to the system board, power supply, disk drives, and adaptor cards.

Amstrad PC1512, PC1640

As steps 1 to 6 for a standard system plus:

7. Disconnect the display power lead and video signal cable from the rear of the system unit. Lift off the display from the recess in the upper case half and move to one side.
8. Depress the two tabs and then lift off the cover fitted to the expansion area at the rear of the system unit.
9. Remove the four long cross-point screws (two at the rear and two at the front fitted under the two snap-off plastic covers).
10. Remove the three smaller cross-point screws that retain the metal plate which secures the expansion cards.
11. Simultaneously slide the front plastic escutcheon forwards and the upper case half upwards, separating the two plastic mouldings in the process.
12. Remove the two-way PCB connector which links the battery holder with the system unit.

Figure 8.10 Internal cabling of a modern tower system

13. Remove the two-way PCB connector which links the front-panel power indicator to the system unit.
14. You will now have access to the system board, power supply, disk drives, and adapter cards.

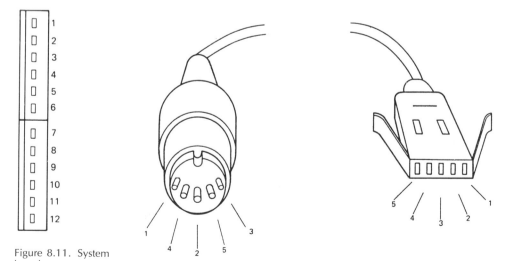

Figure 8.11. System board power connector

Figure 8.12. Pin-numbering for the keyboard connector

Reassembly

System unit reassembly is usually the reverse of disassembly. It is, of course, essential to check the orientation of any non-polarized cables and connectors and also to ensure that screws have been correctly located and tightened. Under no circumstances should there be any loose connectors, components, or screws left inside a system unit!

PC support devices

Each of the major support devices present within a PC has a key role to play in off-loading a number of routine tasks that would otherwise have to be performed by the CPU. This chapter provides a brief introduction to each generic device together with internal architecture and pin connecting details.

Locating and identifying the support devices

The support devices are usually easy to identify as they occupy much larger packages than the RAM devices and other logic circuits. In many cases they may be socketed though they may also be soldered directly to the PCB (without a socket). The support devices are usually marked with the manufacturer's name (or logo), the device coding, and the date of manufacture. Where the functions of several support devices have been integrated into a single device, the chip will generally be surface mounted and soldered directly to the PCB. In this case, specialized SMT handling techniques will be required if the chip is to be removed and replaced.

8087 maths coprocessor

The 8087, where fitted, is only active when mathematics related instructions are encountered in the instruction stream. The 8087, which is effectively wired in parallel with the 8086 or 8088 CPU, adds eight 80-bit floating point registers to the CPU register set. The 8087 maintains its own instruction queue and executes only those instructions which are specifically intended for it. The internal architecture of the 8087 is shown in Figure 8.13. The 8087 is supplied in a 40-pin DIL package, the pin connections for which are shown in Figure 8.14.

The active-low TEST input of the 8086/8088 CPU is driven from the BUSY output of the 8087 NDP. This allows the CPU to respond to the WAIT instruction (inserted by the assembler/compiler) which occurs before each coprocessor instruction. An FWAIT instruction follows each coprocessor instruction which deposits data in memory for immediate use by the CPU. The instruction is then translated to the requisite 8087 operation (with the preceding WAIT) and the FWAIT instruction is translated as a CPU WAIT instruction.

During coprocessor execution, the BUSY line is taken high and the CPU (responding to the WAIT instruction) halts its activity until the line goes low. The two Queue Status (QS0 and QS1) signals are used to synchronize the instruction queues of the two processing devices.

80287 and 80387 chips provide maths coprocessing facilities within AT and '386-based PCs respectively. In '486-based systems there is no need for a maths coprocessor as these facilities have been incorporated within the CPU.

Table 8.2 Pin numbers and typical colour coding convention for the system power connector in an AT-compatible machine (you should *not* rely on this being the same in other machines)

Power connector pin number (see Figure 8.11)	Voltage/signal	Colour
1	Power good	orange
2	+5 V d.c.	red
3	+12 V d.c.	yellow
4	−12V d.c.	blue
5	0 V/common	black
6	0 V/common	black
7	0 V/common	black
8	0 V/common	black
9	−5 V d.c.	white
10	+5 V d.c.	red
11	+5 V d.c.	red
12	+5 V d.c.	red

Table 8.3 Support chips used with 80×86 processors

	CPU type				
	8086	8088	80186	80286	80386 (386)
Clock generator	8284A	8284A	On-chip	82284	82384
Bus controller	8288	8288	On-chip	82288	82288
Integrated support chips				82230/ 82231, 82335	82230/ 82231, 82335
Interrupt controller	8259A	8259A	On-chip	8259A	8259A
DMA controller	8089/ 82258	8089/ 8237/ 82258	On-chip 82258	8089/ 82258	8237/ 82258
Timer/ counter	8253/ 8254	8253/ 8254	On-chip	8253/ 8254	8253/ 8254
Maths coprocessor	8087	8087	8087	80287	80287/ 80387
Chip select/ wait state logic	TTL	TTL	On-chip	TTL	TTL

You can find out whether a coprocessor is fitted to a system without dismantling it. If bit 1 of the byte stored at address 0410 hex. is set, a maths coprocessor is present. If bit 1 is reset, no coprocessor is fitted. You can check the bit in question using DEBUG or by using the QuickBASIC code shown in Listing 8.1.

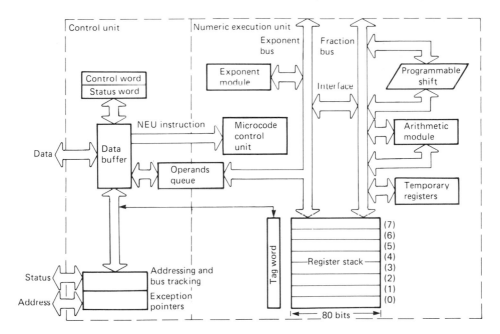

Figure 8.13. Internal architecture of the 8087

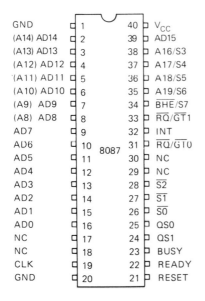

Figure 8.14 Pin connections for the 8087

8237A direct memory access controller

The 8237A DMA controller (DMAC) can provide service for up to four independent DMA
channels, each with separate registers for Mode Control, Current Address, Base Address,

Figure 8.15 IBM PC-XT system board showing 8088 CPU, 8087 maths coprocessor socket, 8288 bus controller, ROM and DIL system configuration switch

Figure 8.16 PC-XT compatible system card showing 8088 CPU and 8087 maths coprocessor socket plus multi-function chip (U62)

```
DEF SEG = 0
byte=PEEK(&H410)
IF byte AND 2 THEN
  PRINT "Coprocessor fitted"
ELSE
  PRINT "No coprocessor present"
END IF
```

Listing 8.1 QuickBASIC program to determine whether a coprocessor is fitted to a PC or compatible system

Current Word Count and Base Word Count (see Figure 8.17). The DMAC is designed to improve system performance by allowing external devices to directly transfer information to and from the system memory. The 8237A offers a variety of programmable control features to enhance data thoughput and allow dynamic reconfiguration under software control.

The 8237A provides four basic modes of transfer: Block, Demand, Single Word, and Cascade. These modes may be programmed as required however channels may be auto-initialized to their original condition following an End Of Process (EOP) signal.

The 8237A is designed for use with an external octal address latch such as the 74LS373. A system's DMA capability may be extended by cascading further 8237A DMAC chips and this feature is exploited in the PC-AT which has two such devices.

The least significant four address lines of the 8237A are bi-directional: when functioning as inputs, they are used to select one of the DMA controllers sixteen internal registers. When functioning as outputs, on the other hand, a sixteen bit address is formed by taking the eight address lines (A0 to A7) to form the least significant address byte whilst the most significant address byte (A8 to A15) is multiplexed onto the data bus lines (D0 to D7). The requisite address latch enable signal (ADSTB) is available from pin 8. The upper four address bits (A16 to A19) are typically supplied by a 74LS670 4 × 4 register file. The requisite bits are placed in this device (effectively a static RAM) by the processor before the DMA transfer is completed.

DMA channel 0 (highest priority) is used in conjunction with the 8253 Programmable Interval Timer (PIT) in order to provide a memory refresh facility for the PC's dynamic RAM. DMA channels 1 to 3 are connected to the expansion slots for use by option cards.

The refresh process involves channel 1 of the PIT producing a negative going pulse with a period of approximately 15 µs. This pulse sets a bistable which, in turn, generates a DMA request at the channel 0 input of the DMAC (pin 19). The processor is then forced into a wait state and the address and data bus buffers assume a tri-state (high impedance) condition. The DMAC then outputs a row refresh address and the row address strobe (RAS) is asserted. The 8237 increments its refresh count register and control is then returned to the processor. The process then continues such that all 256 rows are refreshed within a time interval of 4 ms. The pin connections for the 8237A are shown in Figure 8.18.

8253 Programmable Interval Timer

The 8253 is a programmable interval timer (PIT) which has three independent pre-settable 16-bit counters each offering a count rate of up to 2.6 MHz. The internal architecture and pin connections for the 8253 are shown in Figures 8.19 and 8.20 respectively. Each counter consists of a single 16-bit presettable down counter. The counter can function in binary or BCD and its input, gate and output are configured by the data held in the Control Word

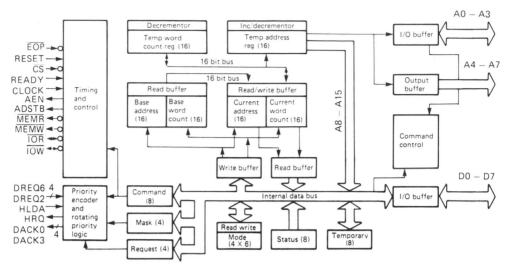

Figure 8.17 Internal architecture of the 8237A

```
         ┌────────┐
IOR    ⊏ 1  ╰─╯ 40 ⊐ A7
IOW    ⊏ 2      39 ⊐ A6
MEMR   ⊏ 3      38 ⊐ A5
MEMW   ⊏ 4      37 ⊐ A4
LOGIC 1 ⊏ 5     36 ⊐ EOP
READY  ⊏ 6      35 ⊐ A3
HLDA   ⊏ 7      34 ⊐ A2
ADSTB  ⊏ 8      33 ⊐ A1
AEN    ⊏ 9      32 ⊐ A0
HRQ    ⊏ 10 8237A 31 ⊐ Vcc  (+5 V)
CS     ⊏ 11     30 ⊐ DB0
CLK    ⊏ 12     29 ⊐ DB1
RESET  ⊏ 13     28 ⊐ DB2
DACK2  ⊏ 14     27 ⊐ DB3
DACK3  ⊏ 15     26 ⊐ DB4
DREQ3  ⊏ 16     25 ⊐ DACK0
DREQ2  ⊏ 17     24 ⊐ DACK1
DREQ1  ⊏ 18     23 ⊐ DB5
DREQ0  ⊏ 19     22 ⊐ DB6
(GND) Vss ⊏ 20  21 ⊐ DB7
```

Figure 8.18 Pin connections for the 8237A

Register. The down counters are negative edge triggered such that, on a falling clock edge, the contents of the respective counter is decremented.

The three counters are fully independent and each can have separate mode configuration and counting operation, binary or BCD. The contents of each 16-bit count register can be loaded or read using simple software referencing the relevant port addresses shown in Table 8.5. The truth table for the chip's active-low chip select (CS), read (RD), write (WR) and address lines (A1 and A0) is shown in Table 8.4.

Table 8.4 Truth table for the 8253

CS	RD	WR	A1	A0	Function
0	1	0	0	0	Load counter 0
0	1	0	0	1	Load counter 1
0	1	0	1	0	Load counter 2
0	1	0	1	1	Write mode word
0	0	1	0	0	Read counter 0
0	0	1	0	1	Read counter 1
0	0	1	1	0	Read counter 2
0	0	1	1	1	No-operation (tri-state)
1	X	X	X	X	Disable tri-state
0	1	1	X	X	No-operation (tri-state)

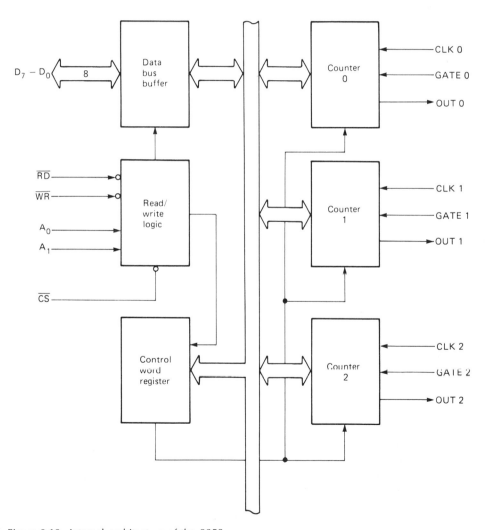

Figure 8.19. Internal architecture of the 8253

Table 8.5 Port addresses used in the PC family

Device	PC-XT	PC-AT, etc
8237A DMA controller	000–00F	000–01F
8259A interrupt controller	020–021	020–03F
8253/8254 timer	040–043	040–05F
8255 parallel interface	060–063	n/a
8042 keyboard controller	n/a	060–06F
DMA page register	080–083	080–09F
NMI mask register	0A0–0A7	070–07F
Second 8259A interrupt controller	n/a	0A0–0BF
Second 8237A DMA controller	n/a	0C0–0DF
Maths coprocessor (8087, 80287)	n/a	0F0–0FF
Games controller	200–20F	200–207
Expansion unit	210–217	n/a
Second parallel port	n/a	278–27F
Second serial port	2F8–2FF	2F8–2FF
Prototype card	300–31F	300–31F
Fixed (hard) disk	320–32F	1F0–1F8
First parallel printer	378–37F	378–37F
SDLC adaptor	380–38F	380–38F
BSC adaptor	n/a	3A0–3AF
Monochrome adaptor	3B0–3BF	3B0–3BF
Enhanced graphics adaptor	n/a	3C0–3CF
Colour graphics adaptor	3D0–3DF	3D0–3DF
Floppy disk controller	3F0–3F7	3F0–3F7
First serial port	3F8–3FF	3F8–3FF

8255A programmable peripheral interface

The 8255A programmable peripheral interface (PPI) is a general purpose I/O device which provides no less than 24 I/O lines arranged as three 8-bit I/O ports. The internal architecture and pin connections of the 8255A are shown in Figures 8.21 and 8.22 respectively. The Read/Write and Control Logic block manages all internal and external data transfers. The port addresses used by the 8255A are given in Table 8.5.

The functional configuration of each of the 8255's three I/O ports is fully programmable. Each of the control groups accepts commands from the Read/Write Control Logic, receives Control Words via the internal data bus and issues the requisite commands to each of the

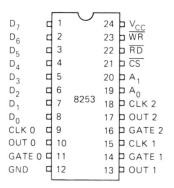

Figure 8.20. Pin connections for the 8253

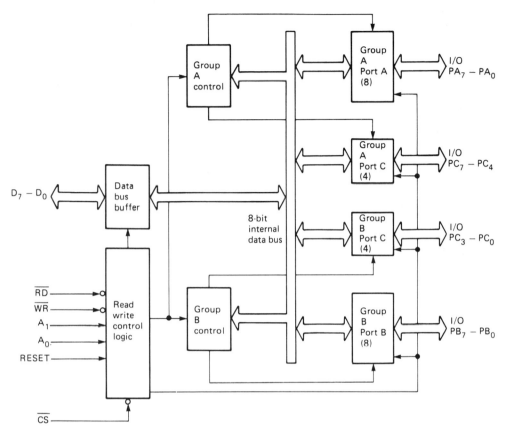

Figure 8.21. Internal architecture of the 8255A

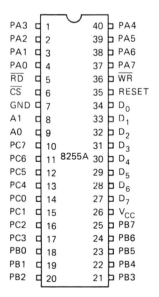

Figure 8.22. Pin connections for the 8255A

Figure 8.23. IBM PC-XT system board showing 8255A, 8237A, 8253 and 8259 devices

ports. At this point, it is important to note that the 24 I/O lines are, for control purposes, divided into two logical groups (A and B). Group A comprises the entire eight lines of Port A together with the four upper (most significant) lines of Port B. Group B, on the other hand, takes in all eight lines from Port B together with the four lower (least significant) lines of Port C. The upshot of all this is simply that Port C can be split into two in order to allow its lines to be used for status and control (handshaking) when data is transferred to or from Ports A or B.

8259A programmable interrupt controller

The 8259A programmable interrupt controller (PIC) was designed specifically for use in real-time interrupt driven microcomputer systems. The device manages eight levels of request and can be expanded using further 8259A devices.

The sequence of events which occurs when an 8259A device is used in conjunction with an 8086 or 8088 processor is as follows:

(a) One or more of the interrupt request lines (IR0–IR7) are asserted (note that these lines are active-high) by the interrupting device(s).
(b) The corresponding bits in the IRR register become set.
(c) The 8259A evaluates the requests on the following basis:
    (i) If more than one request is currently present, determine which of the requests has the highest priority.

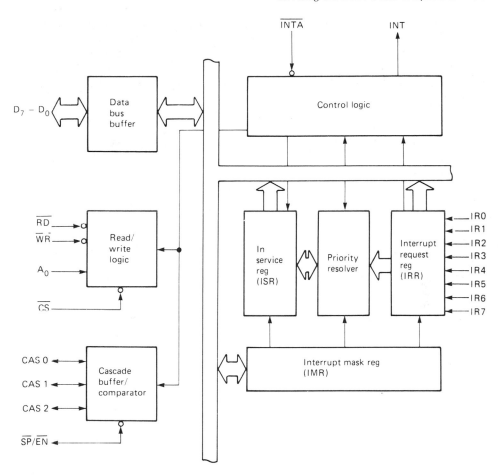

Figure 8.24. Internal architecture of the 8259A

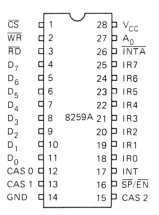

Figure 8.25. Pin connections for the 8259A

(ii)   Ascertain whether the successful request has a higher priority than the level currently being serviced.

(iii)   If the condition in (ii) is satisfied, issue an interrupt to the processor by asserting the active-high INT line.

(d)   The processor ackowledges the interrupt signal and responds by asserting the interrupt acknowledge by pulsing the interrupt acknowledge (INTA) line.

(e)   Upon receiving the INTA pulse from the processor, the highest priority ISR bit is set and the corresponding IRR bit is reset.

(f)   The processor then initiates a second interrupt acknowledge (INTA) pulse. During this second period for which the INTA line is taken low, the 8259 outputs a pointer on the data bus to be read by the processor.

The internal architecture and pin connections for the 8259A are shown in Figures 8.24 and 8.25 respectively.

8284A Clock Generator

The 8284A is a single chip clock generator/driver designed specifically for use by the 8086 family of devices. The chip contains a crystal oscillator, divided-by-3 counter, ready and reset logic as shown in Figure 8.26. On the original PC, the quartz crystal is a series mode fundamental device which operates at a frequency of 14.312818 MHz. The output of the $\div 3$ counter takes the form of a 33% duty cycle square wave at precisely one third of the fundamental frequency (i.e. 4.77 MHz). This signal is then applied to the processor's clock (CLK) input. The clock generator also produces a signal at 2.38 MHz which is externally

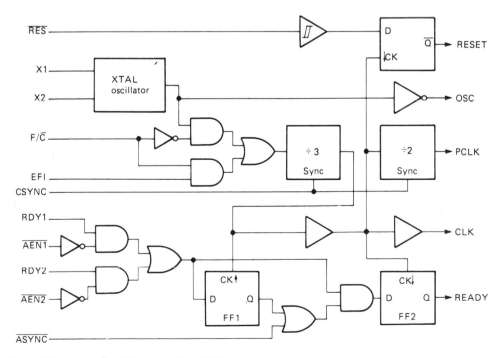

Figure 8.26. Internal architecture of the 8284A

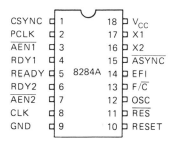

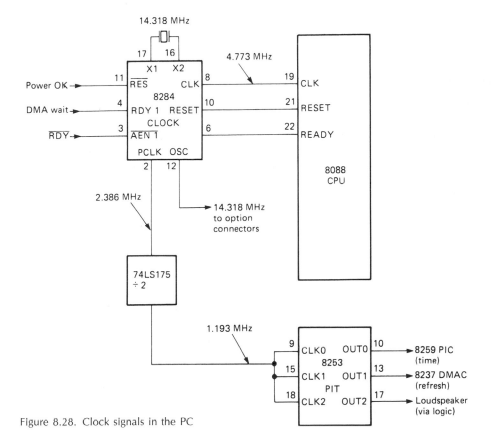

Figure 8.27. Pin connections for the 8284A

Figure 8.28. Clock signals in the PC

divided to provide a 5.193 MHz 50% duty cycle clock signal for the 8253 Programmable Interval Timer (PIT), as shown in Figure 8.28.

8288 bus controller

The 8288 bus controller decodes the status outputs from the CPU (S0–S1) in order to generate the requisite bus command and control signals. These signals are used as shown in Table 8.6.

Table 8.6 8288 bus controller status inputs

| CPU status line | | | Condition |
S2	S1	S0	
0	0	0	Interrupt acknowledge
0	0	1	I/O read
0	1	0	I/O write
0	1	1	Halt
1	0	0	Memory read
1	0	1	Memory read
1	1	0	Memory write
1	1	1	Inactive

The 8288 issues signals to the system to strobe addresses into the address latches, to enable data onto the buses, and to determine the direction of data flow through the data buffers. The internal architecture and pin connections for the 8288 are shown in Figures 8.29 and 8.30 respectively.

Integrated support devices

In modern PCs, the overall device count has been significantly reduced by integrating several of the functions associated with the original PC chip set within a single VLSI device or within the CPU itself. As an example, the Chips and Technology 82C100 XT Controller

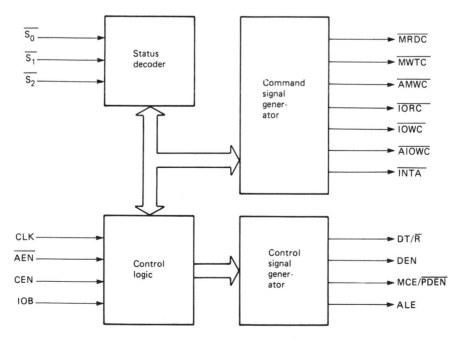

Figure 8.29 Internal architecture of the 8288

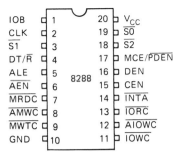

Figure 8.30 Pin connections for the 8288

provides the functionality associated with no less than six of the original XT chip set and effectively replaces the following devices; 8237 DMA Controller, 8253 Counter/Timer, 8255 Parallel Interface, 8259 Interrupt Controller, 8284 Clock Generator, and 8288 Bus Controller.

In order to ensure software compatability with the original PC, the 82C100 contains a superset of the registers associated with each of the devices which it is designed to replace. The use of the chip is thus completely transparent as far as applications software is concerned.

PC memory terminology

The following terminology is commonly used to describe the various types of memory present within a PC or PC-compatible system:

Conventional RAM

The PC's RAM extending from 00000 to 9FFFF is referred to as 'conventional memory' or 'base memory'. This 640K of read/write memory provides storage for user programs and data as well as regions reserved for DOS and BIOS use.

Upper memory area

The remaining memory within the 1 Mbyte direct addressing space (i.e., that which extends form A0000 to FFFFF) is referred to as the 'upper memory area' (UMA). The UMA itself is divided into various regions (depending upon the machine's configuration) including that which provides storage used by video adaptors.

Video RAM

As its name implies, video RAM is associated with the video/graphics adapter. The video RAM occupies the lower part of the upper memory area and its precise configuration will depend upon the type of adaptor fitted.

Extended memory

Memory beyond the basic 1 Mbyte direct addressing space is referred to as 'extended memory'. This memory can be accessed by a '286 or later CPU operating in 'protected mode'. In this mode, the CPU is able to generate 24-bit addresses (instead of the real mode's 20-bit addresses) by multiplying the segment register contents by 256 (instead of 16). This scheme allows the CPU to access addresses ranging from 000000 to FFFFFF (a total of 16 Mbytes). When the CPU runs in protected mode, a program can only access the designated region of memory. A processor exception will occur if an attempt is made to write to a region of memory that is outside of the currently allocated block.

Expanded memory

Expanded memory was originally developed for machines based on 8088 and 8086 CPU which could not take advantage of the protected mode provided by the '286 and later processors. Expanded memory is accessed through a 64K 'page frame' located within the upper memory area. This page frame acts as a window into a much larger area of memory.

Table 8.7 CMOS memory organization

Offset (hex)	Contents
00	seconds
01	seconds alarm
02	minutes
03	minutes alarm
04	hours
05	hours alarm
06	day of the week
07	day of the month
08	month
09	year
0A	status register A
0B	status register B
0C	status register C
0D	status register D
0E	diagnostic status byte
0F	shutdown status byte
10	floppy disk type (drives A and B)
11	reserved
12	fixed disk type (drives 0 and 1)
13	reserved
14	equipment byte
15	base memory (low byte)
16	base memory (high byte)
17	extended memory (low byte)
18	extended memory (high byte)
19	hard disk 0 extended type
1A	hard disk 1 extended type
1B–2D	reserved
2E–2F	checksum for bytes 10 to 1F
30	actual extended memory (low byte)
31	actual extended memory (high byte)
32	date century byte (in BCD format)
33–3F	reserved

```
DIM  cmos%(32)
CLS
PRINT  "Offset",  "Value"
PRINT  "(hex)",  "(hex)"
PRINT
FOR  i%  =  16  TO  31
   OUT  &H70,  i%
   cmos%(i%)  =  INP(&H71)
   PRINT  HEX$(i%),  HEX$(cmos%(i%))
NEXT  i%
```

Listing 8.2 QuickBASIC program to reveal the contents of the second 16 bytes of CMOS RAM

Expanded memory systems are based on a standard developed by three manufacturers (Lotus, Intel and Microsoft). This 'LIM standard' is also known as the Expanded Memory Standard (EMS). In order to make use of EMS, a special expanded memory driver is required. EMS has largely been superseded by the advanced memory management facilities provided by the '386 and '486 CPU chips.

CMOS RAM

The PC-AT and later machines' CMOS memory is 64 bytes of battery-backed memory contained within the real-time clock chip (a Motorola MC146818). Sixteen bytes of this memory are used to retain the real-time clock settings (date and time information) whilst the remainder contains important information on the configuration of your system. When the CMOS battery fails or when power is inadvertently removed from the real-time clock chip, all data will become invalid and you will have to use your set-up program to restore the settings for your system. This can be a real problem *unless* you know what the settings should be!

The organization of the CMOS memory is shown in Table 8.7 (note that locations marked 'reserved' may have different functions in some non-IBM systems).

The QuickBASIC program shown in Listing 8.2 will reveal the contents of the second 16 bytes of CMOS RAM (offset addresses 10 to 1F inclusive). These 16 bytes will tell you how

Offset (hex)	Value (hex)	Comment
10	44	Both drives are 1.44M (type 4)
11	EB	
12	F0	Hard drive 0 is type 15, no hard drive 1
13	9C	
14	4F	2 floppy drives, use display adaptor's BIOS
15	80	
16	2	640K of base memory
17	0	
18	D	3328K of extended memory (4M total)
19	2F	Hard drive 0 extended type 47
1A	0	No hard drive 1
1B	68	
1C	3	
1D	8	
1E	0	
1F	0	

Figure 8.31 Output produced by the program shown in Listing 8.2

the system has been configured (i.e., how much base and extended memory is present and the types of floppy and hard drive). A typical set of CMOS data for these locations is shown in Figure 8.31.

A QuickBASIC program that can be used to save *and* restore the contents of CMOS RAM is shown in Listing 8.3.

BIOS ROM

The BIOS ROM is programmed during manufacture. The programming data is supplied to the semiconductor manufacturer by the BIOS originator. This process is cost-effective for large-scale production however programming of the ROM is irreversible; once programmed, devices cannot be erased in preparation for fresh programming. Hence, the only way of upgrading the BIOS is to remove and discard the existing chips and replace them with new ones. This procedure is fraught with problems, not least of which is compatability of the BIOS upgrade with existing DOS software.

The BIOS ROM invariably occupies the last 64K or 128K bytes of memory (from F0000 to FFFFF or E0000 to FFFFF, respectively). It is normally based on two chips; one for the odd addresses and one for the even addresses.

BIOS variations

Several manufacturers (e.g. Compaq) have produced ROM BIOS code for use in their own equipment. This code must, of course, be compatible with IBM's BIOS code. Several other companies (e.g. American Megatrends (AMI), Award Software, and Phoenix Software) have developed generic versions of the BIOS code which has been incorporated into numerous clones and compatibles.

There are, of course, minor differences between these BIOS versions. Notably these exist within the power-on self-test (POST), the set-up routines, and the range of hard disk types supported.

System board RAM

The PC system board's read/write memory provides storage for the DOS and BIOS as well as transient user programs and data. In addition, read/write memory is also used to store data which is displayed on the screen. Depending upon the nature of the applications software, this memory may be either character mapped (text) or bit-mapped (graphics). The former technique involves dividing the screen into a number of character-sized cells.

Each displayed character cell requires one byte of memory for storage of the character plus a further byte for 'attributes' (see Chapter 13). Hence a screen having 80 columns × 25 lines (corresponding to the IBM's basic text mode) will require 2000 bytes; 1000 for storage of the characters and a further plus 1000 for the attributes.

Bit-mapped graphic displays require a very much larger amount of storage. Each display pixel is mapped to a particular bit in memory and the bit may be a 1 or a 0 depending upon whether it is to be light or dark. Where a colour display is to be produced, several colour planes must be implemented and consequently an even larger amount of memory is required. A VGA graphics adaptor, for example, may be fitted with up to 1 Mbyte of video RAM.

```
REM ** PC Troubleshooting CMOS memory backup **
ON ERROR GOTO warning
DIM cmos%(64)
main:
DO
  CLS
  PRINT "CMOS memory utility"
  PRINT "[B] = backup"
  PRINT "[R] = restore"
  PRINT "[Q] = exit to DOS"
DO
    r$ = UCASE$(INKEY)
  LOOP UNTIL r$ <> "" AND INSTR("BRQ", r$)
  IF r$ = "Q" THEN CLS : END
  IF r$ = "B" THEN
    ' user has selected backup
    PRINT "Backing up CMOS data, please wait..."
    OPEN "A:\CMOS.DAT" FOR OUTPUT AS #1
    FOR i% = 16 TO 63
      OUT &H70, i%
      cmos%(i%) = INP(&H71)
      PRINT #1, cmos%(i%)
    NEXT i%
    CLOSE #1
    PRINT "Done!"
    GOSUB waitkey
  END IF
  IF r$ = "R" THEN
    ' user has selected restore
    PRINT "Restoring CMOS data, please wait..."
    OPEN "A:\CMOS.DAT" FOR INPUT AS #1
    FOR i% = 16 TO 63
      INPUT #1, cmos%(i%)
      OUT &H70, i%
      OUT (&H71), cmos%(i%)
    NEXT i%
    CLOSE #1
  PRINT "Done!"
  GOSUB waitkey
  END IF
LOOP
'
waitkey:
PRINT "Press any key to continue "
DO
  r$ = INKEY$
LOOP UNTIL r$ <> ""
RETURN
warning:
PRINT "An error has occurred!"
GOSUB waitkey
DO
  r$ = INKEY$
LOOP UNTIL r$ <> ""
RESUME main
```

Listing 8.3. QuickBASIC program to backup and restore the CMOS RAM

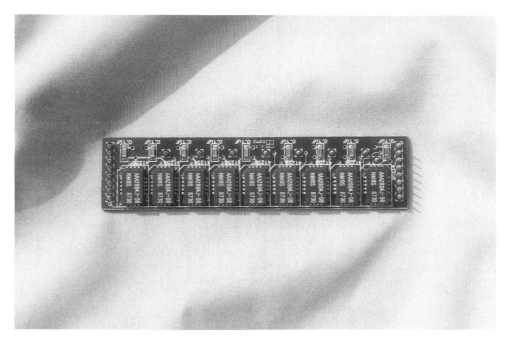

Figure 8.32 256K dynamic RAM module

Figure 8.33 4 × 256K dynamic RAM modules in an AT-compatible system

In modern machines, DIL packaged DRAM devices have been replaced by memory modules. These units are small cards which usually contain surface mounted DRAM chips and which simply plug into the system board.

Single in-line memory modules (SIMMs) are available in various sizes including 256K, 1M, 4M, 8M and 16 Mbytes. The most common type of SIMM (which were first used in the IBM XT-286 machine) has nine DRAM devices and it locates with a 30-pin header. Four of these 256K modules are required to populate a full 1M memory map.

SIMMs are usually inserted into their headers at an angle of about 45 degrees and then simply snapped into place by standing them upright. To remove a SIMM, you should open the locking tabs and gently release the module from its header.

PC memory allocation

The allocation of memory space within a PC can be usefully illustrated by means of a 'memory map'. An 8086 microprocessor can address any one of 1 048 576 different memory locations with its 20 address lines. It thus has a memory which ranges from 00000 (the lowest address) to FFFFF (the highest address). We can illustrate the use of memory using a diagram known as a 'memory map'.

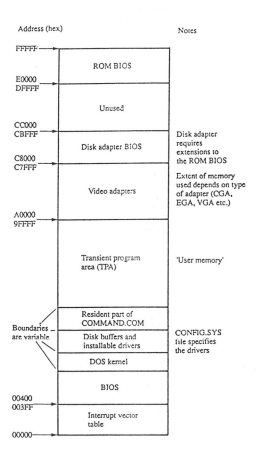

Figure 8.34. Representative memory map for a basic PC

Table 8.8 Memory allocation in a basic specification PC

Address range (hex)	Size (bytes)	Use
00000–9FFFF	640K	Conventional (base) memory
A0000–AFFFF	64K	Video memory (graphics mode)
B0000–B7FFF	32K	Video memory (monochrome text mode)
B8000–BFFFF	32K	Video memory (colour text mode)
C0000–C7FFF	32K	Display adaptor ROM (EGA, VGA, etc)
C8000–DFFFF	96K	Unused (page frame for extended memory, etc)
E0000–FFFFF	128K	BIOS ROM

Figure 8.34 shows a representative memory map for a PC in which the memory is allocated as shown in Table 8.8.

Microsoft's Windows provides you with an excellent utility called MSD (Microsoft Diagnostics). You will find this program in your WINDOWS directory. MSD will provide you with a great deal of useful information on your system, including a complete 'on-screen' memory map. A sample memory map produced by MSD is shown in Figure 8.35.

Alternatively, the DOS MEM command will let you know which programs and drivers are present in memory at any time. The command will also tell you how much extended

```
Microsoft Diagnostics version 2.00 6/27/93   11:10pm        Page 2

                                   Memory

Legend: Available "  " RAM "##" ROM "RR" Possibly Available " ."
EMS     Page    Frame "PP"       Free XMS UMBs "XX"
1024K   FC00    RRRRRRRRRRRRRRRRR    FFFF        Conventional Memory
        F800    RRRRRRRRRRRRRRRRR    FBFF                        Total:    640K
        F400    RRRRRRRRRRRRRRRRR    F7FF                    Available:    560K
960K    F000    RRRRRRRRRRRRRRRRR    F3FF                                  574208 bytes
        EC00    XXXXXXXXXXXXXXXX     EFFF
        E800    #XXXXXXXXXXXXXXX     EBFF        Extended Memory
        E400    ###############      E7FF                        Total:    3328K
896K    E000    ###############      E3FF
        DC00    ###############      DFFF        Expanded Memory (EMS)
        D800    ###############      DBFF                  LIM Version:    4.00
        D400    PPPPPPPPPPPPPPPPP    D7FF        Page Frame Address:    C800H
832K    D000    PPPPPPPPPPPPPPPPP    D3FF                        Total:    3104K
        CC00    PPPPPPPPPPPPPPPPP    CFFF                    Available:    2928K
        C800    PPPPPPPPPPPPPPPPP    CBFF
        C400    RRRRRRRRRRRRRRRRR    C7FF        XMS Information
768K    C000    RRRRRRRRRRRRRRRRR    C3FF                  XMS Version:    3.00
        BC00    ###############      BFFF               Driver Version:    3.00
        B800    ###############      BBFF           A20 Address Line:    Enabled
        B400                         B7FF           High Memory Area:    In use
704K    B000                         B3FF                    Available:    2928K
        AC00                         AFFF        Largest Free Block:    2928K
        A800                         ABFF        Total Free XMS UMB:    30K
        A400                         A7FF      Largest Free XMS UMB:    30K
640K    A000                         A3FF
                                                VCPI Information
                                                        VCPI Detected:    Yes
                                                             Version:    1.00
                                                   Available Memory:    2928K
```

Figure 8.35. A sample memory map produced by MSD

Table 8.9 Useful RAM locations

Address (hex)	Number of bytes	Function
0410	2	Installed equipment list
0413	2	Usable base memory
0417	2	Keyboard status
043E	1	Disk calibration (see Chapter 4)
043F	1	Disk drive motor status (see Chapter 4)
0440	1	Drive motor count (see Chapter 4)
0441	2	Disk status (see Chapter 4)
0442	2	Disk controller status (see Chapter 4)
0449	1	Current video mode (see Chapter 6)
044A	2	Current screen column width (see Chapter 6)
046C	4	Master clock count (incremented by 1 on each clock 'tick')
0472	2	Set to 1234 hex. during a keyboard re-boot (this requires <CTRL-ALT-DEL> keys)
0500	1	Screen print byte (00 indicates normal ready status, 01 indicates that a screen print is in operation, FF indicates that an error has occurred during the screen print operation)

```
DEF SEG = 0
CLS
INPUT "Start address (in hex)"; address
address$ = "&H" + address
address = VAL(address$)
INPUT "Number of bytes to display"; number
PRINT
PRINT "Address", "Byte"
PRINT "(hex)", "(hex)"
PRINT
FOR i% = 0 TO number - 1
  v = PEEK(address + i%)
  PRINT HEX$(address + i%), HEX$(v)
NEXT i%
PRINT
END
```

Listing 8.4. QuickBASIC program to display RAM contents

```
Start address (in hex)? 410
Number of bytes to display? 10

Address      Byte
(hex)        (hex)

410          63
411          44
412          BF
413          80
414          2
415          0
416          18
417          20
418          0
419          0
```

Figure 8.36. Output produced by the program in Listing 8.4

memory you have available. You should use the /CLASSIFY or /DEBUG switches with the MEM command.

Useful PC memory locations

A number of memory locations can be useful in determining the current state of a PC or PC-compatible microcomputer. You can display the contents of these memory locations (summarized in Table 8.9) using the MS-DOS DEBUG utility or using a short routine written in QuickBASIC.

As an example, the following DEBUG command can be used to display the contents of ten bytes of RAM starting at memory location 0410:

D0:0410L0A

(NB: the equivalent command using the DR-DOS SID utility is: D0:410,419)

A rather more user-friendly method of displaying the contents of RAM is shown in Listing 8.4. This QuickBASIC program prompts the user for a start address (expressed in hexadecimal) and the number of bytes to display.

Figure 8.36 shows a typical example of running the program in Listing 8.4 on a modern '486-based computer. The program has been used to display the contents of 10 bytes of RAM from address 0410 onwards.

The installed equipment list

The machine's Installed Equipment List (see Table 8.10) can tell you what hardware devices are currently installed in your system. The equipment list is held in the word (two bytes) starting address 0410. Figure 8.37 and Table 8.11 show you how to decipher the Equipment List word.

Amount of base memory available

The amount of usable base memory can be determined from the two bytes starting at address 0413. The extent of memory is found by simply adding the binary weighted values of each set bit position. Figure 8.38 and Table 8.12 shows how this works.

BIOS ROM release date

The BIOS ROM release date and machine ID can be found by examining the area of read-only memory extending between absolute locations FFFF5 and FFFFC. The ROM release information (not found in all compatibles) is presented in American date format using ASCII characters. Various ROM release dates for various IBM models are shown in Table 8.13.

Machine identification byte

The type of machine (whether PC-XT, AT, etc) is encoded in the form of an identification (ID) byte which is stored at address FFFFE. Table 8.14 gives the ID bytes for each member of the PC family (non-IBM machines may have ID bytes which differ from those listed).

You can display the ROM release date and machine ID byte by using the MS-DOS DEBUG utility or by using the simple QuickBASIC program shown in Listing 8.5. An example of the output produced by this program is shown in Figure 8.39 (the machine in question has an ID byte of FC and a ROM release date of 06/06/92).

Table 8.10 Equipment list word at address 0410

Bit Number	Meaning
0	Set if disk drives are present
1	Unused
2 and 3	System board RAM size:

	Bit 3	Bit 2	RAM size
	0	0	16K
	0	1	32K
	1	1	64K/256K

(NB: on modern systems this coding does not apply)

4 and 5	Initial video mode:

	Bit	Bit 4	Mode
	0	1	40 column colour
	1	0	80 column colour
	1	1	80 column monochrome

6 and 7	Number of disk drives plus 1:

	Bit 7	Bit 6	Number of drives
	0	0	1
	0	1	2
	1	0	3
	1	1	4

8	Reset if DMA chip installed (standard)
9 to 11	Number of serial ports installed
12	Set if an IBM Games Adaptor is installed
13	Set if a serial printer is installed
14 and 15	Number of printers installed

```
Address:   (hex)                0411                0410

Contents:  (hex)            4       2        2       D

           (binary)      0100    0010     0010    1101
                           |       |        |       |
Bit  position:            15       8        7       0
```

Figure 8.37. Deciphering the equipment list

Table 8.11 Example equipment list

Bit position	Status	Comment
0	1 = set	disk drives are present
1	1 = set	this bit is not used
2	0 = reset	these bits have no meaning with
3	0 = reset	systems having greater than 256K RAM
4	0 = reset	initial video mode is 80 column
5	1 = set	colour
6	1 = set	two disk drives installed
7	0 = reset	
8	0 = reset	DMA controller fitted (standard)
9	0 = reset	two serial ports installed
10	1 = set	
11	0 = reset	
12	0 = reset	no IBM Games Adaptor installed
13	0 = reset	no serial printer installed
14	1 = set	one printer attached
15	0 = reset	

```
Address:   (hex)                0414                0413

Contents:  (hex)           0       2       8       0

           (binary)      0000    0010    1000    0000
                          |       |       |       |
Bit position:             15      8       7       0
```

Figure 8.38. Determining the usable base memory

Table 8.12 Determining the base memory

Bit position	Status	Value
9	Set	512K
8	Reset	256K
7	Set	128K
6	Reset	64K
5	Reset	32K
4	Reset	16K
3	Reset	8K
2	Reset	4K
1	Reset	2K
0	Reset	1K

Note: adding together the values associated with each of the set bits gives (512 + 128) = 640K.

PC memory diagnostics

ROM diagnostics

The PC's BIOS ROM incorporates some basic diagnostic software which checks the BIOS ROM and DRAM during the initialization process. The ROM diagnostic is based upon a known 'checksum' for the device. Each byte of ROM is successively read and a checksum is generated. This checksum is then compared with a stored checksum or is adjusted by padding the ROM with bytes which make the checksum amount to zero (neglecting overflow). If any difference is detected an error message is produced and the bootstrap routine is aborted.

RAM diagnostics

In the case of RAM diagnostics the technique is quite different and usually involves writing and reading each byte of RAM in turn. Various algorithms have been developed which make this process more reliable (e.g. 'walking ones'). Where a particular bit is 'stuck' (i.e., refuses to be changed), the bootstrap routine is aborted and an error code is displayed. This error code will normally allow you to identify the particular device that has failed.

The power-on self-test (POST) code within the BIOS ROM checks the system (including system board ROM and RAM) during initialization. The POST reports any errors detected using a numeric code (see reference section, page 350).

Table 8.13 IBM major ROM release dates

ROM date	PC version
04/24/81	Original PC
10/19/81	Revised PC
08/16/82	Original XT
10/27/82	PC upgrade to XT BIOS level
11/08/82	PC-XT
06/01/83	Original PC Junior
01/10/84	Original AT
06/10/85	Revised PC-AT
09/13/85	PC Convertible
11/15/85	Revised PC-AT
01/10/86	Revised PC-XT
04/10/86	XT 286
06/26/87	PS/2 Model 25
09/02/86	PS/2 Model 30
12/12/86	Revised PS/2 Model 30
02/13/87	PS/2 Models 50 and 60
12/05/87	Revised PS/2 Model 30
03/30/87	PS/2 Model 80 (16 MHz)
10/07/87	PS/2 Model 80 (20 MHz)
01/29/88	PS/2 Model 70
12/01/89	PS/1
11/21/89	PS/2 Model 80 (25 MHz)

Table 8.14 ID bytes for various IBM machines

ID Byte (hex)	Machine
F8	PS/2 Models 35, 40, 65, 70, 80 and 90 ('386 and '486 CPU)
F9	PC Convertible
FA	PS/2 Models 25, 30 ('8086 CPU)
FB	PC-XT (revised versions, post 1986)
FC	AT, PS/2 Models 50 and 60 ('286 CPU)
FD	PC Junior
FE	XT and Portable PC
FF	Original PC

```
DEF  SEG  =  &HFFF0
CLS
PRINT  "ROM address",  "Byte",  "ASCII"
PRINT  "(hex)",  "(hex)"
PRINT
FOR  i%  =  &HF0  TO  &HFF
  v  =  PEEK(i%)
  PRINT  HEX$(i%),  HEX$(v),  ;
  IF  v  >  31  AND  v  <  128  THEN
    PRINT  CHR$(v)
  ELSE
    PRINT  ""
  END  IF
NEXT  i%
PRINT
END
```

Listing 8.5. QuickBASIC program to display the last 16 bytes of BIOS ROM

```
ROM address        Byte         ASCII        Comment
(hex)              (hex)
F0                 EA
F1                 5B            [
F2                 E0
F3                 0
F4                 F0
F5                 30            0            ROM  release  date
F6                 36            6            06/06/92
F7                 2F            /
F8                 30            0
F9                 36            6
FA                 2F            /
FB                 39            9
FC                 32            2
FD                 0
FE                 FC                         Machine  ID  byte
FF                 0
```

Figure 8.39. Output produced by the program shown in Listing 8.5

More complex RAM diagnostics involve continuously writing and reading complex bit patterns. These tests are more comprehensive than simple read/write checks. RAM diagnostics can also be carried out on a non-destructive basis. In such cases, the byte read from RAM is replaced immediately after each byte has been tested. It is thus possible to perform a diagnostic check some time after the system has been initialized and without destroying any programs and data which may be resident in memory at the time.

Parity checking

The integrity of stored data integrity can be checked by adding an extra 'parity bit'. This bit is either set or reset according to whether the number of 1s present within the byte are even or odd (i.e., 'even parity' and 'odd parity').

Parity bits are automatically written to memory during a memory write cycle and read from memory during a memory read cycle. A non-maskable interrupt (NMI) is generated if a parity error is detected and thus users are notified if RAM faults develop during normal system operation.

The PC expansion bus

The availability of a standard expansion bus system within the PC must surely be one of the major factors in ensuring its continuing success. The bus is the key to expansion. It allows you to painlessly upgrade your system and configure it for almost any conceivable application. This section introduces you to the ISA and MCA bus standards and explains some of the pitfalls that can occur when you make use of the expansion bus.

Three basic standards are employed in conventional PC expansion bus schemes. The original, and still most widely used standard is called 'Industry Standard Architecture' (ISA). This expansion scheme employs either one or two direct edge connectors and it can cater for an 8 or 16-bit system data bus.

The first ISA connector (62-way) provides access to the 8-bit data bus and the majority of control bus signals and power rails whilst the second connector (36-way) gives access

Figure 8.40 Using a logic probe to check CPU signals in an IBM PC-XT

Figure 8.41 IBM PC-XT system board RAM

to the remaining data bus lines together with some additional control bus signals. Applications which require only an 8-bit data path and a subset of the PC's standard control signals can make use of only the first connector. Applications which require access to a full 16-bit data path (not available in the early original PC and PC-XT machines) must make use of both connectors.

MCA bus

With the advent of PS/2, a more advanced expansion scheme has become available. This expansion standard is known as 'Micro Channel Architecture' (MCA) and it provides access to the 16-bit DATA bus in the IBM PS/2 Models 50 and 60 whereas access to a full 32-bit data bus is available in the Model 80 which has an 80386 CPU.

An important advantage of MCA is that it permits data transfer at significantly faster rates than is possible with ISA. In fairness, the increase in data transfer rate may be unimportant in many applications and also tends to vary somewhat from machine to machine. As a rough guide, when a standard ISA bus AT machine is compared with an MCA PS/2 Model 50, data transfer rates can be expected to increase by around 25% for conventional memory transfers and by 100% (or more) for DMA transfers.

Since MCA interrupt signals are shared between expansion cards, MCA interrupt structure tends to differ from that employed within ISA where interrupt signals tend to remain exclusive to a particular expansion card. More importantly, MCA provides a scheme of bus arbitration in order to decide which of the 'feature cards' has rights to exercise control of the MCA bus at any particular time.

MCA's arbitration mechanism provides for up to 15 bus masters, each one able to exercise control of the bus. As a further bonus, MCA provides an auxiliary video connector and programmable option configuration to relieve the tedium of setting DIP switches on system boards and expansion cards.

EISA bus

Recently, a third bus standard has appeared. This standard is known as 'Extended Industry Standard Architecture' (EISA) and it is supported by a number of manufacturers seeking an alternative to the MCA standard.

EISA is a 32-bit expansion bus. To make the system compatible with ISA expansion cards, the standard is based on a two-level connector. The lowest level contacts (used by EISA cards) make connection with the extended 32-bit bus whilst the upper level contacts (used by ISA cards) provide the 8 and 16-bit connections.

ISA bus

The PC's ISA bus is based upon a number of expansion 'slots' each of which is fitted with a 62-way direct edge connector together with an optional subsidiary 36-way direct edge connector. Expansion (or option) cards may be designed to connect only to the 62-way connector or may, alternatively, mate with both the 62-way and 36-way connectors.

Since only the 62-way connector was fitted on early machines (which then had an 8-bit data bus), cards designed for use with this connector are sometimes known as '8-bit expansion cards' or 'XT expansion cards'. The AT machine, however, provides access to a full 16-bit data bus together with additional control signals and hence requires the additional 36-way connector. Cards which are designed to make use of *both* connectors are generally known as '16-bit expansion cards' or 'AT expansion cards'.

The original PC was fitted with only five expansion slots (spaced approximately 25 mm apart). The standard XT provided a further three slots to make a total of eight (spaced approximately 19 mm apart). Some cards, particularly those providing hard disk storage, require the width occupied by two expansion slot positions on the XT. This is unfortunate, particularly where the number of free slots may be at a premium!

All of the XT expansion slots provide identical signals with one notable exception; the slot nearest to the power supply was employed in a particular IBM configuration (the IBM 3270 PC) to accept a Keyboard/Timer Adaptor. This particular configuration employs a dedicated 'card select' signal (B8 on the connector) which is required by the system motherboard. Other cards that *will* operate in this position include the IBM 3270 Asynchronous Communications Adaptor.

Like the XT, the standard AT also provides eight expansion slots. Six of these slots are fitted with two connectors (62-way and 36-way) whilst two positions (slots one and seven) only have 62-way connectors. Slot positions one and seven are designed to accept earlier 8-bit expansion cards which make use of the maximum allowable height throughout their length. If a 36-way connector had been fitted to the system motherboard, this would only foul the lower edge of the card and prevent effective insertion of the card in question.

Finally, it should be noted that boards designed for AT systems (i.e., those specifically designed to take advantage of the availability of the full 16-bit data bus) will offer a considerable speed advantage over those which are based upon the 8-bit PC-XT data bus provided by the original XT expansion connector. In some applications, this speed advantage can be critical.

The 62-way ISA expansion bus connector

The 62-way PC expansion bus connector is a direct edge-type fitted to the system motherboard. One side of the connector is referred to as A (lines are numbered A1 to A31) whilst the other is referred to as B (lines are numbered B1 to B31).

The address and data bus lines are grouped together on the A-side of the connector whilst the control bus and power rails occupy the B-side. Table 8.15 describes each of the signals present on the 62-way expansion bus connector.

The 36-way ISA bus connector

The PC-AT and later machines are fitted with an additional expansion bus connector which provides access to the upper eight data lines, D8 to D15 as well as further control bus lines. The ISA AT-bus employs an additional 36-way direct edge-type connector. One side of the connector is referred to as C (lines are numbered C1 to C18) whilst the other is referred to as D (lines are numbered D1 to D18). The upper eight data bus lines and latched upper address lines are grouped together on the C-side of the connector (together with memory read and write lines) whilst additional interrupt request, DMA request, and DMA acknowledge lines occupy the D-side. Table 8.16 describes each of the signals present on the 32-way expansion bus.

Power supply limitations

A fully populated AT-compatible system motherboard (including 80287 coprocessor) requires approximately 5 A and 2 A from the +5 V and +12 V rails respectively. An EGA

Table 8.15 Signals present on the 62-way ISA bus connector

Pin no.	Abbrev.	Direction	Signal	Function
A1	IOCHK	I	I/O Channel check	Taken low to indicate a parity error in a memory or I/O device.
A2	D7	I/O	Data line 7	Data bus line
A3	D6	I/O	Data line 6	Data bus line
A4	D5	I/O	Data line 5	Data bus line
A5	D4	I/O	Data line 4	Data bus line
A6	D3	I/O	Data line 3	Data bus line
A7	D2	I/O	Data line 2	Data bus line
A8	D1	I/O	Data line 1	Data bus line
A9	D0	I/O	Data line 0	Data bus line
A10	IOCHRDY	I	I/O channel ready	Pulsed low by a slow memory or I/O device to signal that it is not ready for data transfer.
A11	AEN	O	Address enable	Issued by the DMA controller to indicate that a DMA cycle is in progress. Disables port I/O during a DMA operation in which IOR and IOW may be asserted.
A12	A19	I/O	Address line 19	Address bus line
A13	A18	I/O	Address line 18	Address bus line
A14	A17	I/O	Address line 17	Address bus line
A15	A16	I/O	Address line 16	Address bus line
A16	A15	I/O	Address line 15	Address bus line
A17	A14	I/O	Address line 14	Address bus line
A18	A13	I/O	Address line 13	Address bus line
A19	A12	I/O	Address line 12	Address bus line
A20	A11	I/O	Address line 11	Address bus line
A21	A10	I/O	Address line 10	Address bus line
A22	A9	I/O	Address line 9	Address bus line
A23	A8	I/O	Address line 8	Address bus line
A24	A7	I/O	Address line 7	Address bus line
A25	A6	I/O	Address line 6	Address bus line
A26	A5	I/O	Address line 5	Address bus line
A27	A4	I/O	Address line 4	Address bus line
A28	A3	I/O	Address line 3	Address bus line
A29	A2	I/O	Address line 2	Address bus line
A30	A1	I/O	Address line 1	Address bus line
A31	A0	I/O	Address line 0	Address bus line
B1	GND	n.a.	Ground	Ground/common 0V
B2	RESET	O	Reset	When taken high this signal resets all expansion cards.
B3	+5 V	n.a.	+5 V d.c.	Supply voltage rail
B4	IRQ2	I	Interrupt request level 2	Interrupt request (highest priority).
B5	–5 V	n.a.	–5 V d.c.	Supply voltage rail
B6	DRQ2	I	Direct memory access request level 2	Taken high when a DMA transfer is required. The signal remains high until the corresponding DACK line goes low.
B7	–12 V	n.a.	–12 V d.c.	Supply voltage rail

Table 8.15 *continued*

Pin no.	Abbrev.	Direction	Signal	Function
B8	0WS	I	Zero wait state	Indicates to the microprocessor that the present bus cycle can be completed without inserting any additional wait cycles.
B9	+12 V	n.a.	+12 V d.c.	Supply voltage rail
B10	GND	n.a.	Ground	Ground/common 0 V
B11	MEMW	O	Memory write	Taken low to signal a memory write operation.
B12	MEMR	O	Memory read	Taken low to signal a memory read operation.
B13	IOW	O	I/O write	Taken low to signal an I/O write operation.
B14	IOR	O	I/O read	Taken low to signal an I/O read operation.
B15	DACK3	O	Direct memory access acknowledge level 3	Taken low to acknowledge a DMA request on the corresponding level (see notes).
B16	DRQ3	I	Direct memory access request level 3	Taken high when a DMA transfer is required. The signal remains high until the corresponding DACK line goes low.
B17	DACK1	O	Direct memory access acknowledge level 1	Taken low to acknowledge a DMA request on the corresponding level (see notes).
B18	DRQ1	I	Direct memory access request level 1	Taken high when a DMA transfer is required. The signal remains high until the corresponding DACK line goes low.
B19	DACK0	O	Direct memory access acknowledge level 0	Taken low to acknowledge a DMA request on the corresponding level (see notes).
B20	CLK4	O	4.77 MHz clock	CPU clock divided by 3, 210 ns period, 33 duty cycle.
B21	IRQ7	I	Interrupt request level 7	Asserted by an I/O device when it requires service (see notes).
B22	IRQ6	I	Interrupt request level 6	Asserted by an I/O device when it requires service (see notes).
B23	IRQ5	I	Interrupt request level 5	Asserted by an I/O device when it requires service (see notes).

Table 8.15 *continued*

Pin no.	Abbrev.	Direction	Signal	Function
B24	IRQ4	I	Interrupt request level 4	Asserted by an I/O device when it requires service (see notes).
B25	IRQ3	I	Interrupt request level 3	Asserted by an I/O device when it requires service (see notes).
B26	DACK2	O	Direct memory access acknowledge level 2	Taken low to acknowledge a DMA request on the corresponding level (see notes).
B27	TC	O	Terminal count	Pulsed high to indicate that a DMA transfer terminal count has been reached.
B28	ALE	O	Address latch enable	A falling edge indicates that the address latch is to be enabled. The signal is taken high during DMA transfers.
B29	+5 V	n.a.	+5 V d.c.	Supply voltage rail
B30	OSC	O	14.31818 MHz clock	Fast clock with 70 ns period, 50 duty cycle.
B31	GND	n.a.	Ground	Ground/common 0 V

Notes:
(a) Signal directions are quoted relative to the system motherboard; I represents input, O represents output, and I/O represents a bidirectional signal used both for input and also for output (n.a. indicates not applicable).
(b) IRQ4, IRQ6 and IRQ7 are generated by the motherboard serial, disk, and parallel interfaces respectively.
(c) DACK0 (sometimes labelled REFRESH) is used to refresh dynamic memory whilst DACK1 to DACK3 are used to acknowledge other DMA requests.

graphics adaptor and two standard floppy drives will demand an additional 2.4 A and 1.5 A from the +5 V and +12 V rails respectively. A cooling fan will require a further 0.3 A, or so, from the +12 V rail. The total load on the system power supply is thus 7.4 A from the +5 V rail and 4.1 A from the +12 V rail. With a standard XT power supply, reserves of only 7.6 A from the +5 V supply and a mere 400 mA from the +12 V supply will be available!

Problems which arise when systems have been upgraded or expanded are often caused by excessive loading on the power supply. Under marginal conditions the system will *appear* to operate satisfactorily but it may crash or lock-up at some later time when the system temperature builds up or when one or more of the power rail voltages momentarily falls outside its tolerance limits.

PC video standards

The video capability of a PC will depends not only upon the display used but also upon the type of 'graphics adaptor' fitted. Most PCs will operate in a number of video modes which can be selected from DOS or from within an application.

Table 8.16 Signals present on the 36-way ISA bus connector

Pin no.	Abbrev.	Direction	Signal	Function No.
C1	SBHE	I/O	System bus high enable	When asserted this signal indicates that the high byte (D8 to D15) is present on the DATA bus.
C2	LA23	I/O	Latched address line 23	Address bus line
C3	LA22	I/O	Latched address line 22	Address bus line
C4	LA21	I/O	Latched address line 21	Address bus line
C5	LA20	I/O	Latched address line 20	Address bus line
C6	LA23	I/O	Latched address line 19	Address bus line
C7	LA22	I/O	Latched address line 18	Address bus line
C8	LA23	I/O	Latched address line 17	Address bus line
C9	MEMW	I/O	Memory write	Taken low to signal a memory write operation.
C10	MEMR	I/O	Memory read	Taken low to signal a memory read operation.
C11	D8	I/O	Data line 1	Data bus line
C12	D9	I/O	Data line 1	Data bus line
C13	D10	I/O	Data line 1	Data bus line
C14	D11	I/O	Data line 1	Data bus line
C15	D12	I/O	Data line 1	Data bus line
C16	D13	I/O	Data line 1	Data bus line
C17	D14	I/O	Data line 1	Data bus line
C18	D15	I/O	Data line 1	Data bus line
D1	MEMCS16	I	Memory chip-select 16	Taken low to indicate that the current data transfer is a 16-bit (single wait state) memory operation.
D2	IOCS16	I	I/O chip-select 16	Taken low to indicate that the current data transfer is a 16-bit (single wait state) I/O operation.
D3	IRQ10	I	Interrupt request level 10	Asserted by an I/O device when it requires service.
D4	IRQ11	I	Interrupt request level 11	Asserted by an I/O device when it requires service.
D5	IRQ12	I	Interrupt request level 12	Asserted by an I/O device when it requires service.
D6	IRQ13	I	Interrupt request level 13	Asserted by an I/O device when it requires service.
D7	IRQ14	I	Interrupt request level 14	Asserted by an I/O device when it requires service.
D8	DACK0	O	Direct memory access acknowledge level 0	Taken low to acknowledge a DMA request on the corresponding level.

Table 8.16 *continued*

Pin no.	Abbrev.	Direction	Signal	Function No.
D9	DRQ0	I	Direct memory access request level 0	Taken high when a DMA transfer is required. The signal remains high until The corresponding DACK line goes low.
D10	DACK5	O	Direct memory access acknowledge level 5	Taken low to acknowledge a DMA request on the corresponding level.
D11	DRQ5	I	Direct memory access request level 5	Taken high when a transfer is required. The signal remains high until the corresponding DACK line goes low.
D12	DACK6	O	Direct memory access acknowledge level 6	Taken low to acknowledge a DMA request on the corresponding level.
D13	DRQ6	I	Direct memory access request level 6	Taken high when a DMA transfer is required. The signal remains high until the corresponding DACK line goes low.
D14	DACK7	O	Direct memory access acknowledge level 7	Taken low to acknowledge a DMA request on the corresponding level.
D15	DRQ7	I	Direct memory access request level 7	Taken high when a DMA transfer is required. The signal remains high until the corresponding DACK line goes low.
D16	+5 V	n.a.	+5 V d.c.	Supply voltage rail
D17	MASTER	I	Master	Taken low by the I/O processor when controlling the system address, data and control bus lines.
D18	GND	n.a.	Ground	Ground/common 0 V

The earliest PC display standards were those associated with the Monochrome Display Adaptor (MDA) and Colour Graphics Adaptor (CGA). Both of these standards are now obsolete although they are both emulated in a number of laptop PCs that use LCD displays.

MDA and CGA were followed by a number of other much enhanced graphics standards. These include Enhanced Graphics Adaptor (EGA), Multi-Colour Graphics Array (MCGA), Video Graphics Array (VGA), and the 8514 standard used on IBM PS/2 machines.

The EGA standard is fast becoming obsolete and all new PC systems are supplied with either VGA, 'super VGA', or displays which conform to IBM's 8514 standard. The characteristics of the most commonly used graphics standards are summarized in Table 8.17.

Figure 8.42. IBM PC-XT power supply

Figure 8.43. IBM PC-XT power supply mains input filter and fuse assembly

Table 8.17 Display adaptor summary

Display standard	Approx. year of introduction	Text capability (columns × lines)	Graphics capability (horz. × vert. pixels)
MDA	1981	80 × 25 monochrome	None
HGA	1982	80 × 25 monochrome	720 × 320 monochrome
CGA	1983	80 × 25 in 16 colours	320 × 200 in two sets of 4 colours
EGA	1984	80 × 40 in 16 colours	640 × 350 in 16 colours
MCGA	1987	80 × 30 in 16 colours	640 × 480 in 2 colours, 320 × 200 in 256 colours
8514/A	1987	80 × 60 in 16 colours	1024 × 768 in 256 (PS/2) colours
VGA	1987	80 × 50 in 16 colours	640 × 480 in 16 colours, 320 × 200 in 256 colours
SVGA (XGA)	1991	132 × 60 in 16 colours	1024 × 768 in 256 colours 640 × 480 in 65536 colours

Video modes

It is important to realize at the outset that graphics adaptors normally operate in one of several different modes. A VGA card will, for example, operate in 'text mode' using either 80 or 40 columns, and in 'graphics mode' using 4, 16 or 256 colours.

The graphics adaptor contains one or more VLSI devices that organize the data which produces the screen display. You should recall that a conventional cathode ray tube (CRT) display is essentially a serial device (screen data is built up using a beam of electrons which continuously scans the screen). Hence the graphics adaptor must store the screen image whilst the scanning process takes place.

To determine the current video mode, you can simply read the machine's video mode byte stored in RAM at address 0449. This byte indicates the current video mode (using the hex. values shown in Table 8.18). You can examine the byte at this address using the DEBUG command D0:0449L1 (the equivalent SID command is D0:449,44A).

Graphics adaptor memory

The amount of memory required to display a screen in text mode is determined by the number of character columns and lines and also on the number of colours displayed. In modes 0 to 6 and 8, a total of 16K bytes is reserved for display memory whilst in mode 7 (monochrome 80 × 25 characters) the requirement is for only 4K bytes (colours are not displayed).

In modes 0 to 3, less than 16K bytes is used by the screen at any one time. For these modes, the available memory is divided into pages. Note that only one page can be displayed at any particular time. Displayed pages are numbered 0 to 7 in modes 0 and 1 and 0 to 3 in modes 2 and 3.

The extent of display memory required in a graphics mode depends upon the number of pixels displayed (horizontal × vertical) and also on the number of colours displayed. Provided that a display adaptor has sufficient RAM fitted, the concept of screen pages also applies to graphics modes. Again, it is only possible to display one page at a time.

Table 8.18 Video display modes and graphics adaptor standards

Mode	Display type	Colours	Screen resolution (note 1)	Display adaptors supporting this mode:					
				MDA	CGA	EGA	MCGA	VGA	HGA (note 3)
00	Text	16	40 × 25		•	•	•	•	•
01	Text	16	40 × 25		•	•	•	•	•
02	Text	16	80 × 25		•	•	•	•	•
03	Text	16	80 × 25		•	•	•	•	•
04	Graphics	4	320 × 200		•	•	•	•	•
05	Graphics	4	320 × 200		•	•	•	•	•
06	Graphics	2	640 × 200		•	•	•	•	•
07	Text	Mono	80 × 25	•		•		•	•
08	Graphics	16	160 × 200	(note 2)					
09	Graphics	16	320 × 200	(note 2)					
0A	Graphics	4	640 × 200	(note 2)					
0B	(note 4)								
0C	(note 4)								
0D	Graphics	16	320 × 200			•		•	
0E	Graphics	16	640 × 200			•		•	
0F	Graphics	Mono	640 × 350			•		•	
10	Graphics	16	640 × 350			•		•	
11	Graphics	2	640 × 480				•	•	
12	Graphics	16	640 × 480					•	
13	Graphics	256	320 × 200				•	•	

Notes:
1. Resolutions are quoted in (columns × lines) for text displays and (horizontal × vertical) pixels for graphics displays.
2. Applies only to the PC Junior.
3. The Hercules Graphics Adaptor card combines the graphics (but NOT colour) capabilities of the CGA adaptor with the high quality text display of the MDA adaptor.
4. Reserved mode.

Colour

The basic 16 colour palette for a PC used in the vast majority of DOS applications is based on a 4-bit 'intensity plus RGB' code (see Table 8.19). This simple method generates colours by switching on and off the individual red, green and blue electron beams. The intensity signal simply serves to brighten up or darken the display at the particular screen location. The result is the 16 basic PC colours that we have all grown to know and love!

The 16 colour palette is adequate for most text applications however, to produce more intermediate shades of colour, we need a larger palette. One way of doing this is to make use of a 6-bit code where *each* of the three basic colours (red, green and blue) is represented by two bits (one corresponding to bright and the other to normal). This allows each colour to have four levels and produces 64 possible colour combinations.

A better method (which generates a virtually unlimited colour palette) is to use 'analogue RGB' rather than 'digital RGB' signals. In this system (used in VGA, SVGA and XGA), the three basic colour signals (red, green and blue) are each represented by analogue voltages in the range 0 V to 0.7 V (at the video connector). The number of colours displayed using such an arrangement depends upon the number of bits used to represent the intensity of each colour before its conversion to an analogue signal.

Table 8.19 The PC's 16 colour palette

Hex. code	Binary code				Colour produced
	I	R	G	B	
00	0	0	0	0	Black
01	0	0	0	1	Blue
02	0	0	1	0	Green
03	0	0	1	1	Cyan
04	0	1	0	0	Red
05	0	1	0	1	Magenta
06	0	1	1	0	Yellow
07	0	1	1	1	White
08	1	0	0	0	Grey
09	1	0	0	1	Bright blue
0A	1	0	1	0	Bright green
0B	1	0	1	1	Bright cyan
0C	1	1	0	0	Bright red
0D	1	1	0	1	Bright magenta
0E	1	1	1	0	Bright yellow
0F	1	1	1	1	Bright white

Note:
I = intensity, R = red, B = blue, G = green

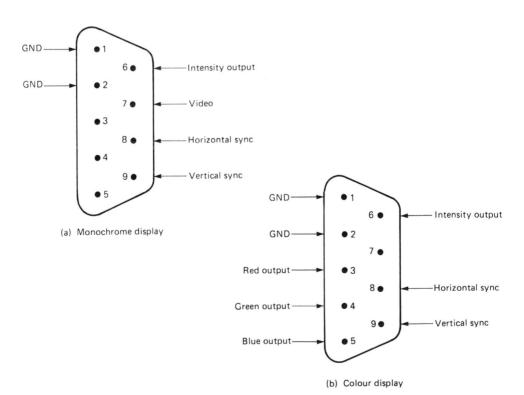

(a) Monochrome display

(b) Colour display

Figure 8.44. Pin numbering for standard CGA and EGA displays

Reference section

Contents

Commonly used symbols

Symbol	Component
	Fixed resistor
	Preset resistor
	Preset potentiometer
	Variable potentiometer
	Fixed capacitor
	Preset capacitor
	Electrolytic capacitor
	Diode
	Zener diode
	Light-emitting diode
	NPN transistor
	PNP transistor
	Buffer
	Inverter
	AND gate
	NAND gate
	OR gate
	NOR gate
	Exclusive–OR gate
	Schmitt inverter

Symbol	Component
	Fixed inductor
	Ferrite cored fixed inductor (RF choke)
	Iron cored fixed inductor (LF choke)
	Preset inductor
	Ferrite cored RF transformer
	Iron cored LF transformer
	Quartz crystal
	Loudspeaker
	Switch (single pole)
	Switch (slide)
	Coaxial socket
	Switched jack socket
	Screening
	Conductors crossing (no connection)
	Conductors joined (connected)
	Common (PCB 0V)
	Earth or chassis

TTL families and device numbering

The most common family of TTL devices is the 74-series in which the device code is prefixed by the number 74. In addition, manufacturers may introduce their own identifying prefix letters. Common examples are:

SN	=	Texas Instruments
DM	=	National Semiconductor
N	=	Signetics
NSC	=	National Semiconductor

Additional letters may be inserted within the device coding to indicate the sub-family to which the device belongs:

H	=	high speed
L	=	low power
S	=	Schottky
LS	=	low power Schottky
ALS	=	advanced low power Schottky
F	=	fast
C	=	CMOS version of the TTL device
AC	=	high-speed advanced CMOS (CMOS input logic level compatibility)
ACT	=	high-speed advanced CMOS (TTL input logic level compatibility)
HCT	=	high-speed CMOS replacement for TTL

A suffix letter may also be added to denote the type of package. The most common is N which describes the conventional plastic dual-in-line package.

Examples

1. SN7400N   is a quad 2-input NAND gate manufactured by Texas instruments and supplied in a plastic dual-in-line package.
2. MM74HC32N   is a quad 2-input OR gate using high speed CMOS technology which is speed, function, and pin-out compatible with 74LS series logic. The device is supplied in a plastic dual-in-line package.
3. N74LS373N   is a low power Schottky octal tristate latch. The device is manufactured by Signetics and supplied in a plastic dual-in-line package.

Abbreviations

The following abbreviations are used in the list of TTL devices:

o.c.	=	open collector
h.v.	=	high voltage
inv.	=	inverting
Sch.	=	Schmitt
str.	=	strobed

00	Ouad 2-input NAND		15	Triple 3-input o.c. AND
01	Quad 2-input o.c, NOR		16	Hex o.c. h.v. inverter
02	Quad 2-input NOR		17	Hex o.c. h.v. buffer
03	Quad 2-input o.c, NAND		20	Dual 4-input NAND
04	Hex inverter		21	Dual 4-input AND
05	Hex o.c. inverter		22	Dual 4-input o.c. NAND
06	Hex o.c. h.v. inverter		23	Dual 4-input str. NOR
07	Hex o.c. h.v. buffer		25	Dual 4-input str. NOR
08	Quad 2-input AND		26	Quad 2-input o.c. NAND
09	Quad 2-input o.c. AND		27	Triple 3-input NOR
10	Triple 3-input NAND		28	Quad 2-input NOR buffer
11	Triple 3-input AND		30	Single 8-input NAND
12	Triple 3-input o.c. NAND		32	Quad 2-input OR
13	Dual 4-input Sch. NAND		33	Quad 2-input o.c. NOR buffer
14	Hex Sch. inverter		37	Quad 2-input NAND buffer

38	Quad 2-input o.c. NAND buffer	110	Single J-K bistable
40	Dual 4-input NAND buffer	111	Dual J-K bistable
42	BCD to decimal decoder	112	Dual J-K bistable
43	Excess 3 to decimal decoder	113	Dual J-K bistable
44	Gray to decimal decoder	114	Dual J-K bistable
45	BCD to decimal o.c. h.v. decoder	116	Dual 4-bit latch
46	BCD to 7-segment o.c. h.v. decoder	118	Hex R-S bistable latch
47	BCD to 7-segment o.c. h.v. decoder	119	Hex R-S latch
48	BCD to 7-segment decoder	120	Dual pulse synchronizer
49	BCD to 7-segment decoder	121	Monostable
50	Dual AND/OR/invert	122	Retriggerable monostable
51	Dual AND/OR/invert	123	Dual retriggerable monostable
52	Single AND/OR	124	Dual voltage controlled oscillator
53	Single AND/OR/invert	125	Quad tri-state buffer
54	Single AND/OR/invert	126	Quad tri-state buffer
55	Single AND/OR/invert	128	Quad 2-input NOR line driver
60	Dual 4-input expander	132	Quad 2-input Sch. NAND
61	Triple 3-input expander	133	Single 13-input NAND
62	Single AND/OR expander	134	Single 12-input tri-state NAND
63	Hex current-sensing interface	135	Quad exclusive-OR/NOR
64	Single AND/OR/invert	136	Quad 2-input exclusive-OR
65	Single AND/OR/invert	138	3 to 8-line decoder
70	Single J-K bistable	139	Dual 2 to 4-line decoder
71	Single J-K bistable	140	Dual 4-input NAND
72	Single J-K bistable	141	BCD to decimal decoder
73	Dual J-K bistable	142	4-bit counter/latch/decoder/driver
74	Dual D-type bistable	143	4-bit counter/latch/decoder/driver
75	Quad bistable latch	144	4-bit counter/latch/decoder/driver
76	Dual J-K bistable	145	BCD to decimal converter
77	4-bit bistable latch	147	Decimal to 4-bit RCD encoder
78	Dual J-K bistable	148	8 to 3-line octal encoder
80	2-bit full adder	150	1-of-16 data selector/multiplexer
81	16-bit RAM	151	1-of-8 data selector/multiplexer
82	2-bit full adder	152	1-of-8 data selector/multiplexer
83	4-bit full adder	153	Dual 4 to 1-line data selector/multiplexer
84	16-bit RAM	154	4 to 16-line decoder
85	4-bit comparator	155	Dual 2 to 4-line decoder
86	Quad 2-input exclusive-OR	156	Dual to 4-line o.c. decoder
87	4-bit complementor	157	Quad 2 to 1-line data selector
88	256-bit ROM	158	Quad to 1-line data selector
89	64-bit RAM	159	4 to 16-line o.c. decoder
90	Decade counter	160	4-bit counter
91	8-bit shift register	161	4-bit counter
92	Divide-by-twelve counter	162	4-bit counter
93	4-bit binary counter	163	4-bit counter
94	4-bit shift register	164	8-bit parallel output serial input shift register
95	4-bit shift register	165	8-bit parallel input serial output shift register
96	5-bit shift register		
97	6-bit binary rate multiplier	166	8-bit parallel/serial input serial output shift register
98	4-bit data selector		
99	4-bit bidirectional shift register	167	Decade synchronous rate multiplier
100	Dual 4-bit latch	168	4-bit up/down synchronous decade counter
101	Single J-K bistable		
102	Single J-K bistable	169	4-bit up/down synchronous binary counter
103	Dual J-K bistable	170	4-by-4 o.c. register file
104	Single J-K bistable	172	16-bit tri-state register file
105	Single J-K bistable	173	4-bit D-type tri-state register
106	Dual J-K bistable	174	Hex D-type bistable
107	Dual J-K bistable	175	Quad D-type bistable
108	Dual J-K bistable	176	Presettable decade counter/latch
109	Dual J-K bistable		

177	Presettable binary counter/latch	275	7-bit-slice Wallace tree
178	4-bit universal shift register	276	Quad J-K bistable
179	4-bit universal shift register	278	4 bit cascadable priority register
180	9-bit parity generator/checker	279	Quad R-S latch
181	Arithmetic logic unit	280	9-bit parity generator/checker
182	Look-ahead carry generator	281	4-bit parallel binary accumulator
183	Dual full adder	283	4-bit binary full adder
184	BCD to binary code converter	284	4 by 4-bit parallel binary multiplier
185	Binary to BCD code converter	285	4 by 4-bit parallel binary multiplier
186	512-bit o.c. PROM	287	IK-bit tri-state PROM
187	1K-bit o.c. ROM	288	256-bit tri-state PROM
188	256-bit o.c. PROM	289	64-bit o.c. RAM
189	64-bit RAM	290	Decade counter
190	BCD synchronous up/down counter	293	4-bit binary counter
191	Binary synchronous up/down counter	295	4-bit bidirectional universal shift register
192	BCD synchronous dual clock up/down counter	298	Quad 2-input multiplexer
193	Binary synchronous dual clock up/down counter	297	Digital phase-locked loop
		299	8-bit bidirectional universal shift register
194	4-bit bidirectional universal shift register	300	256-bit o.c. RAM
195	4-bit parallel-access shift register	301	256-bit o.c. RAM
196	Presettable decade counter/latch	302	2S6-bit o.c. RAM
197	Presettable binary counter/latch	314	1K-bit o.c. RAM
198	8-bit bidirectional universal shift register	315	1K-bit o.c. RAM
199	8-bit bidirectional universal shift register	320	Crystal controlled oscillator
200	256-bit tri-state RAM	321	Crystal controlled oscillator
201	256-bit tri-state RAM	323	8-bit bidirectional universal shift register
202	256-bit tri-state RAM	324	Voltage controlled oscillator
207	1K-bit RAM	325	Dual voltage controlled oscillator
208	1K-bit tri-state RAM	326	Dual voltage controlled oscillator
214	1K-bit tri-state RAM	327	Dual voltage controlled oscillator
215	1K-bit tri-state RAM	348	8 to 3-line tri-state priority encoder
221	Dual monostable	351	Dual 8 to 1-line tri-state data selector
225	Asynchronous FIFO memory	352	Dual 4 to 1-line inv. data selector
226	4-bit parallel latched bus transceiver	353	Dual 4 to 1-line tri-state inv. data selector
240	Octal tri-state inv. buffer/line driver/receiver	362	Four-phase clock generator
		363	Octal tri-state D-type latch
241	Octal tri-state non-inv. buffer/line driver/receiver	364	Octal tri-state D-type latch
		365	Hex tri-state non-inv. bus driver
242	Quad tri-state inv. bus transceiver	366	Hex tri-state inv. bus driver
243	Quad tri-state non-inv. bus transceiver	367	Hex tri-state non-inv. bus driver
244	Octal tri-state non-inv. buffer/line driver/receiver	368	Hex tri-state inv. bus driver
		370	2K-bit tri-state ROM
		371	2K-bit tri-state ROM
245	Octal tri-state non-inv. bus transceiver	373	Octal tri-state D-type latch
246	BCD to 7-segment o.c. h.v. decoder	374	Octal tri-state D-type bistable
247	BCD to 7-segment o.c. h.v. decoder	375	4-bit bistable latch
248	RCD to 7-segment decoder	376	Quad J-K bistable
249	BCD to 7-segment o.c. decoder	377	Octal D-type bistable
251	8 to 1-line tri-state data selector	378	Hex D-type bistable
253	Dual 4 to 1-line tri-state data selector	379	Quad D-type bistable
257	Quad 2-input tri-state non-inv. multiplexer	381	Arithmetic logic unit
258	Quad 2-input tri-state inv. multiplexer	386	Quad 2-input exclusive-OR
259	8-bit addressable latch	387	1K-bit o.c. PROM
260	Dual 5-input NOR	390	Dual decade counter
261	2 by 4-bit parallel binary multiplier	393	Dual 4-bit binary counter
265	Quad complimentary output generator	395	4-bit tri-state universal shift register
266	Quad 2-input o.c. exclusive-OR	398	Quad 2-input multiplexer
270	2K-bit ROM	399	Quad 2-input multiplexer
271	2K-bit ROM .	412	8-bit tri-state buffered latch
273	Octal D-type bistable	424	Two-phase clock generator
274	4 by 4-bit tri-state binary multiplier	425	Quad tri-state buffer

426	Quad tri-state buffer	684	8-bit comparator
428	Bidirectional system controller	685	8-bit o.c. comparator
438	Bidirectional system controller	686	8-bit comparator
446	Quad bus transceiver	687	8-bit o.c. comparator
449	Quad bus transceiver	688	8-bit comparator
470	256 by 8-bit o.c. PROM	689	8-bit o.c. comparator
471	256 by 8-bit tri-state PROM	690	8-bit tri-state decade counter
472	512 by 8-bit tri-state PROM	691	4-bit tri-state binary counter
473	512 by 8-bit o.c. PROM	692	4-bit tri-state decade counter
474	512 by 8-bit tri-state PROM	693	4-bit tri-state binary counter
475	512 by 8-bit o.c. PROM	696	4-bit tri-state decade up/down counter
476	1K x 4-bit tri-state PROM	697	4-bit tri-state binary up/down counter
477	1K x 4-bit o.c. PROM	698	4-bit tri-state decade up/down counter
481	4-bit slice processor	699	4-bit tri-state binary up/down counter
482	4-bit slice controller	740	Octal tri-state inv. buffer/driver
490	Dual decade counter	741	Octal tri-state non-inv. buffer/driver
540	Octal tri-state inv. buffer	744	Octal tri-state non-inv. buffer/driver
541	Octal tri-state non-inv. buffer	804	Hex 2-input line driver
568	Decade tri-state up/down counter	805	Hex 2-input NOR line driver
569	Binary tri-state up/down counter	808	Hex 2-input AND line driver
573	Octal tri-state latch	832	Hex 2-input OR line driver
574	Octal tri-state non-inv. D-type bistable	857	8-line multiplexer
576	Octal tri-state inv. D-type bistable	873	Dual quad latch
580	Octal tri-state inv. latch	874	Dual quad D-type bistable
612	Tri-state memory mapper	878	Dual quad D-type bistable
616	Tri-state 16-bit error detection/correction	880	Dual quad latch
620	Octal tri-state inv. bus transceiver	1000	Buffered 00
621	Octal o.c. non-inv. bus transceiver	1002	Buffered 02
622	Octal o.c. inv. bus transceiver	1003	Buffered 03
623	Octal tri-state non-inv. bus transceiver	1004	Buffered 04
624	Voltage controlled oscillator	1005	Buffered 05
625	Dual voltage controlled oscillator	1008	Buffered 08
626	Dual voltage controlled oscillator	1010	Buffered 10
627	Dual voltage controlled oscillator	1011	Buffered 11
628	Dual two-phase voltage controlled oscillator	1020	Buffered 20
629	Dual oscillator	1032	Buffered 32
630	Tri-state 16-bit error detection/correction	1034	Hex buffer
638	Octal tri-state inverting o.c. bus transceiver	1035	Hex buffer
639	Octal tri-state inverting o.c. bus transceiver	1240	Low power 240
640	Octal tri-state inverting bus transceiver	1241	Low power 241
641	Octal o.c. non-inv. bus transceiver	1242	Low power 242
642	Octal o.c. inv. bus transceiver	1243	Low power 243
643	Octal tri-state inv. bus transceiver	1244	Low power 244
644	Octal o.c. non-inv. bus transceiver	1245	Low power 245
645	Octal tri-state non-inv. bus transceiver	1616	16 x 16 multiplier
646	Octal tri-state bus transceiver	1620	Low power 620
647	Octal o.c. bus transceiver	1621	Low power 621
648	Octal tri-state bus transceiver	1622	Low power 622
649	Octal o.c. bus transceiver	1623	Low power 623
668	Synchronous decade up/down counter	1638	Low power 638
669	Synchronous binary up/down counter	1639	Low power 639
670	4 x 4-bit tri-state register file	1640	Low power 640
673	16-bit SISO shift register	1641	Low power 641
674	16-bit PISO shift register	1642	Low power 642
681	Arithmetic logic unit	1643	Low power 643
682	8-bit comparator	1644	Low power 644
683	8-bit o.c. comparator	1645	Low power 645

CMOS logic devices

4001	Quad 2-input NOR
4002	Dual 4-input NOR
4006	18-bit shift register
4007	Dual CMOS transistor pair/inverter
4008	4-bit full adder
4009	Hex inverter/buffer
4010	Hex buffer
4011	Quad 2-input NAND
4012	Dual 4-input NAND
4013	Dual D-type bistable
4014	8-bit shift register
4015	Dual 4-bit shift register
4016	Quad analogue switch
4017	Decade counter
4018	Divide-by-N counter
4019	Quad 2-input AND/OR
4020	14-bit binary counter
4021	8-bit shift register
4022	Octal counter
4023	Triple 3-input NAND
4024	Seven-stage ripple counter
4025	Triple 3-input NOR
4026	7-segment display driver
4027	Dual J-K bistable
4028	BCD to decimal/binary to octal decoder
4029	Presettable binary/BCD up/down counter
4030	Quad 2-input exclusive-OR
4031	64-bit shift register
4032	Triple serial adder
4033	7-segment display driver
4034	8-bit bidirectional shift register
4035	4-bit PIPO shift register
4036	32-bit RAM
4037	Triple 3-input AND/OR
4038	Triple serial adder
4039	32-bit RAM
4040	12-bit binary counter
4041	Quad inverter/buffer
4042	Quad D-type latch
4043	Quad tri-state R-S latch
4044	Quad tri-state R-S latch
4045	21-bit binary counter
4046	Phase-locked loop
4047	Monostable/astable
4048	8-input multifunction gate
4049	Hex inverter/buffer
4050	Hex buffer
4051	Single 8-input analogue multiplexer
4052	Dual 4-input analogue multiplexer
4053	Triple 2-input analogue multiplexer
4054	BCD 7-segment display decoder/LCD driver
4055	BCD 7-segment display decoder/LCD driver
4056	BCD 7-segment display decoder/LCD driver
4057	Arithmetic logic unit
4059	Divide-by-N counter
4060	14-bit binary counter
4061	256-bit RAM
4062	200-bit shift register
4063	4-bit magnitude comparator
4066	Quad analogue switch
4067	1 to 16-line multiplexer/demultiplexer
4068	Single 8-input NAND
4069	Hex inverter
4070	Quad exclusive-OR
4071	Quad 2-input OR
4072	Dual 4-input OR
4073	Triple 3-input AND
4075	Triple 3-input OR
4076	Quad D-type register
4077	Quad 2-input exclusive-NOR
4078	Single 8-input NOR
4081	Quad 2-input AND
4082	Dual 4-input AND
4085	Dual 2-input AND/OR/invert
4086	Dual 2-input AND/OR/invert
4089	Binary rate multiplier
4093	Quad 2-input NAND
4094	8-stage tri-state register
4095	Single J-K bistable
4096	Single J-K bistable
4097	Dual 8-channel multiplexer/demultiplexer
4098	Dual retriggerable monostable
4099	8-bit addressable latch
4104	Quad level translator
4160	4-bit programmable decade counter
4161	4-bit programmable binary counter
4162	4-bit programmable decade counter
4163	4-bit programmable binary counter
4174	Hex D-type bistable
4175	Quad D-type bistable
4194	4-bit bidirectional shift register
4501	Dual 4-input NAND/single 2-input OR/NOR
4502	Hex str. inverter/buffer
4503	Hex tri-state buffer
4504	Hex TTL-CMOS level shifter
4505	64-bit RAM
4506	Dual AND/OR/invert
4507	Quad exclusive-OR
4508	Dual 4-bit tri-state latch
4510	BCD up/down counter
4511	BCD to 7-segment latch/decoder/driver
4512	8-channel data selector
4513	BCD to 7-segment latch/decoder/driver
4514	4-bit latched input 1 to 16-line decoder
4515	4-bit latched input 1 to 16-line decoder
4516	Binary up/down counter
4517	Dual 64-bit shift register

4518	Dual BCD up-counter
4519	Quad 2-input multiplexer
4520	Dual 4-bit binary counter
4521	24-stage frequency divider
4522	BCD programmable divide-by-N
4524	256 x 4-bit ROM
4526	Binary programmable divide-by-N
4527	BCD rate multiplier
4528	Dual resettable monostable
4529	Dual 4-channel tri-state analogue data selector
4530	Dual 5-input majority gate
4531	12-bit parity tree
4532	8-bit priority encoder
4534	5-decade counter
4536	Programmable timer
4537	256-bit RAM
4538	Dual retriggerable/resettable monostable
4539	Dual 4-channel data selector
4541	Programmable timer
4543	BCD to 7-segment latch/decoder/driver
4544	BCD to 7-segment latch/decoder/driver
4547	BCD to 7-segment latch/decoder/driver
4549	Successive approximation register
4551	Quad 2-input analogue multiplexer
4552	64 x 4-bit RAM
4553	3-digit BCD counter
4554	2-bit binary multiplier
4555	Dual 2 to 4-line decoder
4556	Dual 2 of 4-line decoder
4557	Variable length shift register
4558	BCD to 7-segment latch decoder
4559	Successive approximation register
4560	4-bit BCD adder
4561	9's complementor
4562	128-bit shift register
4566	Time base generator
4568	Programmable counter/phase comparator
4569	Dual programmable BCD counter
4572	2-input AND/2-input NOR/quad inverter
4573	Quad programmable operational amplifier
4574	Quad programmable comparator
4575	Dual operational amplifier/dual comparator
4580	4 x 4 multi-port register
4581	4-bit arithmetic logic unit
4582	Look-ahead carry generator
4583	Dual Sch. trigger
4584	Hex Sch. inverter
4585	4-bit magnitude comparator
4597	8 bit bus compatible latch
4598	8-bit bus compatible latch
4599	8-bit addressable latch

Common TTL pin-outs

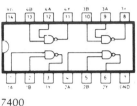

7400
7403
7426
7437
7438

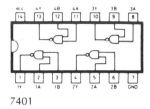

7401

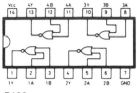

7402
7428
7433

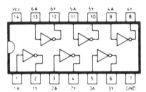

7404
7405
7406
7416

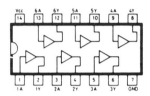

7407
7417

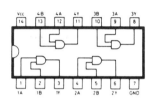

7408
7409

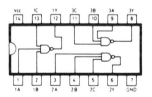

7410
7412

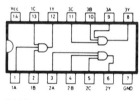

7411
7415

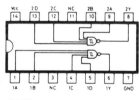

7413

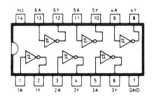

7414

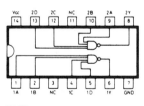

7420
7422

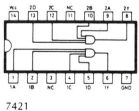

7421
7440

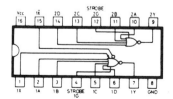

7423

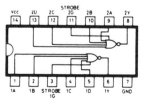

7425

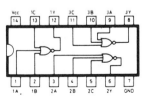

7427

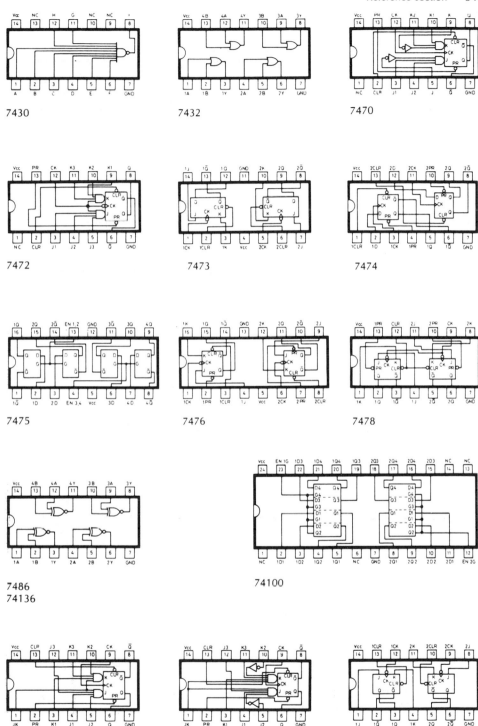

7430

7432

7470

7472

7473

7474

7475

7476

7478

7486
74136

74100

74104

74105

74107

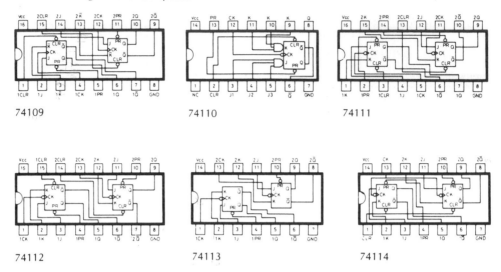

74109

74110

74111

74112

74113

74114

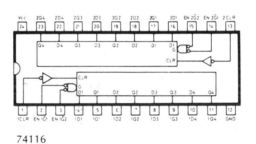

74116

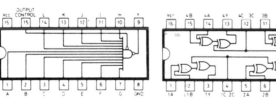

74134

74135

74138

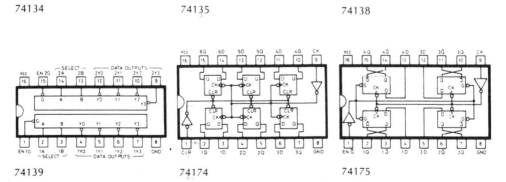

74139

74174

74175

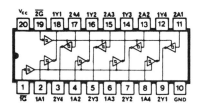

240

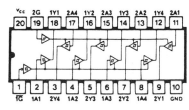

241

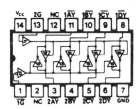

242

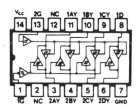

243

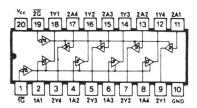

244

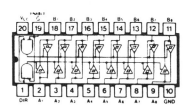

245

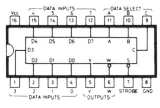

74251

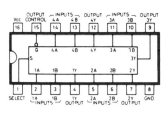

74257

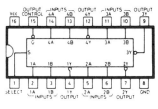

74258

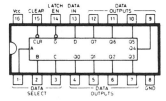

74259

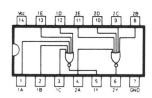

74260

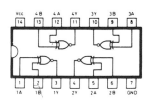

74266

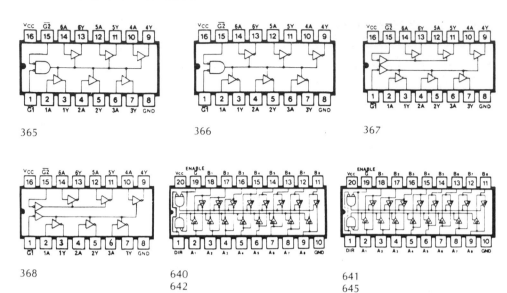

365

366

367

368

640
642

641
645

Equivalent logic functions

AND Gate	OR Gate	A	B	X
		1	1	1
		1	0	0
		0	1	0
		0	0	0
		1	1	0
		1	0	0
		0	1	1
		0	0	0
		1	1	0
		1	0	1
		0	1	0
		0	0	0
		1	1	0
		1	0	0
		0	1	0
		0	0	1
		1	1	1
		1	0	1
		0	1	1
		0	0	0
		1	1	1
		1	0	0
		0	1	1
		0	0	1
		1	1	1
		1	0	1
		0	1	0
		0	0	1
		1	1	0
		1	0	1
		0	1	1
		0	0	1

RAM data

Device	Type	Technology	Size (bits)	Organization	Package
2012A	NMOS	static	1024	IK words x 1 bit	16 pin DIL
2110	ECL	static	1024	IK words x 1 bit	16-pin DIL
2112	ECL	static	1024	256 words x 4 bits	16-pin DIL
2112A	NMOS	static	1024	256 words x 4 bits	16-pin DIL
2114	NMOS	static	4096	IK words x 4 bits	18-pin DIL
2118	NMOS	dynamic	16384	16K words x 1 bit	16-pin DIL
2118	NMOS	static	16384	2K words x 8 bits	24-pin DIL
2142	ECL	static	4096	4K words x 1 bit	20-pin DIL
2147	NMOS	static	4096	4K words x 1 bit	18-pin DIL
2148	CMOS	static	4096	IK words x 4 bits	18-pin DIL
2167	CMOS	static	16384	16K words x 1 bit	20-pin DIL
2168	CMOS	static	16384	4K words x 4 bits	20-pin DIL
2504	TTL	static	256	256 words x 1 bit	16-pin DIL
2510	TTL	static	1024	IK words x 1 bit	16-pin DIL
2511	TTL	static	1024	IK words x 1 bit	16-pin DIL
4116	NMOS	dynamic	16384	16K words x 1 bit	16-pin DIL
4118	NMOS	static	8192	IK words x 8 bits	24-pin DIL
4104	NMOS	dynamic	65536	64K words x 1 bit	16-pin DIL
4256	NMOS	dynamic	262144	256K words x 1 bit	16-pin DIL
4334	CMOS	static	4096	IK words x 4 bits	18-pin DIL
4416	NMOS	dynamic	65536	16K words x 4 bits	18-pin DIL
4464	CMOS	static	65536	8K words x 8 bits	28-pin DIL
4716	NMOS	dynamic	16384	16k words x 1 bit	16-pin DIL
4801	NMOS	static	8192	IK words x 8 bits	24-pin DIL
4802	NMOS	static	16384	2K words x 8 bits	24-pin DIL
4816	NMOS	dynamic	16384	16K words x 1 bit	16-pin DIL
4864	NMOS	dynamic	65536	64K words x 1 bit	16-pin DIL
4865	NMOS	dynamic	65536	64K words x 1 bit	16-pin DIL
5101	CMOS	static	1024	256 words x 4 bits	22-pin DIL
5257	CMOS	static	4096	4K words x 1 bit	18-pin DIL
5516	CMOS	static	16384	2K words x 8 bits	24-pin DIL
5588	CMOS	static	65536	8K words x 8 bits	28-pin DIL
6116	CMOS	static	16384	2K words x 8 bits	24-pin DIL
6117	CMOS	static	16384	2K words x 8 bits	24-pin DIL
6147	CMOS	static	4096	4K words x 1 bit	18-pin DIL
6148	CMOS	static	4096	IK words x 4 bits	18-pin DIL
6167	CMOS	static	16384	16K words x 1 bit	20-pin DIL
6168	CMOS	static	16384	4K words x 4 bits	20-pin DIL
6264	CMOS	static	65536	8K words x 8 bits	18-pin DIL
6267	CMOS	static	16384	16K words x 1 bit	20-pin DIL
10422	ECL	static	1024	256 words x 4 bits	24-pin DIL
10470	ECL	static	4096	4K words x 1 bit	18-pin DIL
10474	ECL	static	4096	IK words x 4 bits	14-pin DIL
10480	ECL	static	16384	16K words x 1 bit	20-pin DIL
41256	NMOS	dynamic	262144	256K words x 1 bit	16-pin DIL
43254	CMOS	static	262144	64K words x 4 bits	32-pin DIL
43256	CMOS	static	262144	32K words x 8 bits	18-pin DIL
50250	NMOS	dynamic	262144	256K words x 1 bit	16-pin DIL
50257	NMOS	dynamic	262144	256K words x 1 bit	16-pin DIL
50464	NMOS	dynamic	262144	64K words x 4 bits	18-pin DIL
55328	CMOS	static	262144	32K words x 8 bits	28-pin DIL
41000	NMOS	dynamic	1048576	IM words x 1 bit	18-pin DIL
41264	NMOS	dynamic	262144	64K words x 4 bits	24-pin DIL
44256	NMOS	dynamic	1048576	256K words x 4 bits	20-pin DIL
424256	NMOS	dynamic	1048576	256K words x 4 bits	20-pin DIL
511000	NMOS	dynamic	1048576	IM words x 1 bit	18-pin DIL

Dynamic RAM equivalents

Organization	Supply	Manufacturer	Device coding
16K x 1	+5V	AMD	AM9016F
	−5V	ITT	ITT4116
	+12V	Mostek	MK4116
		Motorola	MCM4116B
		National	MM5290
		NEC	uPD416
		Texas	TMS4116
		Toshiba	TMM416
64K x 1	+5V	AMD	AM9064
		Fairchild	F64K
		Fujitsu	MB8264A/MB8265A
		Hitachi	HM4864/HM4864A
		Inmos	IMS2600
		Intel	2164A
		Matsushita	MN4164
		Micron Tech.	MT4264
		Mitsubishi	MSK4164
		Mostek	MK4564
		Motorola	MCM6665A
		National	NMC4164
		NEC	uPD4164
		Oki	MSM3764
		Siemens	HY4164
		Texas	TMS4164
		Toshiba	TMM4164
		Tristar	KM4164A
16K x 4	+5V	Fujitsu	MB81416
		Hitachi	HM48416A
		Inmos	IMS2620
		Mitsubishi	MSM4416
		Texas	TMS4416
256K x 1	+5V	Fujitsu	M881256/MB81257
		Hitachi	HM50256/HM50257
		Micron Tech.	MT1256
		Mitsubishi	MSM4256
		Motorola	MCM6256
		NEC	uPD41256/uPD41257
		Oki	MSM37256
		Texas	TMS4256/TMS4257
		Toshiba	TMM41256
		Western Elec.	WCM41256
64K x 4	+5V	Hitachi	HM50464/HM50465
		Micron Tech.	MT4064
		NEC	uPD41256
		Texas	TMS4464

Note: There may be minor variations in refresh requirements and although the devices listed in each group are equivalent, they may not be identical in every respect

Hex, binary, decimal and ASCII/IBM character set

Hex.	Binary	Decimal	ASCII/IBM*
00	00000000	0	
01	00000001	1	^A
02	00000010	2	^B
03	00000011	3	^C
04	00000100	4	^D
05	00000101	5	^E
06	00000110	6	^F
07	00000III	7	^G
08	00001000	8	^H
09	00001001	9	^I
0A	00001010	10	^J
0B	00001011	11	^K
0C	00001100	12	^L
0D	00001101	13	^M
0E	00001110	14	^N
0F	00001111	15	^O
10	00010000	16	^P
11	00010001	17	^Q
12	00010010	18	^R
13	00010011	19	^S
14	00010100	20	^T
15	00010101	21	^U
16	00010110	22	^V
17	00010111	23	^W
18	00011000	24	^X
19	00011001	25	^Y
IA	00011010	26	^Z
IB	00011011	27	^[
IC	00011100	28	^\
ID	00011101	29	^]
IE	00011110	30	^^
IF	00011111	31	^
20	00100000	32	
21	00100001	33	!
22	00100010	34	"
23	00100011	35	#
24	00100100	36	$
25	00100101	37	%
26	00100110	38	&
27	00100111	39	'
28	00101000	40	(
29	00101001	41	)
2A	00101010	42	*
2B	00101011	43	+
2C	00101100	44	,
2D	00101101	45	–
2E	00101110	46	.
2F	00101III	47	/
30	00110000	48	0
31	00110001	49	1
32	00110010	50	2
33	00110011	51	3
34	00110100	52	4
35	00110101	53	5
36	00110110	54	6
37	00110111	55	7
38	00111000	56	8
39	00111001	57	9
3A	00111010	58	:
3B	00111011	59	;
3C	00111100	60	<
3D	00111101	61	=
3E	00111110	62	>
3F	00111111	63	?
40	01000000	64	@
41	01000001	65	A
42	01000010	66	B
43	01000011	67	C
44	01000100	68	D
45	01000101	69	E
46	01000110	70	F
47	01000111	71	G
48	01001000	72	H
49	01001001	73	I
4A	01001010	74	J
4B	01001011	75	K
4C	01001100	76	L
4D	01001101	77	M
4E	01001110	78	N
4F	01001111	79	O
50	01010000	80	P
51	01010001	81	Q
52	01010010	82	R
53	01010011	83	S
54	01010100	84	T
55	01010101	85	U
56	01010110	86	V
57	01010111	87	W
58	01011000	88	X
59	01011001	89	Y
5A	01011010	90	Z
5B	01011011	91	[
5C	01011100	92	\
5D	01011101	93	]
5E	01011110	94	^
5F	01011111	95	_
60	01100000	96	`
61	01100001	97	a
62	01100010	98	b
63	01100011	99	c
64	01100100	100	d
65	01100101	101	e
66	01100110	102	f
67	01100111	103	g
68	01101000	104	h
69	01101001	105	i
6A	01101010	106	j
6B	01101011	107	k
6C	01101100	108	l
6D	01101101	109	m
6E	01101110	110	n
6F	01101111	111	o

Hex.	Binary	Decimal	ASCII/IBM*	Hex.	Binary	Decimal	ASCII/IBM*
70	01110000	112	p	AA	10101010	170	¬
71	01110001	113	q	AB	10101011	171	½
72	01110010	114	r	AC	10101100	172	¼
73	01110011	115	s	AD	10101101	173	¡
74	01110100	116	t	AE	10101110	174	«
75	01110101	117	u	AF	10101111	175	»
76	01110110	118	v	B0	10110000	176	
77	01110111	119	w	Bl	10110001	177	
78	01111000	120	x	B2	10110010	178	
79	01111001	121	y	B3	10110011	179	
7A	01111010	122	z	B4	10110100	180	┤
7B	01111011	123	{	B5	10110101	181	
7C	01111100	124	|	B6	10110110	182	╢
7D	01111101	125	}	B7	10110111	183	╖
7E	01111110	126	¨	B8	10111000	184	╕
7F	01111111	127		B9	10111001	185	╣
80	10000000	128	Ç	BA	10111010	186	║
81	10000001	129	ü	BB	10111011	187	╗
82	10000010	130	é	BC	10111100	188	╝
83	10000011	131	â	BD	10111101	189	╜
84	10000100	132	ä	BE	10111110	190	╛
85	10000101	133	à	BF	10111111	191	┐
86	10000110	134	å	C0	11000000	192	└
87	10000111	135	ç	C1	11000001	193	┴
88	10001000	136	ê	C2	11000010	194	┬
89	10001001	137	ë	C3	11000011	195	├
8A	10001010	138	è	C4	11000100	196	─
8B	10001011	139	ï	C5	11000101	197	┼
8C	10001100	140	î	C6	11000110	198	╞
8D	10001101	141	ì	C7	11000111	199	╟
8E	10001110	142	Ä	C8	11001000	200	╚
8F	10001111	143	Å	C9	11001001	201	╔
90	10010000	144	É	CA	11001010	202	╩
91	10010001	145	æ	CB	11001011	203	╦
92	10010010	146	Æ	CC	11001100	204	╠
93	10010011	147	ô	CD	11001101	205	═
94	10010100	148	ö	CE	11001110	206	╬
95	10010101	149	ò	CF	11001111	207	╧
96	10010110	150	û	D0	11010000	208	╨
97	10010111	151	ù	Dl	11010001	209	╤
98	10011000	152	ÿ	D2	11010010	210	╥
99	10011001	153	Ö	D3	11010011	211	╙
9A	10011010	154	Ü	D4	11010100	212	╘
9B	10011011	155	¢	D5	11010101	213	╒
9C	10011100	156	£	D6	11010110	214	╓
9D	10011101	157	¥	D7	11010111	215	╫
9E	10011110	158	Pt	D8	11011000	216	╪
9F	10011111	159	ƒ	D9	11011001	217	┘
A0	10100000	160	á	DA	11011010	218	┌
Al	10100001	161	í	DB	11011011	219	█
A2	10100010	162	ó	DC	11011100	220	▄
A3	10100011	163	ú	DD	11011101	221	▌
A4	10100100	164	ñ	DE	11011110	222	▐
A5	10100101	165	Ñ	DF	11011111	223	▀
A6	10100110	166	ª	E0	11100000	224	α
A7	10100111	167	º	El	11100001	225	ß
A8	10101000	168	¿	E2	11100010	226	Γ
A9	10101001	169	⌐	E3	11100011	227	π

Hex.	Binary	Decimal	ASCII/IBM*
E4	11100100	228	
E5	11100101	229	
E6	11100110	230	
E7	11100111	231	
E8	11101000	232	
E9	11101001	233	
EA	11101010	234	
EB	11101011	235	
EC	11101100	236	
ED	11101101	237	
EE	11101110	238	
EF	11101111	239	
F0	11110000	240	
Fl	11110001	241	

Hex.	Binary	Decimal	ASCII/IBM*
F2	11110010	242	
F3	11110011	243	
F4	11110100	244	
F5	11110101	245	
F6	11110110	246	
F7	11110111	247	
F8	11111000	248	
F9	11111001	249	
FA	11111010	250	
FB	11111011	251	
FC	11111100	252	
FD	11111101	253	
FE	11111110	254	
FF	11111111	255	

IBM and compatible equipment does not use standard ASCII characters below 32 decimal. These 'non-displayable' ASCII characters are referred to as 'control characters'. When output to the IBM display, these characters appear as additional graphics characters (not shown in the table).

IBM POST and diagnostic error codes

Indeterminate (01x)

01x   indeterminate problem

Power supply (02x)

02x   power supply fault

System board (lxx)

101   interrupt failure
102   BIOS ROM checksum error (PC, XT); timer (AT, MCA)
103   BASIC ROM checksum error (PC, XT); timer interrupt (AT, MCA)
104   interrupt controller (PC, XT); protected mode (AT, MCA)
105   timer (PC, XT); keyboard controller (MCA)
106   system board
107   system board adaptor card or maths coprocessor, NMI test (MCA)
108   system board; timer bus (MCA)
109   DMA test; memory
110   system board memory (ISA); system board parity check (MCA)
111   adaptor memory (ISA); memory adaptor parity check (MCA)
112   adaptor; watchdog time-out (MCA)
113   adaptor; DMA arbitration time-out (MCA)
114   external ROM checksum (MCA)
115   80386 protect mode
121   unexpected hardware interrupt
131   cassette wrap test (PC)
132   DMA extended registers
133   DMA verify logic
134   DMA arbitration logic
151   real-time clock (or CMOS RAM)

152   system board (ISA); real time clock or CMOS (MCA)
160   system board ID not recognized (MCA)
161   system options (dead battery) (CMOS chip lost power)
162   system options (run Setup) (CMOS does not match system)
163   time and date (run Setup) (clock not updating)
164   memory size (run Setup) (CMOS does not match system)
165   adaptor ID mismatch (MCA)
166   adaptor time-out; card busy (MCA)
167   system clock not updating (MCA)
199   incorrect user device list

Memory (2xx)

201   memory error (number preceding 201 indicates specific location)
202   memory address line 0-15
203   memory address line 16-23; line 16-31 (MCA) 204 relocated memory (PS/2)
205   error in first 128K (PS/2 ISA); CMOS (PS/2 MCA)
207   ROM failure
211   system board memory; system board 64K (MCA)
215   memory address error; 64K on daughter/SIP 2 (70)
216   system board memory; 64K on daughter/SIP 1 (70)
221   ROM to RAM copy (MCA)
225   wrong speed memory on system board (MCA)

Keyboard (3xx)

301   keyboard did not respond correctly, or stuck key detected (the hexadecimal number preceding
       301 is the scan code for the faulty key) keyboard interface (MCA)
302   user-indicated error from keyboard test (PC, XT)
302   keyboard locked (AT, models 25, 30)
303   keyboard/system board interface
304   keyboard or system unit error; keyboard clock (MCA)
305   keyboard fuse on system board (50, 60, 80); +5V error (70)
341   keyboard
342   keyboard cable
343   enhancement card or cable
365   keyboard (replace keyboard)
366   interface cable (replace cable)
367   enhancement card or cable (replace)

Monochrome display (4xx)

401   memory, horizontal sync frequency or vertical sync test
408   user-indicated display attributes
416   user-indicated character set
424   user-indicated 80 X 25 mode
432   monochrome card parallel port test

Colour graphics display (5xx)

501   memory, horizontal sync frequency or vertical sync test
508   user-indicated display attributes
516   user-indicated character set

524   user-indicated 80 x 25 mode
532   user-indicated 40 x 25 mode
540   user-indicated 320 x 200 graphics mode
548   user-indicated 640 X 200 graphics mode
556   light pen test
564   user-indicated screen paging test

Diskette drives and/or adaptor (6xx)

601   diskette/adaptor test failure; drive or controller (MCA)
602   diskette test (PC, XT); diskette boot record (MCA)
603   diskette size error
606   diskette verify function
607   write protected diskette
608   bad command; diskette status returned
610   diskette initialization (PC, XT)
611   timeout; diskette status returned
612   bad NEC; diskette status returned
613   bad DMA; diskette status returned
614   DMA boundary error
621   bad seek; diskette status returned
622   bad CRC; diskette status returned
623   record not found; diskette status returned
624   bad address mark; diskette status returned
625   bad NEC seek; diskette status returned
626   diskette data compare error
627   diskette change line error
628   diskette removed
630   drive A: index stuck high
631   drive A: index stuck low
632   drive A: track 0 stuck off
633   drive A: track 0 stuck on
640   drive B: index stuck high
641   drive B: index stuck low
642   drive B: track 0 stuck off
643   drive B: track 0 stock on
650   drive speed
651   format failure
652   verify failure
653   read failure
654   write failure
655   controller
656   drive
657   write protect stuck protected
658   change line stuck changed
659   write protect stuck unprotected
660   change line stuck unchanged

Maths coprocessor (7xx)

702   exception errors test
703   rounding test
704   arithmetic test 1
705   arithmetic test 2
706   arithmetic test 3
707   combination test
708   integer store test

709   equivalent expressions
710   exceptions
711   save state
712   protected mode test
713   voltage/temperature sensitivity test

Parallel printer adaptor (9xx)

901   data register latch
902   control register latch
903   register address decode
904   address decode
910   status line wrap connector
911   status line bit 8 wrap
912   status line bit 7 wrap
913   status line bit 6 wrap
914   status line bit 5 wrap
915   status line bit 4 wrap
916   interrupt wrap
917   unexpected interrupt
92x   feature register

Alternate printer adaptor (10xx)

10xx   adaptor test failure
1002   jumpers (IBM models 25, 30)

Communications device asynchronous communications adaptor system board, asynchronous port (MCA), 16550 internal modem (PS/2) (11xx)

1101   adaptor test failure
1102   card-selected feedback
1103   port 102 register test
1106   serial option
1107   communications cable or system board MCA)
1108   IRQ 3
1109   IRQ 4
1110   modem status register not clear
       16550 chip register
1111   ring-indicate
       16550 control line internal wrap test
1112   trailing edge ring-indicate
       16550 control line external wrap test
1113   receive and delta receive line signal detect
       16550 transmit
1114   receive line signal detect
       16550 receive
1115   delta receive line signal detect 16550 transmit and receive
       data unequal
1116   line control register: all bits cannot be set
       16550 interrupt function
1117   line control register: all bits cannot be reset
       16550 baud rate test
1118   transmit holding and/or shift register stuck on
       16550 interrupt-driven receive external data wrap test

1119 data ready stuck on
      16550 FIFO
1120 interrupt enable register: all bits cannot be set
1121 interrupt enable register: all bits cannot be reset
1122 interrupt pending stuck on
1123 interrupt ID register stuck on
1124 modem control register: all bits cannot be set
1125 modem control register: all bits cannot be reset
1126 modem status register: all bits cannot be set
1127 modem status register: all bits cannot be reset
1128 interrupt ID
1129 cannot force overrun error
1130 no modem status interrupt
1131 invalid interrupt pending
1132 no data ready
1133 no data available interrupt
1134 no transmit holding interrupt
1135 no interrupts
1136 no received line status interrupt
1137 no receive data available
1138 transmit holding register
1139 no modem status interrupt
1140 transmit holding register to empty
1141 no interrupts
1142 no IRQ4 interrupt
1143 no IRQ3 interrupt
1144 no data transferred
1145 maximum baud rate
1146 minimum baud rate
1148 timeout error
1149 invalid data returned
1150 modem status register error
1151 no DSR and delta DSR
1152 no DSR
1153 no delta DSR
1154 modem status register
1155 no CTS and delta CTS
1156 no CTS
1157 no delta CTS

Alternate communications device, asynchronous communications adaptor (ISA), dual asynchronous communications (DAC) adaptor (MCA), 16550 internal modem (12xx)

12xx   Same as 1100-1157 ISA systems, except for PS/2 codes listed below
1202   jumpers (models 25,30)
1202 or 06   serial device (e.g. Dual Asynchronous Adaptor)
1208 or 09   serial device (e.g. Dual Asynchronous Adaptor)
1212   dual async adaptor or system board
1218 or 19   dual async adaptor or system board
1227   dual async adaptor or system board
1233 or 34   dual async adaptor or system board

Game control adaptor (13xx)

1301 adaptor failure
1302 joystick test

Colour/graphics printer (14xx)

1401 printer test failure
1402 not ready; out of paper
1043 no paper; interrupt failure
1404 matrix printer test failure; system board time-out
1405 parallel adaptor
1406 presence test

Synchronous data link control (SDLC) communications adaptor (15xx)

1501 adaptor test failure
1510 8255 port B
1511 8255 port A
1512 8255 port C
5113 8253 timer #1 did not reach terminal count
1514 8253 timer #1 output stuck on
1515 8253 timer #0 did not reach terminal count
1516 8253 timer #0 output stuck on
1517 8253 timer #2 did not reach terminal count
1518 8253 timer #2 output stuck on
1519 8273 port B error
1520 8273 port A error
1521 8273 command/read time-out
1522 interrupt level 4 (timer and modem change)
1523 ring indicator stuck on
1524 received clock stuck on
1525 transmit clock stuck on
1526 test indicate stuck on
1527 ring indicate not on
1528 receive clock not on
1529 transmit clock not on
1530 test indicate not on
1531 data set ready not on
1532 carrier detect not on
1533 clear-to-send not on
1534 data set ready stuck on
1535 carrier detect stuck on
1536 clear-to-send stuck on
1537 level 3 (transmit/receive) interrupt
1538 receive interrupt results error
1539 wrap data miscompare error
1540 DMA channel 1 transmit error
1541 DMA channel 1 receive error
1542 8273 error-checking or status-reporting error
1547 level 4 stray interrupt
1548 level 3 stray interrupt
1549 interrupt presentation sequence time-out

Display station emulation adaptor (DSEA) (16xx)

(NB: try removing non-IBM adaptors and then repeat the POST checks)
1604 or 08   DSEA or system twin-axial network problem
1624 or 34   DSEA
1644 or 52   DSEA
1654 or 58   DSEA
1662   interrupt level switches set wrong or defective DSEA

1664   DSEA
1668   see 1662
1669 or 74   if early version of IBM diagnostics diskette, replace with version 3.0 (or later) and
              repeat diagnostic checks
1674   station address which is set wrong or defective DSEA
1684 or 88   feature not installed, device address switches set wrong, or DSEA

Fixed (hard) disk/adaptor (17xx)

1701   drive not ready (PC, XT)
        fixed disk/adaptor test (AT, PS/2)
1702   time-out (PC, XT); fixed disk/adaptor (AT, PS/2)
1703   drive (PC, XT, PS/2)
1704   controller (PC, XT),
        adaptor, or drive error (AT, PS/2)
1705   no record found
1706   write fault
1707   track 0 error
1708   head select error
1709   bad ECC (AT)
1710   read buffer overrun
1711   bad address mark
1712   bad address mark (PC, AT);
        error of undetermined cause (AT)
1713   data compare error
1714   drive not ready
1730   adaptor
1731   adaptor
1732   adaptor
1750   drive verify
1751   drive read
1752   drive write
1753   random read test
1754   drive seek test
1755   controller
1756   controller ECC test
1757   controller head select
1780   hard disk drive C fatal; time-out
1781   hard disk drive D fatal; time-out
1782   hard disk controller (no IPL from hardfile)
1790   drive C non-fatal error (can attempt to run IPL from drive)
1791   drive D non-fatal error (can attempt to run IPL from drive)

Expansion unit (PC, XT only) (18xx)

1801   Expansion Unit POST error
1810   enable/disable
1811   extender card wrap test failure while disabled
1812   high-order address lines failure while disabled
1813   wait state failure while disabled
1814   enable/disable could not be set on
1815   wait state failure while enabled
1816   extender card wrap test failure while enabled
1817   high-order address lines failure while enabled
1818   disable not functioning
1819   wait request switch not set correctly
1820   receiver card wrap test or an adaptor card in expansion unit
1821   receiver high-order address lines

Bisynchronous communications (BSC) adaptor (20xx)

2001	adaptor test failure
2010	8255 port A
2011	8255 port B
2012	8255 port C
2013	8253 timer #1 did not reach terminal count
2014	8253 timer #1 output stuck on
2015	8253 timer #2 did not reach terminal count
2016	8253 timer #2 output stuck on
2017	8251 data-set-ready failure to come on
2018	8251 clear-to-send not sensed
2019	8251 data-set-ready stuck on
2020	8251 clear-to-send stuck on
2021	8251 hardware reset
2022	8251 software reset command
2023	8251 software error-reset command
2024	8251 transmit-ready did not come on
2025	8251 receive-ready did not come on
2026	8251 could not force overrun error status
2027	interrupt-transmit; no timer interrupt
2028	interrupt-transmit; replace card or planar
2029	interrupt-transmit; replace card only
2030	interrupt-transmit; replace card or planar
2031	interrupt-transmit; replace card only
2033	ring-indicate stuck on
2034	receive-clock stuck on
2035	transmit clock stuck on
2036	test indicate stuck on
2037	ring indicate not on
2038	receive clock not on
2039	transmit clock not on
2040	test indicate not on
2041	data-set-ready stuck on
2042	carrier detect not on
2043	clear-to-send not on
2044	data-set-ready stuck on
2045	carrier detect stuck on
2046	clear-to-send stuck on
2047	unexpected transmit
2048	unexpected receive interrupt
2049	transmit data did not equal receive data
2050	8251 detected overrun error
2051	lost data set ready during data wrap
2052	receive time-out during data wrap

Alternative bisynchronous communications adaptor (21xx)

21xx   as for 2000 to 2052

Cluster adaptor (22xx)

22xx   adaptor test failure

Plasma monitor adaptor (23xx)

23xx   adaptor test failure

Enhanced graphics adaptor systems board video (MCA) (24xx)

2401   adaptor test failure
2402   monitor if colours change, otherwise system board
2408   user-indicated display attributes
2409   monitor
2410   system board
2416   user-indicated character set
2424   user-indicated 80 x 25 mode
2432   user-indicated 40 X 25 mode
2440   user-indicated 320 X 200 graphics mode
2448   user-indicated 640 X 200 graphics mode
2456   light pen test
2464   user-indicated screen paging test

Alternate enhanced graphics adaptor (25xx)

25xx   adaptor test failure

PC/370-M adaptor (26xx)

2601 to 75   memory card
2677 to 80   processor card
2681   memory card
2682   processor card
2694   processor card
2695   memory card
2697   processor card

PC/3277 (27xx)

27xx   emulator test failure

3278/79 emulator, 3270 connection adaptor (28xx)

28xx   adaptor test failure

Colour/graphics printer (29xx)

29xx   printer test failure

LAN (local area network) adaptor (30xx)

3001   adaptor ROM failure
3002   RAM
3003   digital loopback

3005   4V or 12V
3006   interrupt conflict
3007   analog
3008   reset command
3015   refer to PC Network Service Manual
3020   replace adaptor with jumper W8 enabled
3040   LF translator cable
3041   refer to PC Network Service Manual

Primary PC network adaptor (30xx)

3001   adaptor test failure
3002   ROM
3003   ID
3004   RAM
3005   HIC
3006   ±12V dc
3007   digital loopback
3008   host-detected HIC failure
3009   sync fail and no-go bit
3010   HIC test OK and no-go bit
3011   go bit and no CMD 41
3012   card not present
3013   digital fall-through
3015   analog
3041   hot carrier on other card
3042   hot carrier on this card

Alternate LAN adaptor (31xx)

31xx   as for 3000 to 3041
3115 or 40   LF translator cable

PC display adaptor (32xx)

32xx   adaptor test failure

Compact printer (PC, XT only) (33xx)

33xx   printer test failure

Enhanced display station emulator adaptor (35xx)

3504   adaptor connected to twin-axial cable during off-line test
3508   work station address in use by another work station, or diagnostic diskette from another PC
       was used
3509   diagnostic program failure; retry on new diskette
3540   work station address invalid, not configured at controller; twin-axial cable failure or not
       connected; or diagnostic diskette from another PC was used
3588   feature not installed or device I/O address switches set wrong
3599   diagnostic program failure; retry on new diskette

IEEE 488 adaptor (36xx)

3601   adaptor test failure (base address and read registers incorrect, following initialization
3602   write to SPMR
3603   write to ADR or IEEE-488 adaptor addressing problems
3610   adaptor cannot be programmed to listen
3611   adaptor cannot be programmed to talk
3612   adaptor cannot take control with IFC
3613   adaptor cannot go to standby
3614   adaptor cannot take control asynchronously
3615   adaptor cannot take control asynchronously
3616   adaptor cannot pass control
3617   adaptor cannot be addressed to listen
3618   adaptor cannot be unaddressed to listen
3619   adaptor cannot be addressed to talk
3620   adaptor cannot be unaddressed to talk
3621   adaptor cannot be addressed to listen with extended addressing
3622   adaptor cannot be unaddressed to listen with extended addressing
3623   adaptor cannot be addressed to talk with extended addressed
3624   adaptor cannot be unaddressed to talk with extended addressing
3625   adaptor cannot write to self
3626   adaptor cannot generate handshake error
3627   adaptor cannot detect DCL message
3628   adaptor cannot detect SDC message
3629   adaptor cannot detect END with EOI
3630   adaptor cannot detect EOT with EOI
3631   adaptor cannot detect END with O-bit EOS
3632   adaptor cannot detect END with 7-bit EOS
3633   adaptor cannot detect GET
3634   mode 3 addressing not functioning
3635   adaptor cannot recognize undefined command
3636   adaptor cannot detect REM, REMC, LOK, or LOKC
3637   adaptor cannot clear REM or LOK
3638   adaptor cannot detect SRQ
3639   adaptor cannot conduct serial poll
3640   adaptor cannot conduct parallel poll
3650   adaptor cannot DMA to 7210
3651   data error on DMA to 7210
3652   adaptor cannot DMA from 7210
3653   data error on DMA from 7210
3658   uninvoked interrupt received
3659   adaptor cannot interrupt on ADSC
3660   adaptor cannot interrupt on ADSC
3661   adaptor cannot interrupt on CO
3662   adaptor cannot interrupt on DO
3663   adaptor cannot interrupt on DI
3664   adaptor cannot interrupt on ERR
3665   adaptor cannot interrupt on DEC
3666   adaptor cannot interrupt on END
3667   adaptor cannot interrupt on DET
3668   adaptor cannot interrupt on APT
3669   adaptor cannot interrupt on CPT
3670   adaptor cannot interrupt on REMC
3671   adaptor cannot interrupt on LOKC
3672   adaptor cannot interrupt on SRQI
3673   adaptor cannot interrupt on terminal count on DMA to 7210
3674   adaptor cannot interrupt on terminal count on DMA from   7210
3675   spurious DMA terminal count interrupt
3697   illegal DMA configuration setting detected
3698   illegal interrupt level configuration setting detected

Data acquisition adaptor (38xx)

3801   adaptor test failure
3810   timer read test
3811   timer interrupt test
3812   delay, BI 13 test
3813   rate, BI 13 test
3814   BO 14, ISIRQ test
3815   BO 0, count-in test
3816   BI STB, count-out test
3817   BO 0, BO CTS test
3818   BO 1, BI 0 test
3819   BO 2, BI 1 test
3820   BO 3, BI 2 test
3821   BO 4, BI 3 test
3822   BO 5, BI 4 test
3823   BO 6, BI 5 test
3824   BO 7, BI 6 test
3825   BO 8, BI 7 test
3826   BO 9, BI 8 test
3827   BO 10, BI 9 test
3828   BO 11, BI 10 test
3829   BO 12, BI 11 test
3830   BO 13, BI 12 test
3831   BO 15, AI CE test
3832   BO STB, BO GATE test
3833   BI CTS, BI HOLD test
3834   AI CO, BI 15 test
3835   counter interrupt test
3836   counter read test
3837   AO O ranges test
3838   AO 1 ranges test
3839   AI O values test
3840   AI 1 values test
3841   AI 2 values test
3842   AI 3 values test
3843   analog input interrupt test
3844   AI 23 address or value test

Professional graphics controller adaptor (39xx)

3901   adaptor test failure
3902   ROM1 self-test
3903   ROM2 self-test
3904   RAM self-test
3905   cold start cycle power
3906   data error in communications RAM
3907   address error in communications RAM
3908   bad data detected while read/write to 6845-like register
3909   bad data detected in lower hex-E0 bytes while reading or writing 6845 equivalent registers
3910   PGC display bank output latches
3911   basic clock
3912   command control error
3913   vertical sync scanner
3914   horizontal sync scanner
3915   intech
3916   LUT address error
3917   LUT red RAM chip error

3918   LUT green RAM chip error
3919   LUT blue RAM chip error
3920   LUT data latch error
3921   horizontal display
3922   vertical display
3923   light pen
3924   unexpected error
3925   emulator addressing error
3926   emulator data latch
3927   base for error codes 3928-3930 (emulator RAM)
3928   emulator RAM
3929   emulator RAM
3930   emulator RAM
3931   emulator H/V display problem
3932   emulator cursor position
3933   emulator attribute display problem
3934   emulator cursor display
3935   fundamental emulation RAM problem
3936   emulation character set problem
3937   emulation graphics display
3938   emulation character display problem
3939   emulation bank select
3940   display RAM U2
3941   display RAM U4
3942   display RAM U6
3943   display RAM U8
3944   display RAM U10
3945   display RAM U1
3946   display RAM U3
3947   display RAM U5
3948   display RAM U7
3949   display RAM U9
3950   display RAM U12
3951   display RAM U14
3952   display RAM U16
3953   display RAM U18
3954   display RAM U20
3955   display RAM U11
3956   display RAM U13
3957   display RAM U15
3958   display RAM U17
3959   display RAM U19
3960   display RAM U22
3961   display RAM U24
3962   display RAM U26
3963   display RAM U28
3964   display RAM U30
3965   display RAM U21
3966   display RAM U23
3967   display RAM U25
3968   display RAM U27
3969   display RAM U29
3970   display RAM U32
3971   display RAM U34
3972   display RAM U36
3973   display RAM U38
3974   display RAM U40
3975   display RAM U31
3976   display RAM U33
3977   display RAM U35
3978   display RAM U37

3979   display RAM U39
3980   PGC RAM timing
3981   PGC read/write latch
3982   SR bus output latches
3983   addressing error (vertical column of memory; U2 at top)
3984   addressing error (vertical column of memory; U4 at top)
3985   addressing error (vertical column of memory; U6 at top)
3986   addressing error (vertical column of memory; U8 at top)
3988   addressing error (vertical column of memory; U10 at top)
3989   horizontal bank latch errors
3990   horizontal bank latch errors
3991   horizontal bank latch errors
3992   RAG/CAG PGC
3993   multiple write modes, nibble mask errors
3994   row nibble (display RAM)
3995   PGC addressing

5278 display attachment unit and 5279 display (44xx)

44xx   display attachment test failure

IEEE-488 interface adaptor (45xx)

45xx   adaptor test failure

ARTIC multiport/2 interface adaptor (46xx)

4611   adaptor
4612 or 13   memory module
4630   adaptor
4640 or 41   memory module
4650   interface cable

Internal modem (48xx)

48xx   modem test failure

Alternate internal modem (49xx)

49xx   modem test failure

Financial communication system (56xx)

56xx   system test failure

Chip set (Phoenix BIOS only) (70xx)

7000   CMOS failure
7001   shadow RAM failure (ROM not shadowed to RAM)
7002   CMOS configuration data error

Voice communications adaptor (71xx)

7101   adaptor test failure
7102   instruction or external data memory
7103   PC to VCA interrupt
7104   internal data memory
7105   DMA
7106   internal registers
7117   interactive shared memory
7108   VCA to PC interrupt
7109   DC wrap
7111   external analog wrap and tone output
7114   telephone attachment test

3.5 inch diskette drive (73xx)

7301   diskette drive/adaptor test failure
7306   diskette change line error
7307   write-protected diskette
7308   bad command; drive error
7310   disk initialization error; track zero bad
7311   time-out; drive error
7312   bad disk controller chip
7313   bad DMA controller; drive error
7314   DMA boundary error
7315   bad index timing; drive error
7316   speed error
7321   bad seek; drive error
7322   bad CRC; drive error
7323   record not found; drive error
7324   bad address mark; drive error
7325   bad drive controller chip; seek error

8514/A display adaptor/A (74xx)

74xx   adaptor test failure
7426   monitor
744x to 747x 8514 memory module

Page Printer (76xx)

7601   adaptor test failure
7602   adaptor card
7603   printer
7604   printer cable

PS/2 speech adaptor (84xx)

84xx   adaptor test failure

2 Mb extended memory adaptor (85xx)

85xx   adaptor test failure
850x or 851x 80286   Expanded Memory Adaptor/A (model 50)
852x   80286 Expanded Memory Adaptor/A, memory module (model 50)

PS/2 pointing device (mouse) (86xx)

8601   pointing device; mouse time-out (MCA)
8602   pointing device; mouse interface (MCA)
8603   system board; mouse interrupt (MCA)
8604   pointing device or system board

MIDI adaptor (89xx)

89xx   adaptor test failure

Multiprotocol communications adaptor (100xx)

10002 or 06   any serial device, but most likely multiprotocol adaptor
10007   multiprotocol adaptor or communications cable
10008 or 09   any serial device, but most likely multiprotocol adaptor
10012   multiprotocol adaptor or system board
10018 or 19   multiprotocol adaptor or system board
10042 or 56   multiprotocol adaptor or system board

Modem and communications adaptor/A (101xx)

101xx   system board
10102   card-selected feedback
10103   port 102 register test
10106   serial option
10108   IRQ 3
10109   IRQ 4
10110   16450 chip register
10111   16450 control line internal wrap test
10113   transmit
10114   receive
10115   transmit and receive data not equal
10116   interrupt function
10117   baud rate test
10118   interrupt driven receive external data wrap test
10125   reset result code
10126   general result code
10127   S register write/read
10128   echo on/off
10129   enable/disable result codes
10130   enable number/word result codes
10133   connect results for 300 baud not received
10134   connect results for 1 200 baud not received
10135   local analog loopback 300-baud test
10136   local analog loopback 1 200-baud test
10137   no response to escape/reset sequence

10138   S register 13 incorrect parity or number of data bits
10139   S register 15 incorrect bit rate

ESDI fixed disk or adaptor (104xx)

10450   write/read test
10451   read verify test
10452   seek test
10453   wrong device type indicated
10454   controller failed sector buffer test
10455   controller
10456   controller diagnostic command
10461   format error
10462   controller head select
10463   write/read sector error
10464   drive primary map unreadable
10465   controller ECC 8-bit
10466   controller ECC 9-bit
10467   soft seek error
10468   hard seek error
10469   soft seek error count exceeded
10470   controller attachment diagnostic error
10471   controller wrap mode interface
10472   controller wrap mode drive select
10473   error during ESDI read verify test
10480   drive C, ESDI adaptor or system board
10481   drive D seek failure, ESDI adaptor or system board
10482   ESDI fixed disk adaptor
10483   ESDI fixed disk adaptor; controller reset; drive select 0
10484   controller head select 3 selected bad
10485   controller head select 2 selected bad
10486   controller head select 1 selected bad
10487   controller head select 0 selected bad
10488   controlled rg-cmd complete 2
10489   controlled wg-cmd complete 1
10490   drive C format; read failure; controller
10491   drive D format; read failure
10499   controller

5.25 inch external diskette drive or adaptor (107xx)

107xx   drive or adaptor test failure

SCSI adaptor (112xx)

112xx   adaptor test failure

Processor card for model 70, type 3 (129xx)

12901   processor portion of processor board
12902   cache portion of processor board

Plasma display and adaptor (149xx)

14901 or 02   system board or plasma display
14922   system board or display adaptor
14932   display adaptor

6157 streaming tape drive or tape attachment adaptor (165xx)

165xx   adaptor test failure
16520   streaming tape drive
16540   tape attachment adaptor

Primary token-ring network PC adaptor (166xx)

166xx   adaptor test failure

Alternative token-ring network PC adaptor (167xx)

167xx   adaptor test failure

Adapter memory module (194xx)

194xx   adaptor test failure

SCSI fixed disk and controller (210xx)

210xx   disk or controller test failure

SCSI CD-ROM system (215xx)

215xx   CD-ROM system test failure

Hard disk drive characteristics

Manufacturer	Model	Cylinders	Heads	Sectors	Capacity
ATASI	3046	645	7	17	39
	3051	704	7	17	42
	3051+	733	7	17	44
	3058	1024	8	17	71
BRAND-TECH.	BT8085	1024	8	17	71
	BT8128	1024	8	26	109
	BT8170	1024	8	34	142
CONNER	CP-342	981	5	17	42
	CP-3102-A	776	8	33	104
	CP-3102-B	772	8	33	104
	CP-3024	615	4	17	21
	CP-3044	977	5	17	42
	CP-3104	776	8	33	104
CONTROL DATA	9415-519	697	3	17	18
	9415-536	697	5	17	30
	9415-538	733	5	17	31
	94155-48	925	5	17	40
	94155-57	925	6	17	48
	94155-67	925	7	17	56
	94155-77	925	8	17	64
	94155-85	1024	8	17	71
	94155-85P	1024	8	17	71
	94155-86	925	9	17	72
	94155-96	1024	9	17	80
	94155-96P	1024	9	17	80
	94155-120	960	8	26	102
	94155-120P	960	8	26	102
	94155-135	960	9	26	115
	94155-135P	960	9	26	115
	94156-48	925	5	17	40
	94156-67	925	7	17	56
	94156-86	925	9	17	72
	94166-101	969	5	34	84
	94166-141	969	7	34	118
	94166-182	969	9	34	151
	94186-383	1412	13	34	319
	94186-383H	1224	15	34	319
	94186-442H	1412	15	34	368
	94204-65	941	8	17	65
	94204-71	1024	8	17	71
	94205-51	989	5	17	43
	94205-77	989	5	26	65
	94216-106	1024	5	34	89
	94205-77	1024	8	17	71
	94216-106	989	5	17	43
CMI	CM-6626	640	4	17	22
	CM-6640	640	6	17	33
DATA-TECH	DTM-553	1024	5	17	44
	DTM-853	640	8	17	44
	DTM-885	1024	8	17	71
FUJITSU	M2225D	615	4	17	21
	M2227D	615	8	17	42
	M2241AS	754	4	17	26
	M2242AS	754	7	17	45
	M2243AS	754	11	17	72
	M2247E	1243	7	36	160

Manufacturer	Model	Cylinders	Heads	Sectors	Capacity
	M2248E	1243	11	36	252
	M2249E	1243	15	36	343
HITACHI	DK511-3	699	5	17	30
	DK511-5	699	7	17	42
	DK511-8	823	10	17	71
	DK512-8	823	5	17	35
IMPRIMIS	9415-519	697	3	17	18
	9415-536	697	5	17	30
	9415-538	733	5	17	31
	94155-48	925	5	17	40
	94155-56	925	9	17	72
	94155-57	925	6	17	48
	94155-67	925	7	17	56
	94155-77	925	8	17	64
	94155-85	1024	8	17	71
	94155-85P	1024	8	17	71
	94155-86	925	9	17	72
	94155-96	1024	9	17	80
	94155-96P	1024	9	17	80
	94155-120	960	8	26	102
	94155-120P	960	8	26	102
	94155-135	960	9	26	115
	94155-135P	960	9	26	115
	94156-48	925	5	17	40
	94156-67	925	7	17	56
	94156-86	925	9	17	72
	94166-101	969	5	34	84
	94166-141	969	7	34	118
	94166-182	969	9	34	151
	94186-383	1412	13	34	319
	94186-383H	1224	15	34	319
	94186-442H	1412	15	34	368
	94196-766	1632	15	53	664
	94204-65	941	8	17	65
	94204-71	1024	8	17	71
	94205-51	989	5	17	43
	94205-77	989	5	26	65
	94216-106	1024	5	34	89
	94246-383	1747	7	53	331
	94354-135	1072	9	29	143
	94354-160	1072	9	29	143
	9435,1-172	1072	9	36	177
	94354-200	1072	9	36	177
	94355-100	1072	9	17	83
	94355-150	1072	9	26	120
	94356-111	1072	5	36	98
	94356-155	1072	7	36	138
	94356-200	1072	9	36	177
KYOCERA	KC20A	616	4	17	21
	KC20B	615	4	17	21
	KC30A	616	4	26	32
	KC30B	615	4	26	32
LAPINE	TITAN20	615	4	17	21
MAXTOR	XT1065	918	7	17	55
	XT1085	1024	8	17	71
	XT1105	918	11	17	87
	XT1140	918	15	17	119
	XT2085	1224	7	17	74

Manufacturer	Model	Cylinders	Heads	Sectors	Capacity
	XT2190	1224	15	17	159
	XT4380	1224	15	34	319
	XT8760	1632	15	51	639
MICROPOLIS	1323	1024	4	17	35
	1323A	1024	5	17	44
	1324	1024	6	17	53
	1324A	1024	7	17	62
	1325	1024	8	17	71
	1333	1024	4	17	35
	1333A	1024	5	17	44
	1334	1024	6	17	53
	1334A	1024	7	17	62
	1335	1024	8	17	71
	1353	1024	4	34	71
	1353A	1024	5	34	89
	1354	1024	6	34	106
	1354A	1024	7	34	124
	1355	1024	8	34	142
	1551	1224	7	34	149
	1554	1224	11	34	234
	1555	1224	12	34	255
	1556	1224	13	34	277
	1557	1224	14	34	298
	1558	1224	15	34	319
MICROSCIENCE	HH-325	615	4	17	21
	HH-725	615	4	17	21
	HH-1050	1024	5	17	44
	HH-1060	1024	5	26	68
	HH-1075	1024	7	17	62
	HH-1090	1314	7	17	80
	HH-1095	1024	7	26	95
	HH-1120	1314	7	26	122
	HH-2120	1024	7	34	124
	HH-2160	1276	7	34	155
	4050	1024	5	17	44
	4060	1024	5	26	68
	4070	1024	7	17	62
	4090	1024	7	26	95
	5100	855	7	34	104
	7040	855	3	26	34
	7100	855	7	26	79
MINISCRIBE	3053	1024	5	17	44
	3085	1170	7	17	71
	3130	1250	5	34	108
	3180	1250	7	34	152
	3425	615	4	17	21
	3438	615	4	26	32
	3650	809	6	17	42
	3675	809	6	26	64
	6032	1024	3	17	26
	6053	1024	5	17	44
	605311	1024	5	17	44
	6074	1024	7	17	62
	6079	1024	5	26	68
	6085	1024	8	17	71
	6128	1024	8	26	109
	8051A	981	5	17	42
	8425	615	4	17	21

Manufacturer	Model	Cylinders	Heads	Sectors	Capacity
	8438	615	4	26	32
	8450	771	4	26	41
	8450XT	805	4	26	42
	9230E	1224	9	34	191
	9380E	1224	15	34	319
	9780E	1661	15	53	676
MITSUBISHI	MR522	612	4	17	21
	MR535	977	5	17	42
	MR535RLL	977	5	26	65
	MR5310E	977	5	34	85
NEC	D3126	615	4	17	21
	D3142	642	8	17	44
	D3146H	615	8	17	42
	D3661	915	7	36	118
	D5126	615	4	17	21
	D5126H	615	4	17	21
	D5127H	615	4	26	32
	D5146H	615	8	17	42
	D5147H	615	8	26	65
	D5452	823	10	17	71
	D5652	823	10	34	143
	D5655	1224	7	34	149
	D5662	1224	15	34	319
	D5682	1633	15	53	664
NEWBURY DATA	NDR320	615	4	17	21
	NDR340	615	8	17	42
	NDR360	615	8	26	65
	NDR1065	918	7	17	55
	NDR1085	1024	8	17	71
	NDR1105	918	11	17	87
	NDR1140	918	15	17	119
	NDR2190	1224	15	17	159
	NDR4170	1224	7	34	149
	NDR4380	1224	15	34	319
PRIAM	502	755	7	17	46
	504	755	7	17	46
	514	1224	11	17	117
	519	1224	15	17	159
	617	752	11	34	144
	623	752	15	34	196
	630	1224	15	34	319
	V130	987	3	17	25
	V150	987	5	17	42
	V170	987	7	17	60
	V185	1166	7	17	71
PTI	PT225	615	4	17	21
	PT234	820	4	17	28
	PT338	615	6	17	32
	PT351	820	6	17	42
	PT238R	615	4	26	32
	PT25IR	820	4	26	43
	PT357R	615	6	26	49
	PT376R	820	6	26	65
QUANTUM	Q520	512	4	17	17
	Q530	512	6	17	26
	QS40	512	8	17	35
RODINE	203	321	6	17	16
	204	321	8	17	22

Manufacturer	Model	Cylinders	Heads	Sectors	Capacity
	202E	640	4	17	22
	203E	640	6	17	33
	204E	640	8	17	44
	R03000A—NAT	625	5	27	43
	R03000A—XLAT	992	5	17	43
	R03060R	750	5	26	49
	R03075R	750	6	26	59
	R03085R	750	7	26	69
	R05040	1224	3	17	31
	R05065	1224	5	17	53
	R05090	1224	7	17	74
SEAGATE	ST125	615	4	17	21
	ST138	615	6	17	32
	ST138R	615	4	26	32
	ST151	977	5	17	42
	ST157R	615	6	26	49
	ST213	615	2	17	10
	ST225	615	4	17	21
	ST225R	667	2	31	21
	ST238R	615	4	26	32
	ST251	820	6	17	42
	ST250R	667	4	31	42
	ST277R	820	6	26	65
	ST412	306	4	17	10
	ST4026	615	4	17	21
	ST4038	733	5	17	31
	ST4051	977	5	17	42
	ST4053	1024	5	17	44
	ST4096	1024	9	17	80
	ST4144R	1024	9	26	122
SIEMENS	MEGAFILE-1200	1216	8	34	169
	MEGAFILE-1300	1216	12	34	254
SYQUEST	SQ312RD	612	2	17	10
	SQ315F	612	4	17	21
	SQ338F	612	6	17	31
TANDON	TN262	615	4	17	21
	TN362	615	4	17	21
	TN703	578	5	17	25
	TN703AT	733	5	17	31
	TN705	962	5	17	41
	TN755	981	5	17	42
TOSHIBA	MK-53F	830	5	17	36
	MK-53F-R	830	5	26	55
	MK-54F	830	7	17	50
	MK-54F-R	830	7	26	77
	MK-56F	830	10	17	72
	MK-56F-R	830	10	26	110
	MK-134FA	733	7	17	44
	MK-153FA	830	5	34	72
	MK-154FA	830	7	34	101
	MK-156FA	830	10	34	144

IBM PC and PS/2 hard disk drive types

Type	Cyl.	Heads	Write precomp.	Landing zone	Capacity (Mbyte)	Machine support
0	(no hard disk drive)					
1	306	4	128	305	10.16	AT, XT-286, PS/2
2	615	4	300	615	20.42	AT, XT-286, PS/2
3	615	6	300	615	30.63	AT, XT-286, PS/2
4	940	8	512	940	62.42	AT, XT-286, PS/2
5	940	6	512	940	46.82	AT, XT-286, PS/2
6	615	4	None	615	20.42	AT, XT-286, PS/2
7	462	8	256	511	30.68	AT, XT-286, PS/2
8	733	5	None	733	30.42	AT, XT-286, PS/2
9	900	15	None	901	112.06	AT, XT-286, PS/2
10	820	3	None	820	20.42	AT, XT-286, PS/2
11	855	5	None	855	35.49	AT, XT-286, PS/2
12	855	7	None	855	49.68	AT, XT-286, PS/2
13	306	8	128	319	20.32	AT, XT-286, PS/2
14	733	7	None	733	42.59	AT, XT-286, PS/2
15	Reserved (do not use)					
16	612	4	All	663	20.32	XT-286, PS/2
17	977	5	300	977	40.55	XT-286, PS/2
18	977	7	None	977	56.77	XT-286, PS/2
19	1024	7	512	1023	59.50	XT-286, PS/2
20	733	5	300	732	30.42	XT-286, PS/2
21	733	7	300	732	42.59	XT-286, PS/2
22	733	5	300	733	30.42	XT-286, PS/2
23	306	4	All	336	10.16	XT-286, PS/2
24	612	4	305	663	20.32	XT-286, PS/2
25	306	4	None	340	10.16	PS/2
26	612	4	None	670	20.32	PS/2
27	698	7	300	732	40.56	PS/2
28	976	5	488	977	40.51	PS/2
29	306	4	All	340	10.16	PS/2
30	611	A	306	663	20.29	PS/2
31	732	7	300	732	42.53	PS/2
32	1023	5	None	1023	42.46	PS/2
33-255	(reserved)					

Servicing Personal Computers disk offer

The full QuickBASIC source code for a number of useful diagnostic programs has been included within Chapters 5, 6 and 8. These programs have been designed for use with IBM PC, PC-XT, PC-AT, PS/2 and numerous compatible systems.

If you don't have access to Microsoft QuickBASIC, or if you would prefer not to type in the programs, a disk with the source code *and* fully compiled versions of the latest version of each of the program listings is available direct from the author for £5 (UK and EC countries) or £6.50 (USA and overseas). The charge covers the cost of disk, duplication, user instructions, and postage and packing.

The disk also contains a number of additional diagnostic programs which can be used to check and modify the system configuration as well as carry out routine tests and adjustments of such items as disk drives, printers and monitors.

When ordering, please state which one of the following formats is required:

(a) 3.5 inch 1.44M (state 'FORMAT A')
(b) 3.5 inch 720K (state 'FORMAT B')
(c)l 5.25 inch 360K (state 'FORMAT C')

Please allow up to 28 days for delivery and make sure that you have clearly printed your name and address. Cheques, money orders and postal orders should be made payable to 'MIKE TOOLEY'.

Orders should be sent to:

Mike Tooley
Dean of Technology
Brooklands College
Heath Road
Weybridge
Surrey
KT13 8TT
England

Please note that all programs in source code format may be freely adapted, copied and modified. You are encouraged to use them as the basis of your own personalized diagnostic programs. Finally, if you have any suggestions, modifications and/or improvements please let me know so that I can incorporate them in future releases.

Index

Index to semiconductor devices